AUCKLAND
100
YEARS OF RUGBY LEAGUE
1909-2009

AUCKLAND 100 YEARS OF RUGBY LEAGUE
1909–2009

JOHN COFFEY & BERNIE WOOD

First published in 2009 by Huia Publishers and Auckland Rugby League

Huia Publishers
39 Pipitea Street, PO Box 17–335
Wellington, Aotearoa New Zealand
www.huia.co.nz

ISBN 978-1-86969-366-4

Copyright © Auckland Rugby League 2009
Cover design and typeset by Tangerine Design Limited

All rights reserved. No part of this publication may be reproduced, stored in a retrieval system, or transmitted in any form or by any means, electronic, mechanical, including photocopying, recording or otherwise, without prior permission of the publisher.

National Library of New Zealand Cataloguing-in-Publication Data
Coffey, John (John Oliver), 1946-
Auckland, 100 years of rugby league, 1909-2009 / John Coffey
and Bernie Wood.

ISBN 978-1-86969-366-4 (hbk.)

1. Auckland Rugby League—History. 2. Rugby League football—
New Zealand—Auckland (Region)—History. 3. Rugby League football players
—New Zealand—Auckland (Region) —History.

I. Wood, Bernie. II. Auckland Rugby League. III. Title.

796.333809932—dc 22

Note: Where possible, people's full names are given in the book, but often in the early years, only the surname was recorded.

Endpapers:
Front: Panoramic view in early 1921 of the work-in-progress transformation of a market garden to Carlaw Park. *Auckland City Libraries*
Back: Richmond players and officials assembled for a special club photograph in front of the Domain pavilion in 1935, the year the club provided nine New Zealand representatives. *Auckland City Libraries*

Contents

Foreword vii

Acknowledgements ix

Introduction x

CHAPTER ONE
Auckland before the Auckland Rugby League 1

CHAPTER TWO
Rapid Progress: 1909–1919 17

CHAPTER THREE
Triumph and Tragedy: 1920–1929 59

CHAPTER FOUR
Focus on the Clubs: 1930–1939 95

CHAPTER FIVE
Return to Prosperity: 1940–1949 123

CHAPTER SIX
Big Games, Big Wins: 1950–1959 149

CHAPTER SEVEN
Beating the Best: 1960–1969 179

CHAPTER EIGHT
Auckland's Grand Slam: 1970–1979 211

CHAPTER NINE
Changing Times: 1980–1989 249

CHAPTER TEN
The Nervous Nineties: 1990–1999 285

CHAPTER ELEVEN
The Twenty-first Century: 2000–2008 325

Auckland Rugby League Statistics 363

Bibliography 403

Index 405

Major Auckland Rugby League Trophies

Clockwise from top left: Fox Memorial Shield, Roope Rooster, Rukutai Shield, Stormont Shield.
All photographs this page: Auckland Rugby League

Foreword

When the first Auckland Rugby League officials were elected in the Auckland Chamber of Commerce boardroom on 19 July 1909, they started a legacy that would be built upon over the next 100 years. At the beginning of our centennial year, the Auckland Rugby League encompasses thirty-two clubs and seven affiliates, stretching from the Rodney club in the north to the Waiuku club in the south.

Over the course of the past century, the game has evolved considerably both on and off the field. However, the essence of why the game is played and enjoyed by so many remains the same. This story then is testament to all of the players, administrators, officials and supporters who hold the responsibility of retaining the same pioneering spirit that the All Golds team started with their tour of Britain in 1907–08.

The stories and names captured in the following pages highlight the rich history of characters, comradeship, leadership, humour and success that the game has enjoyed. Those involved with the game at every level will be able to look back at their sporting ancestors with pride in how they made the great game it is today.

The core strength of the Auckland Rugby League is the thirty-two current and twenty-nine former clubs of which it is made up and that, over the years, have forged the strongest domestic competition in New Zealand today, the Fox Memorial. With players from this competition, Auckland has built a world-renowned record of success against visiting provinces and nations. The grand slam winning team of 1977 exemplified this when it defeated Australia, Great Britain and France in the space of twenty-one days under the lights of Carlaw Park.

The legacy of Carlaw Park is testament to the work of James Carlaw and his colleagues in 1921, which, eighty-eight years later, has left the game financially secure. For eighty-one of those years, the park stood as the spiritual home of rugby league in New Zealand, and it was the scene of thousands of great matches from the grassroots level to the pinnacle of the international game.

I wish to pay tribute to both Bernie Wood and John Coffey who spent countless hours researching and writing what has developed into a

Cameron McGregor
Chairman
Auckland Rugby League

FOREWORD

colourful record of Auckland's first hundred years. And of course, to all the men, women and children – our future of the game, thank you for your contribution to the sport as we celebrate our centennial year.

Our journey over the next 100 years will have its ups and downs as it has done over the past 100 years, and as can be expected over such a timeframe. The recent decision by the New Zealand game to embrace significant review challenges, which include dividing the current Auckland District into three separate zones, Auckland, Northern and Counties/Manukau, will in itself present challenges never faced before, but as rugby league in Auckland heads towards this new and exciting chapter in 2010, it is the collective responsibility of everybody involved to ensure that we evolve, progress and pass the sport on to the next generation with the same good spirit that was given to us.

Cameron McGregor
Chairman
Auckland Rugby League

Acknowledgements

The authors wish to thank Auckland Rugby League officials Cameron McGregor and Pat Carthy for their confidence and encouragement, and staff members David Blackwell and Sam Panapa for their assistance.

Former Kiwis captain Don Hammond was the hub of a network of experienced New Zealand and Auckland representatives, including Ray Cranch, Des White, Jack Fagan, Peter Brown, Warren Collicoat, Brian Reidy, Bruce Castle, Dennis Stewart and Graeme Norton. This group clarified numerous queries, as did Auckland Rugby League life member Tom McKeown, Kevin Bailey at the New Zealand Rugby League and Richard Becht at the Warriors. Sel Shanks co-ordinated information from clubs and affiliates. British historian Tom Mather supplied correspondence between the fledgling Auckland Rugby League and the Northern Union.

It would not have been possible to gather such a fine array of photographs without the valued help of Elspeth Orwin and Annette Hay at Auckland City Libraries, Trevor McKewen and Gail Selkirk at Fairfax Media, Bryony Lloyd-Fitt at the *New Zealand Herald*, Barry Clarke at *The Star* in Christchurch, Robin Smith from Superleague magazine, and Andrew Cornaga at Photosport. Tricia Wood was untiring in her assistance with photograph identification.

We are also grateful for the support and professionalism of Huia (NZ) staff members Brian Bargh, Jim Firth, Bryony Walker, Melissa Savage and Laryhs Makowharemahihi.

Introduction

Rugby league dominates in northern England, where the game first broke the restrictive rugby union shackles regarding playing laws and player payments. It is all-powerful in the eastern states of Australia. Papua New Guinea calls the thirteen-a-side game its national sport. There are dedicated followers in France and in an increasing number of developing nations. And then there is Auckland, the city and province which for 100 years has made New Zealand competitive against the strongest international opposition.

During a near-century of traditional international tours, itineraries would be scanned to note dates of test matches and other 'special' games. The fans would seek them out with anticipation, while touring players would look with some apprehension for listed fixtures against such invariably tough opponents as Wigan in England, Sydney or New South Wales in Australia, and Auckland in New Zealand.

Auckland against England, 23 July 1910. A general view of Auckland's first international match at Victoria Park during the visitors' 52–9 victory.

Auckland City Libraries

AUCKLAND RUGBY LEAGUE
1909–2009

No matter how many tests the Lions or Kangaroos played in New Zealand, they regarded their clashes with the men in blue and white as an extension of that series. British and French itineraries which often began in the dust and heat of Western Australia or the Northern Territory ended in the wet and cold of a midwinter day or night at Carlaw Park. It was of no comfort to visiting professionals that those waiting to have a last crack at them were only playing for pride and possibly petrol money.

Aucklanders have actually done much to bolster those other strongholds. Wigan, the most famous British club, has hugely benefited from signing players who honed their skills in Auckland, from gifted centre Lance Todd after the original 1907–08 All Golds tour through to great midfield backs Dean Bell and Kevin Iro when the Challenge Cup almost became the club's permanent property. Similarly, Sydney clubs are ever scouting for the next Mark Graham, Kurt Sorensen, Gary Freeman, Sonny Bill Williams or Roy Asotasi.

This book was commissioned to tell the Auckland Rugby League story, to commemorate those who introduced the game to Auckland, those whose talents earned it such a glowing reputation, and the leading officials who nurtured it over its first century. It follows on other centennial books, *The Kiwis: 100 Years of International Rugby League* (2007) and *100 Years Māori Rugby League* (2008), by the same authors.

INTRODUCTION

The initial breakaway from rugby union was no less dramatic in Auckland than in the north of England and Sydney. It occurred in stages, however, with comparatively few players joining Albert Baskerville's pioneering All Golds to tour Britain or Albert Asher's 1908 All Maoris team on tour to Australia. When those teams returned, they set about forming clubs and establishing a provincial administration.

By the end of the 1910 season Auckland had hosted three of the four games on the inaugural Lions tour of New Zealand and made its own promotional tour of the southern North Island and the northern and southern tips of the South Island. Development was far more rapid in Auckland than in other parts of the country, with major centres such as Canterbury and Wellington lying dormant until 1912.

So swift was progress that rugby union historians have conceded that, but for the outbreak of the First World War in 1914, rugby league might well have become the dominant winter sport in Auckland. Karl Ifwersen, champion Grafton and Auckland back, was the biggest sporting drawcard in the city. The 1917 rugby union club champion team changed codes and the Auckland Rugby Union introduced 'Auckland Rules' to brighten up its game in defiance and then with the agreement of a concerned New Zealand union.

In 1920 Auckland was the first to beat a British touring team on New Zealand soil. That was the forerunner of an outstanding record between 1954 and 1990, when Auckland won seven of eleven games against Great Britain. Australia's scalp was first taken in 1961 and on four more occasions through to 1989, while France lost five of its seven games against Auckland between 1951 and 1981.

More recently the northern and southern hemisphere rugby league seasons have run parallel, ending the era of traditional tours. Auckland's influence on the game has changed with the times. During the last twenty-five years, hundreds of Aucklanders have featured in leading overseas club teams. There could be up to half a dozen former Auckland juniors, as team-mates or opponents, involved in British Challenge Cup finals and Super League grand finals or in Australian National Rugby League playoffs.

The New Zealand Rugby League has searched, and struggled, to find a method of levelling the provincial playing field. It tried grouping other provinces to play at inter-districts level and splitting Auckland into pieces for such national competitions as the Lion Red Cup and Bartercard Cup. At various times South Auckland (now Waikato), West Coast, Central Districts and Canterbury have enjoyed some success against Auckland, mostly on their home grounds and never for more than a few seasons.

Auckland beat England 24–16 at the Domain in 1920. Auckland forwards Stan Walters and Jack Wilson are pictured in pursuit of the ball.

Auckland City Libraries

Auckland clubs also did best in national knockout contests for the Rothmans prize money in the 1960s and, in the 1980s, the Tusk Cup and Lion Red League Nationals. At home they have fiercely contested such revered trophies as the Fox Memorial Shield, the Rukutai Shield, the Roope Rooster and the Stormont Shield. Only the very finest teams could aspire to making a clean sweep of that silverware.

Carlaw Park was headquarters for all of this activity from 1921 until 2002. It was the pride of the league and the despair of visiting teams. It was the greatest place to not so much watch as *feel* a bone-crunching clash between two rugged forward packs or marvel at the attacking skills of the game's outstanding backs. Eventually Carlaw Park became an anachronism, but in retirement it provides the Auckland Rugby League with a secure financial future.

This, then, is the story of how Auckland imposed itself on the rugby league world, an influence which is ongoing on the very highest plateau. When New Zealand beat Australia in that momentous World Cup final at Brisbane's Suncorp Stadium on 22 November 2008, the opposing squads included eleven Auckland-born players, five born in Sydney and four born in Brisbane. And there was not a Wigan lad in sight. The World Cup could not have a more appropriate home than Auckland.

INTRODUCTION

Carlaw Park, headquarters of the Auckland Rugby League from 1921 until 2002.

Auckland Rugby League 50th Year Jubilee booklet

Auckland Rugby League board of directors 2009. Back row: Peter Douglas, Taffy Tewheoro (senior management committee), Evelyn Brooker (junior management committee), Steve Brewster, Patrick Carthy (general manager).

Front row: Richard Bolton (deputy chairman), Cameron McGregor (chairman), Cathy Friend.

Farrelly Photos

CHAPTER 01

AUCKLAND BEFORE THE
AUCKLAND RUGBY LEAGUE

CHAPTER ONE

Auckland before the Auckland Rugby League

Return of the All Golds

Auckland was a progressive settlement in the early years of the twentieth century. Electric tramcars were introduced and the first water piped from the Waitakere reservoirs during 1902, the first motor vehicle was registered in 1904, and two years later the Auckland Fire Board was established. In 1908 the Auckland City Council power station began generating electricity from a rubbish-burning plant at Freemans Bay – to all of twelve customers.

Although the population of the Auckland City Council area only increased from 38,400 in 1901 to 40,536 a decade later, the wider Auckland metropolitan area grew from 67,226 to 102,676 during the same period. Auckland's winter sports scene in the early 1900s was dominated by rugby union. Players represented the districts in which they lived: transport was primitive but most could comfortably walk to their home grounds for training. It was the strongest club competition in the country, underpinning a representative team which robustly defended the Ranfurly Shield against other provinces for six years.

But there was growing discontent with the autocratic manner in which the New Zealand Rugby Union ruled the game in this country, yet bowed to the English Rugby Football Union on such contentious subjects as the rigid laws of the game and strict amateur rules. Several provincial unions had advocated rule changes to make the game more enjoyable for players and spectators but were invariably rebuffed by the national body in Wellington.

Ironically, the 1905–06 New Zealand touring team in Britain, which became the first to bear the proud name of All Blacks, provided the catalyst for what was an inevitable breakaway. A good number of those Original All Blacks were angry at being forced to exist on a meagre allowance of three shillings per day during their long and arduous tour. While their sterling efforts on the field drew the crowds which filled the coffers of the English and New Zealand unions, many of the individual players returned home with no money and out of work.

That the All Blacks fashioned such a successful playing record was in part due to England having 'lost' its strongest counties, Yorkshire and Lancashire, ten years earlier. For some years the predominantly working class north had lobbied the middle and upper class south for the introduction of 'broken time' payments for players who could not afford to take Saturdays off work to play rugby. Their pleas were ignored until, at a meeting at the George Hotel in Huddersfield on 29 August 1895, twenty-two of the best clubs broke away to form the Northern Union. Rule changes were implemented to make the game more attractive.

Aucklander George Smith, a brilliant wing and champion athlete, and other All Blacks had watched Northern Union football (then in its last fifteen-a-side season before forward packs were reduced from eight players to six) and been impressed. It was not completely new to Smith. As early as 1902, while competing at the British Amateur Athletics Association's championships, he had declined Yorkshire club Manningham's sign-on offer of £100, plus £3 per week. His interest was renewed during the All Blacks tour.

Back home, Smith assisted the City club to an unbeaten record in the 1906 Auckland senior competition and helped Auckland retain the Ranfurly Shield. At season's end the City team went to Sydney for four games, and Smith and his team-mates socialised with men who held similar opinions of the New South Wales Rugby Union's treatment of its footballers. State representatives were also subjected to the maximum 'three bob a day' allowances when travelling to Queensland and were angry there was no injury insurance cover.

Meanwhile, in Wellington, young postal employee Albert Baskerville was giving considerable thought to the Northern Union. Baskerville was a keen and effective senior rugby player, and a writer and author on the game and its tactics. He dreamed of gathering a strong New Zealand team and taking it to Britain to play the Yorkshire and Lancashire club and county sides that had been excluded from the 1905–06 All Blacks itinerary. Baskerville received an encouraging reply when he wrote to the Northern Union and, with Smith acting as his main contact in Auckland, went about turning his vision into reality.

Among the sportsmen Smith met in Sydney were outstanding cricketer Victor Trumper and livewire entrepreneur James J Giltinan. Significantly, the terms of the tour contracts signed by Baskerville's team were similar to those of privately organised Australian cricket sides to England in that era. Baskerville's players paid £50 towards the costs, and their gamble paid off when they ultimately shared in the profits. Officially titled the Professional All Blacks, the 1907–08 pioneering rugby league tourists were subsequently dubbed the All Golds, an intended derogatory nickname that now holds a proud place in New Zealand sporting folklore.

AUCKLAND RUGBY LEAGUE
1909–2009

George Smith, brilliant wing and champion athlete.

John Haynes: From All Blacks to All Golds: New Zealand Rugby League's Pioneers

CHAPTER ONE

The first half of the 1907 domestic rugby season was rife with rumours, accusations, secret meetings and threats as the national and district rugby unions and major newspapers sought to identify the alleged conspirators. The New Zealand Rugby Union used its influence with the media to accuse the promoter (Baskerville) of seeking financial gain at the expense of the players – the exact crime the players were charging the union itself with. Statements were expressed claiming the tour would never eventuate (to the extent that the New Zealand Government's representative in England dubbed it 'The Phantom Team') and players were grilled individually and collectively about their loyalty.

Baskerville was banned from attending matches. The Rugby Union sought to cut off his supply of players by ordering all those nominated for the 1907 inter-island game, which doubled as the final trial for the All Blacks tour of Australia, to sign legal forms testifying to their amateur status and declaring they would have nothing to do with any rebel tour. Those chosen for the North and South XVs were then required to sign another declaration, repeating their loyalty to the union, and promising to inform on anyone who approached them about the tour and pass on any information they might learn about the preparations. In other words, the union expected them to snitch on their mates.

Twelve Auckland players nominated for the North team were summoned to attend an Auckland Rugby Union management committee meeting at Alexandra Park. To a man they refused to sign, even those who had no intention of straying from the amateur path. In that way they protected those who were going. Others followed their examples in Wellington and Christchurch.

The players received confidential legal advice that the threat of prosecution if they signed the declaration and then joined Baskerville's tour had no basis in law, and they felt more secure about standing firm. In late May 1907, they met Auckland Rugby Union officials again and asked them to amend the wording of the declaration. The union capitulated in a bid to reach a compromise.

While that temporarily kept the champion Auckland team intact, the dozen players had already been banned from the trial match. The union and newspapers announced that they had triumphed over the ogre of professionalism. Less than three months later, five of the twelve Aucklanders left New Zealand as members of the 'phantom' All Golds.

Recruitment for the All Golds and subsequent defections changed the balance of power in Auckland inter-club rugby union. The dominant City club lost Smith, Lance Todd, Billy Tyler and Bill Mackrell and would soon be farewelling outstanding All Blacks forward Charles (Bronco) Seeling to Wigan. The Wynyard brothers, Dick and Billy, joined up from North Shore. Harold Rowe and Bill Trevarthen left Newton. Ponsonby's sole All Gold was Charles Dunning. Although Ponsonby displaced City as top dog, its All Blacks forwards, George Gillett and Arthur (Bolla) Francis, later converted to rugby league.

Auckland was represented by nine pioneering All Golds in England. Training for the third test match at Cheltenham are Dick Wynyard (Auckland), Billy Tyler (Auckland), Edgar Wrigley, Charles Dunning (Auckland), Con Byrne, Bill Trevarthen (Auckland), Dan Gilchrist and Dally Messenger.

NZRL Museum

Not that rugby union was the squeaky-clean amateur sport it claimed to be. In *Ponsonby Rugby Club: Passion and Pride*, the history of the club, author Paul Neazor exposed the club's policies as being 'not quite above board'.

'As was the case in the 1880s, comment was made about players being "looked after", with "billets" (jobs) being provided and time off not hitting pay-packets. As the district scheme required senior players to live within Ponsonby's boundaries, a bit of help in finding a place to live didn't hurt either.' To avoid exposure and possible expulsion, the club did not pick up the tab itself. 'Friends of the club, or prominent business people who liked nothing better than a Ponsonby win each week, helped out where they could.'

The often bitter 1907 season was not the end of the union's problems. Baskerville, Smith and the other All Golds had just sailed off on their nine-month odyssey to Sydney, Ceylon, Britain and Australia when another crack appeared in rugby union's once impregnable wall. Again, it came from within.

The architect was another famous Auckland wing, Albert (Opai) Asher, whose try-scoring records set on the 1903 New Zealand tour of Australia lasted for sixty years. Injury cost Asher the chance of travelling with the All Golds. But a few weeks after they had left, even while he was scoring vital tries in narrow Ranfurly Shield victories over Wanganui and Taranaki, Asher was negotiating, firstly with an individual promoter and later with the fledgling New South Wales Rugby League, for the first of two (1908 and 1909) Māori tours of Australia. His players were mostly drawn from the Bay of Plenty and Auckland areas.

CHAPTER ONE

Supporters of Baskerville's vision continued to be active in Auckland and Wellington while the All Golds were overseas. A United Press Association article out of Auckland on 11 January 1908, told of a wealthy syndicate reportedly prepared to spend the massive sum of £20,000 to 'exploit Rugby football as played under the professional code' but expressed 'astonishment and even doubt' as to the amount of money involved.

'It is known that the movement is being worked up in Auckland in a systematic manner, though the greatest secrecy is being observed in connection with all that is done. Northern Union literature is being disseminated in the city among players and others. From what can be learnt an attempt will be made to get professional football going in Auckland and other parts of the Dominion, especially Wellington, in time for next season and an endeavour will be made to get a ground at Kingsland.'

Had all gone to plan, Baskerville would have returned to Wellington in June 1908 and set about establishing the Northern Union game in his homeland. He was already negotiating a lease of Athletic Park, the main sports ground in Wellington, and was even contemplating assembling another team for a tour of the United States. Baskerville had proved himself to be an extraordinary organiser and charismatic figure. Sadly, he died from pneumonia in a Brisbane hospital on 20 May, surrounded by his grieving team-mates, eleven days after scoring a sensational try in the first trans-Tasman test match in Sydney.

A weakened All Golds beat Australia in two of three tests after English clubs had signed players of the calibre of Aucklanders Smith and Todd. The remarkable Smith had captained the All Golds to their series-deciding victory over the Northern Union and played for Oldham until he suffered a broken leg at the age of forty-two in 1916. Todd served Wigan with distinction as an influential midfield back before achieving fame as Salford's manager and in broadcasting. Todd was killed in a motor accident while returning from a match during the Second World War. Such was the respect in which he was held that the trophy awarded to the Man of the Match in the annual Challenge Cup final was named in his honour.

One can only imagine how different the winter sports scene would have been in New Zealand had Baskerville brought his team home in triumph, with men of Smith's influence and Todd's multiple skills available to build upon what they had achieved on foreign fields. Instead, the first rugby league game on New Zealand soil was played between the remnants of the All Golds and other recruits from rugby union as a benefit to Baskerville's widowed mother. The venue was, fittingly, Athletic Park. But within weeks the Wellington Rugby Union had secured exclusive use of the park, and rugby league was not played there again until 1990.

Twenty-two powerful clubs had broken away from the Rugby Football Union to start the Northern Union competition in 1895, and clubs were formed in the wake of the All Golds to start the Sydney rugby league premiership in 1908. But the individual All Golds were few in number and scattered around New Zealand. All had been banned for life by the New Zealand Rugby Union, and a similar threat hung over the heads of any who would join them. National and provincial rugby unions pressured local councils to deny the 'rebels' use of playing fields.

The second Northern Union fixture played in New Zealand (and the first with an inter-club theme) was staged at Bluff on Wednesday 15 July 1908. A week earlier, the Britannia and Pirates rugby union clubs had refused to venture out of the dressing rooms into freezing sleet for a midweek senior competition game. Pleas by the Southland Rugby Union president were ignored and the 'striking' teams were subsequently suspended. In defiance, the players reassembled for a game under Northern Union rules even though they, and the referee, had only a crude knowledge of the rules. For the record, Britannia won by six points (two tries) to three (one try).

Six of the All Golds who returned to Auckland set about building foundations at club level, acting as tutors to team-mates. Dunning and Tyler played for Ponsonby, Mackrell and Rowe lined up for Newton, and Dick and Billy Wynyard for North Shore. Trevarthen played for Auckland in 1908 but signed for English club Huddersfield a year later. Māori team organiser Albert Asher and his brother, Ernie, formed the City club. The most senior official to emerge was Duncan McLean, a former Auckland Rugby Union administrator.

All that remained was for the new game to kick off in Auckland.

Auckland's first match

The seven Auckland All Golds should have been exhausted after ten months of non-stop playing and travelling, yet immediately arranged a match against their Wellington counterparts. Charles Dunning did not play in the Baskerville testimonial match at Wellington on 13 June 1908, but Harold Rowe and Bill Trevarthen were in the winning side (by 55–20) against Dick Wynyard, Billy Tyler, Billy Wynyard and Bill Mackrell. They were the first Aucklanders to play rugby league in their homeland.

Daniel Fraser, who had been both player and managerial assistant on the All Golds tour, was the Wellington contact. In 1909 Fraser was to manage another privately organised New Zealand team on tour of Australia. A newspaper report described him as secretary of the Wellington Rugby League, though it was to be three more years before a proper inter-club competition was started in the capital.

CHAPTER ONE

Auckland's first match under Northern Union rules was played at Victoria Park on 22 August 1908. Auckland beat Wellington 16–14.

Auckland City Libraries

In late July the Auckland City Council granted the use of Victoria Park for the city's first match under Northern Union rules, to be played on 22 August 1908. Four days earlier the telegraph wires around the country hummed with the news of the first Auckland team:

'Fullback – Dufty; three-quarters – Rowe, W Wynyard, Redwood; five-eighths – W Tyler and S Riley; halfback – R Wynyard; forwards – Mackrell, Dunning, Trevarthen, McDonald, Gladding and Hooper. Of the 13 players chosen, seven toured the North of England and one, S Riley, went across and met the team in Australia, playing several games there. McDonald, Hooper and Dufty are Auckland amateur representatives, while Redwood and Gladding are senior players. The team is in active training.'

According to the *Encyclopaedia of Rugby League Players*, Syd Riley made one first-grade appearance for Newtown in the 1908 Sydney premiership. He thus provided Auckland with an eighth player who was familiar with the thirteen-a-side code, as well as earning the distinction of being the first Aucklander to feature in Australia's premier competition. Riley actually played fullback against Wellington after the late withdrawal of John Dufty. C Dillamore, a regular member of the 1907 Auckland rugby union backline, joined the three-quarters, and Billy Wynyard moved to the five-eighths.

Auckland team.

Back row: P Redwood, W M Trevarthen, W T Tyler, W H C Mackrell, W T Wynyard, F G Gladding, C Dillamore, M J Hooper, T Lang (referee).

Front row: R A MacDonald, C Dunning, H F Rowe, J R Wynyard, S Riley.

Eric Bennetts, NZRL Annual 1933

The teams for the inaugural inter-provincial match were:

Auckland (blue and white): fullback, S Riley; three-quarters, P Redwood, H Rowe, C Dillamore; five-eighths, W Tyler, W Wynyard; halfback, R Wynyard (captain); forwards, W Mackrell, W Trevarthen, C Dunning, R MacDonald, F Gladding, M Hooper.

Wellington (all black): fullback, G Spencer; three-quarters, King, O Instone, D Twohill; five-eighths, J Barber, A House; halfback, A Kelly; forwards, P McGill, C Pearce (captain), C Byrne, J Spencer, D Gilchrist, A Lile.

It was a strong Wellington line-up. Arthur Kelly, Con Byrne, Daniel Gilchrist and Adam Lile, plus Cantabrian Charles Pearce, had toured Britain with the All Golds. James Barber joined them for the Australian leg and was to captain the 1909 New Zealand team across the Tasman. Brothers George and John Spencer had both been All Blacks and were, along with Albert House, also to become members of the 1909 national team. Dan Twohill's switch of codes was a double shock to the Poneke Rugby Club, where he was a prolific try-scorer and the club secretary.

Auckland won 16–14, thanks to Tyler's goalkicking. Wellington scored four tries but converted only one of them. Tyler scored the first Auckland points after only three minutes, kicking a goal after Rowe had marked the ball, a scoring method then permitted. Auckland's first try was claimed by Rowe. Billy Wynyard got the other, and Tyler finished with one conversion, two penalty goals and two goals from marks. Tries were then worth three points and all goals had a value of two points. The game attracted a bumper attendance of 8,000 mostly curious spectators – and contrasting media reaction.

Any praise from *The Observer* reporter was grudgingly given: 'After watching Saturday's display, I cannot admit that it is so much ahead of Rugby that our Northern Union friends would have us believe. The fact of there being no lineout may make the new game somewhat faster, but from a spectacular point of view, it

CHAPTER ONE

The crowd in front of the grandstand.
Auckland City Libraries

was not nearly so interesting as the Ranfurly Shield game between Auckland and Wellington. Although Auckland won by 16 points to 14, they were a trifle lucky in getting home. Towards the end Wellington were having all the best of it, and just on time an excellent chance of scoring was thrown away.'

But the *Auckland Star* scribe was very impressed: 'It cannot but be said that, from a spectacular point of view, the Northern Union game is far ahead of Rugby, and throughout the whole ninety minutes spectators are kept on the qui-vive of excitement, so fast does the ball travel from one end of the ground to the other. Taking a fair and impartial view, there is no doubt that it is considerably faster than the Rugby game, and from a spectator's point of view considerably more exciting. Another strong point in favour of the Northern game is that the risk of accident is considerably minimised.'

The teams were entertained at the Grosvenor Hotel in Hobson Street on the evening of the game, and all speakers paid tribute to the groundwork of the late Albert Baskerville. Mackrell, one of the 1905 All Blacks to join the All Golds, confirmed that it was not the intention for any player to live off the game and that any suggestion of that should be discouraged. However, the new game did provide compensation for any loss of work while on tour.

The Otago Witness published a 27 August Press Association report from Auckland: 'The Northern Union Rugby game seems to be creating quite a stir in local football circles. A prominent member of the Rugby Union said to a reporter: "There is a considerable feeling of unrest in Rugby circles throughout the Dominion. The advent of the Northern Union game has shown the ever-progressive New Zealander that improvement can be made in the national game. Wherever exhibitions of the new game have been given Rugbyites have grown enthusiastic over the possibilities of some of the innovations of the game".'

There was an immediate reaction from the Auckland Rugby Union when it met on 26 August. It unanimously voted to join forces with Otago and demand a special meeting of the New Zealand Rugby Union to discuss rule changes. One look at a rival rugby code was clearly more than enough to increase the clamour to modernise the playing laws.

Your game or your job

Playing for Wellington in the first inter-provincial rugby league match at Auckland cost Adam (Addie) Lile his job in the railways, while fellow All Gold Edward Tyne withdrew from the trip to protect his family's income – such were the sacrifices that rugby league pioneers were forced to make in New Zealand. Their tales were told by the *Hawera and Normanby Star* on 18 September 1908.

'Lile, one of the professionals who toured England under the Northern Union football rules, has a grievance against someone connected with the conduct of the New Zealand Rugby Union, and, secondly, against the Railway Department. Lile was approached to join the Wellington "pro" team to visit Auckland and withheld his answer until he got four days' leave on the ground of "private business".

'Someone – it is alleged that the "someone" was in the same service, but a red-hot amateur – communicated to the Railway Department the nature of the "private business" and, upon Lile admitting he was going to Auckland with the professional team, was told that his leave was cancelled. That was late on Wednesday afternoon and the team was to leave for the north on Thursday morning.

'There was no time to make arrangements for a substitute, and the stationmaster took no notice of the plea that Lile had sunk his cash in the venture only after being given leave of absence, or that he was bound to stand by his fellows.

'Tyne, another railway man in the same predicament, drew out of the team for, being a married man, he could not afford to incur the displeasure of the officials. Lile stood by the team, made the trip, and lost his billet [job] in the railway service.'

Lile had been chosen for the 1907–08 All Golds tour from Wellington. After his return he was prominent in the establishment of rugby league in Taranaki, touring Australia with the 1909 New Zealand team. The Lile Shield, named in his memory, is still the most prized inter-club trophy in Taranaki rugby league.

Adam Lile.

John Haynes, From All Blacks to All Golds: New Zealand Rugby League's Pioneers

Edward Tyne.

John Haynes, From All Blacks to All Golds: New Zealand Rugby League's Pioneers

Auckland accused of 'throwing' game

The 16–14 victory over Wellington on 22 August was the forerunner to three other matches played by the original Auckland representatives, producing a second win, a draw and a loss. Auckland was held to a 13–13 draw by Wellington in the return match at the Petone Recreation Ground on 12 September. Five days later, Taranaki edged out Auckland 5–3 at Western Park, New Plymouth. On 10 October, Auckland reversed that result by 21–18 at Victoria Park.

Wellington was further strengthened for its home game, with All Gold Edward Tyne coming in at wing and forwards Bert King and Henry Knight, who were both to tour Australia with the 1909 New Zealand team, joining the pack. Barclay replaced Gladding in the Auckland forwards, and the loss of Billy Wynyard from the five-eighths was more than compensated for by the inclusion of the irrepressible Albert Asher.

A worried Wellington Rugby Union had hastily arranged a match against Taranaki at Athletic Park as a counter-attraction, but the Auckland–Wellington Northern Union game drew the larger attendance. *The Dominion* newspaper reported the Athletic Park crowd as being 'close to 3000' and that at Petone as 'close upon 4000'. Many had travelled from the city to Petone on special trains. In fine weather, the teams 'marched onto the field accompanied by the dulcet strains of music supplied by the Petone Citizens' Band'.

'Both teams played hard football from start to finish,' said *The Dominion*, 'and the public were well satisfied with the display, but as the ordinary spectator has not thoroughly grasped the rules as yet there was a lack of that enthusiasm which is inseparable from a representative Rugby match. Many of the players seemed unable to forget the old game immediately, so that at times the play was a mixture of Northern Union and Rugby Union rules.

'There was very little to choose between the two teams, the score of thirteen points each being a fair indication of their respective strength. The Auckland backs gave a very fine exhibition of good open play with neat, crisp passing, but their forwards were weak. Wellington forwards, on the other hand, were much stronger than their backs. There was plenty of indication that when the players thoroughly grasp the rules the new game makes for fast play among the forwards as well as the backs.'

Asher had dazzled Australians with his ability to hurdle opponents as they bent to tackle him during the 1903 All Blacks and 1908 Māori tours, and he twice cleared startled Wellington fullback George Spencer in the first half. Spencer learned to remain standing when confronted by Asher and enjoyed greater success in stopping him.

Dan Twohill opened the scoring for Wellington after James Barber caught a high Spencer kick. Auckland's reply was a Harold Rowe try after a Dick Wynyard cross-field kick. Asher ran away for a try, only for Barber to create a Tyne try and an 8–8 halftime score. John Spencer's try and George Spencer's goal made it 13–8 to Wellington before a Matt Hooper try and Billy Tyler goal drew Auckland level.

The Auckland team moved on to New Plymouth. Former Halifax and Swinton professional Alf Chorley (who was to become New Zealand's oldest international player at thirty-six years and ten months in 1910) and Billy Wynyard played against Taranaki in place of Rowe and Asher. The Taranaki team included All Gold Adam Lile and Tom Smith, the two men most responsible for the district becoming an early rugby league stronghold.

The *Hawera and Normanby Star* followed the now familiar line that 'enough was seen to convince the spectators that when they become accustomed to the rules, and are able to understand the finer points of the game, interest and enthusiasm would be the outcome'. A brief summary mentioned that 600 spectators watched the midweek match in very unpleasant weather, and that Arthur Hardgrave's early penalty goal and late try (five points) were sufficient to upset the Aucklanders, whose three points resulted from a Billy Tyler try.

But the *Taranaki Herald* accused Auckland of 'throwing' the game to boost interest in their return fixture a few weeks later. From his tone, the anonymous writer endured a thoroughly depressing afternoon, standing in the pouring rain at the Western Park No.2 ground. He judged the game as 'interesting, but purely on account of its novelty. The play fell far short of what was expected'. He cast grave suspicion on the merits of Taranaki's win.

'The teams were unevenly matched,' he wrote. 'Auckland had a strong team, comparatively accustomed to the game. The Taranaki team was much weaker,

An incident in the second match between Auckland and Taranaki. Auckland won 21–18.

Auckland City Libraries

CHAPTER ONE

and unaccustomed to the Northern Union game. To counterbalance this – and probably with a future match in Auckland between the two teams in view – the Aucklanders were very evidently troubled little about scoring. From their point of view it would have been a serious blunder for them to have beaten the Taranaki men by a large majority of points.'

A clue to his bad day was given in the last paragraph: 'The management committee controlling the match wishes to apologise for no seats having been provided on the ground, the chairs that were ordered not having been delivered through some misunderstanding.' If his feet had stayed dry the journalist's mood might have been more charitable towards the new version of rugby.

He might have reflected that his misfortune at having to attend such an obscure and poorly appointed venue was no fault of the match organisers. The New Plymouth Council had bowed to pressure from the New Zealand Rugby Union and reneged on an agreement to allow the use of the Recreation Sports Ground.

That Auckland only scraped home 21–18 despite enjoying home ground advantage in the return game on 10 October suggests strongly that Taranaki was indeed a worthy opponent. The *Taranaki Herald's* diatribe was surely sufficient to fire up the visitors. Auckland had Asher back in its ranks but was fully stretched to prevent Taranaki from completing a winning double. During the second half Taranaki surged back from 7–14 down to lead 18–16 before conceding the match-winning converted try.

'The game was fast and exciting from the kick-off till play ceased, and was of a very even character, the ball travelling from end to end of the ground at a rapid rate,' said the *Auckland Star Sports*. 'Taranaki looked to have Auckland beaten till about a quarter of an hour before time was called, when the local men livened up, and the visitors were kept on the defensive till the bell rang.'

All Golds Dick Wynyard, Rowe and Tyler, plus MacDonald and Marshall, scored tries for Auckland, and Tyler, Marshall and Thomas Houghton kicked conversions. Houghton was one of two sons of former Northern Union (England) chairman Joseph Houghton who assisted with the introduction of the code to Auckland. The Taranaki tries went to future Kiwis wing Ernie Buckland (two), Gordon Hooker and W McLean, boosted by Arthur Hardgrave's three goals.

Only then, fourteen months after leaving Sydney on the first leg of their All Golds' odyssey, could players such as Dick and Billy Wynyard, Harold Rowe and Billy Tyler hang up their boots. But there was no time to rest. Much work had to be done if Northern Union was to put down roots in Auckland. If it was to become a permanent part of the winter sporting scene, clubs needed to be formed and a competition established under the control of a provincial administration.

Rugby union reaction

Of course, all of this activity caused considerable anxiety and not a little panic around the Auckland Rugby Union boardroom table. In a 1930 *Auckland Star Sports* article published to mark rugby league's twenty-first birthday, Duncan McLean recalled that the Union had even proposed that the self-proclaimed amateur game should turn professional.

'Our first glimpse of what friends in the opposition camp were prepared to do in order to crush the newer code was exemplified at a special conference of the New Zealand Rugby Union held on 10 October, 1908, when the two Auckland delegates supported the payment of their players, if you please,' wrote McLean.

'This fact was reported in both local papers at the time. In spite of that advocacy, what an outcry was made by Rugby against us when we did start and they had the audacity to dub us, by innuendo, professionals! Anything that could detract from Rugby was considered by them almost a sin. I could never see any distinction between Dave Gallaher's 1905 All Blacks receiving three shillings per diem and any League player receiving ten shillings, and the principal remains unaltered.'

Tackling the Māori

On 10 July 1909, only nine days before the meeting held to form the Auckland Rugby League, a representative team met and beat Albert Asher's second Māori touring team 21–14 at Victoria Park. The *Auckland Star* described the encounter as 'an interesting display' and favourably reported the efforts of both teams.

Earlier in the season Auckland had contributed five players to the privately organised New Zealand tour of Australia. All Golds Harold Rowe and Bill Trevarthen made their second overseas excursions and were joined by Arthur Carlaw, the first member of his illustrious family to make a mark in rugby league, English-born Thomas Houghton, and utility Ronald MacDonald, who was to be an influential figure within the game, on and off the field.

Asher was also chosen for the New Zealand team but stayed home to organise a Māori side which was to shock its hosts by opening their itinerary with two victories over New South Wales and a 'test' triumph over Australia in its first three fixtures. The warm-up game against Auckland was vital to the Māori preparations in very wet conditions.

CHAPTER ONE

Charles Dunning, one of Auckland's finest forwards.

Auckland City Libraries

'There was a good attendance of between 2000 and 3000 people at Victoria Park on Saturday to witness the match between teams representing Auckland and the pick of the Maori players in the Auckland province,' reported the *Auckland Star*.

'The natives, wearing "all black" colours, took the field first and gave a haka before the commencement of the game. They are a heavy combination, and their forwards average 13st [83kg], which was about a stone better than their opponents. They played with four three-quarters and two five-eighths, dispensing with the services of a half-back.

'The Auckland thirteen, wearing white jerseys, put up a very good game against the natives, and their exhibition, under Northern Union rules, was watched with interest. The ground was in a soaking condition, and often the ruck was ploughing through a perfect quagmire.'

Ernie Asher, playing under his Māori name of Te Keepa Pouwhiuwhiu, scored the opening try, and Albert Asher produced his favourite party trick by jumping clean over Billy Wynyard's head for the try which put the Māori ahead at 6–5.

Tries for Auckland were scored by Linkhorn (two), Houghton, Charles Dunning and Frank Woodward, and Billy Tyler (two) and Marshall kicked goals. The other Māori tries went to Ariki Haira (Alex Stanaway) and Rewi Maniapoto. Their only goal was kicked by either Haira (according to the *Star*) or Asher (*New Zealand Herald*). Auckland led 8–6 at halftime.

CHAPTER 02

RAPID PROGRESS
1909–1919

CHAPTER TWO

Rapid Progress 1909–1919

The league is formed

Meeting of 150 enthusiasts

The official establishment of rugby league in Auckland was reported in one small paragraph in the *Auckland Star* of 20 July 1909.

'A meeting for the purpose of forming an Auckland Rugby Football League, to play under Northern Union rules, was held in the Chamber of Commerce last evening. There was a large attendance of players and supporters, Mr A E Glover MP presiding. The following officers were elected:– President, the Mayor of Auckland (Mr C D Grey); vice-presidents, Messrs A E Glover MP, J Patterson, W T Thompson, W M Evans, W Somers, and J Bonner; management committee, Messrs G A Wynyard, D W McLean, H G Jones, J Endean jun., and F E N Gaudin; secretary, Mr E Watts; treasurer, Mr W Wynyard. It was decided to hold a practice match on Saturday next. Mr R Eagleton placed at the disposal of the League the use of three playing grounds at Epsom, the offer being gladly accepted. It is expected that there will be four teams playing at an early date.'

The reference to an 'early date' was something of an understatement. Within days meetings were held to form clubs in Devonport, Auckland city and Newton. News quickly spread to other parts of the country, via a Press Association message. The *Weekly Press* in Christchurch and *Otago Witness* in Dunedin carried the following report:

'Auckland, July 22. The Northern Union game has made startling progress during the week. On Monday a meeting was held at which some 150 persons were present, and a league was formed. Since then matters have matured, a meeting being held at North Shore last evening, at which there was a strong attendance and a strong club was formed, having for its officials some leading residents. The club has two teams to put in the field, and has practically taken the pick of the amateur players from their district club.

John Endean, a founder of the Northern Union game in New Zealand, and his child. He was the Auckland Rugby League's first life member.
Auckland City Libraries

'This evening a preliminary meeting was held in the city, about 20 players attending, and steps were taken to form a club. It is stated that a Newton club will be formed next week, there being considerable dissatisfaction among the members of the management of the Auckland Union. The officials of the league have procured a ground at Epsom, and will commence a series of fixtures at once.'

Duncan McLean emerged as the figurehead of the thirteen-a-side code, being elected inaugural chairman of both the Auckland Rugby League and the Devonport United club, later renamed North Shore. The club's eightieth anniversary publication told of how most of the members of the North Shore rugby union senior team literally walked away from their game.

'In early June, on the North Shore No.1 ground, the senior rugby team walked off the field at halftime after Ponsonby was beating them 63–0. They refused in the majority to take the field again. They got dressed and walked out of the shed asserting that they intended playing league football in a club which was to be formed in Devonport. They were later to carry out their intention,' it said.

Encouraged by All Golds Charles Dunning and Billy Tyler, Northern Union enthusiasts in Ponsonby had held gatherings and friendly games in 1908. 'The very first such meeting,' according to the club's website, 'was held in the cellar of the Rob Roy Hotel, but it had to be scheduled for when the Freemans Bay tide was out. The name Ponsonby United Football Club was adopted from a famous junior soccer team playing on old Surrey Hills, now known as Grey Lynn.

'Ponsonby's first formally elected club executive was chosen at a meeting in the local Leys Institute Hall on 30 July, 1909. Mr T A Thompson presided and James Carlaw was elected the first chairman with Barry Brigham the secretary and Percy Ussher club treasurer. Charlie Dunning, Arthur Carlaw, Jack Stanaway, Harry Oakley and S Buick made up the club's executive.' While Ponsonby drew its first recruits from the Herne Bay Rugby Club, they were soon followed by some of the powerful Ponsonby Rugby Club's best players.

Devonport United, City Rovers, Newton Rangers and Ponsonby United thus became the first registered clubs, and there was a sub-league being formed in Rotorua, presumably a by-product of the Māori tours to Australia in 1908 and 1909.

The other significant meetings which firmly established rugby league in Auckland and, indeed, New Zealand occurred in April 1910. The official Auckland Provincial Rugby Football League was formulated at the Suffolk Hotel, College Hill, on 6 April, and nineteen days later the Camden Chambers hosted the first general meeting of the New Zealand Provincial Rugby League.

Harry Oakley, foundation executive member of the Ponsonby club, was later secretary of the Auckland Rugby League 1911–12.
Auckland City Libraries

CHAPTER TWO

Duncan McLean

The 'father' of league football

The 1907–08 All Golds' organiser, Albert Henry Baskerville, is rightly credited with being the man most responsible for lifting rugby league from a regional sport in the north of England onto the international stage. However, it was Devonport resident Duncan McLean who took up the challenge – after Baskerville's untimely death in 1908 – of laying permanent foundations for the code in Auckland and other parts of New Zealand.

The *1933 New Zealand Rugby League Annual*, compiled by Aucklander Eric Bennetts, featured photographs of both Baskerville and McLean on its cover alongside the words '1908 – Pioneers Of The Modern Code – 1909'. That reinforced the point made in a 1928 *Auckland Star* article where McLean was described as the 'father' of league football.

Duncan McLean, chairman of the Auckland Rugby League 1909–10.
Auckland City Libraries

Bennetts wrote that 'the name of the late Mr D W McLean, of North Shore, Auckland, is inevitably linked with that of Baskerville, the player-organiser of the All Golds, as one who, with Mr John Endean, was foremost in laying the official administrative side of the game. Mr McLean, who was for over twenty-one years connected with the code, will never be forgotten as an inspiring, courageous and lovable type of sporting gentleman.

'In the early years he worked with enthusiasm to have the official machinery smoothly operating and in 1912 he toured the Dominion in the interests of the code. He formed the first club (North Shore Albions, now Devonport United), was first Auckland chairman, and was first president of the New Zealand Rugby League, of which he became a life member. With Mr C A Snedden, he represented the Dominion at a Rugby League conference in Sydney in 1928. Mr McLean was also a life member of the New Zealand Commercial Travellers Association.'

Under the headline 'Sportsmen All', the 1928 *Auckland Star* included McLean among a series of personalities 'who have taken more than the average share of the burden of helping Auckland sport to its present good standing'. Describing McLean as 'the man who more than any other may be termed the "father" of League football in Auckland', it expressed regret that he had recently become a less regular attendee at Carlaw Park matches because of failing eyesight.

'He was chairman of the first League Executive Committee formed in Auckland in 1909, and president of the New Zealand League Football Council in 1910. He and the late Mr John Endean were practically the head and front of League football management during the troublesome first three years of its existence. Mr McLean hails from Dunedin, but has been nearly half a century in Auckland. His football interests before 1909 were the Rugby game (as a member of the Auckland Rugby Union management committee from 1905 to 1907).

'Other sports than football have occupied "Mac's" attention. He always took a keen interest in yachting and rowing, and was president of the North Shore Rowing Club when that club instituted the North Shore Orphans Club, which is now such a power in Devonport social life. He is a life member of the North Shore Rowing Club. Of course, "Mac", like most active men who enjoy recreation in the open air combined with genial intercourse, has been a bowler, and has taken part in the politics of bowling as a vice-president of the North Shore club.' He was also active in tennis and hockey clubs based in Devonport.

McLean was president and chairman of the New Zealand Rugby League in its inaugural 1910 season, when it hosted the first England touring team. He served as treasurer in 1911 before returning to the presidency from 1912 to 1914 and 1919 to 1923. He continued his association with the New Zealand Rugby League until reluctantly retiring through ill health in 1930. A newspaper article credited McLean with, after forming the North Shore Albions club, also playing a 'prominent part' in starting the Newton Rangers, Ponsonby and the Northcote Ramblers. It was not long before the far-sighted McLean was looking for further expansion.

When in 1910 the New Zealand Rugby League accepted an invitation to send its first officially sanctioned team to New South Wales and Queensland the following season, it needed to scour the country for candidates. What better way than to send an Auckland team on tour to Wanganui, to the deep south for a triple-header at Bluff, Invercargill and Dunedin, and to Napier and Dannevirke on the way home, under the control of loyal sidekick and secretary Teddy Watts? The upshot was a fully representative New Zealand team to visit Australia, and the subsequent inclusion of four of its members in the 1911–12 Australasian Kangaroos on tour to Britain.

In 1912 McLean addressed public gatherings in Wellington and Christchurch which led to the establishment of the Wellington and Canterbury leagues. Although Wellington provided many players to early New Zealand touring teams and fielded representative sides, neither region had been able to introduce club competitions which would have given the game stability.

Largely because of his opponents' well-publicised alarm, McLean's meetings attracted large attendances. His crusade was a courageous one, taking on a rugby union establishment that had strong influences at national and local government levels and within the media. McLean 'sold' Northern Union on the basis of its progress in Auckland. It was, he claimed, far less brutal than rugby union and its playing laws were more attractive to players and spectators. Much of the emphasis was placed on allaying fears of professionalism, arguing that the payment of expenses to touring players was nothing more than standard practice for the 1905–06 All Blacks.

CHAPTER TWO

A year later McLean again journeyed south, primarily to attend the Australasian conference of Commercial Travellers in Dunedin, but also to assist the fledgling rugby league organisations he had helped create. Wellington and Canterbury were by then under way but he had (in his own words) 'no immediate response' in his old home province of Otago.

Bennetts' 1933 *Annual* was published after McLean's death. He recalled that in 1930 McLean had written a special *Auckland Star Sports* review of the code to mark its twenty-first anniversary, and quoted the following passage to demonstrate the 'splendid character of the "grandfather" of our game in this part of the world':

'We must not forget that the code has a reputation for its chief consideration of players, for the game is the thing, after all. It is the main reason why Rugby League, as an improved science of Rugby, will survive as in the past. As long as it is played with the true spirit of sportsmen, so surely it will progress. I am proud to have had the health and strength to have been able to devote so much time and thought to a game so fine for our young people and so entertaining for the public.' (D W McLean, *Auckland Star Sports*, 14 June 1930.)

Billy Wynyard

From boots to boardroom

The Wynyards had long been a well-known football family before rugby league started in Auckland. Brothers George, Henry and William Wynyard toured Britain and Australia with the 1888–89 New Zealand Natives, that remarkable team which played 107 rugby union matches (plus eight games of Victorian Rules and two of soccer) on an adventure which lasted fourteen months. William, or Tabby as he was known, also represented Auckland and Wellington at cricket and athletics, was a talented golfer, oarsman, billiards player and cyclist, and toured Australia with the 1893 All Blacks.

Their nephews, John Richard (Dick) Wynyard and William Thomas (Billy) Wynyard, played for the North Shore Rugby Club in the early 1900s while continuing a family tradition of working as civil service clerks. Dick was a regular Auckland representative at twenty, playing in the 1905 side which relieved Wellington of the Ranfurly Shield, and Billy, the elder by two years, also wore the blue and white jersey.

But their careers in the fifteen-a-side code came to an end when they paid their £50 fees to join up with the 1907–08 All Golds. The new generation of Wynyards retraced the sprig marks of their uncles on a nine-month tour of Sydney, Ceylon, Britain and Australia. Dick Wynyard appeared in all six test matches in the series triumphs over Britain and Australia, while Billy played in the last two Australian tests.

AUCKLAND RUGBY LEAGUE
1909-2009

The death of Albert Baskerville in Brisbane had left the All Golds, and rugby league in New Zealand, without a leader. Senior players such as George Smith and Lance Todd, and several other team-mates had been, or would be, signed by English clubs. Banned for life by a vengeful New Zealand Rugby Union, those who were left faced great odds when spreading the Northern Union message to their countrymen. Billy Wynyard was among those who were not deterred.

A *Weekly Press* report of 6 October 1909 proved that Billy Wynyard and Wellington-based Daniel Fraser, a forward who had assisted with the All Golds managerial duties, had kept in contact with Northern Union authorities. It quoted the English *Athletic News* in advocating the introduction of an international transfer ban to prevent professional clubs in Britain from fleecing New Zealand and Australia of their best players. The New Zealand Rugby League was not then in existence but the writer said 'both Fraser and Wynyard realise that if the Northern Union game is to flourish in New Zealand those who are conversant with the rules and the style of play favoured by the English professionals should stay in the colonies and play the part of tutors'.

Working alongside Billy Wynyard at P Hayman and Company, an English firm with an Auckland branch on Customs Street East, were Duncan McLean and Teddy Watts. Introducing the rugby league game to Auckland must have occupied at least as much of their time as their work, for when the provincial league was formed in 1909 McLean was chairman, Watts secretary and Wynyard treasurer.

Dick Wynyard, the Auckland captain, in quest of the ball against Wellington in 1909.
Auckland City Libraries

Billy Wynyard (left, rear) as a member of the New Zealand Rugby League council in 1912. The others are Alf Powley (right, rear) and, sitting, Jim Gleeson, Teddy Watts (secretary), Duncan McLean (president), Barry Brigham (treasurer) and Tom MacReynolds.
Eric Bennetts, NZRL Annual 1933.

CHAPTER TWO

A year later McLean and Watts filled the same positions on the newly formed New Zealand Rugby League.

Wynyard stayed on as a member of the national council and occasionally acting as chairman for meetings. He was a New Zealand selector for the first home test against the 1910 British team and remained in that capacity until the 1919 New Zealand team toured Australia. In recognition of his service during rugby league's first decade, Billy Wynyard was made the first life member of the New Zealand Rugby League that same year.

Dick Wynyard died in 1915 at the age of 30. Billy died at 49 in 1932, which prompted an old friend, Ernest Eyre, to pen a 'Tribute to a Good All-round Athlete and Sportsman' – despite Wynyard and Eyre being on opposite sides during the tempestuous times when the rugby league pioneers attempted to break the rugby union monopoly on Auckland's North Shore. Eyre recorded that Billy served in the Boer War and after dabbling in soccer, rowing, yachting and athletics he became a regular in the North Shore backline alongside brother Dick. He was described as protective of his sibling and strong on defence ('he'd have tackled a mountain rather than let it fall on Dick'), 'a ripping good kick with both feet' and, on attack, 'as tricky as a cage full of monkeys'.

First match

North Shore 44 City 24

All Gold Dick Wynyard (North Shore) and future New Zealand representative Arthur Carlaw (City) were the captains for the first match played under the control of the five-day-old Auckland Rugby League at Epsom on Saturday, 24 July 1909. The City team was drawn from players currently in the process of forming clubs on that side of the harbour.

Action from the first match under the control of the Auckland Rugby League, played at Eagleton's Ground, Epsom, North Shore against City. A City player attempting to pass Frank Woodward.

Auckland City Libraries

North Shore led throughout, scoring ten tries and seven goals against six tries and three goals. Try-scorers for North Shore were Seagar (three), Wells (two), Gladding (two), Percival (two) and Neighbour. Woodward kicked seven goals. The City try-scorers were Linkhorn (two), Arthur Carlaw, Billy Tyler, Farrant and George Smith. Smith (two) and Thomas Houghton kicked goals.

The *Auckland Star* reported the winners benefited from having more experienced men and a better combination. City relied heavily on Ponsonby All Golds Charles Dunning and Tyler, the elusive Carlaw, and Englishmen Alf Chorley, who had played for Halifax and Swinton, and Houghton, from St Helens.

'The beauty of the Northern Union game is that even when two teams are brought together, and one is better than the other, the weaker combination is not everlastingly on the defensive. The game rages up and down the field and play is fast and furious all the while,' said the *Star*.

The *New Zealand Herald* concurred: 'On account of the heavy scoring, and the lack of experience on the part of many of the players, particularly in the City team, the game can only be regarded in the nature of a practice match, but nevertheless it gave the spectators an excellent idea of the possibilities of the Northern Union game played by able exponents. The great feature about it is the fast open work, which is often found lacking in ordinary Rugby.'

Other games were arranged between the emerging clubs, such as when Ponsonby United came from a six-point halftime deficit to beat Newton Rangers 16–6 at Victoria Park on 21 August 1909. The *Star* attributed Ponsonby's comeback to Carlaw and Tyler, who 'started to initiate passing runs which were very pretty to watch'.

The Ponsonby club's website history reports that matches were also held against North Shore and City Rovers – 'As many as 32 players passed through the Ponsonby ranks in 1909, clear evidence of the growth of the sport and the number of games the fledgling clubs were arranging amongst themselves.'

The integrated game

Māori involvement in Auckland rugby league, both on and off the field, was very strong from the start. This contrasted with the rugby union attitude of the time. One of Albert Asher's motives in organising the 1908 and 1909 Māori tours to Australia was a lack of representative recognition for Māori players in the fifteen-a-side code. Asher had been an exception as a prolific-scoring All Blacks wing, but it was not until 1910, as a reaction to the Asher tours, that the New Zealand Rugby Union set up a Māori advisory committee.

CHAPTER TWO

The Asher brothers lived their lives in league. Ernie spent sixty years as a player, selector and administrator, and Albert was a long-serving Carlaw Park caretaker. They were instrumental in forming the City Rovers club and its early champion teams included fellow Māori tourists Jim Rukutai and Alex Stanaway. Stanaway's brother, Jack, became New Zealand's first test referee in 1910.

Outstanding All Golds scrum-half Dick Wynyard was the first officially appointed Auckland captain in 1909, and his brother Billy heavily involved himself in selection, coaching and the boardroom. Champion Māori fullback Dick Papakura, from the Rotorua sub-league, and Albert Asher played for Auckland against Wellington that year and were the only New Zealanders invited to represent Australasia against the 1910 British touring team in two Sydney games.

Ernie Asher toured New Zealand with the 1910 Auckland team and the Ashers, Alex Stanaway and Jim Rukutai became Kiwis. Rukutai's international career spanned the First World War, and he is still New Zealand's youngest coach. He was thirty-three when he took the 1921 Kiwis to Australia. Such was his standing in Auckland that the Rukutai Shield was named in his honour soon after his death in 1940.

Annual fixtures between Māori and Pākehā teams were to be features on the Auckland rugby league calendar, raising money for injured players and aiding selectors to finalise their teams. The 1937 New Zealand Māori side provided one of Carlaw Park's all-time highlights by beating Australia 16–5, with famed All Blacks fullback George Nepia making his debut at the ground.

'Donnybrook' at Devonport Domain

Rugby union resentment at the arrival of rugby league on the Auckland sporting scene was at its highest on the North Shore. The *New Zealand Free Lance* reported on 24 July 1909, that 'the North Shore club seems to have suffered the most by the loss of players through the introduction of the professional game in Auckland'.

Apparently the first tentative shots in the North Shore rugby 'war' were fired when Dick Wynyard entered his old rugby club's training shed after the All Golds tour. Wynyard, suspended for life by the New Zealand Rugby Union, refused to leave when asked, saying his North Shore Rugby Club membership was still paid up and he was entitled to be there. A fight broke out and some gas-lights were smashed.

The battle lines were drawn at Devonport Domain, which was coveted by both codes. It was not uncommon for the rugby union club, upon learning that a rugby league game was planned, to rustle up enough players and stage an impromptu match of its own with an earlier kick-off.

One such incident occurred in 1909, when two rugby union sides took the field ahead of a charity rugby league match between North Shore Albions and members of the Devonport Fire Brigade with proceeds to go to the brigade. Both codes started games which inevitably became intermingled and what was described as 'a general Donnybrook' ensued.

In 1910 the rugby union club gained favour with the domain board, shunting the Albions off to a rough and invariably muddy ground belonging to the Takapuna Jockey Club. Rugby union club secretary Ernest Eyre admitted baiting the Albions in August 1911 by spreading the word that the main field at the domain would not be used the next Saturday. Eyre then arranged for two teams to hide in the changing sheds, anticipating that the rugby league players would abandon their quagmire and make for the domain. Just as they came into sight the hidden players ran out and kicked off. Fists were shaken and angry words exchanged as the leaguies turned to trek back through the rain to the racecourse.

On 8 July 1912, a Devonport Domain Board meeting at the borough council chambers ended in chaos when Eyre refused to allow North Shore Albions use of the ground for a major game against Ponsonby United. When matters threatened to get out of control, the mayor ordered his town clerk to summon the police.

As a result of that incident, and to prevent a recurrence, the borough council split the domain into two grounds, one for each code. An uneasy truce lasted until 1958 when the North Shore Albions moved to Bayswater.

Snapshots of the Devonport Domain in 1908, showing rugby union, hockey and soccer games before the introduction of rugby league to the sporting scene.
Auckland City Libraries

CHAPTER TWO

Contact with the Northern Union

After the formation of the Auckland Rugby League, no time was wasted in contacting the Northern Union Rugby League in Leeds, seeking affiliation. According to the minutes of a Northern Union committee meeting on 14 September, the letter from Auckland asked 'that the League be recognised as the ruling body for the whole of New Zealand, and that Leagues forming in other centres throughout the Dominion affiliate to them, the ruling body'.

The Northern Union cabled its acceptance of the application, but in a follow-up letter voiced the opinion 'that it would not be to their interest or the interest of the game to give other provinces the idea that Auckland would take over the entire management of the game in New Zealand, but that the representation of such should be on a broad basis, giving each province an equitable representation'.

Geoffrey Moorhouse, author of the English Rugby League centenary history, wrote that, while well-meaning, the Northern Union's conditional acceptance of the Auckland Rugby League was 'poor advice from men who knew nothing at all of local conditions at the other side of the world. What the fledgling game needed was unity with strong central direction, instead of autonomous and relatively weak parts which could be picked off one by one by their immensely more powerful competitors in the provincial rugby unions.'

The upshot was that rugby league in New Zealand flourished only in the largest and most cosmopolitan city. The Northern Union was to compound its misjudgement in 1910, when the first British touring team restricted itself to playing three matches in Auckland and one in Rotorua. The New Zealand Rugby League had been formed on 25 April 1910, with headquarters in Auckland, and the New Zealand Rugby League and Auckland Rugby League belatedly combined to send a team south on a promotional mission. Valuable time had been lost.

1909 representative games

Despite Auckland leading the way in establishing the code, Taranaki and Wellington were capable of fielding formidable provincial teams, as Auckland discovered when three representative fixtures were played late in the 1909 season. The first team to take the field under the banner of the Auckland Rugby League lost 8–7 to Taranaki at Victoria Park on 7 August. Auckland won the return game 27–11 at the New Plymouth Sports Ground on 16 September, but Auckland was beaten again, 22–19, by Wellington at home on 9 October.

Wigan's All Golds recruit, Lance Todd, was home for a holiday and refereed the first tussle with Taranaki. According to the *Auckland Star*, Victoria Park was wet and heavy 'but the backs on both sides handled the greasy leather [ball] in good style, and the spectators were rewarded with some open and exciting play.' The attendance was estimated at 5,000.

The first officially selected Auckland team (as listed in the *1949 New Zealand Rugby League Annual*) comprised Thomas Houghton at fullback, Alf Chorley, Frank Woodward and Arthur Carlaw in the three-quarters, Dick Wynyard and Ronald MacDonald as the five-eighths, Alf Jackson at half, and forwards Wells, Bill Mackrell, Charles Dunning, Jim Griffen, Linkhorn and George Seagar.

Dunning had the distinction of scoring the first try, capitalising on some wild passing by Taranaki near its own goal-line. Woodward's conversion was the first goal. Auckland went to a 7–0 advantage when Carlaw secured a mark and Neighbour kicked the goal. It stayed that way until the second half.

Several scoring opportunities were narrowly missed by players in both teams, Taranaki scrambling back to cover one particularly incisive Dick Wynyard break

The first representative team to take the field under the banner of the Auckland Rugby League, losing 8–7 to Taranaki at Victoria Park on 7 August 1909.
Auckland City Libraries

An Auckland passing run against Taranaki under Northern Union rules.
Auckland City Libraries

CHAPTER TWO

from a scrum. But Taranaki could not be denied when Ted Haskell and Tom Smith crossed for tries, with Arthur Hardgrave's conversion giving the visitors their 8–7 victory.

'Notwithstanding the heavy, sodden ground, the game was fast and interesting throughout, the ball travelling up and down the field at a great rate, first one side and then the other attacking strongly,' it was reported. 'On the day's play, the Taranaki men should have won by more points than they did, over-eagerness throwing away a number of chances.'

The usually reliable Hardgrave also had an off-day with his goalkicking but was otherwise outstanding as Taranaki's fullback. It was suggested that he would be a valuable acquisition for a British professional club. Instead, Hardgrave was to represent New Zealand from Auckland between 1912 and 1914, his son Roy subsequently becoming a Kiwi in 1928.

In New Plymouth, it conceded a second-minute try to Taranaki centre 'Clews' Moir, and was held to 8–8 at halftime. But Auckland, reinforced by the return from injury of All Golds forward Bill Mackrell, eventually emerged as the comfortable winner. Carlaw, Woodward, Griffen, Wynyard and Mackrell scored Auckland's tries and Bradburn kicked six goals. Lance Todd was again the referee.

Three tries by All Golds captain Hercules (Bumper) Wright spearheaded Wellington to its 22–19 win at Auckland's expense. Wellington claimed six tries to five for Auckland by George Seagar (two), Dick Wynyard, Dunning and Grundy. Conversions were kicked by Billy Tyler and Frank Woodward.

Alex Stanaway (Auckland) gets away on his own in the 22–19 loss to Wellington.
Auckland City Libraries

The Auckland team included Riki Papakura and Albert Asher, the backline stars of the Māori team which had toured Australia earlier in the year. But they came in for their share of criticism in a dysfunctional Auckland three-quarters line. Seagar was described as 'probably the best forward on the field', no small compliment considering the Wellington pack included famed internationals Wright, Tom Cross and Con Sullivan.

A week earlier, Papakura and several other Māori tourists had appeared for Rotorua against an Auckland XIII in the first Northern Union representative fixture in Rotorua, where three clubs had been formed. Selector Billy Wynyard might have under-estimated the opposition. He named his brother, Dick, at halfback, and Woodward was a late addition, but Rotorua over-ran the visitors 33–8. It did not help Auckland that fullback Archie Ferguson suffered a broken leg when a team-mate fell on him.

The second Wellington match ended a momentous season for Auckland rugby league. It was reported that about 200 players were registered, a healthy spectator following had developed, and the next step would be the introduction of inter-club competitions in 1910.

Early referees

Archie Ferguson and Jack Stanaway

According to a contemporary newspaper report, pioneering rugby league referees in Auckland enjoyed a marked advantage over the barrackers on the sidelines – so new was the thirteen-a-side game on the sporting scene that only the referees (and hopefully the players) knew the rules!

That was the situation when J (Tiffy) Lang controlled the representative match between Auckland and Wellington on 22 August 1908, little more than two months after the All Golds had returned to this country with the first rule books. A journalist, who was also rather vague as to what the new-fangled game was all about, reported an attendance of between 7,000 and 8,000 happy but possibly bemused spectators.

'The crowd was enthusiastic about a game in which the ball travelled with bewildering speed from player to player, and from one end of the field to the other,' he wrote. 'Each side took turns to attack, and the game was marked by very few stoppages. Referee Lang did not have to cope with a partisan, knowledgeable crowd as he alone knew the rules, and all accepted his rulings in good part.' It was noted that Lang wore a white jersey and long white trousers, and the players' jerseys carried letters instead of numbers.

According to the Auckland Rugby League's fiftieth anniversary booklet in 1959, the referees association 'as we know it today' was formed on 24 May 1910, at a

J (Tiffy) Lang controlled the first Northern Union game played in Auckland, between Auckland and Wellington on 22 August 1908.
Eric Bennetts, NZRL Annual 1933

CHAPTER TWO

Jack Stanaway, refereeing the first home test match between New Zealand and England at the Auckland Domain.
Auckland City Libraries

Archie Ferguson in charge of the 1910 fixture between Auckland and England at Victoria Park.
Auckland City Libraries

meeting at Cambden Chambers. A year later it adopted its first uniform as white jersey, white shorts and black socks. Appointments were made directly by the Auckland Rugby League.

But a 1985 *League News* article, compiled by Gary Whittle, traced the referees association back to the formation of the Auckland Provincial Rugby League on 6 April 1910, when a group of officials were asked to attend the next meeting to form the association. That was held on 19 April and convened by Matt Hooper, who, Whittle wrote, 'is acknowledged as the founder of the Auckland Rugby League Referees' Association'.

Although inexperience was inevitable among administrators, players, referees and those who would seek to advise the match officials from the sidelines, the first two prominent referees, Jack Stanaway and Archie Ferguson, had played at representative level before taking up the whistle.

Stanaway, under his Māori name of Hone Haira, had not only toured Australia with Albert Asher's original 1908 team but also scored a try in the 20–10 loss to Australia in the only 'test' match on the tour. His brother Alex (Ariki Haira) was also in that team.

From there the brothers took different rugby league paths. Alex returned to Australia with the 1909 Māori team, played for City when club football started in Auckland, and toured Australia with the 1911 New Zealand team. Jack made the transition to refereeing so smoothly that he controlled the first test match on New Zealand soil when the British toured in 1910.

A broken leg while playing for Auckland against Rotorua led to Ferguson's distinguished refereeing career. He was in charge of the 1910 fixture between England and Auckland, the sole test match of the 1914 British tour, and the fourth test when Australia first visited in 1919. Ferguson toured Australia twice with New Zealand teams, as a referee in 1919 and co-manager in 1930, when he was reported as being 'the last remaining active official of the band of men who started the game in Auckland in 1909'.

Ferguson was born in Wellington, where he had been a foundation member of the Selwyn Rugby Club, and linked up with Devonport when he moved to Auckland in 1908. Described as 'a fine forward', Ferguson took a strong fancy to the new code and adopted it. President of the Referees Association for a lengthy period, he remained in administration as the West Coast delegate, and later the Otago delegate, to the New Zealand Rugby League.

King's death delays competition

The scheduled introduction of inter-club rugby league to Auckland on 7 May 1910, was delayed when news reached New Zealand of the death of King Edward VII. In line with other sports organisations, the Auckland Rugby League postponed its matches as a mark of respect to the late monarch. One week later, Ponsonby United and Newton Rangers played at Victoria Park and North Shore Albions met City Rovers at Takapuna racecourse.

Team lists (with a few uncorrected spelling errors) were published in the *Auckland Star* as:

Ponsonby United: R McDonald, H Oakley, S Riley, A Carlaw, C Dunning, W Tyler, F Lynch, J Cholly, H Bettis, S Cole, H Childs, R W McDonald, A Bettis and J C Harley.

Newton Rangers: Houghton, Haswell, Henderson, Bonner, Smith, Armitage, Farrant, Mackrell, Bradburn, Winters, A Smith, F Maki, C Linkhorn, Lupton, Simpson.

City Rovers: C Brett, E Asher, B Blakey, J Lane, A Asher, G Harrison, S Keene, Lowe (2), Haira, Avery, Denize, Blucher, Doran, Dennison, Tobin, Miles.

North Shore Albions: F Taylor, McDonald, Percival, O Miller, A Sutton, Jackson, Hill, B Wells, Griffin, C Wells, Goulter, Baker, Seagar; emergencies, Harrison, F Shaw, E Bailey.

CHAPTER TWO

At Victoria Park the players were addressed by Auckland Rugby League chairman Barry Brigham, who praised the clubs on assembling such fine teams. He said there was no need to caution them about foul play because it was easily detectable in this game. Confirming the visit by the British team, Brigham said it was essential players kept in strict training.

Incredibly, not one goal was kicked in the two games and not a point was scored in the Takapuna match. Despite the presence of such outstanding attacking backs as the Asher brothers, Albert and Ernie, in the City backline, the Rovers and their North Shore rivals were nil-all at fulltime. The heavier Newton forwards, led by Bill Mackrell, paved the way for a 12–6 victory over Ponsonby at Victoria Park. All points came from unconverted tries, to Newton's Farrant (two), Haswell and Winters and Ponsonby's Riley and Cole.

City Rovers won the Myers Cup as the first Auckland club champion in 1910.

Back row: R Denize, W Moki, A Hawthorne, J Rukutai, R Christenson, R Mitchell, A Stanaway, T Avery, E W Watts (treasurer).

Middle row: F Morse, E J Phelan (delegate), A Asher (captain), J Graham (chairman), G Hunt (secretary), H Childs.

Front row: G Graham (mascot), E Asher, G Robinson, A Asher junior (mascot).

NZRL Museum

Myers Cup

The Myers Cup was the original Auckland club championship trophy, won in the first two seasons by City Rovers. It was donated by Arthur (later Sir Arthur) Myers, who was Mayor of Auckland from 1905 to 1909 and a member of Parliament between 1910 and 1921. The Australian-born Myers was responsible for early public works in Auckland, including Grafton Bridge, the Town Hall and Myers Park. He was Auckland Rugby League president from 1914 until his death in 1926.

Asher on the mat

Renowned international wing Albert Asher was the first player to appear before the Auckland Rugby League on a judiciary matter. On 25 June 1910, Asher was warned and then sent off by referee Jack Stanaway (a former Māori team-mate on tour of Australia) for dissent. Stanaway had ruled out a City Rovers 'try' when it trailed Ponsonby United, 11–8, at Victoria Park. The match ended abruptly when the other City players followed Asher off the field. Both Asher and his club apologised at a special midweek meeting of the Auckland Rugby League management committee, and Asher was cautioned, allowing him to leave for Wellington to catch the Sydney boat and play in two matches for Australasia against England.

Sir Arthur Myers.
Auckland City Libraries

1910: Amateurs against professionals

England 52 Auckland 9

A four-match tour by England in 1910 revealed the gulf in standards between the British professionals and New Zealand amateurs. The visitors won all of their matches by wide margins, including a 52–20 victory in the first test match on New Zealand soil. Auckland was beaten 52–9 after trailing 41–3 at halftime.

'The British team played a brilliant game, and many old rugby enthusiasts were carried away by the excitement of the rapidly moving incidents engendered by the new code,' said the Press Association. Ten thousand spectators attended the first international match involving an Auckland team on a fine and calm day, but Victoria Park was very slippery.

'The exhibition of rugby given by the British team was of the highest class, their combination being excellent,' said a special report commissioned by *The Press*. 'Their passing, running and kicking were well above the New Zealand amateur provincial standard, while the tackling by both forwards and backs was of a deadly order.'

CHAPTER TWO

A dribbling rush by the England forwards.
Auckland City Libraries

Another try for England.
Auckland City Libraries

Comments in the *Auckland Star* comparing the British to the All Blacks would have angered the traditionalists: 'Our greatest All Black teams never had a set of forwards who could out-run, out-weigh and out-wit this side, and their best and liveliest backs never could have shown these men anything to speak of in the matter of accurate passing, fast running, straight and strong kicking and safe tackling.' The *Star* said the Aucklanders could not match their opponents in experience, size or pace.

Auckland actually opened the scoring in both halves, when loose forward George Seagar and wing Albert Asher claimed their tries. Prop Jim Griffen completed the scoring with a try just before fulltime.

Fred Jackson, the first man to captain Auckland against an overseas team, had arrived with the 1908 Anglo-Welsh rugby union tourists. After playing in the first test in Dunedin, he was suspended, having been found guilty of professionalism by English authorities. Instructed to return home, Jackson got as far as Sydney before recrossing the Tasman and changing codes. He played for New Zealand against the 1910 Lions before incurring another suspension, this time for striking a rugby league official who insulted Jackson's Māori companion. One of his sons, Everard, was an All Black in the 1930s.

Auckland team (with converted weights): fullback, Alf Chorley (70kg); three-quarters, L Nolan (68kg), G Smith (70kg), Albert Asher (76kg); five-eighths, Alf Jackson (69kg), Ronald MacDonald (76kg); halfback, Len Farrant (64kg); forwards, Fred Jackson (102kg) captain, Charles Dunning (80kg), Jim Griffen (90kg), Alex Stanaway (86kg), H Fricker (80kg), George Seagar (70kg). Emergencies: backs, Syd Riley (73kg), Arthur Carlaw (70kg); forwards, J Bennett (87kg), Jim Rukutai (83kg), Bob Mitchell (81kg).

Touring the nation

Auckland's most extensive tour within New Zealand was not conducted in an age of comfortable air transport or even in plush coaches on modern highways. It occurred in 1910 when, between 20 September and 13 October, a squad of twenty-one players travelled by boat and train to matches in Wanganui, Bluff, Invercargill, Dunedin, Nelson, Napier and Dannevirke. And they even contributed towards the tour costs.

The New Zealand Rugby League, no doubt concerned by the one-sided results during the England tour, had received an invitation to send a team to Australia in 1911 and was eager to unearth talent from around the country. Auckland co-operated by agreeing to send a team south and the players paid £10 each, even though there was no guarantee it would be repaid.

An early draft plan included a game in Christchurch, which did not come to fruition. The itinerary was already strenuous enough. After the three games (in five days) in the deep south the team sailed from Dunedin to Wellington before boarding another steamer to cross Cook Strait and arrive in Nelson on match morning. The players hardly had time to regain their land legs before running onto Trafalgar Park.

The touring team was: Harry Childs, G Harrison, Ernie Asher, W Bonner, Syd Riley, L Nolan, Arthur Carlaw, Alf Jackson, W J Walker (Rotorua), Ronald MacDonald, Sid Kean, J Bennett, S Cole, T Avery, R. Denize, Charles Dunning (captain), H Fricker, George Seagar, Robert Mitchell, H B Oakley, C Brockliss. The team manager was Auckland Rugby League secretary Teddy Watts, and Oakley doubled as his assistant.

CHAPTER TWO

The 1910 Auckland team which toured the Dominion.

Back row: C Brockliss, E Asher, G Harrison, J Bennett, S Riley.

Third row: S Cole, H Fricker, W Bonner. R Mitchell, T Avery, H Childs, W J Walker.

Second row: A Jackson, H Oakley, E W Watts (manager), C Dunning (captain), R A MacDonald (vice-captain), G Seagar.

Front row: R Denize, S Kean, L Nolan, A Carlaw.

Auckland City Libraries

Auckland was travelling into the unknown, the British tourists not having ventured further south than Rotorua. Match results suggest they encountered consistently strong opposition even though they returned home undefeated. Auckland headed off Wanganui (15–14), before sailing south to meet Bluff (42–12), Southland (17–12) and a combined Otago-Southland team (30–18). Next came the long and circuitous trip to Nelson for a 24–13 win. Back on the North Island, they beat Hawke's Bay 19–14 and Dannevirke 28–8.

Try-scoring was obviously a priority. Auckland scored forty-five tries – the individual list headed by Kean (eight), Asher (seven), Seagar (seven) and Nolan (five) – but kicked only twenty goals, eleven of them by Dunning. Kean scored four tries in the Dunedin game and Seagar crossed for four at Bluff, where Carlaw displayed his versatility by refereeing the match.

Dunning went on to captain the 1911 New Zealand team in Australia, with Asher, MacDonald, Kean and Seagar among his team-mates. Happily, the Kiwis returned from Australia with a surplus of £1,182, and all of Auckland's touring players from the previous season had their money refunded.

Northern Union Cup

The 1910 England team managers had brought with them a handsome trophy to present to their New Zealand Rugby League hosts. Made in Bradford, the Northern Union Cup was allocated to inter-provincial competition and initially awarded to Auckland. It is still being contested, having undergone a name change to Rugby League Cup in 1969.

Auckland and Wellington produced a splendid display of the new code in the first challenge match at Victoria Park on 5 August 1911. Wellington led 8–6 at halftime before Auckland dominated the second spell to win 16–8, moving out of range with a try just before fulltime.

On consecutive Saturdays from 19 August, Auckland repelled worthy bids from Hawke's Bay (17–13), Nelson (36–12) and Taranaki (26–15). Hawke's Bay went within an ace of taking the prize home, matching Auckland's three tries and attacking strongly at fulltime. Nelson came north with four New Zealand representatives, Bert Feary, Pat Hannigan, Dave Mason and Charles James, and Taranaki threatened at 18–15 during the second half.

Auckland also beat Lower Waikato 36–22 at Frankton and Hawke's Bay Māori 22–10 at North Shore in a busy representative programme. The Lower Waikato fixture was held on 12 August, and two Ngaruawahia backs, J Kay and Reg Sprague, subsequently played for Auckland in cup matches. Kay scored two tries against Wellington and Sprague toured Australia with the 1911 New Zealand team.

It was the Northern Union Cup that first brought a Canterbury team to Auckland in 1913, the first year of club rugby league in Christchurch. The southerners were competitive for most of the first half and produced flashes of brilliance after that, but Auckland eventually powered away to finish with twelve tries and a 48–12 win. The cup was to remain in Auckland until South Auckland snatched it away in 1922.

Northern Union Cup.
Bernie Wood collection

Auckland Kangaroos

Auckland representatives Arthur (Bolla) Francis, George Gillett, and Charles Savory and Rotorua-based Frank Woodward toured Britain with the 1911–12 Kangaroos, the hosts having invited an Australasian team. Francis top-scored with 125 points and later played professionally for English clubs Wigan and Hull. Like Francis, the versatile Gillett had been an All Black. He is also reputed to have played Australian Rules for Western Australia while living in Kalgoorlie.

CHAPTER TWO

The Auckland representative team which retained the Northern Union Cup in 1911 by beating Taranaki.
Auckland City Libraries

Frank Morse about to start a passing rush from a scrum against Wellington.
Auckland City Libraries

Fullback Alf Chorley gets in his kick, which is followed up by his backs, against Hawke's Bay.
Auckland City Libraries

Auckland half Alf Jackson starting a passing sequence against Taranaki.
Auckland City Libraries

First overseas scalp

With rugby league still in its infancy in Queensland, the New South Wales teams that toured New Zealand before the First World War were virtually full Australian teams. It was all the more to Auckland's credit, then, that it beat the 1912 tourists 10–3, the only loss suffered by the visitors in ten matches, which included an 18–10 win over New Zealand.

It rained 'practically from whistle to bell' and the conditions played into the hands of the Auckland forwards, Jim Rukutai, George Seagar, Charles Dunning, Bob Mitchell and brothers Harold and Morgan Hayward, who hailed from Thames. 'The Auckland forwards quite outplayed the opposition vanguard, and in the second spell there was only one team in it,' reported the Press Association.

Auckland's triumph was overshadowed by accusations of rough play made against the New South Welshmen. Centre Sid Deane was sent off just before the finish for punching Billy Curran three times in the face. Down 3–0 at halftime, Auckland went ahead soon after through a Mitchell try and Arthur Hardgrave conversion. Dunning kicked a penalty goal, and Auckland sealed the victory through a try to Rotorua wing Rukingi Reke. Despite the very wet conditions, more than 7,000 Aucklanders cheered their heroes home.

So impressed was the New Zealand Rugby League that the scheduled second 'test' match was replaced by a return game with Auckland. Sixteen thousand fans converged on the Domain Cricket Ground and expectations were high as heavy morning rain cleared. But Eastern Suburbs wing Dan Frawley ran in four tries as the tourists romped to a 25–2 win.

Auckland City Libraries

Undaunted by thunder storms, a crowd of more than 7,000 saw Auckland beat New South Wales 10–3 at Victoria Park.
Auckland City Libraries

The Auckland side which was beaten 38–16 by the 1912 New Zealand touring team. E Asher, G Seagar, J Griffen, G Lambert, G Smith, R Mitchell, A Stanaway, A Jackson, D Kenealy, H Childs, H Fricker, D Healy, A Blakey.
Auckland City Libraries

CHAPTER TWO

New South Wales, and a still free-scoring Frawley, returned in 1913 to almost replicate that result, beating Auckland 27–2 at the Domain in the course of an unbeaten tour.

Auckland also played matches against the 1911 and 1912 New Zealand teams that had assembled for tours to Australia. So bad was the weather for the 1911 fixture at Takapuna racecourse that city people could not cross the harbour. The Kiwis won 16–14 thanks to a spectacular last-minute try to George Gillett. A year later Auckland led 10–7 at halftime, only to concede nine more tries as the Kiwis charged away to a 38–16 victory.

Billy Curran, the Aucklander punched three times by Sid Deane, who was ordered off.
Auckland City Libraries

New Zealand half Charles Webb breaks away smartly against Auckland in the 1912 clash at Eden Park.
Auckland City Libraries

Auckland against New South Wales in 1913. Snapshots of the 27–2 win by New South Wales at the Domain.
Auckland City Libraries

Thacker Shield

Canterbury Rugby League president Dr Henry Thacker, who also served as Mayor of Christchurch and a member of Parliament, donated a handsome shield in 1913 for competition on a challenge basis between clubs throughout New Zealand. Sydenham, which won the inaugural Canterbury championship that year, became the first defender.

The Sydenham tenure threatened to be very short when Auckland champion North Shore scored the first two tries in Thacker Shield history and led 8–0 at halftime. But Sydenham, spurred on by a large crowd at the Addington Show Grounds, dominated the second spell and replied with three tries, two of them converted, to win 13–8. In 1915 Sydenham easily repelled Athletic (Wellington) in the only wartime shield match.

With the war clouds clearing in 1918, Ponsonby challenged at Sydenham Park. Inside backs Scotty McClymont and Bill Walsh astutely called the shots behind a heavier pack as Ponsonby led 3–0 at halftime after playing into the wind. Two more tries and a penalty goal followed before Ponsonby carried home the shield in triumph as 11–0 victors.

Ponsonby retained possession by beating Federal, of Canterbury, by 29–19 in 1920 and Wellington champion Petone 21–13 in 1921 before matters became complicated. When City won the 1921 Auckland championship, it challenged and beat Ponsonby for the shield. Meanwhile, Sydenham had also lodged a challenge, only to be told by the Auckland Rugby League that no suitable date was available until October.

Controversy reigned, with Dr Thacker, who was still Canterbury's president, wading into the argument. Not all details were released but it is presumed Thacker pointed out the rules stipulated competition between the champion clubs of different provinces rather than between past and present champions of the province where the shield was held.

Ponsonby beat Sydenham 11–0 to win the Thacker Shield in Christchurch in 1918.
(1) W Edwards heads a Ponsonby forward rush.
(2) S Lowrie, I Cadman and L Maddison dribble the ball along the line.
Auckland City Libraries

CHAPTER TWO

Ponsonby United, winner of the senior championship and Thacker Shield in 1919.

Back row: I Cadman, J Brien, A Pooley, W Cross, J Clark, S Lowrie.

Middle row: W Milne, D McCarthy, A Cadman, T McClymont (captain), A Halliday, S McNamara, W Walsh.

Front row: A Rae, F McGregor, F Delgrosso, S Chatfield.

Inset: H Neal.

Absent: A Cross, W Edwards, D Norgrove.

NZRL Museum

The New Zealand Rugby League became involved. It returned the shield to Canterbury and the rules were amended to limit competition between the champion clubs of South Island leagues. Although Christian Brothers (Otago) lost to Hornby in 1926 and Addington beat Waratah (Inangahua) in 1938, the Thacker Shield has since 1923 otherwise been exclusively contested by the top clubs of Canterbury and West Coast.

Auckland Rugby League executive disqualified

The entire fourteen-man Auckland Rugby League management committee was suspended in October 1913, and then disqualified two months later by the New Zealand Rugby League, after a controversy involving renowned footballer and boxer Charles Savory had dragged on for seven months. It still ranks among this country's biggest sporting scandals.

Savory had earned a reputation for ruggedness in both rugby codes, having incurred a two-year suspension for allegedly kicking another player during a rugby union club game for Ponsonby. He toured Australia with the 1911 New Zealand team after switching to rugby league and was one of four New Zealanders who toured Britain with the 1911–12 Kangaroos. But Savory was suspended for the latter half of the 1912 season after being ordered off while playing for Ponsonby United against Newton. That cost Savory a second trip across the Tasman. When he appealed, he was refused a hearing.

For the 1913 season the Auckland Rugby League decided any member of its executive could report incidents of foul play and call players up to explain. Savory had been named in the New Zealand side for another Australian tour shortly before Ponsonby played Manukau at Onehunga. He completed the game but was summoned to an Auckland Rugby League inquiry where he was found guilty of kicking and disqualified for life. Savory argued it was a case of mistaken identity.

On 20 May the New Zealand Rugby League was informed of Savory's ban and he was replaced, reluctantly, in the touring team. When the New Zealand Rugby League received Savory's appeal and heard evidence from him, and from other players and match officials, it decided the harsh sentence was unwarranted. The New Zealand Rugby League referred the matter back to the Auckland Rugby League for reconsideration and permitted Savory to resume playing in the meantime.

The Auckland Rugby League refused to reopen the case and in late June it upset New Zealand Rugby League president Duncan McLean by accusing the national body of acting in an unbusinesslike manner. The New Zealand Rugby League then quashed Savory's conviction altogether. McLean said the sentence had been out of proportion and that the referee and one of the line umpires were of the opinion the injury suffered by Clark, the Manukau player allegedly kicked by Savory, was accidental.

But on 20 August the Auckland Rugby League reaffirmed by nine votes to one that Savory's penalty should stand. Though still 'disqualified for life' by his province, Savory was permitted by the New Zealand Rugby League to play for New Zealand against New South Wales. On 9 October the New Zealand Rugby League received a letter from the Auckland Rugby League which it interpreted as defiance. All Auckland Rugby League committee members were suspended from holding office at any level in the game 'during the pleasure of the council'.

Auckland Rugby League management 1910–11.

Back row: J Graham, G Seagar, E Goulter, M Hooper, J G Jackson.

Front row: A J Powley (secretary), B Brigham (chairman), P S Ussher (treasurer).

Eric Bennetts, NZRL Annual 1933

CHAPTER TWO

In November an Auckland Rugby League delegation was told its powers to suspend players was limited and subject to New Zealand Rugby League endorsement. When the Auckland Rugby League failed to re-register Savory by 4 December its fourteen-man executive, led by chairman Barry Brigham, was disqualified by unanimous vote of the New Zealand Rugby League council. On 15 January 1914, the New Zealand Rugby League approved a 'new' Auckland Rugby League executive and granted it £10 for initial expenses.

Savory's story ended tragically. In 1914 he played for New Zealand against England at the Domain Cricket Ground and shortly before enlisting in the army won the national amateur heavyweight boxing championship. But Lance Corporal Charles Savory died on 8 May 1915, of wounds sustained at Gallipoli. One source claimed Savory was not required to leave his ship but went anyway, wading ashore after announcing 'I am going to fight for my country'.

Most, probably all, of those Auckland Rugby League executives who suspended Savory for life had their own disqualifications lifted by the New Zealand Rugby League within a year or two of the controversy that rocked the code in Auckland.

Percy Ussher, Auckland treasurer 1910–11. While on the New Zealand Rugby League in 1913 his notice of motion led to the disqualification of the entire Auckland Rugby League management committee.
Auckland City Libraries

Motion rescinded

In August 1913 the Auckland Rugby League, by twenty-one votes to seven, reversed a decision of three weeks earlier to urge the removal of the New Zealand Rugby League headquarters from Auckland to Wellington. Newspaper reports said the change of mind occurred because 'the majority of clubs have since instructed their delegates how to vote'.

1914: Against the odds

England 34 Auckland 12

The second England touring team, having retained the Ashes in Australia, proved too big and too strong in beating Auckland 34–12. The *New Zealand Herald* recorded the weights of the teams, with most local players conceding about 12kg to their markers, an amount which took a severe toll on a boggy Domain Cricket Ground. Auckland five-eighth Thomas (Scotty) McClymont tipped the scales at a mere 61kg.

'The weight of the visitors made a considerable difference,' reported the *Herald*. 'The Auckland forwards played a really plucky and praiseworthy game and, in the first half especially, quite held their own. But the local backs were far behind the standard set by the visitors, their lack of weight particularly telling against them. However, the game was always interesting and, although beaten by a large margin, the home team was by no means so outclassed as the score would indicate.'

England jumped out to a 15–0 advantage before two Karl Ifwersen penalty goals reduced the halftime margin to eleven points. The 14,000 spectators, who had paid £650 at the gate, were cheered when Auckland scored within two minutes of the resumption. Ifwersen made ground with a 'neat piece of dribbling' and forward Charles Savory was in support to score. Auckland's other try went to loose forward Jim Clark and Ifwersen's conversion made it 21–12 before England added three more tries.

During the interval a goalkicking competition was held between Aucklanders John Dufty and Ernie Asher, who were not playing in the game, and England tourists Alf Wood and Johnny Rogers, who were playing. It could be argued that the winner, Wood, benefited from having already kicked three goals during the first half.

A view of the 14,000 spectators watching England beat Auckland 34–12.
Auckland City Libraries

CHAPTER TWO

The England defence halts Auckland.
Auckland City Libraries

An evenly contested scrum.
Auckland City Libraries

Auckland had lost gifted fullback George Gillett when he failed a pre-match fitness test. The players, with clubs, were: fullback, Tom Cross (Ponsonby); three-quarters, Charles Woolley (City), Karl Ifwersen (Grafton), Edward Fox (North Shore); five-eighths, Scotty McClymont (Ponsonby), Arthur Hardgrave (Otahuhu); halfback, Charles Webb (Ponsonby); forwards, Charles Savory (Ponsonby), J Bennett (Newton), Stan Walters (North Shore), Bob Mitchell (Grafton), Harold Hayward (Thames), Jim Clark (Ponsonby).

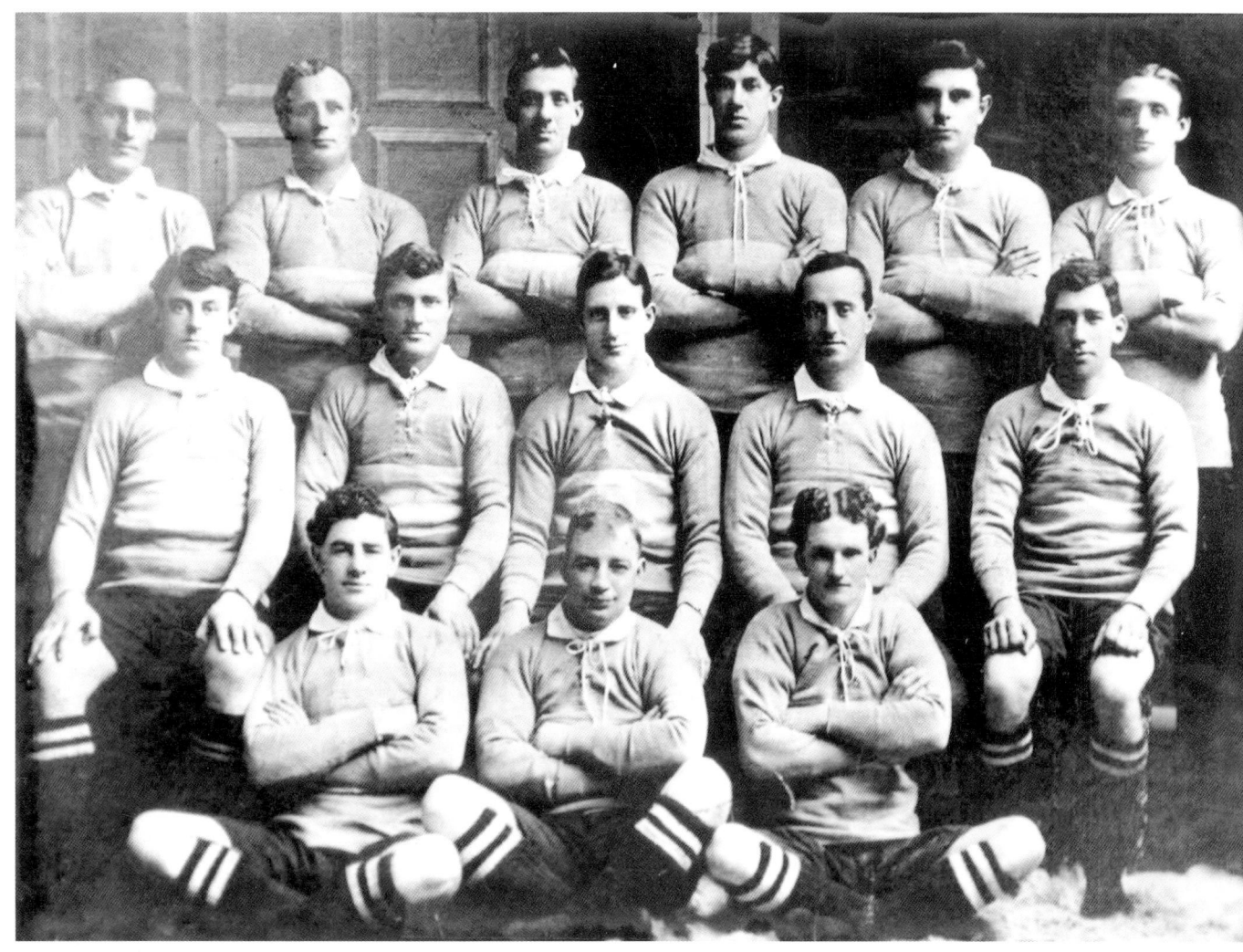

Auckland rugby league representatives in 1914.
Back row: S Walters, C Savory, R Mitchell, H Hayward, J Bennett, J Clark.
Middle row: C Woolley, A Hardgrave, K Ifwersen, H Fricker, T Cross.
Front row: E Fox, C Webb, T McClymont.
Eric Bennetts, NZRL Annual 1933

CHAPTER TWO

Opposing captains in 1912, George Harrison (City Rovers) and George Seagar (North Shore Albions).
Auckland City Libraries

Examining one's conscience

The First World War crippled rugby league's expansion in New Zealand, with several burgeoning provinces being forced into recess as the events in Europe drained this country of its young, fit and unattached men. Indeed, historians have regularly attributed the war to saving rugby union's status as this country's national sport.

In *The Shield: A Century of the Ranfurly Shield*, Lindsay Knight wrote: 'Shield matches played in the 1905–13 era confirm some of the problems rugby was having in competing with league. In 1912 Auckland survived a torrid challenge for Otago with a five-all draw. This match was played at Alexandra Park in Epsom before a crowd of just 3,000. At the same time a league 'test' was being played a little closer to the city between New Zealand and New South Wales at the Domain in Grafton. This match attracted a crowd of about 15,000.

'League's progress in these years was such that there seems little doubt that had it not been for the outbreak of World War I in 1914, when all organised [rugby union] football as such ceased for the next four years, league might have become certainly Auckland's, and perhaps even New Zealand's, premier winter sport.'

The Auckland Rugby Union's centenary book recalled that in 1916 its clubs were restricted to players under 20 years, the official age of military call-up. 'All this caused many former players to seek other avenues for their recreation. Though the restriction was made for patriotic reasons, it caused a setback to the rugby game from which only a slow recovery was made during the early post-war years.' The union's gates were well down and its financial year closed with a bank overdraft of £808.

Rugby league imposed no such age restriction, following the lead of its counterpart in Sydney. It was argued in the media that 'most senior players have already enlisted, and those participating this year will either be underage, or married, and ineligible men' and 'that it is the duty of the State, not of football organisations, to judge the qualifications of men to serve their country.'

On the eve of the 1916 season, newspapers speculated about the public reaction and did not have to wait long to find an answer. Two thousand spectators attended the main Victoria Park match between City and Ponsonby, and there were good turn-outs as Grafton overcame Newton and North Shore travelled to Otahuhu to gain a hard-earned win. Editorials were in favour of the league's actions, provided club officials examined the credentials of the players who were wearing their colours and their own consciences.

The Auckland Rugby League was constantly raising funds for the war effort. A 1914 fancy-dress procession through the main city thoroughfares culminated with a gala at the Domain Cricket Ground. In 1915 all six senior clubs took part in a round-robin seven-a-side tournament and auction on behalf of the Hospital Ship and Wounded Fund. Successful bidders at the auction kept donating their prizes back with the result that darkness fell before North Shore and City could complete the final.

The 1916 Roope Rooster semi-final replay between City and Newton drew 2,500 fans on a wet day, the entire takings being given to charity. As an additional means of swelling the gate, the league held a ballot to find the public's favourite player. Ponsonby captain Scotty McClymont won the gold medal prize with 714 votes, ahead of City's Albert Asher (547) and Grafton's Karl Ifwersen (230).

In a letter to the *Auckland Star* in September 1918, Duncan McLean wrote: 'In Auckland it is well known the attendances at club matches average between 5000 and 6000 a Saturday, and although for the most part no gate charges are made, receipts from other sources have enabled the Auckland Rugby League during the past three years to donate the sum of £1300 to patriotic and charitable purposes, representing the net profit during that period.'

During and immediately after the war the New Zealand Rugby Union softened its attitude towards players who changed codes by introducing a general amnesty to those who wished to return from rugby league.

City Rovers 1912. M Harrison, R Denize, A Stanaway, Hunt, E Asher, G Harrison (captain), H Childs, R Mitchell, James, Phillips, Warner, W Moki, Martin.
Auckland City Libraries

CHAPTER TWO

Roope and his Rooster

Although Dick Roope, who served briefly as Auckland Rugby League chairman before moving to live in Australia, donated the Roope Rooster for a knockout competition in 1915, he did not actually see the unique trophy for another fifty-four years.

The unusual story emerged when Roope visited Carlaw Park in 1969. It was only then that he, at the age of eighty-three, held the coveted prize, which had cost thousands of players so much sweat and blood, and caused so many tears and cheers, for more than half a century.

'All he saw of the trophy before he left permanently for Australia was a wax model from London,' reported the *Auckland Star*. 'This is Mr Roope's first visit to Auckland since 1915.'

'His reasons for giving the trophy: "When it came to representative matches the vast majority of players were sidelined with nothing to do. In order they could have more football I conceived the idea of having a knockout competition".

'Why a rooster?: "So the team that won it would have something to crow about – which is very bad sportsmanship, I suppose".'

The *Star* reported that Roope had planned his return to Auckland so that he could look up old-timers in the game, travel on to New Plymouth where his family had been pioneer settlers, and renew his acquaintance with the Rutherford family of whom nuclear scientist Ernest was a son. It noted he had been talking with schoolboy control board officials with the intention of donating another trophy.

Dick Roope in 1969.
Fairfax Media

Off the rails

Railway, a combination of the former Marist Brothers Old Boys and City rugby union teams, won the 1917 Auckland rugby union championship at its first attempt. With both clubs finding themselves chronically short of players because of the war, they had amalgamated at season's start under the guidance of Marist secretary Conrad McDevitt and City captain Doug Stewart, who both worked at the railway workshops in Newmarket.

But there was an air of revolt within the ranks, and in late September a meeting was called to secede from the Auckland Rugby Union and apply to the Auckland Rugby League for affiliation. Railway also somewhat cheekily issued a challenge to Ponsonby United, the Auckland Rugby League champion, for a match at the Domain Cricket Ground the following Saturday.

Inevitably, there was uproar, for Railway was already scheduled to play University at Eden Park that day for the rugby union Charity Cup. On consecutive midweek mornings the *New Zealand Herald* published conflicting statements – first by the union that Railway would indeed fulfil its Charity Cup obligation and then by McDevitt that the champion team was actually in training to play Ponsonby. No wonder the sporting public was confused.

Both matches eventuated. University beat Railway 15–13 at Eden Park, and the novice Railway rugby league team upset Ponsonby 12–3 at its own game. The Railway XV was clearly below strength, with most of the leading players having switched codes, and Ponsonby suffered at the Domain when Spencer Jones suffered a broken leg.

The Railway XIII next took on the 1916 Auckland Rugby League championship and Roope Rooster-winning City Rovers and was soundly beaten by 18–6. Among the Railway players in those two matches was a teenaged Ces Dacre, a future New Zealand cricket representative.

By the following April, the fledgling Railway Rugby League Club found itself again short of playing personnel and decided at a gathering at John Endean's Waitemata (later Great Northern) Hotel to amalgamate with the Grafton Athletic club. Despite the presence of the great Karl Ifwersen, Grafton finished among the also-rans in 1918.

McDevitt, the man who had placed the advertisement for Railway's breakaway from rugby union in 1917, lodged another notice of meeting with the *Auckland Star* in April 1919. This time it was to form the Marist Brothers Old Boys club to play under the jurisdiction of the Auckland Rugby League.

Captained by McDevitt, Marist initially struggled, losing 28–3 to Newton on debut and sometimes taking the field with less than thirteen players. But Marist recovered to win its first championship in 1924 and has produced many outstanding internationals since it evolved from the 'rebel' Railway XV.

CHAPTER TWO

'Auckland Rules'

So desperate was the Auckland Rugby Union to combat the rugby league threat that it introduced its own rule amendments in 1917, giving up on years of trying to legislate changes through the traditional channels of the New Zealand Rugby Union and the Rugby Football Union in England.

'Auckland, being the city where league was strongest, had problems' wrote Paul Neazor in *Passion and Pride*. 'Rugby union was seen as a slow, pedestrian game when compared to its counterpart. Auckland decided to introduce variations to the playing conditions, which became known as "Auckland Rules". Basically, they were four in number and designed to speed the game up, making it more interesting for both players and spectators.'

'Auckland Rules' eliminated the wing forward, provided for absolute free kicks, modified the rule relating to kicking into touch, and required strict enforcement of the rule as to lying on the ball. In effect, the Auckland Rugby Union was belatedly following the lead of the Northern Union from 1895 in making its game more attractive. It was also heralding changes that later became rugby union law.

The 'Auckland Rules' caused internal eruptions. A furious New Zealand Rugby Union threatened to expel Auckland for breaking ranks, and there were resignations from the more conservative Auckland Rugby Union management committee members. When the Wellington Rugby Union voted to play Auckland under the modified rules in 1918, it too earned the wrath of its parent body and had to pacify many of its own representative players who initially refused to play under the amended laws. When some rule variations were used in the game, including having the referee feed the scrums, the New Zealand Rugby Union was not amused and instigated an enquiry.

Eventually, at its annual meeting in May 1921, the national union backtracked and granted Auckland dispensation to continue with its new rules. All the while the rugby league community could only look on with some amusement at the furore its presence had caused in Auckland.

'Genius of back play'

Many outstanding Auckland footballers changed codes to bolster the new game in the years before the First World War. Karl Ifwersen, whose illustrious career spanned the war years, fashioned a record which arguably placed him above all others. The Grafton Athletic inside centre and goalkicker toured Australia with the Kiwis in 1913 and 1919, and played at home against New South Wales in 1913, England in 1914, Australia in 1919 and England in 1920.

Sportswriter Sir Terry McLean attributed the changes made to the Auckland Rugby Union's playing laws as being 'to combat the popularity which that genius of back play, Karl Ifwersen, was generating in rugby league'. He also wrote that rugby league's threat to become Auckland's most popular winter sport 'diminished when Karl Ifwersen, reckoned by renowned All Black Mark Nicholls to be the greatest of five-eighths, was reinstated to rugby'.

Having permanently banned so many players who had changed codes, the New Zealand Rugby Union not only bent its own rules to welcome Ifwersen back in 1921, it rushed him into the All Blacks team for the deciding test match against the Springboks at Wellington. But not even Ifwersen could overcome a flooded Athletic Park in a scoreless draw. Ifwersen would have toured Britain with the 1924–25 Invincibles had British rugby union authorities not barred the thirty-one year old because of his rugby league background.

Former Kiwis captain and long-serving coach Scotty McClymont, who saw all of the finest players over rugby league's first sixty years, described Ifwersen as 'a born footballer. He was a natural who couldn't help playing brilliantly. It was just no effort to him.' Karl Ifwersen was inducted into the New Zealand Rugby League Legends of League in 2000.

The Ifwersen family accepting their uncle and great uncle's NZRL Legends of League citation in Auckland in 2000.
Photosport

CHAPTER TWO

Garden of Eden

Eden Park, best known as an international cricket and rugby union venue, hosted Auckland's 1919 Northern Union Cup defence against Hawke's Bay. Craddock Dufty kicked seven goals and scored a try in Auckland's 38–13 walkover. The 1919 Auckland team for that historic match was: Frank Delgrosso, George Davidson, Dougie McGregor, George Iles, Craddock Dufty, Bert Laing, George Neal, Keith Helander, Sam Lowrie, V Thomas, Tom Haddon, L Newdick and Bert Avery.

Rugby league had previously been played at Eden Park in 1912, by arrangement with the cricket association's trustees. Duncan McLean recalled in 1930 that 'this was because the soccer authorities were unable to pay the rent. Our presence there, however, was feared and we were subsequently outbid for the area – and with no regrets as it happens.' After 1919, it was not until the 1988 World Cup final that Eden Park was again used for rugby league.

Ponsonby United, which beat Manukau 19–5 as part of a triple header at Eden Park on 11 May 1912.
Auckland City Libraries

Ponsonby in action against Manukau Rovers.
Auckland City Libraries

The North Shore Albions team that beat City Rovers. E Bailey, O Miller, S Paul, B Cargen, E Rogers, S Weston, A Stevenson, C Clark, W Wynyard, D Law, A Jackson, A Haddon, F Pearson.
Auckland City Libraries

North Shore Albions (13) and City Rovers (9) played the main game of three at Eden Park on 11 May 1912.
Auckland City Libraries

> ## Ponsonby's treble
>
> Ponsonby completed a treble of Auckland championship titles from 1917 to 1919, in addition to winning the Roope Rooster in 1917 and bringing the Thacker Shield from Christchurch in 1918. Halves Bill Walsh and Scotty McClymont, forward Jim Clark and hooker Sam Lowrie all represented New Zealand in 1919. Secretary Ivan Culpan told the *Weekly Press* in Christchurch in 1918 that the club was in good heart despite the First World War having made great inroads on their membership. It was then fielding six teams, one in each of the top four grades and two in the fifth grade competition. Ponsonby ran its own insurance scheme to assist injured players and was drawing crowds of between 4,000 and 7,000 for club matches against Maritime, Grafton, Newton and archrival City.

1919: Rampant Kangaroos

Australia 32 Auckland 8

Australia sent its national team across the Tasman for the first time in 1919. The Kangaroos blazed a path through the country, faltering only in the second test match at Christchurch. They comfortably won the other three tests and rattled on ninety-three points against Wellington. The Auckland game at the Domain followed Australia's 32–2 romp in the fourth test.

With legendary players such as wing Harold Horder, centre Les Cubitt, scrum-half Duncan Thompson and forward Frank Burge in the ranks, this was one of the most powerful Australian teams to visit New Zealand. Auckland was given no chance of winning, and so it proved. Burge, with four tries, was the individual star in a 32–8 result.

Auckland led early through a Karl Ifwersen penalty goal and again at 5–3 when loose forward Bert Avery touched down for his try. But, after Australia was ahead 13–5 at the break, Burge piled on the points with three consecutive tries. Fullback Bill Davidson crossed for Auckland's other try.

'The Australians again displayed their superiority, but the match was a great deal more interesting than the scores would indicate,' said the *New Zealand Herald*. 'The Auckland team was much faster than that which represented New Zealand on the previous Saturday and tackled with a great deal more vigour.' The crowd was estimated at 20,000.

CHAPTER TWO

Auckland team: fullback, Bill Davidson; three-quarters, Dougie McGregor, Scotty McClymont, Karl Ifwersen, George Davidson; halves, Ivan Stewart, Billy Ghent; forwards, Stan Walters, Sam Lowrie, Bill Williams, Bert Avery, Bob Mitchell, Nelson Bass. Reserves: backs, George Iles, Frank Delgrosso; forwards, Jim Clark, Ernie Herring. Only Ghent and George Davidson did not play for New Zealand during their careers.

Three prominent members of the Australian team, Frank Burge, who scored four tries against Auckland, Claude O'Donnell and Les Cubitt.
Auckland City Libraries

CHAPTER 03

TRIUMPH AND TRAGEDY
1920–1929

CHAPTER THREE

Triumph and Tragedy 1920–1929

1920: 'Beer truck forwards and racing-car backs'
Auckland 24 England 16

Years after the momentous 24–16 victory over England in 1920, Auckland fullback Bill Davidson wrote that it was achieved through perfect teamwork by a combination of 'beer truck forwards and racing-car backs'. It was the last season of international rugby league at the Domain Cricket Ground and the official attendance of 35,000 on a sunny July day was not surpassed until the 1988 World Cup final at Eden Park.

It was the opening game and the only loss of England's ten-match tour. England went on to win all three test matches, though a late converted try was needed to preserve that record in the third test at Wellington. The 1920 Auckland side was indeed a great one. Of the thirteen players and four reserves, only Lower Waikato second-row forward Jack Wilson did not wear the Kiwis jersey – and he was not available for the 1920 test series.

The *Auckland Star* captured the excitement of the occasion: 'From the fame that had preceded the visiting players it was anticipated that the "All Whites" of England would prove too classy a combination for the blue and white representatives of Auckland. How different was the realisation! In the first three minutes the Auckland players brought the crowd to fever heat by registering the first score. The game thereafter was a continuous delirium of excitement.'

Auckland cleared out to a fourteen-point halftime lead and the tension rose throughout the second spell as England surged back. England was unfortunate to lose stand-off Johnny Rogers with a broken leg after ten minutes. Adhering to their own no-replacement rule, the Lions soldiered on one man short. Yet when Rogers' marker, Ivan Stewart, damaged a collarbone soon afterwards he was replaced by Scotty McClymont. England had only eleven men for a time while Frank Gallagher was treated on the sideline for a shoulder injury.

Much of the credit for the first loss by an England team on New Zealand soil was given to Auckland forwards Stan Walters, Wally Somers, Bill Stormont, Bert

Auckland City Libraries

Avery, Jack Wilson and Nelson Bass. 'The Auckland forwards had easily the better of the first spell and the local team was attacking all the time,' said the *Star*. 'After the interval the position was reversed as the brilliant British backs came out in shining fashion. In great measure the victory was due to the superiority of the home pack, and to the safe work of the backs, of whom Davidson, the fullback, played a great defensive game.'

Auckland was awarded an early penalty try when centre Charles Woolley, having bustled England fullback Gwyn Thomas into dropping the ball, was obstructed when about to touch down. England led briefly at 5–3 before Auckland took control with tries to hooker Somers, replacement McClymont, prop Walters and wing Bill Cloke. Davidson's two goals made it 19–5 at the break.

England steadily cut into that advantage, getting as close as 19–13 before Walters took Auckland to comparative safety with his second try, after a passing move involving backs Woolley, Eric Grey, Clarrie Polson, McClymont and Karl Ifwersen. Davidson's conversion ensured Auckland of its 24–16 victory despite conceding a late try. Scoring tries was not out of character for front-rower Walters – in eight test matches he registered five tries.

Auckland team: fullback, Bill Davidson; three-quarters, Bill Cloke, Karl Ifwersen, Eric Grey; five-eighths, Charles Woolley, Ivan Stewart; halfback, Clarrie Polson; forwards, Stan Walters, Wally Somers, Bill Stormont, Bert Avery, Jack Wilson, Nelson Bass. Reserves: backs, Scotty McClymont (replaced Stewart), Norm Loveridge; forwards, Ernie Herring, George Paki.

(1) Auckland half Clarrie Polson being tackled by brilliant England inside back Jonathan Parkin.
Auckland City Libraries

(2) A group of interested spectators. Seated at left are Dr Henry Thacker, MP and Mayor of Christchurch, and Mrs Thacker. Billy Wynyard is in conversation with the keen Canterbury sportsman.
Auckland City Libraries

(3) Albert Johnson (England) tackling an Aucklander after the break-up of a scrum.
Auckland City Libraries

CHAPTER THREE

James Carlaw.
Auckland City Libraries

Sir Arthur Myers.
Eric Bennetts, NZRL Annual 1933

Auckland's home patch

Carlaw Park is gone, but it will never be forgotten. From its opening in 1921 it was rugby league's field of dreams – and occasional nightmares – as players at club, provincial and international levels experienced their glory days and disasters. Even the kids who played at halftime in the big games never forgot the experience. Fans relished the intimacy. The media loved the rickety old press box on the grandstand roof. Since its closure in 2002, 'Carlaw' has left an ongoing legacy which enriches the Auckland Rugby League's coffers.

When the Sydney Cricket Ground hosted Australia's 2008 Centenary match against New Zealand it moved two clear of Carlaw Park as the most-used test venue anywhere in the rugby league world. Carlaw's sixty-eight tests extended from the 1924 tour by England to a one-off match against Tonga in 1999. By then it had already been overtaken by larger and more modern stadiums at Albany and Penrose.

Auckland's first five test matches from 1910 to 1920 were played at the Domain Cricket Ground. As early as 1914 far-sighted James Carlaw had taken note of the Chinese market garden nestled in the lee of the domain and within easy walking distance of the city centre. His eagerness to negotiate a sale was tempered by another leading official, Arthur Myers, who was then Minister of Munitions and advised nothing be done until the war ended.

Carlaw became Auckland Rugby League chairman in 1918. There was another delay while Myers steered a Bill through Parliament legalising an exchange of land which would allow room for two playing fields. In January 1921 the Auckland Rugby League took possession, though not without objections from the Ah Chee family, who lived in a house on the property. When that was solved, volunteers and construction gangs moved in. Progress was swift.

Myers, as president of the Auckland Rugby League, officially opened the park on 25 June 1921, after bad weather had forced a one-week postponement. In a 1922 match programme, secretary Ivan Culpan wrote capital expenditure had been £4322. Up to the opening of Carlaw Park, the league was dependent for its revenue on a few charge days at the Domain and voluntary contributions at Victoria Park.

City Rovers beat Maritime 10–8 on that opening afternoon in front of 7,000 people, with Maritime's Herb Lunn scoring the first try and Eric Grey kicking the first goal. Ivan Littlewood's try for Maritime created an 8–0 halftime lead. The winning second-half points for City came from tries to Harry Hawkes and Harry Francis and two goals by Minogue. The teams, refereed by Archie Ferguson, were:

City Rovers: backs, R Harley, B Davidson, W Minogue, R Clarke. M Wetherill, J Mitchell, T Peckham; forwards, V Thomas, A Townsend, G Reid, H Francis, H Hawkes, E Mackie.

Maritime: backs, Flynn, I Littlewood, J McGregor, G Davidson, E Grey, G Yardley, H Lunn; forwards, W Arndt, Meller, J Brien, Ballantyne, Dance, Webb.

Terraces had been built, the original 640-seat grandstand was doubled in size in 1922, and hot showers were available in time for the first test match two years later. A larger wooden grandstand was completed in 1934, the terraces were concreted and covered in 1954 and twenty years later Auckland Rugby League chairman George Rainey oversaw the purchase of the park for what became a bargain $200,000. Floodlighting followed a year later, the embankment behind the Railway Stand was purchased in 1994 for $35,000 and the road access from Stanley Street cost $239,500 in 1993. That all added up to a multi-million dollar investment.

Overseas teams hated Carlaw Park, and not just because they were guaranteed a bruising reception from the Kiwis and Auckland forwards and a roasting from the local supporters. For decades the low-lying ground looked more like a paddy field than a former market garden. Exasperated French manager Antoine Blain famously scooped up a handful of sodden turf and chanted 'mud, mud, mud'. That problem was eventually solved when sand-slitting technology came into vogue in the 1980s. The largest (estimated) test crowd was 28,000 during the 1928 England tour. In later years capacity was reduced to 17,000.

Auckland City Libraries

Opening day at Carlaw Park on 25 June 1921, when City played Maritime in the first club fixture.
Auckland City Libraries

Carlaw Park's largest test crowd of 28,000 for the first England test match of 1928.
Auckland City Libraries

CHAPTER THREE

New Zealand won thirty-three test matches, lost thirty-two and drew one at Carlaw Park. Great Britain and France also twice met there in world tournaments. Auckland city and provincial teams beat Great Britain seven times in twenty-one meetings (including seven of the last twelve), beat Australia in five of thirteen matches (five of the last nine), beat France in five of seven matches, and enjoyed one-off victories over Wales and South Africa. No wonder the visitors stepped across the touchline with more than a little trepidation.

Carlaw Park was leased for many diverse events, including international hockey and soccer, Gaelic football, supercross motorcycling, professional boxing, rodeos, outdoor movies, golf driving ranges and the crusade of American evangelist Billy Graham. The second playing field, which ran at right angles to the main ground at the Stanley Street end, was used for club games until 1993.

Many great test matches were played at Carlaw, such as the 16–15 heart-stopper with the 1951 Frenchmen and the 18–0 shutout of the 1985 Kangaroos. Auckland's five defeats of Australia were achieved by margins ranging from one to five points, thrillers all of them. The 5–4 victory over the 1954 Lions ranks with the most brutal contests of all time. And in the glorious month of June 1977, the Bill Sorensen-coached blue and whites in turn humbled Australia, Britain and France.

The grand old park's days were numbered even before the Warriors opted to stay at Mount Smart Stadium. Initially disappointed, the Auckland Rugby League redirected its energies towards commercial development. Care was taken to maximise the property's value and capitalise on the spadework of earlier administrations. Freehold rights were sold for the No.2 ground, but the main field was leased in perpetuity to guarantee a significant annual income.

George Rainey signs the Carlaw Park purchase document in October 1974, flanked by solicitor J Goldstine and Auckland Hospital Board chairman Sir Harcourt Caughey.
NZ Herald

Ode to Carlaw Park

From the *Auckland Rugby League News*, 16 May 1925, attributed to 'F C Parnell'

There's a neat little Park in Parnell.
Of its picturesque beauties I'd tell,
Overlooked by the trees
As they wave in the breeze
On whose branches the singing birds dwell.

It's a beautiful place to behold,
Nicely sheltered from winds that are cold,
This novel of freeland
The gem of New Zealand
And its worth can't be measured by gold.

To protect it the walls are built high,
Just to hide from the view of the spy
Who never is willing
To part with a shilling
For what others are anxious to buy.

High upon its long terraces grand,
Where a great many thousands can stand,
There they all get a view
And a thrill through and through
As the boys play the game at command.

There's an artistic fence all around,
That encircles the main playing ground,
Where our young athletes
There perform the great feats
Of endurance that doubt all astound.

It's a bit of this world made anew,
And a place of enjoyment for you,
'Twill hold when completed,
Both standing and seated,
A full thirty-five thousand clear view.

Rugby League is the game that they play,
Rugby League is the game come to stay,
Where the public of sports,
By the thousands resort,
Get full measure for all that they pay.

When the game to its full end has come,
And the critic has used his small comb,
Then just outside the gate,
There the tramcars all wait
To take players and spectators home.

CHAPTER THREE

Fire stops play

On the day that Carlaw Park was opened, Fire Brigade and Marist were drawn to meet at the adjacent Domain Cricket Ground. But, reported the *Auckland Star*, the call of duty in the form of a warehouse fire prevented the Fire Brigade players from arriving on time. They eventually made an appearance but were obviously tired after their strenuous battle with the flames, and Marist agreed that the match should be postponed.

Family dynasty

Jack McGregor, who played for Maritime on Carlaw Park's opening day, was one of four brothers, all of them wings, who during their careers occasionally filled all four wing positions, as team-mates and opponents, in the same game. They established a rugby league family dynasty, being followed by Jack's son, Ron, who was a fine footballer and even more renowned administrator, and grandson, Cameron, the Auckland Rugby League chairman since 2001.

James Carlaw and his nephews

Carlaw Park was named after James Carlaw, the prime mover in its purchase and construction and the senior figure in one of rugby league's most prominent families. His extensive terms as office holder of both the Auckland and New Zealand leagues were among a number of services to a community he graced throughout his adult life.

Born in Newcastle-upon-Tyne, England, in 1854, Carlaw arrived in Auckland with his family as a nine-year-old. He was to be employed by the Auckland City Council for forty-six years, twenty-five of those as waterworks engineer, and he would be responsible for many major works until his retirement in 1925.

His first sporting endeavours were in lawn bowls. A lifelong member, one-time champion, president and life member of the Auckland club from 1891, Carlaw helped establish a second club at Ponsonby in 1896 and in 1918 founded the Auckland Veterans Bowling Association.

Meanwhile, Carlaw and his nephews, Arthur Edward Carlaw and William Owen (Owie) Carlaw had become deeply involved in rugby league.

Arthur Carlaw was among Ponsonby's first players, proving to be a versatile and skilful back. He toured Australia with the privately organised 1909 New Zealand team and returned there with the 1912 and 1913 sides. In 1912 he was promoted

Arthur Carlaw.
Auckland City Libraries

AUCKLAND RUGBY LEAGUE
1909–2009

A montage of Auckland Rugby League officials during James Carlaw's presidency.
Eric Bennetts, NZRL Annual 1933

CHAPTER THREE

to the captaincy when tour captain Arthur Francis left for England in mid-tour to start a contract at Wigan. Arthur Carlaw died in Christchurch in 1934 after a long illness caused by war disabilities.

Owie Carlaw directed his energies towards administration, first as auditor to the Auckland Rugby League in 1911. He was treasurer of the New Zealand Rugby League from 1913 to 1920 – a period interrupted by four years of war service – and its secretary between 1921 and 1948. Owie Carlaw was widely praised for his judgement, knowledge and unflagging energy as he guided the sport through difficult financial times.

The elder statesman of the Carlaw clan at provincial and national rugby league levels was undoubtedly James. He was New Zealand president from 1914 to 1919, Auckland chairman from 1918 to 1921, New Zealand president again from 1921 to 1926, and both Auckland president and New Zealand patron from 1926 until his death in 1935 at the age of eighty-one.

While Carlaw Park was James Carlaw's shining achievement, his greatest disappointment was the disastrous 1926–27 New Zealand tour of Britain, when seven forwards were cast adrift after a tour-long dispute between them and the management. Carlaw retired as New Zealand Rugby League president at the 1927 annual meeting and could not be persuaded to continue.

He said at the time he had looked forward to the 1926–27 tour for ten years and every endeavour had been made to send a thoroughly prepared and competitive team. He told the delegates he believed they would have won ninety per cent of their matches had it not been for the internal troubles.

A tour which promised to return a profit of £7,000 was wrecked, and instead of a profit a serious loss has to be faced, Carlaw said. Instead of having a sizeable surplus with which to promote the sport, the New Zealand Rugby League was in deficit and even owed the Otago Rugby League £847.

It was a tribute to the work of James Carlaw that for seventy years crowds flocked through the turnstiles of the park named in his honour to refill those coffers and restore New Zealand's reputation as a rugby league nation.

In the 1946 silver jubilee booklet of Carlaw Park, Auckland Rugby League secretary Ivan Culpan wrote that James Carlaw was 'the man whose keen foresight, tireless energy, and magnanimous assistance had made all this possible … who happily lived to enjoy for many years the fruits of his planning and to realise that, for all time, the game near and dear to his heart was solidly based.'

Ivan Culpan, secretary

Though he invariably deflected praise towards the chairmen with whom he worked, no individual exerted more influence over the first four decades of the Auckland Rugby League than long-serving secretary Ivan Culpan, who filled the position from 1918 until he stepped down at the 1949 annual general meeting.

Culpan was a sports official even longer than that, having been secretary of the Australian Rules game in Auckland from 1906 to 1910. When Rules faded and rugby league emerged, Culpan became secretary of the Ponsonby club from 1914 and was manager of the team that captured the Thacker Shield from Canterbury champion Sydenham in 1918.

When James Carlaw was elected Auckland chairman he head-hunted Culpan as secretary and Australian-born Fred Ellis as treasurer, setting up an office at the old Tattersall club on Swanson Street. Together, Carlaw and Culpan controlled the voluntary 'working bees' which transformed the Ah Chee market garden into the stadium that became Carlaw Park. Wet or fine, every Sunday from January to June, they toiled away to have the grounds ready for opening day.

Culpan presided over leasing of the park, and learned it was more profitable to stage rodeos than outdoor movies. Strong fences were erected to protect the public from an Australian-owned rodeo's 'wild' animals. The crowd held its collective breath as the first two bulls were unleashed from the pens, only for the beasts to amble out and contentedly chew the grass. But fifteen per cent of a healthy gate was collected from the promoters before they hurriedly returned to Sydney. In contrast, a company staging open-air movies went broke after one night's gross takings of four shillings and six pence.

Top: View of the terraced portion of Carlaw Park.

Bottom: Carlaw Park in May 1923 during the presentation ceremony when Mayor J H Gunson accepted the freedom of the park of behalf of the citizens of Auckland.

E F Andrews, I Culpan (secretary ARL), W J Hammill, (chairman ARL), A G Lunn, J H Gunson (mayor), J L Smith (city councillor), G Baildon (city councillor), N Culpan, E J Phelan, J S Dickson MP, A E Powell.

Auckland City Libraries

CHAPTER THREE

In the *League News* report of Culpan's retirement, the selfless secretary gave credit to the chairmen he was associated with – 'James Carlaw, whose name is time-honoured; Mr W J Hammill, who further improved the ground; Mr George Rhodes, reformer of the Board of Control and wise administrator; Mr G Grey Campbell, an unassuming, business-like administrator under whose guidance the present stand was built; Mr J W Watson, tried and found true during the arduous and turbulent war years; and the present chairman, Mr D A Wilkie, who rose all the way from the ranks.'

It was with no little sadness that Culpan retired. But he told the *League News* that in keeping with the growth of the game, there should be a secretary in regular attendance at the office. He endorsed his successor, former Kiwis three-quarters Ron McGregor, as 'the right man in the right place'.

The *1949 New Zealand Rugby League Annual* published several tributes to Culpan. Auckland chairman Dave Wilkie said Culpan had watched rugby league grow from humble beginnings to a proud position as one of Auckland's premier sports. 'He is one of those persons so gifted that he could combine organising ability with an outstanding personality which carried him through his lengthy career to leave him with a legacy of a host of friends.'

Flying the flag

In August 1921, Auckland flew the flag around and against other provinces. Ivan Culpan managed the touring team which beat Wellington (23–21), West Coast (47–7) and Canterbury (39–14 after scoring 29 unanswered points in the second half). Meanwhile, another Auckland team beat King Country 58–25 at home, with Bert Avery scoring five tries, but a third was tripped up, 18–15, by Hawke's Bay in Napier. Culpan and his players were guests at the Canterbury Rugby League's annual smoke concert. *The Press* reported him saying Auckland expected the tour to cost it £250, but regarded that as money well spent in promoting the code around the country.

League ladies turned away

In 1921 the Auckland Rugby League management committee risked accusations of being spoil sports when they not only banned betting from Carlaw Park but also declined a request from the Parnell Girls' Club to play there. Parnell offered to use modified rules, and explained that three matrons, two of them trained nurses, were in charge of its sixty-five members. All to no avail. The committee also agreed with a complainant that it was not a good look for players to be mingling with punters at the park before matches.

AUCKLAND RUGBY LEAGUE
1909–2009

The Auckland team that beat Canterbury 39–14.
Back row: A Morris (referee), J Wood, H Hawkes, G Cargill, G Smith (NZRL), A Eustace, W Stormont, V Thomas, C James.
Middle row: I Culpan (manager), A Townsend, B Davidson, M Wetherill (captain), G Yardley, J McGregor, A Freeman.
Front row: M McNeill, R Littlewood (reserve), T Peckham, N Flynn.
Auckland City Libraries

Auckland and Canterbury at Sydenham Park in September 1921.
(1) G Yardley sends the ball out to A Eustace, the Auckland three-quarters.
(2) W Stormont tackled by a Canterbury player.
(3) Canterbury half R Watts gets the ball away smartly from a scrum.
(4) J Sanders scores Canterbury's first try.
(5) T Peckham, the Auckland half, gets around quickly on Watts, who sends the ball out to his backs.
Auckland City Libraries

CHAPTER THREE

Dominant City side

City Rovers, the club formed in the Waitemata Hotel laundry room and winner of the first two Auckland championships in 1910 and 1911, clinched a unique treble in 1921 – the Monteith Shield (then the championship trophy), Roope Rooster and Thacker Shield. The Rovers were well represented in New Zealand teams of that era. Bill Davidson and Bert Laing toured Australia in both 1919 and 1921, Ivan Stewart and Harry Tancred in 1919, and George Paki in 1921. City went on to win the championship again in 1922, 1923 and 1925 and the Roope Rooster in 1924.

The victorious 1923 City Rovers, winners of the Auckland championship for the third year in succession. Crewther, Bert Gallagher (referee), Casey, Wetherill, McDonald, Wilson, Mitchell, McLaughlin, Mackie, Thomas, Reid, B Davidson, G Davidson, W Davidson (captain).
Auckland City Libraries

(1) Ben Davidson (City) saves with a timely force.
(2) F Wilson (City), despite being tackled by C Webb (Grafton), sends the ball out to G Reid.
(3) A view of the terraces at Carlaw Park showing a portion of the big crowd which witnessed the championship cup final. City won 8–7.
Auckland City Libraries

Laing a Kangaroo

As in 1911–12, the Rugby Football League invited an Australasian team to tour Britain in 1921–22. During the 1921 season, a New Zealand team played New South Wales and Queensland in what were virtually tour trials. New South Welshmen dominated the third Kangaroos, with only four Queenslanders picked and Auckland inside back Bert Laing the sole New Zealander. Laing scored four tries in ten appearances on tour. In 1922 he played again for the Kangaroos, in an exhibition game against a combined Australia and New Zealand team at Carlaw Park. Laing also toured Australia in 1919 and as captain in 1925.

Bert Laing leads Auckland on to the field against New South Wales at the Domain in September 1922.
Auckland City Libraries

CHAPTER THREE

Northern Union Cup goes south

Rugby league clubs were first formed in South Auckland after Auckland chairman Barry Brigham's visit to Ngaruawahia in 1910, and the game flourished there until the First World War took a heavy toll. When normality returned, the game was rebuilt and the South Auckland Rugby League was constituted on 28 April 1921. Within seventeen months the lusty newcomer had ended Auckland's tenure of the Northern Union Cup.

'The visiting team is credited with being a formidable combination, having a fine record in representative matches,' previewed the *New Zealand Herald* on 2 September 1922. 'An idea of the standard of play in the Waikato this season is furnished by the fact that South Auckland scored a victory over the Australian University team. On this form it is anticipated the side will be hard to beat.' The *Herald* lamented the absence from the Auckland backs of injured brothers Bill and Ben Davidson and the unavailable Eric Grey.

Auckland's team was still stacked with former, current and future Kiwis. Among the few known personalities in the South Auckland team were fullback Tonga Mahuta, a brother of the Māori king, wing Brownie Paki, who played for Sydney club St George in 1923, and inside back Wilson Hall, who was to make two Kiwis tours as a prelude to a professional career in England.

When Auckland dashed to a 12–2 lead it seemed the cup remained in safekeeping. Mahuta chipped into that lead with two more penalty goals and the conversion of a Paki try to make the halftime score 12–11. South Auckland went ahead at 16–15 thanks to a Hall interception try. But Auckland scrum-half Clarrie Polson dashed over from a scrum and the cup holder was back in front at 20–16. With time running out, Hall sparked a move that ended with Paki diving across to score near the corner flag.

It all came down to Mahuta's sideline conversion. His good mate Paki recalled decades later that he was anxiously looking on and offering some well-meaning advice. 'I stood behind him and told Tonga that he was aiming more for the terraces than the posts,' he said. 'Tonga turned around and told me that *he* was taking the kick, went back three paces, and booted it over the middle of the crossbar.' Final score: South Auckland 21, Auckland 20. The cup awarded to Auckland in 1910 was heading south.

That was no fluke. When Auckland travelled to Steele Park, Hamilton, four weeks later it was beaten 26–18 and its 1923 cup challenge was deterred when the sides drew 20–20 at the same venue. The *New Zealand Herald's* Hamilton correspondent witnessed 'brilliant passing rushes on the part of the city backs and deadly tackling by the South Auckland forwards'. This time it was Auckland which finished on attack, after trailing 10–20 at halftime.

It was not until 1925 that Auckland retrieved the cup, by 24–16, benefiting from a home challenge. All six Auckland tries went to the three-quarters, two each to wings Ivan Littlewood and Ben Davidson and centre George Gardiner, with Clarrie Polson (two) and Gardiner kicking goals. Later in the season Auckland surged from 8–11 down at the break to win a return game 36–19, and when the Aucklanders thrashed their southern neighbours 49–15 in 1926 it seemed that big brother had put his little sibling very much in his place.

However, South Auckland returned to Carlaw Park in 1927 and swept aside a below-strength Auckland 29–12. The *Herald* scribe felt that Maurice Wetherill was the only Auckland back to perform up to standard, while the South Auckland forward pack, which included future internationals in double try-scorer Tom Timms, Jim Jones and hooker Bob Stephenson, dominated in and out of the scrums.

This time South Auckland's tenure lasted only eight months, until it brought the cup to Carlaw Park in June 1928. A far more powerful Auckland combination – ironically, Wetherill was the notable absentee – cruised to a 22–3 victory after scoring all 22 points in the first half. Centre Claude List scored two of Auckland's six tries. In 1929, Auckland pounded Canterbury 47–18 but was kept busy repulsing two border raiders, winning 11–8 over South Auckland and 22–19 over Northland, which was then in its first full season of rugby league.

'[Northland] delighted the crowd with a surprisingly good exhibition of the League code, and the game was fast and open,' reported the *Herald*. 'Northland's backs repeatedly overshadowed the local men, who were beaten for pace in passing bouts. But for the fine individual play of Delgrosso and Seagar Auckland would have been outclassed.' Northland led three times before, at 19–19, Auckland scored a 'lucky' winning try. According to the *Herald*, 'both Delgrosso and Francis knocked the ball on before Campbell touched down'.

There was no video referee in those days, though a draw would have been enough to hold the cup. So the 1920s ended with the Northern Union Cup still, if only just, in Auckland's trophy cabinet.

CHAPTER THREE

The Auckland team which lost 40–25 to New South Wales. B Laing (captain), C Dufty, I Littlewood, W Somers, F Delgrosso, C Polson, W Hanlon, N Bass, H Douglas, G Davidson, H Hawkes, B Avery, M Wetherill.
Auckland City Libraries

(1) A portion of the large crowd at the Domain.
(2) Bert Avery scores a try for Auckland.
(3) A group of officials and supporters, G Baildon, J Carlaw, W Wallace, F Whittaker, H Mackenzie, H Cotter.
Auckland City Libraries

Unstoppable

Legendary Australian loose forward Frank Burge twice scored six tries against New Zealand opposition in 1922 – for Sydney Metropolis against New Zealand Māori at Sydney and for New South Wales against Auckland at the Domain, where he added three goals for good measure. The visitors won that game 40–25. Four days later they got home by only 21–20 in the return game. Burge's contribution was one try and two goals before he was sent off for dissent just before fulltime. It was not a good season for Auckland against trans-Tasman rivals. Australian University also beat Auckland twice, by 13–12 and 18–7.

Transfer troubles

Inter-club transfer wrangles have dragged numerous Auckland Rugby League committee meetings into the late hours. But few, if any, have been as dramatic, or involved a bigger personality in the game, that that between the City and Newton clubs over brilliant young wing Lou Brown in 1924.

Brown made his Auckland debut as a seventeen-year-old replacement against New South Wales in 1922, scored three tries and was immediately stamped for greatness. After spending 1923 with Newton he went to Wigan, where he played as an amateur in several reserve team games. When Brown got home he joined City. Newton's inevitable protest was upheld by both the Auckland and New Zealand leagues. Yet Brown lined up for City in a 32–7 win over Richmond at Carlaw Park, scoring three tries. The dispute became national news.

'On all sides the playing of Brown is considered a direct challenge to the ruling of the controlling body, and it will be interesting to see the outcome,' reported the *Weekly Press* in Christchurch. 'The City club contends that the clearance given to Brown before he made a trip to England, where he played for Wigan, was absolute, and left him open to join any club on his return.

Lou Brown sprinting for a brilliant try in the corner on debut against New South Wales in 1922.
Auckland City Libraries

CHAPTER THREE

'Newton contends the clearance was given and understood to be on the condition that Brown again threw in his lot with Newton. The application for Brown's transfer to City was refused by the ARL, whose decision was upheld by the New Zealand council. In the face of these decisions City played Brown last Saturday. The next move must come from the New Zealand council.'

Brown was suspended, and the impasse lasted three weeks. When it was resolved the public announcement said only an 'amicable settlement' had been reached and the suspension was lifted in time for Brown to take the field for Newton against Marist. In the midst of the dispute, rumours circulated that City would withdraw from the competition or even switch to rugby union. That was serious stuff. City boasted four New Zealand team members and two reserves.

In hindsight, Brown might have preferred a longer suspension, for he had three near-tries ruled out against Marist. The first two were denied for a knock-on and then a forward pass. Later, Brown left his rivals standing in a long run near the sideline, only for the referee to set a scrum on the grounds the line umpire had signalled he had stepped into touch. Too late it was discovered the referee's eye had actually been caught by the elevated arm of a St John Ambulance man as he ran down the sideline to attend an injured player. Marist won 13–2.

But Brown had few such fruitless days. After touring Australia in 1925 and Britain in 1926–27 with the Kiwis, he again joined Wigan, this time as a professional, and was a try-scorer when it won the first Wembley Challenge Cup final in 1929. Brown also played for Halifax and York before returning to Auckland and playing in home test series against the Australians (1935) and British (1936). The nomad then had further stints with French and British clubs before suffering the illness that caused his death in Auckland in 1947.

1924 and 1928: Lions four-peat

The fourth and fifth British teams

Auckland could not repeat its 1920 triumph when Wakefield Trinity half Jonty Parkin led Ashes-winning England teams on tours of New Zealand in 1924 and 1928. His sides experienced mixed results at test level, but the visitors won all four games against Auckland city and provincial opposition at Carlaw Park.

Local officials adopted two English rule interpretations for the 1924 match with Auckland City – no goals would be allowed from marks, as permitted in Auckland, and scrums instead of penalties would result from forward passes. England did not need any help, winning comfortably by 24–11 after being held to 13–8 at halftime. Ben Davidson (two) and Nelson Bass scored Auckland's tries, and Craddock Dufty kicked a goal.

Auckland City Libraries

(1) Nelson Bass makes a determined effort to break through the England defence

(2) Part of the large crowd on the northern bank at Carlaw Park.

(3) Rival captains Jonty Parkin and Nelson Bass with the ball boys.

(4) Clarrie Polson beats an England player for the ball.
Auckland City Libraries

Auckland Province included South Auckland wings Johnston and Brownie Paki. Like the City XIII, it conceded six tries and scored three in losing 28–13. From 20–5 at the interval, Auckland got back to 20–13 before the British finished ahead. Johnston, Hec Brisbane and Frank Delgrosso were Auckland's try-scorers and Dufty kicked two goals.

Dufty also played against the 1928 Lions and his goalkicking was a feature of both games. He kicked three penalty goals, two from near halfway, as Auckland Province lost 14–9 after being 9–8 ahead. Wing Len Scott was Auckland's try-scorer. South Auckland and Kiwis prop Joe Menzies was the only Auckland player from outside the city club competition.

The 1924 Auckland City team which played England, Nelson Bass, Craddock Dufty, Ben Davidson, Maurice Wetherill, Charles Gregory, Frank Delgrosso, Hec Brisbane, George Gardiner, Ernest Herring, Bert Avery, Clarrie Polson, Wally Somers, Bill Stormont.
Auckland City Libraries

CHAPTER THREE

A forty-yard field goal and two conversions were Dufty's contribution in Auckland City's 26–15 loss to the British. His display compared favourably with that of great Welshman Jim Sullivan, who finished with four goals. An estimated 25,000 fans sensed an Auckland victory when the home side held an 8–3 halftime advantage and later went ahead 15–6. Once again, the Lions finished over the top of their opponents. Roy Hardgrave, Len Scott and Alan Clarke touched down for Auckland.

Auckland teams against the British in the 1920s were:

1924 Auckland City: fullback, Charles Gregory; three-quarters, Ben Davidson, Hec Brisbane, Frank Delgrosso; five-eighths, Maurice Wetherill, Craddock Dufty; halfback, Clarrie Polson; forwards, Bill Stormont, Wally Somers, Ernie Herring, George Gardiner, Bert Avery, Nelson Bass (captain).

1924 Auckland Province: fullback, Craddock Dufty; three-quarters, Brownie Paki (South Auckland), Hec Brisbane, B Johnston (South Auckland); five-eighths, Maurice Wetherill, Scotty McClymont; halfback, John Lang; forwards, Jim O'Brien, Sam Lowrie, Ernie Herring, Bert Avery, Bill Te Whata, Hec McDonald.

1928 Auckland Province: fullback, Craddock Dufty; three-quarters, Len Scott, Claude List, Beattie; five-eighths, W Hanlon, Jim Amos; halfback, Bill Peckham; forwards, Joe Menzies (South Auckland), Neville St George, Dick Moisley, Trevor Hall, J Payne, R Jenkinson.

In 1928 England beat Auckland City 26–15. An Auckland passing run breaks down when Len Scott misses the ball. Jim O'Brien and Trevor Hall are in support.
Auckland City Libraries

England wing Alf Ellaby secures the ball after a scrum breaks up.
Auckland City Libraries

1928 Auckland City: fullback, Craddock Dufty; three-quarters, Len Scott, Claude List, Roy Hardgrave; five-eighths, Maurice Wetherill, Stan Prentice; halfback, Frank Delgrosso; forwards, Jim O'Brien, Wally Somers, Lou Hutt, Trevor Hall, J Payne, Alan Clarke.

Seeing double

1925 Queensland tourists

The try which drew Auckland City level at 18–18 with the great 1925 Queensland touring team was attributed by the *Auckland Star* to O'Brien. Unfortunately, the writer did not say which O'Brien followed up Maurice Wetherill's in-goal kick to touch down. We know it was Jim O'Brien and that he was a prop. But there were two Jim O'Briens, both props, in the Auckland team. One came from Marist and the other from Devonport.

Auckland's draw was a particularly significant result, for this Queensland side is regarded as one of the finest overseas teams to visit these shores. Queensland dominated New South Wales in that era and was expected to do the same in this country. But it lost 25–24 to New Zealand in the first match and, back at Carlaw Park four days later, Auckland had nine starting Kiwis in its line-up. After that the Queenslanders ran rampant over all opposition, including New Zealand (35–14) and Auckland Province (54–14).

While Auckland City was credited with adhering to the winning New Zealand formula of having the forwards smash into the Queensland defence to counter the visitors' brilliant backline, Auckland also played a more all-round game. As on the previous Saturday, Queensland struggled with the rule interpretations of a referee named Ripley and conceded many penalties. Captain and loose forward Bert Avery (two), scrum-half Stan Webb and one of the Jim O'Briens scored tries, and Frank Delgrosso kicked three goals.

The O'Briens clashed when Devonport beat Marist 25–19 at Carlaw Park in September 1924. G Smith (Devonport), in centre, being supported by Jim O'Brien (on left) while Jim O'Brien (Marist) is on the right, during a tussle for the ball.
Auckland City Libraries

Ivan Littlewood (Auckland) endeavours to fend off an opponent as 18,000 spectators witness a 41–17 victory by the 1925 New Zealand side. This game was played prior to the arrival of the Queenslanders.
Auckland City Libraries

CHAPTER THREE

A month later Auckland Province, with four of the Auckland City forwards but only Delgrosso among the backs, and some South Auckland input, was never in contention against a Queensland side reinforced by champion centre Tom Gorman. Avery was awarded an obstruction try when about to force the ball, Arthur Singe scored the only legitimate try and there were four goals from Delgrosso. It was 28–6 by half-time and no more competitive after that.

Auckland teams:

Auckland City: fullback, Charles Gregory; three-quarters Ivan Littlewood, Frank Delgrosso, Lou Brown; five-eighths Jack Kirwan, Maurice Wetherill; scrum-half Stan Webb; forwards, Jim O'Brien (Marist), Neville St George, Jim O'Brien (Devonport), Ernie Herring, Arthur Singe, Bert Avery (captain).

Auckland Province: fullback, George Raynor; three-quarters, B. Johnston, George Gardiner, A Jackson; five-eighths, Frank Delgrosso, Brian Riley; halfback, Bill Peckham; forwards, Jim O'Brien (Marist), Alf Townsend, Ernie Herring, Joe Menzies, Arthur Singe, Bert Avery. Replacements: Bill Te Whata, Len Mason.

Auckland also played the returning New Zealand team after its tour of Australia in 1925. On a fine day at Carlaw Park the Kiwis carved through for nine tries, three each to Avery and Wetherill, and Delgrosso converted seven of them to embellish a 41–17 scoreline. Auckland replied with tries to Ben Davidson, St George and Riley and four Singe goals.

The brothers Davidson

When Ben Davidson ran onto Carlaw Park as a replacement in New Zealand's first match against the 1925 Queenslanders, he completed a notable treble of national representation. Elder brothers Bill and George had previously attained the highest recognition in rugby league and athletics, respectively, with George also utilising his sprinting ability as a prolific scoring Auckland representative wing.

Bill Davidson converting a try for Auckland against Hawke's Bay in 1921.
Auckland City Libraries

Ben Davidson in action for Auckland against New Zealand in 1925.
Auckland City Libraries

George Davidson supporting Bert Avery (on the ground) during Auckland's 1922 game against New South Wales.
Auckland City Libraries

While that trio's deeds have survived the test of time, there were actually five Davidson brothers on the Auckland sporting scene just before and after the First World War. The oldest of them, Charles, was killed at Messines in 1917. Nicknamed Bunny, he had captained the first Auckland junior representative rugby league team against Waikato in 1914. Charles also won an Auckland amateur boxing title before enlisting.

William John (Bill) Davidson was an outstanding fullback and goalkicker who captained City when it reigned over the Auckland club scene. He toured Australia with the 1919 and 1921 New Zealand teams and played for Auckland and New Zealand against the 1919 Kangaroos and 1920 Lions. Bill was a senior player for City from 1914 until 1923, apart from time spent in camp at Trentham.

A more than useful sprinter and swimmer, Bill later served those sports as well as rugby league in official capacities. Not just around the board table either, for

CHAPTER THREE

he was regarded as an expert with an athletics starting gun. Bill represented his City club on the Auckland Rugby League and Canterbury on the New Zealand Rugby League. For many years he wrote match reports and feature articles for the Auckland newspapers and compiled three annuals from 1947 to 1949.

George Davidson was the undisputed fastest man in New Zealand from 1919 to 1921. He finished fifth in the 200 metres final at the 1920 Olympic Games in Antwerp after winning his heat and beating illustrious American Charlie Paddock in a quarter-final. George started and finished his rugby league club career at City, either side of a stint with Maritime. He represented Auckland from 1919 until 1922, and legend has it that he would have joined brothers Bill and Ben on the Kiwis Roll of Honour had work not prevented him from being available for two Australian tours.

Benjamin Alfred (Ben) Davidson inherited his family's speed. At the Auckland Domain in 1921 George was first, Ben second and Bill third in a classic 100 yards sprint. After his brief international debut against the 1925 Queenslanders, Ben toured Britain with the 1926–27 Kiwis as a centre and wing – scoring fourteen tries in twenty-three appearances and playing in three of the four test matches – and caught the eye of Wigan officials.

He made a try-scoring debut for Wigan against Warrington on 27 August 1927, and scored again in his last game against Wakefield Trinity on New Year's Day 1930. Ben secured a release from his contract and left Central Park with a record of thirty-one tries in sixty-nine appearances. He resumed playing in Auckland, scored a try for the province against the 1932 Lions, and was recalled to the Kiwis for the second test at Christchurch.

A 1936 *Auckland Rugby League Gazette* recalled that a fifth Davidson sibling, Reg, was playing sufficiently well as a City fourth grader in his youth for some observers to predict that he would follow his brothers through to a high level. 'However, it was destined not to be, as a severe accident cut short the career of what promised to be another top-liner in one of the most noteworthy sporting families in the Dominion.'

The oldest of the five Davidson brothers, Charles, lost his life at Messines during the First World War.
Alexander Turnbull Library

In Memory of
Private CHARLES KENNETH DAVIDSON

21225, 15th Coy. 2nd Bn., Auckland Regiment, N.Z.E.F
who died age 23
on 07 June 1917
Son of Charles and Alice Davidson, of 74, Franklin Rd., Auck
New Zealand.
Remembered with honour
WULVERGHEM-LINDENHOEK ROAD MILITARY
CEMETERY

Commemorated in perpetuity by
the Commonwealth War Graves Commission

Stormont Memorial Shield

Front-row forward Bill Stormont became Marist's first New Zealand international in all three test matches against England in 1920, having played strongly in Auckland's victory over the tourists. In 1924 he captained his club to success in the Auckland championship, before falling ill, leading to his death in June 1925, aged just twenty-six. Stormont's family donated the William Stormont Memorial Shield which the Auckland Rugby League attached to the annual champion of champions fixture. Marist was beaten 23–22 by Roope Rooster winner Ponsonby in September 1925 as a prelude to Ponsonby becoming the first shield-holder after a 35–3 victory over championship winner City.

In 1924 Marist, captained by Bill Stormont, beat Devonport 20–17 to win its first championship. Scenes from one of their clashes.

(1) Marist team, Lang, Nelson, Foss, Stewart, Brisbane, Gregory, Sweeney, O'Brien, J Stormont, Gardiner, Neal, Johnson, W Stormont.

(2) Bert Laing (Devonport) accepts a pass from his half, Garrett.

(3) 'Stacks on the mill' as the pack collapses.

(4) Devonport team, Goddick, Garrett, O'Brien, Scott, Seagar, Harper, Taylor, J Laing, Webb, Veart, St. George, B Laing, Douglas.

Auckland City Libraries

CHAPTER THREE

Contrasts with Canterbury

Auckland suffered its first loss to Canterbury, by 6–5 on a recently opened but very muddy Monica Park in Christchurch in 1925, but achieved its highest ever total over the same opponent, 66–26 at Carlaw Park, three years later.

There were mitigating circumstances for Auckland losing its unbeaten record. A dozen leading players stayed in Auckland to represent New Zealand against Queensland at Carlaw Park on the same day, though a more than useful squad was sent south. After beating West Coast 22–15 at Greymouth, Auckland led Canterbury 5–0 at halftime through a try to Bill Te Whata. It was 5–3 in the seventy-eighth minute, until the Canterbury forwards launched a desperate attack which resulted in Stan Polaschek scoring the winning try from a grubber to the in-goal area.

Full retribution was exerted during Canterbury's 1928 Northern Union Cup challenge. Roy Hardgrave led the charge with five tries and Craddock Dufty and Allan Seagar claimed three each as the slick Auckland backline monopolised all sixteen of their team's tries. Six players shared the nine successful conversions. Ted Spillane, a test reserve who was soon to be signed by Wigan, replied with three tries of his own for an outgunned Canterbury.

In 1928 Auckland beat Canterbury 66–26.
(1) Maurice Wetherill leads the Auckland team on to Carlaw Park.
(2) 'Will he sell the dummy?' Allan Seagar, the Auckland stand-off, in one of his characteristic passing runs against Canterbury.
Auckland City Libraries

Suspended for life

Marist second-rower Arthur Singe was the sole Aucklander among seven players suspended for life after the 1926–27 New Zealand team (dubbed the 'All Blacks') toured Britain. The others were vice-captain Neil Mouat and Jack Wright from the West Coast, Alphonsus Carroll from Wellington, and Bill Devine, Lou Petersen and English-born Frank Henry from Canterbury.

Disputes with manager George Ponder and Australian coach Ernest Mair widened the crack to a chasm as the tour progressed, and the seven 'strikers' withdrew their services. They were cut adrift and the rest of the team soldiered on with only five specialist forwards. Auckland backs George Gardiner, Craddock Dufty and Jim Parkes were drafted into the pack for some games.

All concerned swore an oath of secrecy and no public comment was ever made, although a journalist who toured with the team painted Mair as the villain when interviewed on his return. The English Rugby Football League had some sympathy for the players. At one stage officials persuaded Mair to temporarily step down as coach to achieve a temporary peace, and they were later accused of siding with the estranged players when giving them £10 each for the boat trip home. Henry stayed in England and was allowed to play on.

The New Zealand Rugby League, acting on legal advice, never released the managers' version of the dispute when it banned the seven players for life in March 1927. In 1962 the New Zealand Rugby League administration lifted the suspensions. By then four of the six New Zealand-domiciled players, including Singe, had died.

There was a postscript to the tour when an Auckland representative team beat the 'Auckland All Blacks' by 24–21 in April 1927 at Carlaw Park. Irrepressible wing Lou Brown crossed for three tries to give the 'All Blacks' a 19–10 halftime lead but Auckland centre, Maurice Wetherill, who had been unavailable for the tour, starred in a winning second-half surge.

Captain courageous

There was no shortage of immensely skilled players to brighten the Saturdays of football fans during the depression years of the 1920s. But Bert Avery was the finest of them all, and had a great career which extended at representative level from 1919 to 1927. He was the inspiring captain of an otherwise disastrous New Zealand tour of Britain in 1926–27.

Undaunted by the loss of seven forwards in a dispute which split the team, loose forward and captain Avery played in twenty-nine of the thirty-four fixtures and scored twenty-three tries. Only wings Phillip Orchard (twenty-seven tries in

CHAPTER THREE

Bert Avery receives a pass from Clarrie Polson during Auckland's clash with England in 1924.
Auckland City Libraries

1971) and Vern Bakalich (twenty-six in 1955–56) have scored more tries on a Kiwis tour. Included in Avery's total were tries in all three test matches against England and five in the match against Broughton Rangers.

James Goldthorpe wrote in the *Yorkshire Evening News*: 'In Avery, the captain, the team has a man who has throughout played a magnificent game. His skill is far in excess of any league forward, in spite of the weight of care he has had to carry.'

After serving in the First World War, Avery played for Maritime (later Grafton Athletic) and made his international debut against the 1919 Kangaroos, scoring in two of the four tests. From then on he was an automatic selection for Auckland and the Kiwis, in home tests against the British in 1920 and 1924, on tour to Australia in 1921 and 1925, and as captain against Queensland in 1925. He later selected Auckland and New Zealand teams and was inducted into the New Zealand Rugby League Legends of League in 1995.

Schoolboys competition

An unofficial schoolboys competition was held in 1926 between teams from Newmarket, Otahuhu, Papatoetoe and Parnell. That was sufficiently encouraging for a primary school management committee to be set up in 1927, with delegates from Newmarket, Otahuhu, Papatoetoe, Richmond, Onehunga School and Onehunga Convent. Teams from Newton and Newmarket B joined them in a late season knockout.

Otahuhu, coached by former Auckland and New Zealand representative Jim Clark, won that inaugural competition. By 1930 the number of teams had doubled to twelve; there were thirty in 1937 and seventy-eight in 1939. The Auckland Rugby League jubilee booklet reported another sizeable increase to 150 teams in 1946, by which time an independent schoolboy board of control had been formed, and to 326 in 1959.

But playing rugby league in schools, whether they be primary or secondary, has long been a vexed question. Rugby union authorities have always sought to protect their monopoly at schools level, while rugby league has had little influence from within the education system. It did not take long for problems to arise in 1927.

The *Auckland Rugby League Gazette* of 7 May reported: 'Those enthusiasts who have undertaken to establish League football among the younger generations are having a pretty rough time at the hands of some of the schoolmasters.' Officials who went to schools to verify players' ages were made all too aware that some headmasters did not approve of their sport or were left waiting for hours before the information was supplied.

'But the best of the lot was where the schoolmaster called the bigger boys together and told them that if they played League he would not give them the "recommendation" which is usually given by a headmaster when a boy leaves school,' said the *Gazette*. 'It is absolutely astounding to think that people who are servants of the State – and well paid ones at that – are going to be allowed to dictate to the boys what form of sport they will follow in their own time.'

Southern sojourn

In September 1927 Auckland mounted its most extensive internal tour for seventeen years, taking the Northern Union Cup on the road and successfully defending it against Canterbury at Christchurch (24–13), West Coast-Buller at Greymouth (44–15), Otago at Dunedin (20–13) and Wellington at Wellington (41–23).

The Auckland squad included: backs C Dufty (Newton), C Gregory (Marist), G Wade (City), M Little (Newton), C List (Kingsland), J Wilson (Mangere), M Wetherill (City, captain), S Webb (Devonport) and H McIntyre (Newton); and forwards, J O'Brien (Devonport), W Somers (Newton), H Dixon (Devonport), L Hutt (Ponsonby), T Hall (Newton), J Payne (Ponsonby), A Clarke (Newton) and N Bass (City).

Centres Wetherill and Gregory, with fullback Dufty, were credited with giving the Canterbury backs a lesson in how to bamboozle a defence. Hooker Somers held the upper hand, or foot, in the scrums and Canterbury's 13–11 halftime lead was partly attributed to its having the wind advantage. A try by List had Auckland ahead soon after the restart and the margin was increased with further tries to Hutt and Dixon.

Auckland rugby league selectors in 1927, Ernie Asher, Edward Fox and Alan Blakey.
Auckland City Libraries

'Wetherill was the outstanding player on the field,' reported *The Press*. 'His ability to draw the defence and then evade it was a source of delight to the spectators.' Dufty, Gregory and wings List and Little were also praised for their attacking prowess, and the writer said, 'all the forwards could handle like backs, Payne, Hutt and Clarke being the best'.

CHAPTER THREE

Auckland totalled twelve tries in easily accounting for West Coast-Buller, which had done well to restrict the visitors to a 17–10 halftime lead. Wilson grabbed three first-half tries on one wing, but there is uncertainty how many Little finished with on the other, the *Christchurch Star* crediting him with three and the Press Association with two. Only four tries were converted, preventing Auckland from reaching a half-century.

Rugby league had made a bold revival in Otago a few years earlier. Indeed, touring British teams played test matches in Dunedin in 1924 and 1928, and the Otago Rugby League was wealthy enough to loan money to the New Zealand Rugby League. Auckland had to work harder than even the locals expected for its seven-point success. By halftime it was 15–8, Otago scored next, and victory was not clinched until Dufty converted Webb's try.

The Wellington stopover was less stressful, even though the game was as close as 23–15 midway through the second spell, with Auckland toiling into the wind. Dixon, a snowy-haired second-rower, was in his element, scoring four of Auckland's nine tries. Auckland returned home still in possession of the Northern Union Cup, eyeing two home defences.

Buller, playing as a single entity, was not expected to threaten Auckland and eventually suffered a 60–33 thumping. But the little league, which lasted only a few years, did provide an outstanding prospect in rugged second-rower Vern Goodall, who scored two tries, kicked six goals and was picked for the Kiwis in 1928. Auckland, overall, had too much experience, combination, speed and skill. Gregory, List and Beattie collected three tries apiece of the sixteen scored, twelve of them by the backs.

After such a triumphant march through the south, followed by an apparently useful training run against Buller, it was all the more surprising that South Auckland should come north and beat a not unduly changed Auckland side as convincingly as the 29–12 result indicated. The cup spent the summer in the Waikato.

Newton Rangers won a second and last championship in 1927, defeating Ponsonby 6–3, before 13,000 spectators.

(1) Team. Back row: T Hall, C Dufty, A Clark, G Rhodes, W Somers, W Henry, R Tucker (trainer), R Stack.

Front row: A McIntyre, M Little, M Herewini, R Hardgrave, G Morman (captain), W Kerr, A McLeod.

(2) Ivan Culpan (secretary ARL) and George Rhodes (chairman ARL).

(3) T Tuohey and R Pollock (NZRL council).

(4) Newton wing M Little endeavouring to evade J Payne (Ponsonby).

(5) W Henry (Newton) gets in a left-footer.

(6) Little is well covered by Payne (immediately behind) and S Ussher (about to tackle).

Auckland City Libraries

Souths' five-man pack

In 1929 South Sydney showed the way for many other Australian clubs by tripping across the Tasman for late-season feature matches. Sydney champions for the previous five seasons, the Rabbitohs were pitted against top Auckland club Marist over consecutive Saturdays. Honours were shared with Marist, and Souths decisively beat Huntly midweek. Souths travelled without Kangaroos

CHAPTER THREE

Harry Finch, 'Mick' Kadwell, Paddy Maher, Eddie Root and George Treweek, who were touring Britain.

Marist had won the Roope Rooster and beaten Ponsonby 28–14 in the champion of champions showdown two weeks before taking on Souths. The Marist backline included outstanding internationals Hec Brisbane and Charles Gregory (both future New Zealand captains), and future Kiwis Norm Campbell at fullback and Wilf Hassan at scrum-half. Prop Jim O'Brien was a current test player, and hooker Gordon (Stump) Campbell wore the Kiwis jersey in 1932.

Gregory was the hero of the first clash, providing all of his team's points from two tries, a conversion and a penalty goal in a 10–9 Carlaw Park thriller. His first try came on the back of a move by Hassan and forwards Dick Moisley and Alan Clarke. In the next play, Gregory cleverly wrong-footed the defence to score. His winning try came after good lead-up work by Phil Brady and Brisbane.

'The South Sydney team took the field with five forwards and eight backs, playing three halves and four three-quarters,' reported the *New Zealand Herald*. 'After the first few minutes Marist countered this by taking Clarke from the scrum and placing him inside Hassan and Gregory. For a commencement this movement somewhat upset the Marist combination, as Clarke was a little too slow in getting the ball away. Nevertheless he improved as the game progressed and for a forward played a fine game in his new position.'

Another 15,000 attendance was registered when the clubs lined up again a week later but the second match – a 21–5 victory to the Rabbitohs – failed to reproduce the excitement of the first. Once again, Souths used only five forwards and the ploy worked for them. Marist this time maintained orthodox positioning. Souths dominated the ball, not only from the scrums but also from the many Marist mistakes, which cost them points and possession. George Batchelor scored Marist's sole try, and Gregory kicked a penalty goal.

Charles Gregory (on ground) scores the first try for Marist.
Auckland City Libraries

AUCKLAND RUGBY LEAGUE
1909–2009

Five times Sydney champion South Sydney lost to Marist 10–9 in a Carlaw Park thriller.

(1) Brady (Marist) about to tackle a South Sydney back.

(2) The Marist team. Back row: H Donovan (trainer), Duane, Gregory, O'Brien, Clarke, Johnston, N Campbell, McDonald, Batchelor, J Kirwan (coach). Front row: Flett, Brisbane, Graham, Moisley, (captain), Hassan, Brady, G Campbell.

Auckland City Libraries

Marist won its second consecutive Roope Rooster by beating championship winner Ponsonby 28–14.

(1) A young mascot sets the ball rolling.

(2) Batchelor (Marist) is securely tackled.

(3) Rival captains Charles Gregory (Marist) and Frank Delgrosso (Ponsonby) with George Rhodes (chairman ARL) and referee Vic Simpson.

(4) Moore (Ponsonby) about to be tackled by Hassan.

(5) Skelton (Ponsonby) sends out a good pass before being tackled by Batchelor.

(6) Section of the crowd on the terraces.

Auckland City Libraries

CHAPTER THREE

Two trebles

Classy outside backs Roy Hardgrave and Hec Brisbane recorded try-scoring trebles for Auckland when Otago bravely made the long journey north to Carlaw Park in September 1928. It was an illustration of Otago's confidence and seemed justified when it closed up to 15–16 late in the first half. But centre Brisbane scored just before the break and, after wing Hardgrave had raced back to make a try-saving tackle, fellow wing Len Scott utilised an overlap on the blind side of a scrum to reignite the home side's scoring. Auckland won 42–22.

Snapshots of the Otago v Auckland clash at Carlaw Park in September 1928, won by Auckland 42–22.

(1) Claude List (Auckland) passes the ball to Len Scott before being tackled by Bert Eckhoff.

(2) An Otago back attempting to stop Dick Moisley's progress.

(3) An Otago player well tackled by Moisley.

(4) The Otago representative touring team.

Auckland City Libraries

CHAPTER 04

FOCUS ON THE CLUBS
1930–1939

CHAPTER FOUR

Focus on the Clubs 1930–1939

'Bright future' predicted

The *1933 New Zealand Rugby League Annual*, which provided a valuable insight to the early days of the game but was never followed up by a promised second edition, predicted a bright future for the sport in general, and Auckland in particular, during the 1930s. Whether that occurred is debatable as the game and the nation battled through the depression years, though most of the doubt resulted from factors out of Auckland's control.

New Zealand played no overseas test matches between the disastrous 1926–27 tour of Britain until the Kiwis returned there in 1947–48. Although New Zealand sides visited Australia in 1930 and 1938, they had to be content to meet state, city and country opposition. At least Australia made its first tour of New Zealand for sixteen years in 1935, and the 1937 Kangaroos stopped over for three games in Auckland on their way to Britain. The only international constants were the four-yearly tours by the British in 1932 and 1936.

The 1938 Kiwis were the first to be officially bestowed with that title, and the first to wear a white vee on the traditional black jersey. Their Australian tour was seen as a stepping stone towards mounting another major tour of Britain in 1939. A powerful team was assembled and confidence was high. But Europe exploded into the Second World War around the time the Kiwis arrived in England, and they returned home after winning two club matches.

Auckland's internal activities were subdued. The Northern Union Cup was lost to South Auckland in 1930. From there it went to North Auckland, back to South Auckland, and to the South Island. There was no great enthusiasm to chase it. Indeed, when Auckland met and beat cup holder Canterbury at Christchurch in 1935, the trophy was not at stake because the 30 June challenge deadline had not been met. The cup did not come back to Auckland until 1950. Canterbury and West Coast played in Auckland only once each in the 1930s, and rugby league was struggling for survival in Wellington.

But the *1933 Annual* had good reasons to be optimistic for the game in Auckland. A perceived slump in football quality between 1927 and 1930 had been arrested, standards were rising appreciably and crowds were of record proportions. In 1931, the administration structure had changed from an executive of club delegates to a board of control 'to eliminate partisanship in administration'. The number of senior clubs was reduced to seven, City, Devonport, Ellerslie, Marist, Newton, Ponsonby and Richmond. They received a share of the gate-takings to reduce their dependence on the generosity of honorary vice-presidents.

'G Grey Campbell, a prominent Auckland business and public man – member of the City Council and Transport Board, community singing leader, church worker and widely known as "Uncle Cam" over the radio – became chairman and trustee in succession to George Rhodes. Mr Campbell, previously a rugby union referee, has been a rugby league enthusiast for some years and his first season as chairman has earned for him the admiration of the growing thousands who support the code in Auckland.'

Despite the scarcity of international and national competition, the Auckland club scene was hotly contested. Richmond fielded arguably the most successful team of all time and had every right to call itself Australasian champion, Devonport and Marist were strong, and the charismatic Steve Wātene assembled a Manukau side which won the Fox Memorial Shield and Roope Rooster at the first attempt in 1936. Sydney clubs crossed the Tasman, staying for several games and engaging in many rousing encounters with Auckland's best.

Fox Memorial Shield

Auckland's inter-club rugby league championship winners have for the last seventy-seven years been the recipients of the Fox Memorial Shield, named in honour of Edward Vincent Fox, who died in 1930 after finally succumbing to wounds suffered during the First World War. Fox was an outstanding member of pre-war North Shore backlines and represented Auckland against the 1914 England touring team before enlisting in the army. While overseas he was awarded the Military Medal and promoted to the rank of sergeant but suffered leg wounds that ended his playing career. The indomitable Fox was appointed to the Auckland Rugby League executive and became an Auckland and New Zealand selector.

CHAPTER FOUR

Francis (Auckland) kicks into touch.
Auckland City Libraries

South Auckland wins cup

That the Northern Union Cup was sitting somewhat uneasily in Auckland's trophy cabinet became evident when Northland almost snatched it away in May 1930. The northerners led 8–0 and were still ahead 12–11 at halftime. An interception try to Maurice Wetherill got Auckland in front but Northland never fell far off the pace and it was 21–16 at the finish. Ted Meyer was to be Northland's first Kiwi on tour to Australia that year.

It stood to reason, then, that South Auckland would be a tougher proposition two weeks later. The Waikato district was to have six players, four of them forwards, on the Kiwis tour, comparing more than favourably with the eight from Auckland, of whom only two were forwards. Auckland's selectors made multiple changes between the two cup games but that did not prevent South Auckland from winning 13–12.

The *New Zealand Herald* had predicted the threat posed by the South Auckland pack and confirmed it in its match report. 'The Waikato forwards again proved a very formidable combination and throughout controlled the game. The solid scrum formation of the visitors gave them a decided advantage and time and again they

Auckland retained the Northern Union Cup by beating Northland 21–16. The Auckland team, Ruby, Clarke, List, Carter, Seagar, O'Brien, Francis, Brady, Wātene, Pascoe, Campbell, Shortland, Wetherill (captain).
Auckland City Libraries

South Auckland takes the Northern Union Cup from Auckland, 13–12.

(1) Tittleton, the South Auckland wing, makes a dash for the line.

(2) Paki (South Auckland) carries the ball into touch.

(3) Auckland's Brisbane (left) and Perry in midfield.

(4) Paki scores the visitors' second try after a herculean dash as Brisbane and Clarke tackle him.

Auckland City Libraries

won the ball.' Hec Brisbane was described as 'easily Auckland's best back' but the *Herald* said the backs, as a unit, lacked the teamwork to save the day.

It was 13–7 to South Auckland at halftime and Auckland did its utmost to get back on level terms. Craddock Dufty missed a penalty goal from close range and the only second-half scoring came from a Wetherill high kick leading to a try to second-rower Len Barchard, who was making his representative debut, and Allan Seagar's conversion.

Captain Charles Gregory, Steve Wātene, Stan Clark, Seagar, Barchard, Brisbane, Dufty and Wetherill were the Auckland representatives in the Kiwis touring team. The first five of them lined up for New Zealand again in a 34–27 victory over Auckland at Carlaw Park on their return. But the stars of the game were South Auckland scrum-half Edwin Abbott, who scored four tries from eager support play, and Canterbury stand-off Jim Amos, who made the breaks for most of them. Amos had spent the 1928 season with City in Auckland. He was to coach the Kiwis to consecutive test series victories over Australia in 1952 and 1953.

Curiously, when the cup changed hands again at Carlaw Park in 1931 it was Northland that successfully challenged South Auckland (16–8) to start its only tenure of the symbol of inter-provincial supremacy. It was the first match on the park between two neutral provinces. To prove that was no fluke, Northland returned to Carlaw Park (without the cup) and drew 19–19 with a strong, though not full-strength, Auckland team. In 1932, South Auckland regained the cup from Northland at Ngaruawahia, only to be beaten by West Coast the next season.

Prominent officials of the Auckland Rugby League at Carlaw Park in 1930. Fred Ellis (treasurer), Ivan Culpan (secretary), George Rhodes (chairman), Bill Hammill (former chairman) and John A Lee MP (future president).
Auckland City Libraries

CHAPTER FOUR

Donovan's find

During a senior match on 9 May 1931, Marist hooker Jack Donovan was locked in the midst of a swirling, sweating scrum on a wet No.2 ground at Carlaw Park. The Ellerslie scrum-half was about to feed the ball when Donovan spied a shilling piece lying on the turf.

Donovan slipped an arm loose, reached down and picked up the coin. He was promptly penalised by the referee for not binding correctly. Undeterred, the hooker strolled to the fence and passed the shilling to a spectator.

The penalty did not stop Marist winning 39–3, nor did it deter Donovan from taking up refereeing after his retirement; he was in charge of the sole test match when the 1946 British touring team lost to the Kiwis 13–8 on the adjacent main field at Carlaw Park.

Clubs combine to beat Easts

It took the combined talents of the Devonport United and Marist clubs to subdue Sydney side Eastern Suburbs in 1931. They were the leading Auckland clubs of the era: Marist had won the 1931 championship; the first for the Fox Memorial Shield; and Devonport the Roope Rooster and Stormont Shield. The roles were to be reversed in 1932 and Devonport was to claim another championship and the champion of champions trophy in 1933.

There have been few teams in Sydney premiership history which boasted so many brilliant youngsters as that Easts squad. Centre Dave Brown, five-eighth Ernie Norman, halfback Viv Thicknesse and forwards Ray Stehr and Sid (Joe) Pearce were aged between eighteen and twenty. Within two years all were wearing the Australian jersey, and they toured New Zealand again with the 1935 Kangaroos. Easts, runner-up to South Sydney in 1931, was developing the combination which won three consecutive Sydney titles from 1935 to 1937.

Devonport United and Marist combined to beat Sydney Eastern Suburbs 14–13.

(1) Mike Nixon (Eastern Suburbs) gathering up the ball which has been dropped by team-mate Bill Dyer.

(2) Alan Clarke (combined) gets his kick in on being tackled.

Auckland City Libraries

Easts accepted a five-match itinerary and started with wins over Northland (23–11) at Whangarei, Devonport (41–27) and South Auckland (23–14) at Hamilton. The tour finished with an 18–13 victory over Auckland Colts. The decision to play a combined Devonport and Marist team in the fourth game rather than the Auckland representatives captured the imagination of the public, and Carlaw Park was packed for the occasion.

The combined team won a 14–13 thriller. Devonport wing Len Scott scored a try in the first minute and three goals to Marist loose forward Alan Clarke left Easts with a nine-point deficit in the opening quarter. Brown spearheaded the revival with two tries, both converted by Morrie Boyle, and Easts led 10–9 at the break.

Devonport's Allan Seagar and Marist's Hec Brisbane then fused their attacking skills for the latter to score, and Clarke's third penalty goal had Combined out to 14–10. Easts fought back, with Pearce giving right wing Fred Tottey room to dummy and step his way through the defence. Brown's failure to convert proved crucial, for there was no further scoring as Devonport-Marist rebuffed a series of frantic goal-line assaults.

'In a tense, wavering and fast struggle Eastern Suburbs met their first defeat in New Zealand but they went down gloriously, making such determined and clever efforts in the fading moments to snatch victory that the crowd was on its feet cheering them as, in the same breath, it looked with some confidence to the defensive skill of the home thirteen,' reported the *Auckland Star*.

'Highlights of the game were the consistently good goalkicking of Clarke (Auckland) and Boyle (Sydney), the magnificent anticipatory play of the visiting centre three-quarter Dave Brown, the towering exhibition of the Eastern Suburbs forward S Pearce, and the fine collaboration of Brisbane and Seagar in attack and defence. Campbell's hooking for the winners was also praiseworthy.'

1932: Tackling the Lions

England 19 Auckland 14

Auckland fielded twelve players who had or were to wear the Kiwis jersey – as did all three reserves – against the 1932 England team. The exception was speedy Marist wing Pat Meehan, who had scored four tries for North in the 1931 inter-island game. But this British combination, captained by legendary Welsh and Wigan fullback Jim Sullivan, had already won the Ashes in Australia and was to be unbeaten in New Zealand. Its toughest contests were against Auckland (19–14) and the third test match (20–18).

The *New Zealand Herald* revealed in its preview that Auckland, like the Kiwis, had 'indulged in extensive training' under Bill Kelly, who had represented both

CHAPTER FOUR

Rugby League Football.
CARLAW PARK.
England v. Auckland.
Kick-off at 3 p.m.
Curtain Raisers from 12 noon.
Book Seats at E. Asher, Tobacconist, Shortland St.
ADMISSION, SEE DAILY PAPERS.

Auckland City Libraries

New Zealand and Australia before being wounded in the First World War and turning his attention to coaching in Sydney. 'Providing the Auckland forwards gain a fair share of the ball, which seems very doubtful owing to England's superior weight, the backs are expected to make better combination than the New Zealand [first test] rearguard.'

(1) Auckland team led onto the field by Hec Brisbane.

(2) Stan Smith (England) tackles Bert Cooke. The other Auckland players are Wilf Hassan (left) and Ray Lawless.

(3) England led out by legendary fullback Jim Sullivan.

(4) Alec Fildes effectively tackles Bert Cooke with Wilf Hassan coming up in support.

(5) Auckland fullback Norm Campbell collared by a hefty Englishman.

Auckland City Libraries

For its part, England fielded its entire test backline and three of the six forwards who had shared in the 24–9 defeat of the Kiwis the previous Saturday. The *Herald* noted that the tourists outweighed the Aucklanders by a stone (6.5kg) per man across the field.

When England scored all thirteen points registered in the first half it seemed likely to be a no-contest. But Auckland got on the board through an Alan Clarke penalty goal and a spectacular Ben Davidson try. From a scrum, Bert Cooke short punted, Claude List ran through and secured the ball, and Davidson finished it off. But England kept its points ticking over, staying out of range as Auckland fullback Norm Campbell kicked a field goal, Clarke added another penalty goal, and Cooke chipped through to score near the posts for Clarke to convert. But 19–14 was as close as the home side got.

The *Herald* conceded England was the better side, on the basis of its scoring five tries to two and overcoming a 27–9 disadvantage in penalties. Auckland hooker Gordon (Stump) Campbell earned himself selection for the last two tests when he raked the ball from twenty-nine of the sixty-three scrums against the bigger England pack. Second-rower Ray Lawless was another to catch the eyes of the national selectors, while the *Herald* praised the backline efforts of Cooke, in particular, Davidson, List and scrum-half Wilf Hassan.

Auckland team: fullback, Norm Campbell; three-quarters, Pat Meehan, Ben Davidson, Claude List; five-eighths, Bert Cooke, Hec Brisbane; halfback, Wilf Hassan; forwards, Stan Clark, Gordon Campbell, Lou Hutt, Alan Clarke, Ray Lawless, Trevor Hall. Reserves: backs, Allan Seagar, Len Scott; forward, Neville St George.

Bert Cooke wowed the fans

Bert Cooke had made his return to rugby league only two months before his outstanding performance for Auckland against England in 1932. At thirty-one, his illustrious career in rugby union had ended in controversial circumstances, and he was working in a Hastings dairy factory when astute Auckland businessman and future New Zealand Rugby League president Jack Redwood persuaded him to join his club, Richmond. It was a sensational capture, for Cooke was truly a rugby union icon.

Within a matter of weeks he was racing away for three tries in the inter-island match which doubled as a Kiwis trial. In addition to his try for Auckland against England, he also scored in the first and third test matches at Carlaw Park. There was clearly plenty of firepower left in the man who had already registered thirty-eight tries in forty-four appearances for the All Blacks from 1924 to 1930. The slightly built Cooke was blessed with rare vision at fullback or centre. He was fearless, fast and a gifted tactical kicker.

Bert Cooke, the famous All Black who donned a Richmond jersey in the 1932 Auckland rugby league competition.
Auckland City Libraries

CHAPTER FOUR

New Zealand did not play in 1933 or 1934, and Cooke had to be content with wowing the crowds in club and provincial football. When West Coast visited Carlaw Park in 1933, Cooke crossed for three of Auckland's six tries in a 28–22 victory and he helped make Richmond the dominant club of the mid-1930s. But Cooke had to wait until the Australians toured in 1935 to prove that, even at thirty-four, he was still not a spent force at the highest level. He captained New Zealand from fullback in the first test before a late tackle in the second test knocked him out of the series.

Northern migration

The depression years of the 1930s led to the loss of some fine players to Britain, where they could earn a living through their sporting prowess. In one mini-migration, wing Roy Hardgrave, loose forward Lou Hutt and second-rower Trevor Hall went to St Helens. All of them appeared in the second Challenge Cup final at Wembley Stadium, losing 10–3 to Widnes. Hardgrave (a son of 1912–14 Kiwi Arthur) went on to score 173 tries in 212 matches for the Saints. While the others stayed in England, Hutt returned home and played for Auckland and New Zealand against England in 1932 and Australia in 1935.

Six of the best

When Marist provided six players to the New Zealand team for the third test match of the 1932 series against England at Carlaw Park it was thought the club had set a record which would last for decades. What is more, there were seven Marist players featuring in the series and seven Marist men in the tour fixture against Auckland.

Yet only three years later Richmond supplied six of its players for both the first and third tests against the Australians and bettered Marist's series record by having nine players wear the Kiwis jersey that season. Richmond also had seven in the Auckland team against the Kangaroos.

Both clubs also provided test captains, Marist's Hec Brisbane in 1932 and Richmond's Bert Cooke for the first two 1935 tests before he missed the third through injury. The respective club records were:

Marist in 1932. New Zealand v England: first test (two players), Hec Brisbane (captain), Claude List; second test (four), Hec Brisbane (captain), Claude List, Wilf Hassan, Gordon Campbell; third test (six) Hec Brisbane (captain), Claude List, Norm Campbell, Gordon Campbell, Jim Laird, Alan Clarke.

Auckland v England (seven): Hec Brisbane (captain), Claude List, Wilf Hassan, Alan Clarke, Norm Campbell, Gordon Campbell, Pat Meehan.

Richmond in 1935. New Zealand v Australia: first test (six players), Bert Cooke (captain), Ted Mincham, Stan Prentice, Roy Powell, Cliff Satherley, Harold Tetley; second test (four), Bert Cooke (captain), Ted Mincham, Roy Powell, Cliff Satherley; third test (six), Stan Prentice, Cliff Satherley, Harold Tetley, Alf Mitchell, Eric Fletcher, Ray Lawless. Auckland v Australia (seven): Bert Cooke, Ted Mincham, Stan Prentice, Roy Powell, Bill (Snow) Telford, Cliff Satherley, Harold Tetley.

Auckland and Marist half Wilf Hassan tackles big forward Bill Horton but cannot prevent him passing to Billy Williams during the 1932 England game.
Auckland City Libraries

Two of Marist's seven representatives in action against England. On the ground losing the ball is Gordon Campbell and Alan Clarke is the nearest Auckland player on the left.
Auckland City Libraries

CHAPTER FOUR

The Dragon slayers

St George played four games at Carlaw Park in 1933 and one at New Plymouth, where it beat Taranaki 22–14. The Dragons overcame Devonport 19–8 and Newton 30–23 but were beaten by both Richmond (5–3) and Marist (25–11). Marist scored five tries to three but its task was made easier when St George lost halfback Hans Mork (a guest player from fellow Sydney club Newtown) and centre Norm Tipping through injuries, finishing with eleven men. Richmond and St George engaged in what one publication called 'the roughest game since Carlaw Park was opened,' after the visitors took exception to Richmond being awarded a penalty try for obstruction. Capitalising on the public interest, the Auckland Rugby League subsequently arranged a special match between the Dragon slayers, won 31–8 by Richmond after Marist had led 8–6 at halftime.

Marist and St George at Carlaw Park.
(1) Herb Carter (Marist) downs a St George player.
(2) Mick Ward and Tom Killiby (St George) wait for a Marist forward to play the ball.
(3) Len Schultz (Marist) evades the tackle of Jim Rutherford.
Auckland City Libraries

Len Schultz (Marist, at left) is too late to stop Bernie Martin, of St George, from scoring during the home team's 25–11 win.
Auckland City Libraries

Richmond's golden era

Richmond became the first club to win the Fox Memorial (championship), Roope Rooster (knockout) and Stormont Shield (champion of champions) treble in 1934. The Richmond Rovers retained the Fox and Stormont shields in 1935, won the Stormont Shield in 1936, regained the Fox Memorial in 1937 and captured the Roope Rooster and Stormont Shield in 1938. They were also unbeaten in four matches against visiting Australian club teams from 1934 to 1939.

Few would argue that Richmond was Australasia's top club in 1934. It beat Sydney champion Western Suburbs not once but twice (18–16 and 10–3) at Carlaw Park to ram that claim home. In the first game Richmond did the unthinkable by coming from 13–0 down to score eighteen unanswered points. A try by celebrated Kangaroos five-eighth Vic Hey from forty metres out got Wests back within two points, but Percy Williams, a guest player from South Sydney, missed the conversion to draw the game.

In 1938 Richmond edged out Sydney runner-up Eastern Suburbs 11–9, despite conceding a try from the opening kick-off. Consecutive tries to Jack Satherley, Watkins and Mills, plus a Bramley conversion, made it 11–3 at halftime. Easts attacked through its backs, was rewarded with corner tries to Rod O'Loan and Balmain guest Frank Hyde, but the Richmond defence otherwise held magnificently to the finish.

Newspapers reported that Richmond held the upper hand for most of its 1939 game against an Easts Combined team, racing to a 17–3 lead thanks to two tries by George Mitchell and one by Devine. Devine and Furnell kicked two goals each before the combined side produced a late scoring burst to get as close as 17–16.

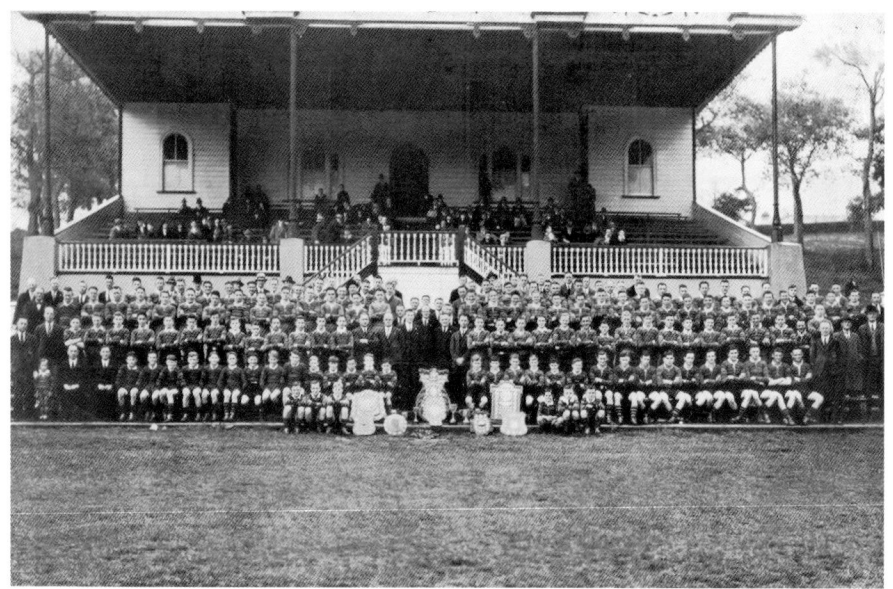

Richmond players and officials assembled for a special club photograph in front of the Auckland Domain pavilion in 1935, the year the club provided nine New Zealand representatives.
Auckland City Libraries

CHAPTER FOUR

It has already been recorded that Richmond provided nine players to the Kiwis for their 1935 three-match test series against Australia. Actually, the Richmond influence went much deeper than that, for no less than sixteen of the club's players wore the national jersey during the 1930s: Stan Prentice, Bert Cooke, Ray Lawless, Ted Mincham, Roy Powell, Cliff Satherley, Harold Tetley, Alf Mitchell, Eric Fletcher, Wally Tittleton, Noel Bickerton, Jack Satherley, Jack McLeod, Dave Solomon, Laurie Mills and George Mitchell.

Richmond beating Western Suburbs (Sydney) in 1934.

(1) Harold Tetley scores for Richmond.

(2) Western Suburbs fullback Jimmy Sharman eludes Clarrie McNeil.

(3) Cliff Satherley and Bill Telford in a forward dribbling rush.

(4) Western Suburbs forward Alan Blake pursued by Ted Mincham (left) and Cliff Satherley (far right).

Auckland City Libraries

The Second World War interrupted that incredible run. But it restarted immediately when international rugby league resumed in 1946, with Maurie Robertson, Ron McGregor, Clarence (Sandy) Hurndell, Abbie Graham, Allan Laird, Dave Redmond and Tommy Baxter becoming Kiwis before the end of that decade. As a team, Richmond resumed where it had left off by beating Sydney club champion Balmain 17–9 in 1946 in what was described as 'the best game seen in Auckland this season'.

The mastermind behind all that success was Thomas (Scotty) McClymont, an international inside back and captain for Ponsonby between 1919 and 1924. He first coached the Kiwis against England in 1928 and his appointment as Richmond selector and coach in 1931 preceded its rise to prominence via a 1933 Roope Rooster triumph. McClymont coached the Kiwis on their 1938 tour to Australia, the 1947–48 and 1951–52 tours to Britain and France, and in home tests against all of the major rugby league nations.

McClymont's influence extended for many years after his retirement. One of his pupils in Richmond teams of the 1930s, and an Auckland representative prop, was Bill (Snow) Telford, who coached the Kiwis for twenty-eight tests in three terms from 1955 to 1965. In 1979, Telford was persuaded by Ron McGregor, then New Zealand Rugby League president, to convene the national selection panel and assist the Kiwis regain their winning ways. What worked for the Rovers in the 1930s was still being applied to the Kiwis fifty years later.

Southern double

Auckland made its only South Island tour of the 1930s in September 1935, beating West Coast by 32–14 at Victoria Park in Greymouth and Canterbury by 26–13 at Christchurch's Monica Park. Although Auckland's forwards encountered rugged resistance on both sides of the Southern Alps, and wily Canterbury hooker Reg Ward monopolised scrum possession, the Auckland backs were too slick for their opponents. Veterans Bert Cooke and Lou Brown were the stars, with Brown's four-try haul at Greymouth the single highlight. He also touched down twice in Christchurch. Auckland used the tour to prepare for its showdown with Australia the next weekend.

1935: Rare Kangaroo sighting

The Kangaroos were a rare species on New Zealand rugby league grounds before the Second World War. Their 1935 tour was only the second, sixteen years after the first. Five of the six matches were played in Auckland, the other in Wellington. For the last time, both Auckland City and Auckland Province were included on an itinerary.

Maurie Robertson, Kiwis captain 1950–52.
E Gibson. The Kiwis 1947–1948

Thomas (Scotty) McClymont.
E Gibson. The Kiwis 1947–1948

CHAPTER FOUR

Those highly promising youngsters who visited Auckland with Eastern Suburbs in 1931 had grown up. Centre Dave Brown was his country's captain, Ernie Norman and Viv Thicknesse were partners in the halves, and prop Ray Stehr and second-rower Sid (Joe) Pearce had become integral members of the Australian pack. Brown arrived fresh from scoring a phenomenal thirty-eight tries – a record which still stands – in the Sydney club season.

Scenes from Australia's 16–8 victory over Auckland City in 1935.

(1) and (5) The opposing teams before kick-off at Carlaw Park.

(2) Vic Thicknesse tackled by Auckland's Roy Powell.

(3) Bert Cooke tackles Ross McKinnon as the ball flies free to Kangaroos captain Dave Brown.

(4) Australian managers Jack Chaseling and Harry Sunderland.

(6) Jim Gibbs, surrounded by Auckland's Harold Tetley (on ground), Arthur Kay and Bert Cooke, clears the ball to Frank Curran.

(7) Ivan Culpan, Auckland secretary.

(8) 'Owie' Carlaw, NZRL secretary.

Auckland City Libraries

Australia's 16–8 victory over Auckland City after leading 11–3 at halftime was rated by the *New Zealand Herald* as 'a brilliant exhibition of football' and 'a thrilling game' before 15,000 spectators. It told its readers that Auckland looked a beaten side at the break, yet in the second spell 'the local backs rose to the occasion splendidly and at one stage a win looked likely'. Only a late converted try enabled Australia to slip out of range again, and Auckland rued the four goal attempts which were missed from close range. Brown scored two of Australia's four tries and was prominent in the moves which led to the other two. He also kicked two goals.

Lou Brown, on the Auckland wing, replied creating Auckland's first-half try for centre Ted Mincham. After Mincham got within a metre of Australia's goal-line in the second half, prop Snow Telford snapped up the ball to score. Mincham completed Auckland's scoring with a penalty goal. Two dazzling touchline runs by Brown failed to produce tries only because of a forward pass and then a knock-on. Former Auckland and Kiwis back Maurice Wetherill was the referee.

New Zealand, with Lou Brown scoring three tries, won the first test 22–14 before the Kangaroos comfortably claimed the other two. The tour was completed by the Wednesday encounter with Auckland Province, which had enlisted the Tittleton brothers, George and Wally, from South Auckland. Only centre Arthur Kay and forwards Lou Hutt, Cliff Satherley and Harold Tetley had played for the city team in the tour opener and Dave Brown was missing from the Australian line-up.

Auckland Province started promisingly, loose forward Tetley capitalising on a fumble to score the first try and scrum-half Eric Fletcher kicking three goals for a 9–0 advantage. But the Kangaroos bounded away with the result by rattling on the next twenty-three points on their way to a 36–18 victory. Fletcher kicked three more goals, the last of them a conversion of his own try to give him a personal haul of fifteen points. The *Herald* credited fullback Claude Dempsey, Fletcher and forwards Tetley and Des Herring as being the best local players.

The 1935 Kangaroos completed their itinerary with a victory over Auckland Province. Left: Auckland stand-off Brian Riley breaks upfield with Harold Tetley (left) and Arthur Kay in support. Right: Tetley claims his try.
Auckland City Libraries

CHAPTER FOUR

The Auckland teams were:

Auckland City: fullback, Bert Cooke; three-quarters, Lou Brown, Ted Mincham, C Hall; five-eighths, Arthur Kay, Stan Prentice; halfback, Roy Powell; forwards, Lou Hutt, W Quirke, Bill Telford, Cliff Satherley, Jim Laird, Harold Tetley.

Auckland Province: fullback, Claude Dempsey; three-quarters, George Tittleton (South Auckland), Wally Tittleton (South Auckland), Arthur Kay, Alf Mitchell; halves, Brian Riley, Eric Fletcher; forwards, Lou Hutt, J Flanagan, Des Herring, Ray Lawless, Cliff Satherley, Harold Tetley.

The brothers Brimble

Among the personalities in 1930s Auckland rugby league were the three Brimble brothers, two playing for Newton and one for Manukau, who all went on to represent New Zealand. Edward appeared in one 1932 test against England and Walter and Wilfred toured Australia in 1938. They were inside backs and shared the second Christian name of Pierrepont.

Of dusky complexion, the Brimbles were also chosen for various Māori teams. But they were not Māori, and few knew their exotic backgrounds. They were the sons of Harold Pierrepont Brimble, an English railways electrician from Bristol who went with friends to South Africa at the age of seventeen in search of work.

While there Harold enlisted in the British army and was severely wounded in the Boer War. He was nursed back to health by a young Bantu woman, Jane (her English name) Depua Mahadna, whose uncle was head of her tribe. Romance blossomed, and when they were married Jane signed the certificate with an X. They were to have seven sons on a roundabout route to Auckland.

After living in Molteno, Cape Province, the family left apartheid South Africa for Sydney on 9 March 1912. Harold and Jane by then had five children, John (aged six), Cyril (four), Edward (two) and twins Walter and Lionel (four months).

Australia's 'whites only' settlement law caused them to move again, and they lived for two years in Honolulu, where Wilfred was born. In 1914 the Brimbles settled in Onehunga and welcomed their seventh son, Amyas. Tragically, both Harold and Amyas died during a Spanish influenza epidemic.

Two of the Brimble brothers – Wilfred and Edward in Newton club gear, and Wilfred in his 1938 Kiwis jersey.
Harold Brimble collection

The Brimbles were a multi-talented rugby family. In addition to Edward, Walter and Wilfred achieving international rugby league honours, John played rugby union for Manukau and Auckland and Cyril represented Canterbury. Five of the brothers served in the New Zealand Army during the Second World War.

1936: Another close call

England 22 Auckland 16

In 1936 Auckland further enhanced its reputation of providing British touring teams with an extra 'test' match. These Lions, having retained the Ashes in Australia, were unbeaten in their eight New Zealand matches. Only in the first test against the Kiwis (10–8) were they more seriously extended than in the 22–16 victory over Auckland which opened the tour.

'It was a hard and close game,' said the *Auckland Star*. 'England, with their "man mountain" type of forwards, overshadowed the Auckland six, while the English backs showed more pace and strategy than their opponents. In the open play alone could Auckland hope to match their opponents, and the home side opened up whenever they got a chance. The best constructive try of the day came Auckland's way as the outcome of brilliant interplay and backing up.'

The *Star* described the move thus: 'From midway, [Lou] Brown broke clear and sailed down the right wing, with [Arthur] Kay and [Wally] Tittleton trailing for position. The next pass was to Kay, and thence to Tittleton, and the latter whipped the ball to Brown, who came up on the inside. The Auckland wing raced across amid excitement and scored. [Steve] Wātene kicked a beautiful angle goal to make the score England 17 Auckland 16.'

But, with five minutes remaining, Auckland could not finish off the tourists. Instead, Salford halves Billy Watkins and Bert Jenkins conspired for Jenkins to

Auckland's representatives line up for the 1936 clash. Captain Lou Brown (right foreground) waits to toss with England captain Jim Brough.
Auckland City Libraries

CHAPTER FOUR

score the match-clinching try, which was converted by club-mate Gus Risman. Auckland's earlier try, which provided a temporary 7–0 lead, resulted from prop Bill Breed capitalising on loose forward Harold Tetley's alertness in swooping on a spilled ball. Wātene kicked three penalty goals to add to his two conversions.

'Outweighed forward, and faced with a back division that was fast and singularly elusive at times, Auckland put up a good showing against the English team, which showed themselves to be an attractive combination, with finesse and skill, with an exceptionally clever pair of halfbacks,' said the *Star*.

'Although overshadowed most of the way, Auckland played to form, with L Brown the most constructive back, and Kay and Stockley defending well in the five-eighths line. All the Auckland forwards were worthy of their places, with Gault, Wātene and Breed showing up all the way.' Lou Brown was then thirty-one – fourteen years on from his Auckland debut against New South Wales. He played in both test matches before resuming his professional career with French club Bordeaux.

Top, England fullback Jim Brough eludes the Auckland defence. Below, Auckland half Roy Powell kicks for position. Supporting Powell at left is Frank Pickrang.
Auckland City Libraries

Auckland team: fullback, Claude Dempsey; three-quarters, R. Bright, Wally Tittleton, Lou Brown (captain); five-eighths, W. Stockley, Arthur Kay; halfback, Roy Powell; forwards, Angus Gault, Jack Satherley, Bill Breed, Steve Wātene, Frank Pickrang, Harold Tetley.

Marvellous Manukau

Manukau's achievements in winning the 1936 Fox Memorial championship and Roope Rooster knockout were extraordinary, considering the team did not even exist at the end of the previous season. Had it not been for the high calibre of the Richmond team that beat Manukau in the Stormont Shield champion of champions play-off, the newcomer would have swept to an incredible treble triumph at its first attempt.

The catalyst behind the formation of the mostly Māori Manukau squad was Steve Wātene, an inspiring Kiwis utility who that season also became the first of his race to captain New Zealand. Wātene not only had to build a team from scratch, he needed to convince Auckland Rugby League officials that his untested combination would be competitive in the top grade. The Manukau story is told in Bill Davidson's *1947 New Zealand Rugby League Annual*.

'One of the most attractive and popular teams to entertain the crowds at Carlaw Park was undoubtedly Manukau, which was formed at a meeting in October 1935 in the Foresters' Hall, Onehunga. The late [Auckland Rugby League chairman] Mr Grey Campbell attended, and after a lengthy discussion agreed to admit Manukau into the Auckland Rugby League competition in the 1936 season,' wrote Davidson.

Steve Wātene (left, in headgear), the inspiration behind Manukau's amazing 1936 season, playing for Auckland against England.
Auckland City Libraries

CHAPTER FOUR

'Mr Steve Wātene and the late Mr "Shorty" Cowan did the spade work in the organisation. Steve Wātene did a lot of travelling around the country in the summer months of 1935–36. He gave me some interesting references from a notebook setting out the history of the team, which was intended to be composed mainly of Maoris.

'Strong opposition came from some of the Auckland senior clubs to the administration of Manukau. In spite of the opposition, Wātene convinced the chairman, Mr Campbell, that the personnel of the team was good enough to win the championship honours for the first season.

'Wātene told the League management that he had travelled all over the North Island, and visited Maori settlements in Hawkes Bay, Wairarapa, Otaki, Palmerston North – and to see that the players already secured did not get "cold feet." He had long talks with the tribal elders and, sympathetic though they were to the idea, they asked Steve not to take players from any of the existing Maori rugby teams, particularly in the Hawkes Bay district.

'He then confined his activities to the Wairarapa district, and his main captures were Jack Hemi and Joe Broughton. On his way back to Auckland, Wātene visited the King Country and gathered in Len Kawe, a New Zealand Maori representative of 1925, and also Frank Pickrang.

'The same week Mr Cowan received word that Tom Trevarthan, of Otago rugby fame, was on his way to join up with Manukau. Angus Gault, a very fast and rugged forward, intimated his wish to play and he came from Waitomo. From North Auckland came A Hollis, a smart five-eighth, and W Davis, from Kaikohe. J Brodrick, also a New Zealand Maori rep., and Peter Mahima came to "town" and the stage was set for Manukau.' Later recruits included Rangi and Tom Chase from Taihape.

Early action in the 1936 club season.

(1) The Devonport team which beat Mount Albert 10–5.

(2) Alan Clarke (Marist) over-runs the ball, which is gathered in by Edward Brimble (Newton) in Marist's 11–0 win.

(3) The newly promoted Manukau team which shocked champion Richmond 14–8.

(4) Claude List runs onto a pass from Mount Albert team-mate J Schultz.

(5) Philp, the Manukau half, smothers his Richmond rival as Steve Wātene breaks from the scrum.

Auckland City Libraries

It was not long before many of Wātene's recruits were also wearing the Kiwis jersey, Hemi, Trevarthan and Pickrang in 1936, Gault, Brodrick and Rangi Chase in 1937, Hemi, Rangi Chase, Gault and Brodrick on tour to Australia in 1938, and Tom Chase on the aborted 1939 tour of Britain.

A by-product of Wātene's recruitment was his captaining the New Zealand Māori to their historic 16–5 victory over the 1937 Kangaroos at Carlaw Park. By then famous All Blacks fullback George Nepia was home from playing professionally in England. Other Manukau men to share in that triumph were Broughton, Hemi, the Chase brothers, Mahima and Brodrick.

All rounder

Surely only one man has played sport at Carlaw Park and Eden Park on the same day. In April 1937 the *Auckland Rugby League Gazette* noted the enthusiasm of Verdun Scott, a young North Shore three-quarter, who dashed off after his game at Carlaw Park to knock up twenty-two runs in the final cricket match of the season at Eden Park. Scott was to achieve the highest honours in both sports. He travelled to Britain with the 1939 Kiwis as a fullback and centre, only for the tour to be cancelled after two games because of the Second World War. Ten years later Scott went back to England with the New Zealand cricket team, establishing an outstanding opening partnership with fellow Aucklander Bert Sutcliffe. He is the only New Zealand double international at cricket and rugby league.

New Zealand Herald

Verdun Scott in his dual international sporting roles of rugby league and cricket, wearing his 1939 Kiwis jersey and opening the batting for New Zealand with Bert Sutcliffe (left) at Headingley, Leeds, in 1949.

Don Neely collection

CHAPTER FOUR

Anderson's day

Marist captain and loose forward John Anderson dominated the Stormont Shield finale to the 1937 season between his Roope Rooster winning club and Fox Memorial champion Richmond. Although Richmond was missing the Tittleton brothers, George and Wally, it still fielded a powerful combination in quest of a fourth consecutive shield tenure. But Anderson took control, through a penalty goal, a first-half try which he converted himself, a blockbusting second try through the midst of the Richmond defence and, in the last minute, a smartly snapped field goal. The scoreboard should have read Anderson 12, Richmond 5. Anderson had joined Marist from West Coast club Blackball after injury cost him New Zealand test selection in 1935. With his Stormont Shield performance still vivid in many minds, it was no surprise when he toured Australia with the 1938 Kiwis. Nor, perhaps, when he returned home as the leading try-scorer.

John Anderson (sixth from left) in the Auckland team which met Wellington on King's Birthday 1936. H G Tetley (captain), L S G Hutt, A Quirke, E Simpson, E Morgan, Anderson, C Hall, W J Tittleton, C Dempsey, A G Kay, B Riley, E T Mincham, R H S Powell and A E Cooke (coach).
Auckland City Libraries

Hired gun

Queenslander Brent Webb, the Warriors fullback, was not the first expatriate Australian to be selected for the Kiwis when he played at the 2004 Tri-Nations tournament in Britain. There had been a notable precedent just before the Second World War. South Sydney stand-off half Bob Banham crossed the Tasman as a player-coach in 1938 and was called up by the New Zealand selectors after his second season.

Banham, aged twenty-five, was brought to Auckland by the Mount Albert club. The Auckland and New Zealand leagues, both conscious of a lack of depth in the pivot position, gave the club some assistance. While Banham spent time at other clubs – such as when he travelled to Christchurch with Newton – he rewarded Mount Albert for its enterprise and confidence by guiding it to Fox Memorial and Stormont Shield successes in 1939.

Late in the 1939 season Banham, who had represented Auckland, was appointed vice-captain of the New Zealand team for the tour to Britain. The other stand-off was Dave Solomon, a Fijian-born former All Black who had changed codes earlier in the year and clinched his selection with two tries for North Island. Unfortunately for both, the tour was cancelled after two games because of war.

In September 1940, just before the Roope Rooster semi-finals, Banham returned to Sydney with the intention of joining the Australian forces. He played a few more games for Souths in 1941, but the war effectively ended a highly promising career.

Club v Province

It was not unusual for Auckland clubs to play representative teams when they made trips to some provinces, but Newton took that trend a step further by meeting Canterbury XIIIs at home and away in 1938. Newton took its senior side to Christchurch in July, with Mount Albert's Australian player-coach Bob Banham standing in for unavailable former Kiwis stand-off half Edward Brimble, and drew 16–16 with a Canterbury XIII at Monica Park. A highlight was the tussle between Newton's current Kiwis scrum-half Wilfred Brimble and Canterbury's Len Brown, who went to Britain with the 1939 Kiwis. The top Canterbury team was in Greymouth that weekend, where it unsuccessfully challenged West Coast for the Northern Union Cup.

When Canterbury travelled to Auckland three weeks later most of its leading players stayed over for a Wednesday game against Newton. This time Newton, with Banham contributing three tries, won 22–12. Auckland had to settle for a smaller winning margin over Canterbury, with Rangi Chase's three tries and five Jack Hemi goals featuring in a 28–22 victory.

CHAPTER FOUR

Archie Ferguson, pioneer referee and later chairman of the Auckland Rugby League Referees Association.
NZRL Museum

Honours board

Fourteen stalwarts of the game were recognised when an honours board, presented by R H Wood in memory of Mrs Edith Wood, was unveiled at the 1939 Auckland annual meeting. The list comprised J Carlaw, D W McLean, E K Asher, R Benson, A Campny, J Clark, I Culpan, A Ferguson, M J Hooper, M Liversidge, B Longbottom, W Mincham, C Raynes and F Thompson. 'The board bears the names of those who have served the League continuously for the past twenty-five years, or whose services have been of outstanding value to the code,' said the *Auckland Rugby League Gazette*. 'Followers who have been with League since, say, 1913, appreciate just what a dour, self-sacrificing struggle the sponsors of League waged, and all will applaud the action of the Board of Control in thus recording for all time the gentlemen who rendered such sterling stewardship.' (Chapter 12 includes a list of the names on the honours board in February 2009.)

Kiwis captains

Between 1919 and 1938 fifteen Auckland representatives captained every Kiwis test and touring team, from Karl Ifwersen (1919) to Stan Walters (1920), Henry Tancred (1921), Scotty McClymont and Frank Delgrosso (1924), Bert Laing (1925), Bert Avery (1926–27), Maurice Wetherill (1928), Charles Gregory (1930), Hec Brisbane (1932), Bert Cooke and Lou Brown (1935), Steve Wātene (1936–37), Harold Tetley (1937) and Bill McNeight (1938) – a sequence never to be repeated by Auckland or approached by any other district. Not all were home-bred. Tancred was a transplanted Australian and McNeight had been a 1936 Kiwi from the West Coast before joining Auckland club Newton.

War looms

Auckland's dominance of New Zealand rugby league had been obvious when eighteen of the twenty-two Kiwis who toured Australia in 1938, plus both managers and coach Scotty McClymont, hailed from the Queen City. That was a reflection of the strength of Auckland's club competition and mirrored several one-sided inter-island games. Auckland Rugby League president John A Lee MP touched on that subject in his address to the 1939 annual meeting.

'The past season was truly one of the most remarkable on record, and this will be true again this year. In quality of play, quantity of players and public esteem, the code continues its steady advance,' said Lee. Referring to the domestic scene, he said 'the high standard of club football is reflected in the calibre of representatives; hence my urge to build the code through the clubs'. With junior standards ever improving, more and more senior players were coming from rugby league nurseries rather than as recruits from rugby union.

Lee also reminded delegates that the Auckland Rugby League had been mindful of the financial problems faced by many of its supporters. 'When we consider the fact that one shilling remains the utmost charge for the average patron, one appreciates the fact that football is the one commodity which has remained low in price. Though the quality of play has improved, the tariff is unchanged.'

Thirteen years after the previous touring team had been torn apart by internal strife, the Rugby Football League had at last invited the Kiwis to return to Britain. Seventeen of the twenty-six selected players were from Auckland clubs. Hopes were high that an exhaustive series of trials and some resourceful recruiting had produced a team capable of beating the British semi-professionals.

Much of the money required to finance the tour had been raised through public subscription, which was to be repaid from the anticipated profits. It is history now that war was declared soon after the Kiwis arrived in England. They met and beat St Helens and Dewsbury before freely giving of their labour to assist the war effort while they waited for their homeward passage. Only one of the players, Arthur McInnarney, returned to Britain with the 1947–48 Kiwis. Another of the Auckland outside backs, Laurie Mills, was killed in action during the Egyptian campaign in 1941.

Former All Black Dave Solomon tackling Middleton (Ponsonby) while playing for Richmond in 1939. Rushing to Middleton's aid is Ponsonby's Frank Bell, a recent arrival from Sydney. Solomon was selected for the ill-fated Kiwis tour of Britain.

Fairfax Media

CHAPTER FOUR

Action in the September 1935 provincial clash between Wellington and Auckland, played at Newtown Park, Wellington. The Wellington forwards are jubilant as referee Vic Simpson awards a try.
Auckland City Libraries

A Wellington forward endeavours to pick up the ball with Auckland forwards Keane (left) and Herring awaiting developments. Auckland won 39–27.
Auckland City Libraries

CHAPTER 05

RETURN TO PROSPERITY
1940–1949

CHAPTER FIVE

Return to Prosperity 1940–1949

The war years

Rugby league in Auckland was just entering its fourth decade when, for the second time, New Zealand was drawn into a world war. Britain's declaration of war on Germany coincided with the start of what was to have been the third New Zealand tour of Britain and the first visit to France. The Kiwis, each issued with his own gas mask, filled sandbags at a hospital near their Harrogate hotel while they waited for a naval gun to be installed on the *Rangitiki*, the ship which carried them around the world for just two games.

It was inevitable that the game would struggle again, both financially and for man power, at a time when it was still recovering from the gigantic setback that had been the 1926–27 'strike' tour of Britain and the depression years. Once again,

NZRL Museum

Auckland was best placed of all the provinces to ride out the storm. But this time it had a serious on-field rival: most of the finest West Coast players were coalminers in townships such as Blackball and Runanga, and were therefore exempt from war service because of their occupations.

In 1942, amalgamations were introduced to the Auckland senior club competition. It was decreed that Manukau, Ponsonby and Richmond would stand alone, but there would be amalgamations between Marist and North Shore, Mount Albert and Newton, and City and the newly promoted Otahuhu. North Shore, the 1941 champion, was a reluctant marriage participant, and Marist soldiered on alone for several weeks before they were eventually united. Manukau won that championship and then made a clean sweep of the four major trophies when all nine clubs became separate entities again in 1943. City was the dominant side in 1944 and Otahuhu won the Fox Memorial for the first time in 1945.

Otahuhu Rovers stalwart Morrie Ritchie recalled the war years in the club's seventy-fifth anniversary booklet in 1986. 'We never knew from day to day who would be available to play. Players in camp getting leave to play on Saturday – then, with a troop departure, perhaps half the team gone in a week. Many anxious times at Carlaw Park waiting for a full team to assemble. Sometimes some of the players were [absent without leave] with the [military police] breathing down their necks. On one occasion the MPs hustled one of our best players back to camp, complete with football gear at the conclusion of a game, after heeding a plea by yours truly at halftime to let him finish the game.' It was a situation replicated at football grounds across the city every weekend.

When normality returned, rugby league in New Zealand not so much recovered quickly, as soared to unprecedented heights. The Kiwis beat Great Britain in a one-off test at Carlaw Park, that Lions team earning the nickname The Indomitables after the aircraft carrier which transported them as far as Fremantle. New Zealand then made a highly profitable tour of Great Britain and France, getting within one point of the British in their test series and sharing the two tests with the French. Two drawn series followed against Australia, on tour in 1948 and at home in 1949. Those remarkable results achieved by New Zealand amateurs against overseas professionals were largely gained by combining slick Auckland backs with unyielding South Island forwards. War-weary fans flocked to watch their new heroes in all four major rugby league nations.

CHAPTER FIVE

All Blacks in league

The significance of Marist's 22–17 victory over Ponsonby on 16 April 1941 did not become apparent until after the Second World War when nineteen-year-old Marist forward Johnny Simpson and twenty-year-old Ponsonby fullback Bob Scott went on to become renowned All Blacks.

Army service was responsible for them switching to rugby union, where they initially gained fame as team-mates on the 1945–46 New Zealand Army team's tour of Britain, France and New Zealand. When they were demobbed they joined up with the Ponsonby Rugby Union Club.

Simpson went on to play nine test matches for the All Blacks until a serious knee injury ended his career at the age of twenty-eight in 1950. Scott's career continued through to 1954 and included seventeen tests in an illustrious and prolific scoring career.

In later life Scott demonstrated his kicking prowess by landing goals from halfway in bare feet. Yet in that 1941 rugby league encounter with Simpson, it was Arthur Kay, and not Scott, who was Ponsonby's preferred goalkicker on the day.

Jack Hemi, Manukau's ace goalkicker.
J Coffey & B Wood, 100 Years Māori Rugby League

Size does matter

Manukau's heavyweight forward pack paved the way for it to be New Zealand's top club team after beating West Coast champion Blackball 23–9 at Carlaw Park in October 1943. The Manukau trophy cabinet was already bulging with the Fox Memorial Shield, Rukutai Shield, Roope Rooster and Stormont Shield, while Blackball had beaten the best clubs in Canterbury and Wellington.

The *Auckland Star* reported Manukau had fielded such formidable characters as Pita Ririnui (111kg), Steve Wātene (105kg) and Aubrey Thompson (97kg). 'In the set scrums [Manukau] was able to get possession by the simple expedient of walking over the ball.' They were very big men for that era, and even the hooker Te Tai tipped the scales at 90kg. It mattered not that Blackball had two future Kiwis forwards in lightweight hooker Bob Aynsley and hard-tackling loose forward Ken Mountford.

There were actually three Mountfords in the Blackball line-up. Centre Bill Mountford also represented New Zealand. But the man who attracted most attention that day was Cecil Mountford, who was to take his enormous talent to Wigan, where he was rated the best stand-off half in what was then rugby league's most professional competition. The *Star* praised their individual efforts against Manukau but nothing could halt the juggernaut.

'All the best features of League football were shown at Carlaw Park when, after a fast, bright and open game, Manukau, the Auckland champion, beat Blackball, the South Island champion club team from the West Coast. The visitors gave the most brilliant exhibition of handling seen in Auckland for many years. They were a young, fast and light team but were up against a much heavier team which on occasions developed combination of a high order.

'The Blackball players tried to keep possession, but scarcely more than twice in the game did they get the ball from a set scrum. In the second half of the game Manukau got three converted tries in quick succession. [Jack] Hemi scored a try and kicked four goals, one a field goal. There was a record attendance for the season, one of the spectators being the Minister of Mines, Mr Webb.'

Murray (two), Butler, Taumata and Hemi scored tries for Manukau. Cecil Mountford was Blackball's sole try-scorer and future Kiwis fullback Ray Nuttall kicked three goals. Manukau led 5–4 at halftime before Mountford's try gave Blackball a 9–5 advantage. That lasted twelve minutes before Manukau's monopoly of the scrums took its toll. The crashing runs of Ririnui and Wātene had the Blackball defence back-peddling and the Manukau backs grabbed their try-scoring chances.

CHAPTER FIVE

Family pack

When Otahuhu Rovers won their first Auckland major championship in 1945 the team included four Johnson brothers, Ivan, Joffre, Mick and Norm, in the forwards, and Jack and Royce Speedy in the halves. The captain was Jim Fogarty. Fogarty was later joined by his brother Dick. It was not unusual for the entire pack to be composed of the four Johnsons and two Fogartys, with the Speedy siblings as the halves.

Joffre Johnson and rugby union recruit Claud Hancox became Otahuhu's first Kiwis when chosen for the 1947–48 tour of Britain and France.

Otahuhu, with the four Johnson brothers, won its first Auckland championship in 1945.
Back row: D Hardy, R Keat, C Wellm, R Ritchie (secretary), N Sanderson, D Smith, C Riley.
Third row: J Parry (treasurer), R Halsey, M Johnson, J Johnson, N Johnson, I Johnson, R Seymour, E McManus (masseur).
Second row: S Johnson (manager), E Pattillo, J Fogarty (captain), C Hall (coach), H Brady (vice-captain), K Simons, W Rodger (club captain).
Front row: R Martin, R Speedy, J Speedy.
Otahuhu 75th Jubilee Year booklet

Auckland unbeaten in 1945

Auckland was unbeaten when provincial football returned to the rugby league calendar in 1945, but it was a close call. The blue and whites thrashed South Auckland (46–7) and Wellington (also 46–7) at Carlaw Park and won return matches in Wellington by 47–17 and in Huntly 26–13. But their sole encounter with West Coast was a thriller, a very late penalty goal by fullback Warwick Clarke getting Auckland home, 8–7, at Carlaw Park.

The Coasters had the better of the first half, leading 7–0 from penalty goals by Jock McNaughtan and Cecil Mountford and a try to Bill Mountford just before the interval. But Auckland struck back when Roy Clark's break led to a try for wing Brian Nordgren soon after the resumption, and Roy Nurse, who had replaced Bernie Lowther on the other wing, cut the deficit to one point with his try into the final quarter.

Nurse's appearance caught the visitors by surprise. Auckland local rules permitted halftime substitutions but that was apparently not the case on the West Coast. There was no dispute, however, that replacements were not allowed in the second spell, and when both Nordgren and rival wing Jack Forrest were injured in the same tackle, the teams were each reduced to twelve players. West Coast was briefly down to eleven men when second-rower Charlie McBride 'dropped like a log' after running into the massive Pita Ririnui.

Auckland was dominating territory by that stage, and two minutes from fulltime Clarke goaled the penalty which put the home side ahead. In the closing seconds Auckland loose forward Travers Hardwick, who had switched to wing to fill the gap left by Nordgren, was pushed into the corner flag after taking a crosskick and making a bold bid for the try-line.

Warwick Clarke.
NZRL Year Book 1962

CHAPTER FIVE

North Shore Albions, winner of the Roope Rooster and Stormont Shield in 1945.
Back row: J Le Scelle (selector), H Hunt, A Read, C Petersen, B Graham, I Stirling, W James (masseur).
Third row: A Young (steward), H Thomas, V Scott, T Field, H Mackintosh, R Smith (coach).
Second row: M Coghlan (secretary), C E Smith, R Clark (captain), A Ferguson (president), J Rutherford (vice-captain), A Taylor, H Mann (chairman).
Front row: E Chatham, J Russell-Green, S Gow.
Absent: L Pye.
NZRL Museum

One that got away: Brian Nordgren

Wigan has never been slow in signing players from down under and the Lancashire club cleverly signed Ponsonby and Auckland wing Brian Nordgren, along with West Coast stand-off half Cecil Mountford, in December 1945. When the New Zealand Rugby League protested, Wigan pointed out the international transfer ban imposed in 1937 had lapsed in December 1941. Because of the Second World War no-one else had noticed. Both players proved to be outstanding buys.

Nordgren had amassed a national record 267 points for Ponsonby in 1945. He was in Wigan teams which won a string of Championship, Lancashire League and Lancashire Cup titles but experienced mixed emotions in his two Challenge Cup finals at Wembley Stadium. In 1946 Nordgren scored two tries but missed all seven goal kicks as Wigan lost 13–12 to Wakefield Trinity. Five years later he shared in the 10–0 defeat of Barrow, when Mountford won the Lance Todd Trophy. In all, Nordgren scored 312 tries, plus 109 goals for 1,154 points, in 294 appearances for Wigan and represented Other Nationalities against France.

He was also a remarkable man in his private life. Born in Greymouth in 1926, Nordgren spent most of his first ten years in a Christchurch orphanage and in 1940 joined the army by claiming he was 'almost eighteen'. In 1944 he was awaiting shipment to Europe when family members revealed he was only seventeen and not twenty-one. Despite having no formal secondary education, Nordgren studied at Liverpool University and qualified as a lawyer in 1951. He returned to New Zealand in 1955, coached his old Ponsonby club, and practised law in Auckland and Hamilton.

Brian Nordgren scoring a try at Carlaw Park before the Wigan scouts pounced.
Fairfax Media

CHAPTER FIVE

1946: Lessons from abroad

'Indomitables' win twice in Auckland

The presence of eleven Welshmen in the 1946 England touring team undoubtedly had much to do with their name change to Great Britain for future visits. Led by legendary centre Gus Risman, the Lions beat Australia in two tests and drew the other, but lost to West Coast and New Zealand in the only test. They out-scored Auckland twice, by 9–7 and 22–9, the latter match being Risman's farewell to international football after fourteen years.

Even what the *New Zealand Herald* described as 'the worst possible conditions' did not deter more than 15,000 spectators attending Carlaw Park for the first Auckland game. It was played 'in heavy driving showers of rain on a ground which was almost a sea of mud'. The *Herald* praised the standard achieved by the sodden, mud-caked participants, though the conditions ensured the 'many bright flashes of play (were) confined generally to individual efforts'.

After Auckland fullback Warwick Clarke goaled from a penalty, all three England tries resulted from the visitors' superb kicking skills. The 19st (121kg) prop Frank Whitcombe dribbled through for wing Arthur Bassett's try, forwards Owens and

The Auckland forward pack which opposed England in 1946. Front row: Bruce Graham, John Rutherford, Joffre Johnson. Second row: Les Pye, Des Ryan. At back: Travers Hardwick.
Fairfax Media

Conditions deteriorated markedly when Auckland met England at Carlaw Park in 1946.

(1) In the early stages a still spotless Ernest Ward (England) and Roy Nurse (Auckland) led the chase after the ball.

(2) Midway through the second half the ball eluded the very muddied Travers Hardwick (Auckland, left) and Tommy McCue (England).
Auckland City Libraries

Nicholson both had the ball at toe before the latter scored, and Bassett was across again after kicking ahead. Just when it seemed the game was over, Auckland half Rex Cunningham followed through to claim a try which Clarke converted. But the British confidently defended their 9–7 lead.

It was not only the touring backs who were restricted by the conditions. Outstanding attackers such as stand-off Roy Clark and centres Maurie Robertson and Ron McGregor had to be content with tackling for most of the game. 'There was no better forward on the field than [Travers] Hardwick, the Auckland breakaway,' said the *Herald*. 'Others conspicuous in Auckland's front line were Graham, Johnson, Pye and Rutherford.'

Auckland team: fullback, Warwick Clarke; three-quarters, Arthur Read, Ron McGregor, Roy Nurse; five-eighths, Maurie Robertson, Roy Clark (captain); halfback, Rex Cunningham; forwards, Joffre Johnson, John Rutherford, Bruce Graham, Les Pye, Des Ryan, Travers Hardwick.

Carlaw Park was still soft but there was no rain when England and Auckland clashed sixteen days later. The 12,000 fans who found their way to the Monday afternoon match were delighted by the clever play of the British backs after three Clarke goals provided the home team with a 6–2 halftime advantage. The Lions ran in four second-half tries against a solitary reply by Nurse after Graham had broken through and set the backline alight.

'In the second spell England's backs revealed brilliant offensive movements,' reported the Press Association. 'Passing bouts were started from any position, and they outplayed Auckland with superior speed and better positional play.' Loose forward Ike Owens and scrum-half Tommy McCue were the masterminds behind Britain's victory, fullback Ernest Ward kicked four goals from wide out and negated Auckland's more promising attacks, while veteran Risman bowed out in style.

The *Auckland Star* singled out former North Sydney wing Frank Collins, the defensively secure Robertson, nippy half Cunningham and tidy all-rounder Clarke as Auckland's best backs. Collins, who had joined Ponsonby from Norths, twice bumped off Risman with powerful runs. Graham and Hardwick 'did grand work in the Auckland pack, all members of which worked hard from start to finish,' said the *Star*. However, England won the ball in eighteen of the twenty-two scrums after halftime and the backs put it to good use.

Auckland team: fullback, Warwick Clarke; three-quarters, Roy Nurse, Trevor Bramley, Frank Collins; five-eighths, Maurie Robertson, Roy Clark (captain); halfback, Rex Cunningham; forwards, Joffre Johnson, John Rutherford, Bruce Graham, Les Pye, Des Ryan, Travers Hardwick.

CHAPTER FIVE

Wharfies walk-off

Under headlines such as 'Watersiders Prefer Football To Work', newspaper readers around the country read the following Press Association report (dateline Auckland, 12 August 1946): 'About 130 waterside workers discharging southern produce from the *Waiana* left the ship at three o'clock this afternoon to attend the Rugby League match between England and Auckland at Carlaw Park. The vessel was left idle until six o'clock, when the men returned to work the evening shift. A request was made by the Auckland Waterside Workers' Union for leave for all its members to see the game, but permission was refused by the Waterfront Control Commission. Only the men on the *Waiana* left their work, a separate request from them also having been declined.'

Bruce Graham.
J Coffey & B Wood, The Kiwis: 100 Years of International Rugby League

New heroes

Auckland prop Bruce Graham wore the Kiwis jersey only once. But he was New Zealand's first post-war rugby league hero after scoring the winning try in the 13–8 test victory over the British at Carlaw Park. The scores were level at 8–8 when fullback Warwick Clarke's attempt to kick a fifth penalty goal struck an upright. The ball rebounded into the arms of Graham, who was unstoppable as he hurled himself across to score between the posts. Clarke's conversion completed the scoring. The Kiwis were captained by stand-off half Roy Clark and included fellow Aucklanders in Clarke, wing Roy Nurse, centres Len Jordan and Maurie Robertson, scrum-half Rex Cunningham and loose forward Travers Hardwick. Ron McGregor was the reserve back.

Grief in Greymouth

Auckland experienced contrasting results in 1946 when it ventured to the South Island for the first time in eleven years. A strong Auckland squad lost to West Coast at Greymouth 10–7 but out-played Canterbury 51–28 in Christchurch two days later.

Although West Coast held the Northern Union Cup, it was not at stake because Auckland had not lodged a challenge. The match programme suggested that it might have been a wise move. It described the cup as 'a liability to the West Coast as with no challenges it is of no interest and the Coast League has only to bear the insurance cost from year to year'. The writer hoped the New Zealand Rugby League would inject new life into the trophy.

The Auckland team consisted of: backs, Warwick Clarke, Arthur Read, Trevor Bramley, Roy Nurse, Maurie Robertson, Ron McGregor, Roy Clark (captain), Abbie Graham, Rex Cunningham; forwards, Jim Fogarty, Des Ryan, Joffre Johnson, Don Hardy, Fred James, Les Pye, Clarrie Petersen, Travers Hardwick. Original selections Len Jordan and John Rutherford withdrew and were replaced by Bramley and Hardy.

The Press reporter in Greymouth wrote that the rain that fell throughout negated some of the effectiveness of the Auckland backs, allowing the West Coast forwards to win the day. The home pack included John Newton, Bob Aynsley, Charlie McBride, Arthur Gillman and Ken Mountford, all destined to be Kiwis. Hardwick scored Auckland's try, and Clarke kicked two goals. Nurse, McGregor and Cunningham were rated the best Auckland backs and Petersen the outstanding forward.

It was a different story at the Addington Show Grounds as Auckland sprinted away to a 36–16 halftime advantage. Clarke finished with nine goals and Graham (two), Fogarty (two), Clark (two), Cunningham (two), Read, Pye and Hardwick scored tries. *The Press* reported on Auckland's 'consistent backing up by forwards and backs in brilliant bouts of passing'. Clarke's tactical kicking was a revelation, and when he chose to run he ignited many attacks by the three-quarters.

Auckland's 1946 team which toured West Coast and Canterbury.

Back row: Fred James, Les Pye, Clarrie Petersen, Travers Hardwick, Des Ryan, Joffre Johnson.

Middle row: Warwick Clarke, Arthur Read, Jim Fogarty, Roy Nurse, Maurie Robertson, Abbie Graham, Rex Cunningham.

Front row: Don Hardy, Trevor Bramley, Ted Knowling (manager), Roy Clark (captain), Ivan Stonex (manager), Ron McGregor, Dave Wilkie (board member)

NZRL Museum

CHAPTER FIVE

Tigers toppled

Balmain crossed the Tasman to take on Auckland's best club teams after winning the 1946 and 1947 Sydney premierships. Richmond enhanced its already outstanding record against Australian clubs when it beat the Balmain Tigers 17–9 in the 1946 clash of the championship winners. Coach Scotty McClymont was credited by the *Auckland Star* with producing a superbly fit Richmond side which lifted its teamwork on defence and attack to levels even higher than those attained during the domestic season. However, Balmain edged out Mount Albert 16–11 in the 1947 'Australasian' showdown. Star of the match was nineteen-year-old wing Bobby Lulham, who scored three of Balmain's four tries. Mount Albert's try-scorers included Roy Nurse and Ray Cranch. The 1947 Tigers did not have it all their own way, losing to Otahuhu and Marist before winning a return game with Otahuhu and then being beaten next day by Waikato Māori at Huntly.

Clarence (Sandy) Hurndell.
E Gibson,
The Kiwis 1947–1948

1947–48 Kiwis: Best of both worlds

New Zealand selectors Ernie Asher, Scotty McClymont (both from Auckland) and Jim Amos (Canterbury) largely adopted a formula of blending Auckland backs with West Coast forwards in selecting the 1947–48 Kiwis team to tour Britain and France. Ten of the fourteen backs were chosen from Auckland clubs, alongside two each from Canterbury and West Coast. Of the twelve forwards, six were from Auckland and five from West Coast. The only 'outsider' in the pack was front-rower and captain Pat Smith from Canterbury. McClymont was coach, and the managers were Jack Redwood (Auckland) and Lance Hunter (West Coast).

It was a truly great tour, erasing any lingering nightmares of the disastrous tour of 1926–27 and the disappointment of the abandoned 1939 tour. The Kiwis drew massive crowds in Britain, where the population was still living on war rations and had been equally starved of top-level sport. They were unfortunate not to win the test series. The outcome eventually rested on Britain's 11–10 victory in the opening match at Headingley. The Kiwis struck back to win at Swinton, but the home team won the decider at Bradford. The two-test series in France was shared one-all.

Only fifteen of the Aucklanders actually reached London's Tilbury Docks, however. Richmond second-rower Clarence Hurndell took ill at Panama and could not continue on the voyage. Happily, he recovered his fitness and form to tour Australia with the 1948 Kiwis and play home tests against the Kangaroos and Lions in the next two years.

Richmond also provided three of the backs: vice-captain and stand-off half Abbie Graham, whose tour was to be blighted by injury, and centres Ron McGregor and Maurie Robertson. All three had advanced through the Richmond junior ranks and seemed poised for long and illustrious international careers. But the gifted Graham was restricted to three tests in 1948 and 1949, and McGregor was injured in the 1948 tour trials before turning his energies towards administration. Robertson was to fulfil all of his promise, captaining the 1951–52 Kiwis in Britain and France.

The other backs and their senior clubs were: fullback, Warwick Clarke (City); three-quarters, Arthur McInnarney (Mount Albert), Doug Anderson (Point Chevalier) and Len Jordan (Ponsonby); and halves, Roy Clark (North Shore), Des Barchard (Marist) and Rex Cunningham (City). Their pen-pictures credited Ellerslie with fostering Clarke and McInnarney in their junior days, Northcote as Jordan's junior club, and Mount Albert as Cunningham's previous club.

Auckland's Kiwis forwards were hooker George Davidson (Marist), Les Pye (North Shore), Joffre Johnson (Otahuhu), Claud Hancox (Otahuhu), Travers Hardwick (Ponsonby) and the unfortunate Hurndell. A future Kiwis captain and coach, Hardwick hailed from Dunedin and played rugby union in Wairarapa before he discovered rugby league on arriving in Auckland. Davidson's career lasted longest of all the sixteen Aucklanders, culminating with the away and home test series triumphs over Australia in 1952 and 1953.

Jack Redwood: From junior player to national chairman

The highly successful 1947–48 Kiwis tour of Britain and France was a superb tribute to the administrative skills and tenacity of Jack Redwood, who rose through the ranks from the Richmond club's fourth grade team to become a truly outstanding president and chairman of the New Zealand Rugby League.

Thames-born, Redwood discovered rugby league as a youngster in 1917 and was among Richmond's keenest and most capable players in its early senior years. On hanging up his boots he just as enthusiastically moved into administration – as Richmond team manager, committee member and chairman, and as the club's representative on the Auckland Rugby League before the formation of the Board of Control.

In 1934 Redwood was appointed as West Coast's New Zealand Rugby League council delegate under the chairmanship of Cyril Snedden. An Auckland solicitor, Snedden worked hard in difficult economic times to recover the respect lost through the disastrous 1926–27 tour of Britain. When he retired in 1937, the reins were handed to Redwood.

Jack Redwood.
Auckland Rugby League 50th Jubilee booklet

CHAPTER FIVE

'The new president, though quite a young man, has had a sound business training and as managing director of the Auckland Glass Company brings to the table of the Council practical knowledge which should be to the advantage of the code in general,' said the *Auckland Rugby League Gazette* in 1937.

Nine years later another *Gazette* described Redwood's slogans as 'energy and sincerity' and praised his achievements to date. 'Cautious in his approach, Mr Redwood examines every project at first hand; once convinced of the necessity for action of any nature, he goes to the task with relentless courage. Mr Redwood it was who advised the tour to Australia in 1938, as a prelude to the 1939 assault upon the citadel of England.'

New Zealand had not toured Australia since 1930 and had not been invited back to Britain since seven rebellious forwards were banished from the 1926–27 tour. Redwood restored his country to the international scene. That 1938 tour was significant for two reasons – at Redwood's insistence the tourists were officially named the Kiwis for the first time and the now-familiar white vee was added to the traditional black jersey.

Great hopes were held for the 1939 Kiwis when Redwood and fellow Aucklander and long-serving national councillor Bob Doble set off for Britain as co-managers. With the code still strapped for cash, the tour had largely been financed through debentures taken out by supporters, and no-one was more distraught than Redwood when it was cancelled after two games because of the outbreak of the Second World War.

Redwood was determined to take the Kiwis back to Britain at the first opportunity, and made such a favourable impact on his English counterparts that New Zealand was invited ahead of Australia when peace was restored. Once again, Redwood's planning was meticulous, with an exhaustive series of regional and national trials leading up to the team selection. Captained by Pat Smith, the amateur 1947–48 Kiwis came within one point of sharing the test series with the British professionals and tied the inaugural two-test series against France.

Even more important to Redwood, the Kiwis attracted huge crowds as the war-weary British public found release in sport. All of the investors who had taken out debentures in 1939 were repaid, the game was back in a sound financial state, and an international cycle of tours had been established involving New Zealand, Great Britain, Australia and France.

When Redwood retired from the New Zealand Rugby League presidency in 1953, his close associate Bob Doble, then deputy chairman, also vacated his position. The *League News* said Doble 'has probably been more closely associated with Mr Redwood through the bad times and the good than any other official, for he had already served the N.Z. Council for a considerable period when Mr Redwood arrived.' Doble had spent almost thirty years travelling by ferry from Devonport to attend weekly meetings of the New Zealand and Auckland leagues.

'Rugby League in Auckland, throughout New Zealand and even over the world is indeed indebted to these two capable gentlemen,' said the article. Redwood, however, was to return to his provincial roots, being elected Auckland Rugby League president in 1956 and serving in that capacity during the fiftieth anniversary celebrations three years later.

Redwood's other sporting passion was tennis, in which he was an enthusiastic participant and typically earnest administrator. In 1959 his company was the first naming rights sponsor of the New Zealand Open. A grandstand at the Stanley Street courts, adjacent to Carlaw Park, was named in his honour.

Keeping ahead

Weakened Auckland and West Coast teams were involved in notable provincial fixtures after the departure of the 1947–48 Kiwis. While West Coast was beaten 11–4 by Wellington at Greymouth, ending fourteen years of Northern Union Cup tenure, Auckland had sufficient depth to remain unbeaten against Canterbury at Carlaw Park. But, at 22–20, it was a close call. Auckland led 6–5 at the break, and spurted ahead with quick tries to Eric Chatham and Teddy Allen and a Ray Cranch conversion. Canterbury briefly led 15–14 before the Auckland backs regained some control with further tries to Eddie Kay and Tommy Rae and another goal by Cranch to make it 22–15. Canterbury forward Joe Duke crashed over for a try and Zac Beri kicked a penalty goal but the Auckland defence thereafter stayed firm until fulltime.

Kiwis crash

Being pitted against Auckland in June 1948 proved to be a bridge too far for a Kiwis team which, according to newspaper reports, showed tiredness and was without key players in vital positions. No wonder, for most of the Kiwis had been on the thirty-five-match 1947–48 tour to Britain and France and had virtually no off-season before departing for their eight-match tour of Australia. They had put New Zealand back on the international map with test wins in all three countries but a fresh Auckland side was more than they could handle.

Auckland won 30–9, with tries to Jack Lepper (two), Doug Price, Ray Cranch, Bill McCook and Len Jordan. Des White kicked six goals. The best the Kiwis could manage in reply was captain Pat Smith's try and fullback Warwick Clarke's three goals. 'The Kiwis were beaten in all departments of forward play and the backs were out-paced by their opponents,' said the *New Zealand Herald*. Auckland scrum-half Jack Russell-Green was identified as the outstanding individual player, while Cranch and Price were 'splendid' Auckland forwards.

CHAPTER FIVE

The ball flies into the hands of Doug Anderson (Kiwis), as Doug Gibson (Auckland) and Allan Wiles (Kiwis) fall to the ground. Covering at right is Len Jordan (Auckland).
Fairfax Media

Busy weekend in '48

Auckland spread its talents during a weekend in July 1948 when seventeen players went south to play Canterbury and West Coast on consecutive days and another team stayed home to take on South Auckland. The travellers had the much tougher task. After winning comfortably in Christchurch, they were decisively beaten by a West Coast side which boasted five current or future Kiwis forwards. Meanwhile, South Auckland was thrashed at Carlaw Park.

Earlier in the year, Auckland had provided five of the seven newcomers to the Kiwis team that toured Australia. They were fullback Morris Rich, wing Dave Redmond, centre Allan Wiles, stand-off Vic Belsham and loose forward Allan Laird. Prop Clarence Hurndell also made his on-field debut, after having been invalided home during the previous year's voyage to Britain.

The Auckland selectors included in their southern squad current Kiwis Rich, Cunningham, Hurndell and Doug Anderson, along with 1947–48 tourists Len Jordan (captain) and Arthur McInnarney and future Kiwis Jack Russell-Green, Roy Roff and Ray Cranch.

On their way south they played and beat Wellington 14–5, but the Northern Union Cup, which Wellington had wrested from West Coast after the Kiwis had left for Britain the previous year, was hidden away. Wellington had accepted challenges only from easy-beats Wanganui and Taranaki as the venerable old trophy sank further into insignificance. It did not return to prominence until 1956, when the New Zealand Rugby League ruled that it be at stake in all of the holder's matches, home and away, apart from special tournaments.

Rich, with seventeen points from a try and seven goals, and fleet-footed wing Doug Gibson, who claimed three of Auckland's six tries, provided most of the points in the 32–22 victory over Canterbury at Athletic Park. Forwards Doug Price and Bill McCook crossed for the other tries. At one stage of the second half Auckland led 22–4, but Canterbury cut that deficit to just three points before McCook and Rich restarted Auckland's scoring.

It was never going to be easy against West Coast at Wingham Park the next day. According to newspaper reports, West Coast produced its most convincing display since beating England two years earlier. After ten minutes the Coasters were ten points up and their fast-breaking forwards, spearheaded by Kiwis Ken Mountford and Charlie McBride, harassed the Auckland backs throughout. At fulltime it was 18–2, Auckland's only positive return being a Rich penalty goal.

Test fullback Warwick Clarke had a field day as Auckland hammered South Auckland by 60–9, converting eleven of his team's twelve tries and adding a penalty goal for twenty-four points. The try-scoring list testified to the strength of the Auckland combination. Roy Nurse got three, Des Barchard two, and Vic Belsham, Sid Gow, Dave Redmond, Joffre Johnson, Travers Hardwick, George Davidson and Maurie Robertson one each. Of them all, only Gow did not play for his country.

The 1948 Auckland team which went south to play Wellington, Canterbury and West Coast.

Back row: Doug Price, Ray Cranch, Roy Flinkenberg, Steve Rogers, Bill McCook, Clarence Hurndell.

Middle row: Don McLeod, Tommy Rae, Rex Cunningham, Stan Prentice (coach), Roy Roff, Morris Rich, Arthur McInnarney.

Front row: Dave Wilkie (manager), Doug Gibson, Jack Russell-Green, Len Jordan, Doug Anderson, Jack Lepper, Bill Telford (manager).

NZRL Museum

CHAPTER FIVE

Auckland defended its proud home record against West Coast either side of that 1948 away loss. In 1947 the provinces drew 13–13 at Carlaw Park, scoring three tries apiece in a match played after the Kiwis had departed for Britain. West Coast fullback Joe Soster was just astray with what would have been the match-winning conversion. Auckland won 9–3 in the mud in 1949. Maurie Robertson (two) and Neil Clarkin were Auckland's try-scorers and Frank Mulcare replied for the Coast. Despite the slippery conditions, it was crystal clear that nineteen-year-old Auckland centre Tommy Baxter and eighteen-year-old West Coast stand-off half George Menzies would have big futures in top company.

Tamaki Makaurau

Māori rugby league in Auckland was first put on a sound administrative footing in the late 1940s under the guidance of Jack and Sally Ewe. Tamaki Makaurau rugby league and netball teams were entered in the coronation tournaments, with most of the footballers coming from Manukau and other established clubs. Many people still involved with the game can trace family members back to those days. After the Ewe era there was a general decline because of date clashes between Māori tournaments and Auckland's regular inter-club competitions. In 1983, at a meeting hosted by Greg Whaiapu, an enthusiastic group set up a committee to resume and revitalise Māori rugby league in the Tamaki Makaurau area. They are affiliated to the Auckland Rugby League, providing a springboard for young players to participate in their own tournaments and fostering the game at grassroots level.

For club and country

Marist did not have matters all its own way in Auckland in 1948, despite winning the Fox Memorial Shield. It shared the Rukutai Shield with Richmond and was beaten by Mount Albert in both the Roope Rooster knockout and in the Stormont Shield showdown. But, as Auckland champion, it set out to add national and trans-Tasman titles to its credit.

Veteran Kiwis forward John (Chang) Newton brought his Runanga team from the West Coast to Carlaw Park. Marist proved too strong, winning 23–10 after having conceded the first seven points of the game. The slick halfback partnership between Des Barchard and Laurie Rae, two tries to centre Pat Kirwan, George Davidson's superior hooking, and a dogged forward effort got Marist home with something to spare.

Sydney champion Western Suburbs set up camp in Auckland after extinguishing Balmain's hopes of a third consecutive premiership. Although the Kangaroos were touring Britain, only controversial captain Col Maxwell had been chosen from Wests, and they had won their championship without him.

Some of the gloss was taken off the 'Australasian' title bout when Wests lost to Ponsonby, Mount Albert and, inevitably, Richmond in lead-up matches. Richmond thus continued its mastery over Sydney sides, this time by 18–6 through tries to Graham Burgoyne (two), Dave Redmond and Bill Spence and goals by Redmond (two) and Maurie Robertson.

Perhaps the Sydneysiders were foxing. They saved their best form for Marist, winning 19–15. It became a contest between a spirited Marist backline, which manufactured tries for Pat Kirwan, Jimmy Edwards and Jack Fisher, and a dominant Wests pack led by captain Jack Walsh. Eventually the ascendancy of the visiting forwards told, enabling future Kangaroos halves Keith Holman and Frank Stanmore to dictate play. Holman scored two of his team's tries but the four-point margin was provided by Bill Keato's five goals against three by Morrie Brockliss.

Ron McGregor: Rugby league statesman

Ronald George McGregor climbed every rugby league mountain, scaling the highest peaks as a player before moving on to be one of the finest administrators in the history of the New Zealand game. In a lifetime's devotion to his sport, he was a brilliant centre and wing in an all too brief Kiwis career, a thoroughly efficient Auckland Rugby League secretary, and a highly respected and responsible New Zealand Rugby League president.

A nephew of All Blacks and Kiwis wing Alwin (Dougie) McGregor, young Ron advanced through the junior grades with the Richmond club and represented Auckland at senior level in 1942. Army service required a change of codes, one he performed seamlessly, for he was named in the *New Zealand Rugby Almanack* as one of its players of the year. Returning to rugby league, McGregor was the non-playing reserve back for the Kiwis' sole home test match against the 1946 British team and, at twenty-three years of age, an automatic choice for the 1947–48 tour to Britain and France.

McGregor's tour pen-picture read that 'though slightly built [at 1.75m and 67kg], he has agility considerably above average. [He] has faithfully served the Richmond club in the position of centre, where with [Abbie] Graham and [Maurie] Robertson, a copybook attack was perfected which has delighted watchers and amassed high winning totals for his teams.' Graham and Robertson were team-mates on the 1947–48 tour.

In twenty-three appearances, McGregor scored ten tries. Three of his tries, two against Great Britain and one in New Zealand's first match on French soil, came in his five tests. A long and illustrious international career stretched ahead of

Ron McGregor in 1946.
NZRL Museum

CHAPTER FIVE

him – until his jaw was broken in two places during a trial for the 1948 tour to Australia. That injury, combined with family and other responsibilities, persuaded McGregor to retire and turn to administration.

An urge to serve rugby league off the field had its genesis on the 1947–48 tour when team manager Jack Redwood acknowledged that McGregor had just completed his accountancy degree by putting him in charge of the financial records. Years later McGregor said he had been so impressed with the trust in which he was held that 'I made a commitment then and there to put something back into the game'.

He did that, and more, over the next half-century. In 1949 he became Auckland's secretary, succeeding a legendary figure in Ivan Culpan. Any thoughts of playing again ended when a majority of clubs invoked a constitutional by-law that he could not even belong to a club, let alone play for one, while serving in that capacity. McGregor co-managed the 1956 Kiwis in Australia, where he noted that country's emerging professionalism being fuelled by the recently introduced poker machines. He remained Auckland's secretary until 1962.

Ron McGregor receives his OBE from Governor General Sir David Beattie in 1983.

Bernie Wood collection

When he stepped down, it was to become the minor leagues' delegate to the New Zealand Rugby League, an involvement with the national body which was to last until 1986. In 1970 McGregor began a seventeen-year term as president and chairman, and enjoyed immediate success when the 1971 Kiwis completed a grand slam of victories over Australia at home and Britain and France on tour.

Within weeks of their return, Australian clubs began signing New Zealand's best players. McGregor knew then it would be necessary for the Kiwis to have access to their overseas-based players if they were to stay competitive, though it took a long and frustrating time to gain support around the International Board table. Once that was achieved, McGregor presided over the golden years of the mid-1980s.

McGregor was also in the chair when the old, parochial system of Auckland-based regional delegates running the game was abandoned and replaced by a board of directors, with an appointed executive director handling the day-to-day affairs.

His tireless work was deservedly recognised over the years – by the awarding of a Queen's Jubilee Medal in 1977, New Zealand Rugby League life membership in 1978, the Order of the British Empire (OBE) in the 1983 Queen's Honours, and a Queen's Service Medal (QSM). On each occasion he humbly and modestly accepted on behalf of his sport.

Ron McGregor also spent a decade as secretary of the International Rugby League Board, which elected him as a life member in 1999.

1949: Second half slide

Australia 36 Auckland 18

Auckland fell from an 18–14 halftime lead to lose 36–18 to the 1949 Kangaroos at Carlaw Park in a match marred by some ugly scenes for which the local newspapers blamed the Australians and local referee George Kelly. It did not help the crowd's mood when Auckland centres Maurie Robertson and Tommy Baxter were injured soon after the biggest flare-up, Robertson requiring treatment for a shoulder injury and Baxter leaving the field with a black eye.

Once they settled to their work, the Kangaroos overcame a 20–10 penalty deficit to finish over the top of their smaller opponents, whose valiant defensive effort weakened in the face of the onslaught. In the second half the Australian backline turned on the speed and the backs and forwards combined in passing moves which led to an avalanche of tries. Three of them went to big wing Ron Roberts, who was to famously end Britain's thirty-year tenure of the Ashes at the Sydney Cricket Ground in 1950.

'The light Auckland pack had done well in backing-up in the first spell and, with W S Clarke in extraordinary touch with his kicking, the Australians by no

CHAPTER FIVE

George Davidson.
NZ Herald

means seemed certain to win. Until the outbreak of the fighting, Auckland was holding its own,' reported the *New Zealand Herald*. Clarke had kicked six goals by halftime to complement tries by Doug Anderson and Bill Spence, but the Australians were to rattle on twenty-two unanswered points.

'Clarke's defensive failings of the second half somewhat modified his truly splendid goalkicking of the first. Baxter, the young centre, was outstanding, particularly for speed and defensive work, while Robertson demonstrated his experience in several movements. His grubber kick across to the wing to enable Anderson to score was beautifully judged. Russell-Green, the halfback, was the smallest of the Auckland team but the most efficient in orthodox low tackling,' said the *Herald*.

'Laird, the backrow forward, was outstanding in the Auckland pack both for defensive play and attacking runs with the ball. Spence, who scored a fine try with a clever dummy, and Davidson, the hooker, were also prominent in a pack which lacked the weight, size and vigour to counter the Australians.'

Auckland played the Kangaroos in a Saturday match between their 26–21 loss to the Kiwis in the first test at Wellington and their 13–10 Carlaw Park victory to level the two-match series. Russell-Green made his debut for the Kiwis in the absence of injured halves Jimmy Haig (Canterbury) and Des Barchard, while Len Jordan, who had come out of retirement to assist his Ponsonby club, was re-called at stand-off for the second test after Abbie Graham suffered a career-ending knee injury while scoring two tries in the win at Wellington.

Auckland team: fullback, Warwick Clarke; three-quarters, Dave Redmond, Tommy Baxter, Maurie Robertson, Doug Anderson; halves, Abbie Graham, Jack Russell-Green; forwards, Clarence Hurndell, George Davidson, Bill Spence, Ra Rogers, Graham Burgoyne, Allan Laird.

One for the boys

Australian officials agreed to a tenth match in the 1949 Kangaroos' itinerary, against the Auckland Colts at Carlaw Park. Unfortunately, the home side had no opportunity to train together before the game, and in the circumstances the 30–16 losing score line was respectable.

The *New Zealand Herald* reporter conceded the youngsters 'did as well as might be expected' while condemning some of their defence against the hardened, semi-professional Australians. The tourists fielded such quality backs as fullback Clive Churchill, wing Johnny Graves and scrum-half and stand-in captain Billy Thompson, and current test forwards Len Cowie, Jack Holland, Jack Rayner and Roy Bull.

Colts team: fullback, Des White; three-quarters, Harold Moore, Jack Fisher, Bill Brooking, Neil Clarkin; halves, Jack Lepper (captain), Bill Tocker; forwards, Jack Wright, John Herring, Colin McNicol, Ray Cranch, Steve Rogers, Vic Barchard. Other squad members were Bill Bailey, Norman Dodds, Morrie Cooke, Eddie Kay. Forwards Peter Dormer and Sid Gow were withdrawals from the original team.

White was to prove the star graduate of the Colts, though the *Auckland Star* gave him a mixed review in 1949. Within twelve months White was the Kiwis test fullback against Great Britain, and he went on to establish national and international points-scoring records. Opposing White on that Monday afternoon was the legendary Churchill in what was a prelude to their clashes in the unforgettable 1952 and 1953 trans-Tasman test series.

Only one other Colt advanced to Kiwis honours – the second-rower Cranch, who the *League News* described as 'easily the best Auckland forward, showing the devil which some of the senior representatives seemed to lack'. Cranch set up a try for Rogers, while Barchard scored the Colts' other try and White kicked five goals. Centre Ian Johnston scored one of Australia's six tries and kicked six goals.

The *Star* said Tocker 'came through with credit, sending out fair passes and making useful breaks around the scrum. Lepper played up to form and Clarkin compared favourably with Australian test wing Pat McMahon. There was no better Auckland forward than the rugged McNicol, one of the most improved packmen in Auckland this season.'

Des White.
Fairfax Media

CHAPTER FIVE

Roy Nurse has his progress stopped by Cyril Clarke during Auckland's 22–20 victory over Canterbury in 1947.
Fairfax Media

Inter-club action in the late 1940s. Ponsonby forward Doug Richards-Jolley has his path blocked by Mount Albert's Allan Wiles.
Fairfax Media

CHAPTER 06

BIG GAMES, BIG WINS
1950–1959

CHAPTER SIX

Big Games, Big Wins 1950–1959

1950: Slow start by Auckland

Great Britain 26 Auckland 17

The early 1950s have long been regarded as among the finest years in New Zealand rugby league history. The Kiwis beat Great Britain two–nil in 1950, pipped the volatile 1951 Frenchmen in an unforgettable clash at Carlaw Park, and achieved away and home series victories over Australia in 1952 and 1953. There were tough times too, with the Kiwis making minimal impact on the 1954 and 1957 World Cup tournaments, and twice being unable to emulate the All Golds by winning a test series on British soil. The decade ended with a tantalisingly close series loss in Australia.

Enterprising British stand-off Dicky Williams makes a break as Des White, the Auckland fullback, moves across to tackle.
Auckland City Libraries

Aucklanders played leading roles in all of those highs and lows, while the Auckland team itself was always a threat to visiting teams. Great Britain was beaten 5–4 in a brutal 1954 match, and France was conquered 17–15 a year later.

At provincial level, the Wingham Park hoodoo continued to haunt Auckland. By 1952 it had lost to West Coast at Greymouth on four consecutive occasions. But that was redressed on three biennial visits from 1954. The Fox Memorial Shield was shared around, with only Richmond, in 1955 and 1956, winning consecutive championships – and being rewarded in that second season with seven Kiwis chosen to tour Australia. In 1959 the controversial district scheme was introduced.

On reflection, in 1950 Auckland would probably have benefited from making its southern tour before the game with Great Britain. Awarded the Saturday game played between the Kiwis' two test wins, Auckland seemed to be caught short of a run in the first half. It was down 18–5 at the break after a poor defensive display, and eventually beaten by a much more respectable 26–17. The tourists finished with six tries to three in a fast, open game on a firm Carlaw Park surface.

Britain's backs received the most praise from the *New Zealand Herald*, the halves Dicky Williams and Tommy Bradshaw and captain Ernest Ward receiving credit for setting up Ward's fellow centre, Tom Danby, for his try-scoring treble. Nor were there any weak links in the Lions pack. Auckland's most effective backs, according to the *Herald* writer, were Des White, Jimmy Edwards, Tommy Baxter and Ossie Stewart, while Jack Wright, Doug Price and Cliff Johnson were singled out for praise among the forwards. Maurie Robertson (two) and Wright were Auckland's try-scorers, and White kicked four goals.

Auckland team: fullback, Des White; three-quarters, Jimmy Edwards, Tommy Baxter, Maurie Robertson, Bevan Hough; halves, Des Barchard, Ossie Stewart; forwards, Don McLeod, George Davidson, Bill Spence, Jack Wright, Cliff Johnson, Doug Price.

White, Baxter, Robertson (captain), Hough, Barchard, Davidson and second-row forward Clarence Hurndell were the Auckland representatives in the New Zealand teams that won the tests 16–10 at Christchurch and 20–13 at Carlaw Park. White made his debut all the more memorable by kicking a penalty goal from near halfway in the first minute. When compared with those results, Auckland's performance was disappointing.

CHAPTER SIX

Spreading the talent

A month after the game with Great Britain, Auckland sent a squad of seventeen on a three-match southern tour and fielded another team against South Auckland at Carlaw Park. There were no easy games. The travellers headed off Wellington 13–10 on a Thursday afternoon, beat Canterbury 17–8 two days later and lost to West Coast 8–5 on the Sunday. The 'other' Auckland was fully extended by South Auckland before winning 29–26.

Des White captained the southbound side, which also included Jimmy Edwards, Neil Clarkin, Bob Robertson, Billy Dunn, Bob Hayward, Terry Nixon, Des Dodds and Ossie Stewart in the backs, and forwards Roy Roff, Bill Spence, Don McLeod, Jack Wright, Bill McCook, Peter Dormer, Clarence Hurndell and Ray Storey.

Auckland battled into a strong wind and driving rain at Wellington to lead 8–7 at halftime and resorted to kick and chase tactics to protect its advantage. Nixon (two) and Clarkin scored the tries, and White kicked two goals. *The Dominion* newspaper praised White and Stewart for best adapting their play to the conditions and also the efforts of Hurndell and McCook in the tough forwards exchanges. The home side, it said, had erased memories of a 41–4 beating in Auckland earlier in the season.

Despite the nine-point margin, Auckland only scored three tries (by Nixon, Wright and Edwards) to the two scored by Canterbury's Atkinson brothers, Alister and Neville, on a blustery day in Christchurch. White's four goals made

The Auckland team which played at Wellington, Christchurch and Greymouth in 1950.

Back row: Ken Lipscombe, Neil Clarkin, Jimmy Edwards, Roy Roff, Ken McIver (referee).

Third row: Peter Dormer, Don McLeod, Bill Spence, Bill McCook, Clarence Hurndell, Jack Wright.

Second row: Jim Clark, Bob Robertson, Percy Rogers (manager), Des White (captain), Arthur Chapman (manager), Ray Storey, Terry Nixon.

Front row: Ossie Stewart, Bob Hayward, Billy Dunn, Des Dodds.

NZ Herald

the difference. The Auckland skipper was described by *The Press* as the best back on the field (with Canterbury's Lory Blanchard the best forward) and, with hooker Roff dominating the scrums, Stewart, Edwards, Hurndell and Wright also stood out in the winning side.

The weather and playing surface in Greymouth were atrocious. That, and stubborn defence by the West Coast forwards, denied Auckland throughout a scoreless second half as they spent almost all of the time on attack. West Coast won thanks to tries by Kiwis Jack Forrest and John Newton and Ray Nuttall's goal, against a Clarkin try and White goal.

In contrast, Auckland's three-point defeat of South Auckland was one of the brightest games at Carlaw Park all season, in the words of the *Auckland Star*. Although Auckland only snatched victory in the closing minutes through a Bill Tocker try, it would have been unlucky to lose after scoring seven tries to four. The team comprised Dave Walker, Bevan Hough, Tommy Baxter, Bill Sorensen, Doug Anderson, Laurie Rae, Tocker, Cliff Johnson, John Herring, Ray Cranch (captain), Doug Richards-Jolley, Graham Burgoyne, Doug Price, and the reserves Jack Fisher, Jim Somerville, Bill Bailey and Bill Goulin.

Empire Games long jump silver medallist Bevan Hough breaks away for one of his three tries for Richmond against City in 1950, the year of his athletics success.
Fairfax Media

CHAPTER SIX

> ### Blackball backlash
>
> Seven years on, West Coast club Blackball returned to Carlaw Park in October 1950 and this time achieved the result it wanted, a 35–15 victory over Fox Memorial, Rukutai Shield and Roope Rooster winner Mount Albert. The *Auckland Star* labelled Blackball the national club champion, the Coasters having already thrashed Canterbury champion Sydenham by a Thacker Shield record scoreline of 53–13. Blackball's forwards scored eight of their team's nine tries and ruled the scrums. Current or future Kiwis Bob Aynsley, Bill McLennan and Bob O'Donnell crossed for two tries each. Allan Wiles, Ray Cranch and Bill Tocker were Mount Albert's try-scorers and Roy Moore kicked three goals. In the curtain-raiser, City retained its senior first division status after a two-round playoff with challengers Zora and Ellerslie.

1951: Against the 'greatest'

France 15 Auckland 10

Many Australian old-timers still rate the 1951 Frenchmen as the greatest team to tour down under. In New Zealand they are remembered with mixed feelings, largely because of the dramatic one-off test match at Carlaw Park. After eighty minutes of brutality and brilliance the match ended with Kiwis fullback Des White kicking a penalty goal from a difficult angle after the fulltime siren had sounded to clinch a 16–15 victory.

No-one quite knew what to expect when France returned to Carlaw Park two days later to take on Auckland, but the *New Zealand Herald* reckoned as many as 30,000 spectators assembled on that Monday at 3.15pm to find out. Hundreds of others were shut out. Some might have been disappointed, for 'not a blow was struck nor a hand raised' as France held off the locals to win 15–10. Instead, the crowd 'obtained satisfaction out of a match played at a good speed and which had considerable excitement when Auckland made a late run'.

Backs White, Tommy Baxter and Bevan Hough, hooker George Davidson, and forwards Cliff Johnson and Doug Richards-Jolley backed up from the torrid test match. The *Herald* claimed some showed signs of tiredness, yet added 'Auckland's best period was in the last 20 minutes, when it scored two capital tries'. Ironically, goalkicking hero White missed four close-range penalties and substitute Davidson was astray with another.

'The New Zealand forwards, Johnson and Richards-Jolley, were often prominent in the Auckland pack, and Wiles at lock covered a good deal of ground,' reported the *Herald*. 'Hurndell, a popular figure because of his recent omission from the New Zealand touring team, made some dashing runs and hard tackles.' Hurndell,

A race between the outside backs as Frenchman Jo Crespo attempts to out-pace Bruce Robertson and Jimmy Edwards.
NZ Herald

French hooker Martin Martin tries to out-flank Auckland defenders Cliff Johnson (headgear) and Allan Wiles.
NZ Herald

CHAPTER SIX

who missed the 1947–48 tour because of illness, had recently been left out of the 1951–52 Kiwis squad for Britain and France.

The *Herald* continued: 'If the Auckland backline had failings, it nevertheless produced a sturdy defender in Barchard, the captain and halfback, a young centre with a likely eye for an opening in Eastlake, and speedy wings in Edwards and Hough, both of whom were dangerous. Baxter, whose form was generally below that of Saturday, co-operated in an excellent try.' From second division club Ellerslie, Eastlake had replaced an injured Maurie Robertson for what proved to be a stepping stone to international stardom.

Auckland team: fullback, Des White; three-quarters, Jimmy Edwards, Tommy Baxter, Cyril Eastlake, Bevan Hough; halves, Bruce Robertson, Des Barchard (captain); forwards, Cliff Johnson, George Davidson, Graham Burgoyne, Doug Richards-Jolley, Clarence Hurndell, Allan Wiles. The Auckland points came from Johnson and Hough tries and two goals from White.

The fourteen Aucklanders named for the 1951–52 Kiwis tour were backs White, Eastlake, Hough, Edwards, Baxter, Maurie Robertson (captain), Bruce Robertson, Bill Sorensen and Barchard, and forwards Davidson, Johnson, Richards-Jolley, Ray Cranch and Graham Burgoyne. Despite a series of frustratingly narrow test losses, the experience gained and the teamwork developed served the Kiwis very well in the immediate years ahead.

White's world record

Ponsonby fullback Des White kicked a world test record eleven goals, from fourteen attempts, when the Kiwis blitzed the Kangaroos 49–25 at the Brisbane Cricket Ground in 1952. It was the most remarkable scoreline in an era when only the 'big four' nations had test match status. Australia had won the first test at Sydney by a seemingly comfortable 25–13 before coach Jim Amos devised the tactics which captain Travers Hardwick and the players implemented to embarrass the Australians on their home soil. Four days after the big win in Brisbane the Kiwis clinched the series 19–9 back in Sydney.

Auckland representatives in that massive win at Brisbane were White, wings Jimmy Edwards and Cyril Eastlake, centre Tommy Baxter and hooker George Davidson. Hardwick had transferred from Auckland to Waikato two years earlier and young Taranaki centre Ron McKay later played for Auckland. The other Auckland players on tour were fullback Roy Moore, three-quarters Bevan Hough, Cliff Harris and Alan Riechelmann, scrum-half Jack Russell-Green, hooker Roy Roff, and front-row forward Joe Ratima.

The Kiwis formula of pairing Auckland backs with South Island forwards had again proved successful in Australia, but it left Auckland short of experienced international forwards when it went south later in the 1952 season. Two tries each by Edwards and Bill Sorensen got Auckland home 18–8 after conceding the first eight points to Canterbury, but West Coast furthered its proud Wingham Park record with a 19–12 win the following day. On the club scene, White's Ponsonby side made a clean sweep of the four major trophies.

The Meates Cup

In 1953 the Meates Cup was presented for competition between Auckland and West Coast. Interestingly, it was donated by West Coast official Bill Meates on a day when one of the Auckland second-rowers was his son, Jack. Auckland won 12–2 on a waterlogged Carlaw Park, with Kiwis wings Vern Bakalich (two) and Jimmy Edwards scoring three of the four tries. Match reports said Auckland's play was of a surprisingly good standard, the forwards rising to the occasion and the backs capitalising on the opportunities given them. So bad were the conditions for goalkicking that world record breaker Des White missed all six of his shots and the West Coast kickers managed one from five attempts.

The Meates family produced four football-playing brothers – Billy and Kevin were All Blacks, while Vince (West Coast) and Jack (Wellington and Auckland) played representative rugby league.

1953: Auckland 'inept'

Australia 26 Auckland 4

Although New Zealand completed an historic back-to-back series victory over Australia when the Kangaroos toured in 1953, the visitors had no trouble beating Auckland 26–4 in what was expected to be the other feature match. Both the *New Zealand Herald* and the *League News* condemned the performance of the Auckland forwards, the latter saying they had been 'outplayed and outsmarted in the first half' and 'almost routed in the second'.

The *New Zealand Herald* – under the subheading 'Inept Auckland Team Thrashed By Aggressive Australians' – was less than happy with both teams, criticising the Auckland pack but also lambasting the Australians for their 'rough-house play'. That culminated with referee George Kelly ordering off second-rower Albert Paul just before fulltime for punching Doug Richards-Jolley. By then the Australians had run in eight tries, three to wing Noel Pidding, against two penalty goals by Auckland fullback Des White.

CHAPTER SIX

Auckland wing Don Clapp goes head to head with Australian Noel Pidding in 1953. Behind Clapp are George Davidson and Des White.
Auckland City Libraries

'Under the circumstances the Auckland backs went quite well. But that was hardly surprising as the line included five test players,' said the *League News*. That muted praise was qualified by criticism that, given George Davidson's slight advantage in the scrums, the backs might have been more adventurous when in possession. The writer then conceded that the inside backs, captain Des Barchard and Bill Sorensen, took a battering from the fast-breaking Australian forwards.

'The man who made the most of the few opportunities he received was winger Vern Bakalich. Twice his speed carried him past McGovern but both times he slipped in the mud when trying to go inside Churchill.' Bakalich also impressed the New Zealand selectors and was elevated into the Kiwis team for the third test match.

Up front, the much-maligned Auckland forwards were unable to lift themselves to the level maintained by an Australian pack led by rugged front-rower Roy Bull. 'They were hopelessly outclassed,' said the *Herald*. 'Davidson got his share of the ball, but only Meates, Wright and Richards-Jolley provided any opposition.' Auckland's weather and Carlaw Park's muddy surface did nothing to lift the mood of the match.

Auckland team: fullback, Des White; three-quarters, Don Clapp, Tommy Baxter, Cyril Eastlake, Vern Bakalich; halves, Bill Sorensen, Des Barchard (captain); forwards, Jack Wright, George Davidson, Jack Meates, Henry Maxwell, Doug Richards-Jolley, Barry Singe.

1953: Kiwi 'all stars'

Auckland 54 United States All Stars 26

Having captained Auckland against the Australians, scrum-half Des Barchard changed sides and played for the United States All Stars against his former team-mates only three weeks later. Alongside him were three other guest players, Auckland hooker Roy Roff, Waikato loose forward Travers Hardwick and West Coast second-rower Frank Mulcare. Auckland fullback Roy Moore was enlisted for other tour matches.

This was surely the most remarkable rugby league touring team of all time. Gathered together by former American football star Mike Dimitro, they were a group of talented athletes from various sports. But only Dimitro, during navy service in Australia, had even seen the game played before. In the early stages of their Australian itinerary, they drew crowds of up to 65,000. As inexperience, injuries and fatigue took their toll they clearly needed help, hence the recruitment of New Zealanders to bolster their ranks.

Because of the presence of Barchard, Roff, Hardwick and Mulcare in the red, white and blue, the *New Zealand Herald* informed its readers that Auckland had beaten an 'all-nations' team by 54–26. Even at that late stage of the tour the Americans had little idea of cover defence, allowing Auckland backs Cyril Eastlake and Bill Sorensen ample room to make breaks and set up tries. The best of the Americans were the unrelated backs, Alvin E Kirkland (who later played for Parramatta and Leeds) and Alfred D Kirkland. The *Herald* described organiser Dimitro as 'a hustling type of forward'.

'Three new players in representative football in K Graham (halfback), J Riddell and W Goulin (forwards) succeeded for Auckland,' said the *Herald*. 'Graham gave a good display, sending out clean and snappy passes, and Riddell and Goulin justified their selection. Eastlake and Sorensen made splendid openings and Baxter, at centre, was sound and constructive. At fullback, D White gave a sound display. Among the forwards, J Meates and D Richards-Jolley stood out.'

Auckland team: fullback, Des White; three-quarters, Jimmy Edwards, Tommy Baxter, Cyril Eastlake, Vern Bakalich; halves, Bill Sorensen, Keith Graham; forwards, Henry Maxwell, George Davidson, Jack Meates, Jim Riddell, Doug Richards-Jolley, Bill Goulin. Scorers of Auckland tries were Edwards (two), Eastlake (two), Davidson (two), Baxter (two), Riddell, Richards-Jolley, Graham and White, and White converted nine of them.

NZRL Museum

CHAPTER SIX

Warming to Wingham

It took five attempts over eight post-war years, but Auckland finally laid the Wingham Park hoodoo to rest by beating West Coast 30–14 in June 1954. The Auckland squad was packed with current and future Kiwis, and the forwards were strengthened by the return to representative play of Cliff Johnson. A new centre star had emerged in Christchurch the previous day when Ron Ackland scored three of Auckland's seven tries in a 35–15 defeat of Canterbury. That was no mean feat, for the Canterbury pack included five Kiwis and there was a likely lad named Mel Cooke at scrum-half.

Ackland completed a prosperous weekend by crossing for two more tries at Wingham Park. Newspaper reports credited stand-off half Bill Sorensen with being the star of the show. Sorensen outplayed celebrated fellow international George Menzies, and his combination with Cyril Eastlake was too slick for the West Coast defence to counter. Ian Grey and Jim Austin also returned try-scoring doubles, and Des White kicked six goals to add to his seven in Christchurch.

That mini-tour catapulted Ackland into the Kiwis and, appropriately, he made his debut in the 20–14 second-test defeat of Great Britain at Wingham Park. It is history now that Ackland re-emerged as a blockbusting second-row forward on tour to Australia in 1956. He later fashioned a famous Kiwis loose-forward trio with fellow Aucklander Don Hammond and Canterbury's Mel Cooke. The latter, like Ackland, had forsaken a highly promising career as a back for an outstanding one in the pack.

Ron Ackland.
Christchurch Star

Pacific Island influx

The now very marked Pacific Islands' influence on rugby league in Auckland extends further back than many people realise. During the pre-war years there had been a few Pacific players, such as brothers Alf and George Mitchell, who both represented New Zealand in the late 1930s. Tongan-born Bill Sorensen was a dominant figure at all levels of the game throughout the 1950s. He launched a family dynasty, with brother Dave and nephews Dane and Kurt also becoming Kiwis and son Bill junior making a New Zealand XIII. The 1969 Marist jubilee book written by Terence Hyland recalled an influx of Pacific Islanders at the club fifteen years earlier. They enjoyed immediate success in the junior grades. The outstanding senior graduate from that squad was John Ah Loo, who went on to be chosen for Auckland and New Zealand Māori. Pacific Island players were frequently chosen in local and national Māori teams until there were sufficient numbers to represent their various homelands in the reformed Pacific Cup tournament of 1986.

1954: Triumph over thuggery

Auckland 5 Great Britain 4

Auckland's second victory over Great Britain, and first for thirty-four years, was marred by thuggery, which led to the dismissals of British forwards Nat Silcock and Jack Wilkinson, and a grossly illegal tackle by centre Dougie Greenall, which inflicted serious injury on Auckland fullback Des White. It was a grim affair as the home side successfully battled to retain a 5–4 advantage throughout the scoreless second half.

'Auckland Wins R.L. Brawl' pronounced the *Auckland Star* headlines, and the match report began: 'Britain's Rugby League tourists left Auckland by air last night for Australia – and not before time! Their tour will be remembered as the roughest of any since World War II. The merit of Auckland's win was overshadowed by the toughness of the play. British pressmen rated the game as the dirtiest of the tour, far worse than the called-off match against New South Wales.'

The hometown hero was Ian Grey, who moved from loose forward to fill in as fullback and goalkicker. White suffered a split spleen early in the match when the ruthless Greenall charged in to deliver something more akin to a drop kick than a tackle. One of the Lions who played alongside Greenall that day later described his team-mate's typical tackling style as 'ball and all – it included knees, elbows, and all that sort of thing'.

In an era of no replacements, playmakers and goalkickers were prime targets for the game's hit men. Britain's entire tour had been liberally sprinkled with unsavoury incidents, the ultimate disgrace being a match against New South Wales that was abandoned after fifty-six minutes because of fighting. White underwent surgery to have his spleen removed, and his illustrious international career was put on hold for two years.

This was the tour finale, held two days after Great Britain had won the deciding test match on an appropriately stormy Auckland day. At least the *New Zealand Herald* found one 'feel good' story amid the chaos: '[Usually] a lock forward, Grey filled the fullback position with astounding success. He handled well and his kicking suffered little in comparison with that of the redoubtable [British dual rugby international] Lewis Jones, who had an outstanding match. Grey's father was in the Auckland side which beat England 34 years ago.'

Despite the heavy ground and low scoring, both sets of backs handled the slippery ball surprisingly well and mounted many adventurous movements. The *Herald* commended 'all the Auckland backs' who 'did some useful work and matched the enterprise of the English set with a solid and safe defence'. Prop Joe Ratima and second-rower John Yates were judged to be the best of the Auckland forwards, while 'Richards-Jolley, a central figure in several of the incidents, made some good breaks'.

Angry spectators react to an incident in the match between Auckland and Great Britain. The newspaper photograph was headlined, 'Send him off! Send him off!'
Auckland City Libraries

Trouble in the 1954 tour match was traced by one newspaper to the action of Britain's Nat Silcock pushing Doug Richards-Jolley face-first into the deep mud. It did not go unnoticed by another Auckland forward, Cliff Johnson.
Auckland City Libraries

CHAPTER SIX

Family double. Hometown hero Ian Grey emulated the deeds of his father, Eric, thirty-four years earlier when he played in the 1954 Auckland triumph over Great Britain.
Fairfax Media

Neville Denton.
Christchurch Star

Hooker Roy Roff was the unlikely try-scorer when he and Ratima capitalised on a British handling error after nineteen minutes. Jones, Grey, and Jones again, exchanged penalty goals to complete the scoring before halftime. Referee George Kelly had more to contend with than keeping the combatants apart, sending Silcock (after thirty-eight minutes) and Wilkinson (fifty-four minutes) to the showers after both were involved in incidents with Auckland forward Doug Richards-Jolley. The *Herald* reported Kelly was on his fourth whistle by fulltime without explaining why.

Auckland team: fullback, Des White; three-quarters, Jim Austin, Ron Ackland, Tommy Baxter, Jimmy Edwards; halves, Cyril Eastlake, Len Eriksen; forwards, Joe Ratima, Roy Roff, Cliff Johnson, Doug Richards-Jolley, John Yates, Ian Grey. All thirteen players were Kiwis during their careers.

First World Cup

Rugby league became the second sport, after soccer, to embrace World Cup tournaments, even if it took French Rugby League president Paul Barrière two years to convince Australian, British and New Zealand officials of the value of such a venture. When held in late 1954, the inaugural World Cup marked the twentieth anniversary of the game in Barrière's homeland.

Auckland provided eight of the nine Kiwis backs in Doug Anderson, Jimmy Edwards, Neville Denton, Jim Austin, Ron McKay, Cyril Eastlake (captain), Bill Sorensen and Len Eriksen. The exception was West Coaster George Menzies. Among the forwards were Aucklanders Cliff Johnson, John Yates and Ian Grey.

Six seasoned internationals were not available to travel for one reason or another, including injured fullback Des White. In his absence, and as the injury list grew, Anderson, Denton and Grey all took a turn at fullback. Both southern nations suffered from being out of season as a much-changed Great Britain side from that which had previously toured Australasia beat France 16–12 in the final. New Zealand and Australia played exhibition matches at Los Angeles and Long Beach, California on their way home.

Provincial stalemate

Auckland went perilously close to losing a home match to a South Island province for the first time in May and June 1955 when it drew 19–19 with West Coast and 18–18 with Canterbury. The Auckland *League News* analysed the results as 'not an indication of any deterioration in the local representative standard, but a healthy and gratifying sign of the big progress the code is making in the south'.

West Coast was 'the superior team on the day' whose 'honest efforts deserved a more favourable score,' said the *News*. This time George Menzies had the better of yet another memorable duel with Bill Sorensen, and big Kiwis prop Bill McLennan was singled out as the best forward. Among Auckland's most effective players were centre Ron McKay and loose forward Ian Grey.

Canterbury scored a late converted try to draw level but the New Zealand Press Association claimed 'on the run of play, Canterbury should have won, particularly because of the splendid manner in which the forwards overcame the bad ground conditions'. The *News* was full of praise for Sorensen's masterly display and nominated the uncapped Point Chevalier wing Royce Craike and City-Newton hooker Arch McInteer for the Kiwis to play France. Sadly for them, the national selectors did not take the hint.

1955: Out-foxing the French

Auckland 17 France 15

The 1955 French tourists shared the two-match test series with New Zealand, before completing their itinerary with a 17–15 loss to an enthusiastic Auckland side. Auckland's secret weapon was Cyril Eastlake, who had taken the year off international football, including the 1955–56 tour to Britain and France, but was still available for his club and province. Eastlake created two of Auckland's three try-scoring chances and regularly rattled the French defence.

'There was a sting in the back play that New Zealand sides had lacked in the tests,' said the *Auckland Star*. 'Eastlake, playing against the Frenchmen for the first time on tour, was directly responsible for this. Time and again he cut through to send centre Baxter and the wingers, Bakalich and Craike, racing for the line. That Auckland did not score more in the second half was a tribute to the French defence.'

Newspaper reports rated the tempo of the game as being far above the two comparatively dour test matches for skill and action. France suffered a setback when centre Victor Larroude was injured late in the first half and had to carry on with twelve men. Despite that, the tourists briefly led 10–8 in the second spell before Dick Haggie's goalkicking and a Jim Riddell try gave Auckland a lead which France's third try in the final minute could not run down.

Riddell, who had been a reserve for the first test and made his Kiwis debut in the second, was acclaimed as 'the outstanding forward on the field' by the *New Zealand Herald*. 'Fast on attack and defending tenaciously, Riddell was always

CHAPTER SIX

on the ball and deserved to score Auckland's final try.' Eastlake and Haggie had combined in the lead-up to Riddell's try, and Haggie's conversion from a wide angle secured victory for the home side.

'For brilliance on attack, Eastlake, the Auckland second five-eighths, had no rival. Threading his way through the French defence, he made Auckland's last two tries and came within a few yards of scoring himself on one occasion after an electrifying burst. Baxter, the Auckland captain, also played one of his best games. Controlling the attack intelligently, he positioned his wings well and showed unexpected speed to burst through gaps in the defence. Tackling hard and often, Baxter also gave a great display on defence.'

The *Herald* rated Bakalich the best of the wings on display, favourably mentioned Haggie's fine form on attack and improved defence, and was impressed by the individual and combined efforts of halves Belsham and Sorensen. Up front, Ratima put the French on the back foot with his early try and loose forward Grey hunted far and wide on cover defence to discourage the French backs.

Auckland team: fullback, Dick Haggie; three-quarters, Vern Bakalich, Tommy Baxter (captain), Cyril Eastlake, Royce Craike; halves, Bill Sorensen, Sel Belsham; forwards, Joe Ratima, Arch McInteer, Henry Maxwell, Jim Riddell, Keith Bell, Ian Grey. Ratima, Craike and Riddell scored Auckland's tries and Haggie kicked four goals.

Outstanding Auckland centre Cyril Eastlake is, for once, cornered by French defenders Jacques Fabre and Maurice Voron.
NZ Herald

Bakalich's 26 tries

Richmond wing Vern Bakalich crossed for a record twenty-six tries on the 1955–56 New Zealand tour of Britain and France, a number exceeded only by Bay of Plenty's Phillip Orchard on the corresponding tour in 1971. The Kiwis were savaged by injuries, so much so that only twelve players could originally be considered for the last test match in Paris. In a pre-match fitness test, Canterbury scrum-half Keith Roberts was found to be less handicapped than Bakalich and played as a makeshift wing.

Fourteen Auckland representatives toured, even after Cyril Eastlake was unavailable and Cliff Johnson became a late withdrawal (replaced by Henry Maxwell). Tommy Baxter captained a squad which included provincial team-mates in backs Dick Haggie, Roy Moore, Bakalich, Bruce Robertson, Neville Denton, Ron McKay, Bill Sorensen and Sel Belsham, and forwards Maxwell, John Yates, Rex Percy, Jim Riddell and Ian Grey. The coach was Aucklander Harold Tetley.

Because of the long injury list there were many examples of players going well beyond the call of duty, none more so than Sorensen, who appeared in thirty-three of the thirty-seven fixtures, the last nineteen in a row. Baxter (thirty-two games) and Bakalich (thirty) were close behind. Maxwell justified his late call up by playing twenty-seven times, including all six tests. Considering the circumstances, Baxter's men did well to win test matches in both Britain and France.

Vern Bakalich chased by rival British wing Billy Boston during his record-breaking 1955–56 Kiwis tour.
Christchurch Star

CHAPTER SIX

Night match in Dunedin

Bevan Hough, still retaining much of the pace which had earned him Empire Games selection as a long jumper in 1950, ran in four tries at Tahuna Park when Auckland beat Otago 51–11 in the first floodlit rugby league match in Dunedin in June 1956. The game had only been revived in Otago a few years earlier, and the home side did well enough to restrain Auckland to an 18–4 lead at halftime. Keith Bell converted nine of the eleven tries.

That match was held on a Thursday night, and Auckland backed up for the traditional Saturday and Sunday games against Canterbury and West Coast. Both were strongly contested before Auckland won 13–5 at Christchurch and 9–7 in Greymouth. A smartly taken try by scrum-half Keith Graham completed the scoring against Canterbury and outside backs Owen Hill (two) and Dennis Moon provided the tries to keep the Coasters at bay on a very muddy Wingham Park.

Auckland's team was: backs, Neville White, Dennis Moon, Bevan Hough, George Turner, Owen Hill, Jim Ackland, Brian Campbell, Bobby Draper, Keith Graham; forwards, Harold Moore, Keith Bell, Alan Riechelmann, Simon Yates, Bill Woolsey, Arch McInteer, Lionel Ford, Nelson Johnson.

The 1956 Auckland players alongside their National Airways Corporation aircraft at Dunedin airport.

Back row: Local manager, Simon Yates, Harold Moore, Alan Riechelmann, Lionel Ford, Owen Hill, Dennis Moon, George Turner, Neville White, Ken Gillam (manager), Des Barchard (coach), Bobby Draper, Jim Ackland.

Front row: Keith Bell, Nelson Johnson, Arch McInteer, Brian Campbell, BevanHough, Bill Woolsey, Keith Graham.

NZRL Museum

The Kiwis were touring Australia at the same time, under Tommy Baxter's captaincy and with fullback Des White making both a return and a farewell to the international scene. Other Auckland tourists were Vern Bakalich, Gordon Moncur, Tom Hadfield, Ron Ackland, Cyril Eastlake, Bill Sorensen, Sel Belsham, John Lasher, Cliff Johnson, Henry Maxwell, John Yates, Duncan MacRae, Joe Murray, Jim Riddell and Rex Percy.

Former Richmond and Auckland forward Bill (Snow) Telford made the first of his five tours as Kiwis coach, and former Richmond, Auckland and Kiwis outside back Ron McGregor was manager. Fittingly, Richmond's 1955 and 1956 Fox Memorial wins earned tour selection for seven players, Bakalich, Baxter, Belsham, Murray, Lasher, Johnson and Riddell.

Educated football

The first Auckland University Rugby League Club was formed in 1957, initially operating on an invitation basis and playing in a Sunday friendly league. In its second year, University fielded a proper Saturday competition team but, possibly because it was affiliated to the Ellerslie club, it seemed to lack its own identity. As a consequence, the initial enthusiasm dwindled and the club died a natural death in 1959. Among the original University players were Murray Patterson, Allen Gore, Frank Dodds, Bruce Pert, Rex Billington, Kevin and Gerald Ryan, Roger Douglas and Owen Mooney.

Transfer ban stays

An Auckland bid to have the overseas transfer ban changed to allow dispensations was beaten by seven votes to four at the 1957 New Zealand Rugby League annual meeting. The remit proposed that limited clearances be given to players on educational trips to register as amateurs in overseas countries for a maximum period of one year, and that players who had represented New Zealand in at least twelve test matches and had reached twenty-five years of age be allowed to negotiate for professional contracts, a maximum of two to be granted in any one year.

'The present transfer ban goes too far,' argued Ron McGregor (Auckland). 'It is morally wrong to interfere too much with a person's private life.' But Auckland-based West Coast delegate Bill Swift referred to the just-announced balance sheet. 'The £50,000 that our assets have increased by since 1947 is here only because we have the teams good enough to earn it. Our first duty is to amateur rugby league in New Zealand. If we lifted the ban, we would be reduced to a feeding ground for wealthy Australian clubs.' Much more was to be heard on this subject in the years ahead.

CHAPTER SIX

Junior tour

Captain Brian Reidy and fellow outside back Gary Phillips were the outstanding graduates of the Auckland junior representative team which travelled to Australia in 1957. Only two years later Reidy and Phillips recrossed the Tasman as fully fledged internationals with the Kiwis. Reidy went on to fashion a long and illustrious career in the black and white jersey, and Phillips would have emulated him had he not been cut down by injury. Managed by Lou Pearson and George Batchelor, the 1957 juniors won their matches with Illawarra and Western Suburbs and twice beat Eastern Suburbs. Quite a number of other players went on to achieve senior provincial honours or became prominent club footballers.

Members of the 1957 Auckland junior touring team listen avidly to former Kiwis captain Tommy Baxter (right). Second from the right at back is Brian Reidy and next to Baxter is Gary Phillips, both future Kiwis.
NZ Herald

1958: Lions win thriller

Great Britain 24 Auckland 17

The Ashes-winning 1958 Great Britain team was beaten 15–10 in the first test against the Kiwis. But the Lions struck back to tie the series 32–15 as a prelude to meeting Auckland in the last of their thirty matches in Australasia. Wing Tom Hadfield and loose forward Rex Percy, who between them had scored five of the six New Zealand tries in the two tests, plus centre George Turner were ruled out through injuries.

Auckland selectors Maurie Robertson, Des Barchard and Des White omitted Kiwis prop Henry Maxwell and made two notable positional changes. Kiwis fullback Cyril Eastlake was moved to stand-off half, and former Kiwis back Ron McKay, by then playing regularly in the forwards, was recalled at fullback. Bill Sorensen, overlooked by the Kiwis selectors, came into the centres. But the biggest surprise was Point Chevalier stand-off Ray Webber at wing ahead of Les Cherrie. Webber had played for North Island in the five-eighths.

Referee Vic Belsham is about to caution fiery British forward Vince Karalius, who, in turn, points the finger at Auckland's Cliff Johnson. Hooker Jim Patterson supports Johnson.
Auckland City Libraries

The latter decision was almost a master stroke. Five minutes from fulltime, with Auckland trailing by 17–19, Eastlake sent speedy centre Neville Denton away from deep inside his own territory. Denton kicked ahead, and in the scramble over the British goal-line Webber fell on the ball for an apparent winning try. In horror he then saw a touch judge's flag raised back near halfway, having ruled that Denton had stepped out in the act of kicking. Just on fulltime the Lions claimed a converted try to complete a 24–17 scoreline.

It was an incident-packed encounter, with referee Vic Belsham prominent. He awarded Britain a penalty try when livewire half Alex Murphy broke through in midfield and was obstructed by McKay after kicking over the Auckland fullback's head. Later, Belsham spotted a British forward leaning on a goal post as Ian Grey missed a conversion. Grey was given a second kick, which he goaled and Auckland led 17–10. The Lions were not amused.

Vern Bakalich, pictured playing for Richmond, scored a long-range try against the 1958 Lions.
NZ Herald

CHAPTER SIX

Joe Ratima, taking the ball up for Ponsonby.
NZ Herald

Auckland wing Vern Bakalich raced seventy-five metres for the most spectacular try of the match. Sorensen jinked his way through to score the first Auckland try and made the opening which enabled Denton to use his pace and score the other. Grey kicked three goals and Sorensen one. Tough prop Joe Ratima played on for an hour despite suffering a broken rib. But Britain had plenty of stars, too, in the likes of Murphy, centre Phil Jackson, fullback Eric Fraser and rugged backrow forwards Vince Karalius and Dick Huddart.

Sorensen 'made a wonderful difference to the Auckland backline, either twisting through tackles or slamming into Englishmen in cover defence,' reported the *New Zealand Herald*. An unnamed Lion was quoted as rating Sorensen as 'the best centre in New Zealand'. There was praise for the solid McKay, the elusive Eastlake, and fleet-footed Bakalich. 'Forward play seemed far better than in the test. Aucklanders such as Johnson, Yates and hooker Patterson gave the Englishmen little leeway,' said the *Herald*.

Auckland team: fullback, Ron McKay; three-quarters, Vern Bakalich, Neville Denton, Bill Sorensen, Ray Webber; halves, Cyril Eastlake, Len Eriksen; forwards, Joe Ratima, Jim Patterson, Cliff Johnson, John Yates, Keith Bell, Ian Grey.

First grand final

Championship playoffs, culminating in a grand final, were introduced to decide the Fox Memorial winner in 1958. They have been held every season since then with the exception of 1964, a transitional year between the district scheme and a return to club football when the first-past-the-post system was temporarily restored. Ponsonby beat Otahuhu 16–7 in the inaugural grand final on Saturday, 13 September 1958.

The teams were:

Ponsonby: fullback, Jack Fagan; three-quarters, Les Cherrie, Ron Smyth, Bill Sorensen (captain), Rex Percy; halves, Mal Barber, Len Eriksen; forwards, Arthur Tomlinson, Ted Johnson, Joe Ratima, Graham Keys, Graham Bint, Keith Bell.

Otahuhu: fullback, Dick Haggie; three-quarters, Owen Wright, Joe Gibbons, Jack Te Kawa, Alan Sanderson; halves, John Te Kawa, Joe Wright (captain); forwards, John Yates, Allen Gore, Barry Giltrap, Simon Yates, Bill Hattaway, Joe Jujnovich.

Percy and Smyth scored tries for Ponsonby, both converted by Sorensen, who also kicked three penalty goals. Gibbons was Otahuhu's try-scorer and Haggie kicked two penalty goals. Ponsonby led 6–5 at halftime. The referee was Vic Belsham.

Auckland beat West Coast 31–11 and Canterbury 36–15 on its 1958 southern tour.
Back row: Les Cherrie, Kevin Ngawati, Hona Rakena. Jim Patterson, Bill Snowden.
Middle row: Dick Haggie, Doug Sanderson, Bruce Owen, Rex Percy, Keith Bell, Alan Riechelmann.
Front row; George Turner, Neville Denton, Lou Hutt (manager), Henry Maxwell (captain), Tom Hadfield (vice-captain), Des White (coach), Ted Johnson. Absent: Rex Billington.
NZRL Museum

CHAPTER SIX

Three off in three minutes

Fox Memorial winner Ponsonby finished its 1958 Stormont Shield match against Roope Rooster winner Marist reduced to ten men after three Kiwis had been sent off by referee Vic Belsham, himself a former Kiwis inside back. During the first half the Ponies had lost hooker Ted Johnson through injury, though he was replaced, and another forward was battling an injury. But, trailing only 16–12 after sixty minutes, they were still very much in what had been an exciting game – and with a full complement of players.

Entering the last quarter, rival players Len Eriksen (Ponsonby) and Neville Denton (Marist) were wrestling for possession of the ball when massive Ponsonby prop Joe Ratima leapt into the air and brought both of them crashing to the ground. Referee Belsham sent Ratima off. Team-mate Keith Bell disputed the decision, and he was also dismissed. Play had only just restarted when scrum-half Eriksen late-tackled Marist forward Alan Riechelmann, and Belsham again pointed towards the sideline. Three sent off in three minutes must surely be an Auckland, if not a world, record for any match, let alone a showcase season's finale.

Remarkably, Graham Bint and Bill Sorensen responded with tries for the Ponies to go ahead at 20–16. Future Kiwi Brian Reidy, making his senior debut, then scored his first try. It was converted by Ron McKay, and Marist led 21–20. A Sorensen penalty goal swung it back to Ponsonby at 22–21. But the admirable effort told on the ten survivors and their three-man scrum, and they could not prevent prop Sam Edwards and wing John Ah Loo running in the tries which gave the champion of champions trophy to Marist by 29–22.

Ponsonby won the Fox Memorial and Rukutai Shield in 1958. Bill Sorensen has repelled one defender and eyes Trevor Lye as his next target while playing for Ponsonby against Ellerslie at Carlaw Park.

Fairfax Media

Manly on the move

Manly-Warringah added a new dimension to end-of-season Sydney club visits in 1958 by first playing in the South Island, where it beat Canterbury 27–5 and an under-strength West Coast 36–5. Coached by Ken Arthurson and captained by Ron Willey, Manly had finished third in its minor premiership, and included international backs Peter Diversi and Ray Ritchie and forwards Roy Bull and Rex Mossop.

Mossop was sent off for disputing a decision of referee Vic Belsham in Manly's first Auckland match, but that did not prevent the Sydneysiders from hammering Auckland runner-up Otahuhu by 42–12. That was not the worst incident, however. The *New Zealand Herald* reported Manly hooker George Lenon having a little finger bitten 'pretty well to the bone', for which the Otahuhu forward responsible later apologised. That same forward eventually left the field by stretcher just before fulltime, 'although not severely injured'.

The only loss of Manly's six-match tour was in midweek. The Maurie Robertson-coached Ellerslie contained internationals Cyril Eastlake and Brian Campbell in its backline and a forward pack reinforced by guest players Ron Ackland (Eastern City Districts) and Don Hammond (Mount Albert) to fill gaps created by a rash of injuries. Ellerslie upset the tourists 16–15. The margin would have been greater had loose forward Barry Singe passed the ball when Hammond had a clear run to the goal-line late in the game. It was not long before Ackland and Hammond, both transplanted centres, were sharing the Kiwis second-row positions.

Ponsonby, the 1958 Auckland champion, could not emulate Ellerslie three days later, losing 18–5 and registering only a Rex Percy try and a Jack Fagan goal. The tour ended on a somewhat festive note a day later with Manly beating an All Stars selection, comprising former and current Kiwis, by 26–10.

District scheme 1958–1963

Ted Gibson, writing in the *League News* in October 1958, used the decisive Manly victory over Otahuhu to argue the Auckland Rugby League's controversial case for changing from a club to a district system in its top grades. He pointed out that Manly, neither winner nor runner-up in its own competition, had been far too classy for the second-ranked Auckland club team and that standards needed to be raised.

Although club loyalty, an understandable and even commendable consideration, had stalled the introduction of the district scheme, Gibson said it was inevitable in a rapidly expanding Auckland. 'One can look backward to clubs such as Eden, Grafton, Newton, City, Kingsland and Athletic, all of which were swallowed up in the city and code growth. To refuse to step with this growth will stunt the code.'

CHAPTER SIX

Western United captain Tommy Baxter dives over for a try ahead of Northern Districts defender Dave Probert in 1959.
Fairfax Media

Progress on the district scheme had been outlined by John Buckingham in an August edition of *League News*. He also noted the resistance: 'the attitude of a number of our clubs to the district scheme has a similarity to that of suburban borough councils to the master transport plan – they recognise the necessity but are not prepared to meet the cost! It is quite obvious that some clubs are playing possum while others hint at adopting a "try and make us" approach.'

Buckingham recalled that when the scheme was adopted by the Auckland Rugby League, it was prepared for its implementation to take some years. Clubs were given first opportunity to negotiate and submit suggested districts. If at the end of the allotted time clubs had not complied then the Auckland Rugby League would step in and complete the job. By 1958 two district clubs had been established, Northern Districts (representing North Shore and Northcote) and Eastern City Districts (City-Newton and Eastern Suburbs). Negotiations for Mount Albert and Point Chevalier to combine as Western Districts had been completed. Other discussions between individual clubs had come to nothing.

'Northern Districts, although only in their first season, are a good example of the value of the district principle. In 1957 [there were] two clubs not contributing anything worthwhile to the senior competition, North Shore and Northcote.

Cyril Eastlake has his eye on the goal-line while spearheading Eastern United to victory over Northern Districts in 1960.
Fairfax Media

In 1958, as a district side, [it is] well up the ladder, a side to be reckoned with and already a drawcard – in short, an asset to rugby league.' Buckingham ended his article by imploring the reluctant clubs to 'recognise progress and get on with the job. This scheme is the shot in the arm the code has been searching for, for the last 20 or 30 years.'

Playing against Northern Districts, which also had the undoubted asset of master coach Scotty McClymont, and Eastern City Districts in the 1958 competition were established clubs Ellerslie, Glenora, Marist, Mount Albert, Otahuhu, Ponsonby, Point Chevalier and Richmond.

By the start of the 1959 season there was an eight-team premiership. Northern Districts and Eastern Districts had been joined as combined sides by Southern Districts (Otahuhu, Papakura and Papatoetoe) and Western United (Mount Albert and Point Chevalier). Ellerslie, Glenora and Marist were still playing solo. So was Richmond, but only because Ponsonby refused to amalgamate and instead took its championship winning team and rich array of Kiwis into the senior second division.

While Western United won the first Fox Memorial championship under district rules in 1959, Eastern United was to be a dominant force over the next four years, winning or sharing an incredible thirteen of the sixteen major trophies (Fox Memorial, Rukutai Shield, Roope Rooster, Stormont Shield). Ellerslie, as an individual entity, had already won the Roope Rooster and Stormont Shield in 1959.

In 1960 Ponsonby relented and joined Richmond as Central Districts. The retitled Eastern United was strengthened by the addition of Ellerslie, and Midland Districts (initially known as Manlane-Roskill, a union of Mount Roskill and Manukau-Greenlane) became the eighth side in the top grade. The status quo remained through the next two seasons, but as 1963 advanced there was growing pressure from clubs. A vote was eventually taken in August with the inevitable result that the district scheme was abandoned.

To 'unwind' from the various amalgamations, it was decided to give senior status to fourteen clubs in 1964 – the virtually unchanged Glenora, Marist, Midlands and Otahuhu, plus City-Newton, Eastern Suburbs, Ellerslie, Mount Albert, Northcote, North Shore, Point Chevalier, Ponsonby, Richmond and Southern Districts.

The top eight finishers qualified for the 1965 competition, they being City-Newton, Ellerslie, Glenora, Marist, Midland, Mount Albert, Otahuhu and Ponsonby. Only then did rugby league life in Auckland settle back into its traditional pattern.

CHAPTER SIX

New breed rising

Very few New Zealand touring teams have introduced so many outstanding young players to international football as that which toured Australia in 1959. The tour was preceded by a highly successful national coaching school at Palmerston North, and a team from that school all but upset the established Kiwis, who had tied the 1958 test series with Great Britain, in the final trial.

The thirteen test players were retained for the tour, and they were joined by twelve debutants plus a revitalised Ron Ackland, who had made the transition from the centres to second-row. Among the old hands from Auckland were Cyril Eastlake, Neville Denton, Tom Hadfield, George Turner, captain Cliff Johnson, Henry Maxwell, Joe Ratima and Rex Percy.

Auckland's newcomers were fullbacks Gary Phillips and Brian Reidy, wing Murray Paterson, centre Brian Campbell, scrum-half Bill Snowden, hooker Bill Schultz, and backrow forwards Don Hammond and Bill Hattaway. Phillips was the first to show through, appearing in all three test matches, and Campbell played in the first two tests after an injured Turner had been ruled out of the first international.

Phillips, Reidy, who switched to wing, Snowden and Hammond, along with Canterbury loose forward Mel Cooke and West Coast utility back Graham Kennedy, were to become stalwarts of the Kiwis side for years to come. Paterson scored four tries in consecutive country games to be top try-scorer on the 1959 tour, and Schultz was recalled to tour Britain and France in 1965.

Because there was so much talent among the emerging players, the 1959 Kiwis recorded the most impressive record (thirteen wins in fifteen games) of any Kiwis side across the Tasman, and finished off with a rousing victory in the third test match at the Sydney Cricket Ground. Eight of the 1959 Kiwis – Ackland, Cooke, Eastlake, Hammond, Johnson, Kennedy, Snowden and West Coaster George Menzies – captained the Kiwis at test level during their careers.

Gary Phillips in action for Auckland against West Coast.
NZ Herald

Beating the 'unbeaten'

Australian reference books will testify that St George was unbeaten in 1959, a season in which it claimed the fourth of its incredible eleven consecutive Sydney premierships. But the Saints did drop one decision, to Auckland champion Western United (Mount Albert and Point Chevalier combined) at Carlaw Park in late September. The home team won by 8–7 on the back of a last-minute try which was converted by a concussed part-time goalkicker!

Admittedly St George was below full-strength, having supplied seven players to the Kangaroos tour of Britain and France. But the side which crossed the Tasman included international forwards Norm Proven, Harry Bath and Ken Kearney. Not surprisingly, the visitors turned the match into a dour forward struggle with Proven, Bath, Kearney and Monty Porter dominating possession and, according to the *New Zealand Herald*, luring Western into locking horns with them.

'Outstanding players for Western United were particularly Kem, the irrepressible Maori halfback, the five-eighths Penney, and the winger, Rae, who scored the winning try,' reported the *Herald*. 'All the Western forwards played heroically and two of particular merit were Hammond and R McRae. Hammond, although concussed to the extent he was not quite sure where he was, kicked the conversion to Rae's try.'

Centre Ted Penney scored after eight minutes for the only first half points. St George went ahead 7–3 through a try to replacement forward Peter Armstrong and two goals by Bath. In the dying seconds Peter Rae broke clear on the left wing and stepped inside two defenders to touch down by the posts. Western was without regular kicker Don Raisbeck because of a knee injury, and Hammond put over the most important of his few career goal kicks. He had little memory of the event and required a mate to drive his car home.

With Tommy Baxter as player-coach, Western triumphed in a national club championship held to mark the Auckland Rugby League's fiftieth anniversary. Western was a convincing winner, beating Papanui (Canterbury) 23–17, Huntly South (Waikato) 42–13 and Papanui again in the final 39–14. Its major local rival was Ellerslie (soon to become the backbone of the formidable Eastern United), which won the Roope Rooster and beat Western for the Stormont Shield.

CHAPTER SIX

The champion Western United team in 1959.

Back row: Doug Moselen, Peter Rae, Danny Proffit, Trevor Jamieson (steward), Ron McRae, Tai Rakena, Ray Webber.

Third row: Ron Andrews, Jack Whorskey (masseur), Henry Maxwell (vice-captain), Laurie Olliff, Morrie Costello (steward), Duncan McRae.

Second row: Don Raisbeck, Jim Sinclair (secretary), Tommy Baxter (captain), Bert Humphries (chairman), Don Hammond, Jack Sparnon (manager), Ted Penney.

Front row: Graham Clark, Billy Kem, Graham Humphries.

Don Hammond collection

CHAPTER 07

BEATING THE BEST
1960-1969

CHAPTER SEVEN

Beating the Best
1960–1969

1960: France falls first

Auckland 14 France 5

Auckland made a sensational start to the 1960s when it recorded consecutive-season victories over France, Australia and Great Britain at Carlaw Park. It had become the custom for touring teams to back up against Auckland on the Monday or Tuesday after the final test match. There could have been few tougher assignments in the rugby league world – akin to the Kiwis facing Wigan or New South Wales – at a time when the visitors were either celebrating or suffering the outcome of their test series with New Zealand.

The tourists would inevitably be thinking of home – the French and British having made long treks through Australia even before arriving in New Zealand

Nelson Johnson tries to brush past the outstretched arm of French forward Majoral.
NZ Herald

– and many teams no doubt struggled to raise the enthusiasm needed to run out onto an often muddy field to again take on a team of near-test strength. But many Auckland players inevitably had test commitments, preventing the provincial team from training together and increasing the possibilities of injuries further disrupting Auckland's preparation.

In 1960, France decided to use fresh players for the tour finale. The side was fortunately injury free and only called upon stand-in captain Jean Barthe to back up from the side that had lost a closely contested two-test series. Auckland had the luxury and the depth to field twelve Kiwis (past, current or future). Cyril Eastlake was switched from his test role of fullback to stand-off half, allowing Ponsonby fullback Jack Fagan to wear the number one jersey.

The *New Zealand Herald* described Carlaw Park's surface as 'having the consistency of thick porridge', yet 'strangely enough, it was in the backs Auckland gained its greatest superiority' in going on to win 14–5. 'The main factor in this was the play of Eastlake and Sorensen. Eastlake, by the intelligent use of the blind [side], kept the French defence guessing all day, while Sorensen was as brilliant on attack as he was solid on defence. The other star of the Auckland backs was Fagan, who used every opportunity available to attack from the fullback position.'

Forwards shared in the praise: 'Ackland's play capped off a series of fine performances in the three matches he has played against the tourists. In the second-row yesterday he possibly eclipsed even his tremendous display in the second test. Ackland not only seemed to be on hand for every [attacking] movement, he also defended with great purpose. The other Kiwi in the Auckland pack, Maxwell, was also in fine form. Tearing into tackles like a small army tank, he did much to wear down the Frenchmen. McKay, in the back row, also had a good game, while Riddell worked hard.'

French emotions had spilled over in the last minutes of the test series the previous Saturday, but there was no hint of lingering bad blood in the Auckland match. Barthe led his men in the manner expected of France's best forward, and slightly built fullback Pierre Lacaze was both footballer and showman in entertaining the crowd. Auckland's tries were scored by Fagan, Denton, Sorensen and Riddell, with Sorensen converting one.

Auckland team: fullback, Jack Fagan; three-quarters, Neville Denton, George Turner, Cyril Eastlake, Murray Patterson; halves, Bill Sorensen, Bill Snowden; forwards, Henry Maxwell, Jim Patterson, Nelson Johnson, Ron Ackland, Jim Riddell, Ron McKay.

CHAPTER SEVEN

Two formidable warhorses on a collision course at Carlaw Park, Auckland captain Cliff Johnson and West Coast's Jock Butterfield.
Fairfax Media

Auckland coach Des White talks to his players on the eve of a 1961 match against Canterbury. From left, Rata Harrison, Laurie Olliff, Don Hammond (partly obscured), Bruce Castle, Bill Sorensen, Paul Schultz and Reg Cooke.
Fairfax Media

Match under threat

Auckland's Monday match against the 1960 Frenchmen was under threat of cancellation until a few hours before kick-off. Only then did French manager Antoine Blain name hooker Andre Vadon and wing Alain Perducat as the players who had assaulted referee Vic Belsham in the fiery final minutes of the second test at Carlaw Park two days earlier. The New Zealand Rugby League had demanded Blain identify them or the Auckland fixture would be cancelled. Vadon and Perducat were subsequently banned from playing again in New Zealand. All concerned were relieved there were no further incidents during Auckland's 14–5 victory, the *Auckland Star* headline announcing 'France ends with loss – only thing dirty was the mudbath' after a clean game on a churned-up field.

Cup lost and regained

Auckland finally lost its unbeaten home record against South Island teams when West Coast came to Carlaw Park, triumphed 22–18, and captured both the Northern Union Cup and the Meates Cup. The Coasters received some local assistance. Down 13–2 at half-time, they returned to score twenty points in twenty-one minutes after receiving timely advice from long-serving Kiwis coach Snow Telford. Among the West Coast try-scorers were Kiwis Graham Kennedy, Trevor Kilkelly and Reese Griffiths, with Kennedy kicking five goals, while Tom Hadfield, Ron Ackland, Jim Patterson and Peter Rae claimed Auckland's tries and Cyril Eastlake kicked three goals.

But the Coasters' tenure was to be short-lived. Auckland regained the two trophies with a 19–4 victory in Greymouth when trekking south over Queen's Birthday weekend. George Turner, with three tries, led the way in what local newspapers called 'strong and vigorous backline play' despite a wet ball. Tom Hadfield and Neville Denton also scored tries and Bill Sorensen kicked two goals. On the Monday, Auckland successfully defended the Northern Union Cup, 8–2, against a formidable Canterbury team, with Murray Paterson and Bill Sorensen scoring tries and Sorensen adding a goal. During the same weekend Auckland B downed Waikato by 11–8.

In 1961 both southern provinces challenged for the Northern Union Cup at Carlaw Park, only to be repelled by Auckland's try-scoring firepower. Don Hammond touched down three times and Reg Cooke, Neville Denton and Ron Ackland twice each in the 38–4 rout of Canterbury, while Tom Hadfield and Gary Phillips scored two tries apiece in the 16–7 win over West Coast.

1961: Kangaroos conquered

Auckland 13 Australia 8

Auckland defended a 13–8 lead for the last thirty-three minutes of its first victory over Australia. The 1961 Kangaroos had been held to one-all in the test series with both matches closely contested and decided by two-point margins. Auckland fullback Gary Phillips was the hero of the first test when his field goal, a rarity then worth two points, broke a deadlock that had lasted most of the second half. The Kiwis result was satisfactory, given the spate of international retirements, including Auckland stalwarts Cliff Johnson, Cyril Eastlake, Henry Maxwell and Bill Sorensen, that followed the 1960 World Cup.

The Australians were hit by injuries and forwards Ron Lynch and Jack Sinclair were named in the centres for the Auckland match, while another backrower, Bill Owen, alternated between the pack and the backline during the game. Eight of the Aucklanders, Phillips, Tom Hadfield, George Turner, Bill Snowden, Ron Ackland, Maunga Emery, Jim Patterson and Tom Reid, had appeared in the second test match two days earlier. They were joined by former internationals Sorensen and Neville Denton, future Kiwis Doug Ellwood and Bruce Castle, and late replacement Ted Johnson.

Johnson was called into the second-row, alongside Kiwis captain Ackland, after original squad members Brian Lee and Laurie Olliff withdrew on the day of the match. It was a daunting task for the newcomer, but he earned an honourable mention in newspaper reviews. Castle had already been included in the New Zealand team to tour Britain and France as loose forward understudy to Canterbury's Mel Cooke, while Ellwood was to make his international debut in Australia in 1963.

Inevitably, the state of Carlaw Park featured high in the *New Zealand Herald* match report, being described as 'churned up in the two test matches' and 'devoid of grass and very muddy between the 25-yard lines'. Steady rain fell throughout the first half, after which Auckland held a tenuous 8–3 advantage.

Emery, who went on to form one of the Kiwis' most daunting front-row combinations with fellow prop Sam Edwards and hooker Jock Butterfield, had made his test debut even more notable by scoring a try. He repeated that effort for Auckland, from a Sorensen centre kick. Phillips gained the second Auckland try. Hadfield had broken away down the touchline and kicked infield for Castle to trap Australian wing Ken Irvine near his goal-line. As Irvine played the ball back, Phillips dived around from marker to secure possession and score.

Australian forward Jack Sinclair can be identified by his touring number (20) but his Auckland opponent has disappeared into the Carlaw Park slush.
NZ Herald

CHAPTER SEVEN

Australia levelled up through a converted try only one minute after the resumption but Auckland went clear in the forty-seventh minute when Ackland scooped up a loose ball and passed to the unmarked Denton. Sorensen's conversion was his second goal of the match. Australia took its turns on attack, but the Auckland defence held firm to the finish, much to the delight of an estimated 17,000 fans.

The *Herald* described wily veteran Sorensen as 'the most incisive player in the Auckland backline' with his clever tactical kicks. Phillips' try was 'just reward for his enterprising runs as the extra man into the backline' – the hallmark of his brilliant but injury-plagued short international career. Ellwood was said to have played a sound game, with Snowden again prominent and particularly strong on defence. Castle, Ackland and Johnson were singled out among the forwards.

Auckland team: fullback, Gary Phillips; three-quarters, Tom Hadfield, George Turner, Bill Sorensen, Neville Denton; halves, Doug Ellwood, Bill Snowden; forwards, Maunga Emery, Jim Patterson, Tom Reid, Ron Ackland, Ted Johnson, Bruce Castle.

Bailey blitzes Britain

Roger Bailey blitzed the British on his Kiwis debut, the 1961 tour of Great Britain and France. The nineteen-year-old Ponsonby centre topped the try-scorers with nineteen from his twenty-one appearances (five more than Marist wing Brian Reidy). Included in Bailey's total were two tries in the second British test at Bradford, two more in the series-deciding second French test at Perpignan, and another in the drawn third test at Paris. The tour launched Bailey on a dazzling career, laced with brilliant performances.

New Zealand's prospects of challenging Britain and France did not appear bright when circumstances forced the selectors to send an inexperienced team. There had been a raft of retirements after the 1960 World Cup. Auckland centre George Turner and West Coast stand-off half George Menzies were not available and, after the team was named, test captain Ron Ackland, wing Neville Denton and fullback Gary Phillips withdrew over a dispute about allowances. There were sixteen debutants, including Roger Bailey and his brother Gary, also a centre.

Don Hammond succeeded Auckland and New Zealand second-row partner Ackland as captain. Hammond had toured Australia with the 1959 Kiwis but missed much of the next season through injury and made his test debut the same month as being elevated to the tour captaincy. But Hammond proved to be an inspired choice, leading his team in twenty of the twenty-nine matches, including all six tests. The highlights were a 29–11 thrashing of a shocked British side in the first test at Leeds and the one–nil (with two drawn) series' victory in France.

Even without Turner, Ackland, Denton, Phillips, rejected test prop Tom Reid and 1960 World Cup forward Laurie Olliff, the touring team included sixteen players from Auckland: backs, Jack Fagan, Jim Ford, Tom Hadfield, Brian Reidy, Roger Bailey, Gary Bailey, Reg Cooke, Ken McCracken and Bill Snowden; hooker, Jim Patterson; and forwards Maunga Emery, Rata Harrison, Ron Duffy, Don Hammond, Brian Lee and Bruce Castle. Auckland also provided manager Colin Siddle and coach Bill Telford, who were both Kiwis selectors.

Rising star Roger Bailey (centre) flanked by his brothers Gary, Bob, David and Kevin.
NZ Herald

CHAPTER SEVEN

Rival captains Mel Cooke and Don Hammond with the Northern Union Cup before Canterbury's surprise win in 1962.
NZRL Year Book 1963

Shock in Christchurch

Canterbury gained its second victory over Auckland, and its first for thirty-seven years, when scrum-half Bob Irvine scored a last-minute try to secure a 16–13 result at the Addington Show Grounds in 1962. The earlier loss had involved an under-strength Auckland team because of the 1925 Queensland tour. But this time there were no excuses, with Auckland's twelve internationals including players of the calibre of Brian Reidy, Roger Bailey, Ken McCracken, Neville Denton, Ron Ackland and Don Hammond. The only non-international was loose forward Stu Hunter.

Inspiring loose forward Mel Cooke, stand-off half Jim Bond and wing Allen Amer were Canterbury's only 1961 Kiwis. Auckland seemed to have the Northern Union Cup in safe keeping when leading 13–6 after sixty-four minutes. But Canterbury fullback Tony Smith kicked his fourth penalty goal and a break by Cooke ultimately led to wing Pat White sprinting fifty metres to score. Smith's conversion made it 13–13. As the game entered injury time, Bond feigned a field goal, dashed to his right, and centre John Walshe gave the speedy Irvine room to cross at the corner flag. Auckland's tries were scored by Ackland, at the end of a magnificent seventy-metre run, Hammond and McCracken, and Reg Cooke kicked two goals.

A day earlier Auckland had held West Coast try-less while winning 11–4 in Greymouth. Ackland, Bailey and Reg Cooke crossed for the Auckland tries, and Cooke kicked one goal. Before the season was over, however, the Northern Union Cup was back in Greymouth, tries by veterans George Menzies and Reese Griffiths giving the Coasters a 6–4 home win over Canterbury.

Auckland's Brian Campbell in possession at Christchurch. Awaiting developments from right are Peter Smith (Canterbury), Reg Cooke and Roger Bailey.
Christchurch Star

1962: Wounded Lions put to sword

Auckland 46 Great Britain 13

The 1962 Great Britain Lions were among the finest to tour Australia, comfortably winning the first two tests, beating New South Wales twice, and losing the third test by one point to prevent a clean sweep of the major matches. But injuries hit them hard in New Zealand, and the unsympathetic Kiwis enjoyed nineteen-point winning margins in both test matches at Carlaw Park. Lions captain Eric Ashton and champion scrum-half Alex Murphy did not play in this country, and the tourists had problems filling some specialist positions.

Either side of the second test, the Lions recorded their highest-ever total in New Zealand by embarrassing Bay of Plenty 81–14 and then suffered their biggest-ever defeat, 13–46 to a rampant Auckland. The Aucklanders coasted home on the back of a twelve-try bonanza and would have topped the half-century had their kickers been more on target.

Britain fielded eight forwards (including Laurie Gilfedder on the wing and the superb Dick Huddart in the centres) and five backs, the *New Zealand Herald* reporting they were the only fit players left. But it must be said that the presence of Huddart, Dave Bolton, Neil Fox, Harold Poynton, stand-in captain Derek Turner, Jack Wilkinson and Bill Sayer made this a still-formidable combination. And the British were, after all, professionals up against amateurs. Tour manager Stuart Hadfield did his players little service by commenting, 'What could you expect from a team of crocks?'

'Strangely enough it was not the injured players [forwards Wilkinson and Ken Noble suffered further knocks during the game] who let Britain down,' said the *Herald*. 'They played as well as they could. It was the lack of determination by the fit players who did not seem to put their full effort into the game which cost them the match.'

This Auckland outfit would have been a problem for any rival. There were twelve current or future internationals, the only exception on this occasion being second-rower Arthur Carson. But of the Auckland forwards, only Ackland played more than a handful of tests during his career, and it was a surprise the home pack outplayed its far more experienced opponent.

Auckland was also buffeted by injuries from the second test, losing front-row bookends Maunga Emery (leg) and Sam Edwards (shoulder) and second-rower Don Hammond (shoulder). Yet even when Britain brought Huddart into the pack after halftime, the balance of forward power clearly stayed with Auckland. For most of the unheralded Auckland forwards, this was their finest hour.

In contrast, the Auckland line-up of wings Brian Reidy and Neville Denton, and centres Roger Bailey and captain Bill Sorensen, supported by such a penetrative

CHAPTER SEVEN

fullback as Gary Phillips, would rate among the finest of all time. Inside them were emerging stand-off half Doug Ellwood and test scrum-half Bill Snowden. Ten of the twelve tries went to the backs, with only Phillips not getting his name on the scoreline.

Auckland team: fullback, Gary Phillips; three-quarters, Brian Reidy, Roger Bailey, Bill Sorensen (captain), Neville Denton; halves, Doug Ellwood, Bill Snowden; forwards, Rata Harrison, John Lasher, Graham Mattson, Arthur Carson, Ron Ackland, Bruce Castle.

Try-scorers for Auckland were Denton (three), Bailey (two), Ellwood (two), Reidy, Sorensen, Snowden, Harrison and Mattson. Phillips kicked three goals and Sorensen two. In reply, Britain managed three tries and two goals. Auckland led 17–3 at halftime. It remains Auckland's most decisive victory over an international team.

Referee Bert Payne is about to whistle up a try for Bill Sorensen in Auckland's record defeat of the 1962 Lions.
NZ Herald

Neville Denton touches down for one of his three tries against Great Britain.
NZ Herald

Brian Reidy has beaten Neil Fox but is about to be claimed by Dave Bolton with Gary Phillips rushing up.
Brian Reidy collection

Auckland clubs dominate

Cigarette manufacturer Rothmans sponsored a £1,000 national inter-club tournament from 1962 to 1964, after which it changed to an inter-provincial tournament, and Auckland clubs (or districts) Eastern United, Southern Districts and Otahuhu carried off the prize money. The beaten finalist every time was the Canterbury champion, Hornby (twice) and Linwood.

Eastern had over-filled its trophy cabinet in 1961 by winning the Fox Memorial Shield, Rukutai Shield, Roope Rooster and Stormont Shield. But it was not quite as dominant in 1962, being held to a 17–17 draw by Glenora in the Fox final. Eastern had won the Rukutai Shield as minor premier and retained the Roope Rooster, but Glenora was a 13–10 winner of the champion of champions. Seeded straight to the Rothmans final, Eastern was too good for Hornby with Ron Ackland and Reg Cooke scoring two tries each in a 25–2 victory.

Few would argue that Eastern was again the top Auckland club in 1963. It kept the Roope Rooster, was outright Fox champion with an 8–0 defeat of Southern Districts, and regained the Stormont Shield. The only trophy it missed was the Rukutai Shield, trailing Southern by two points. But the Rothmans format had altered, and the Auckland nominee was required to be named early and play in all rounds. Southern Districts accounted for Te Mahoe (Bay of Plenty) 53–4, Ngaruawahia (Waikato) 26–9 and Waitara (Taranaki) 53–17. Linwood was just as superior in the South Island, but tries to Ken George (two) and Roy Christian provided Southern with a comfortable 15–2 victory in the national final at Carlaw Park.

Ron Ackland slides across to score for Eastern United in a national tournament match against Canterbury champion Hornby at Carlaw Park.
Christchurch Star

CHAPTER SEVEN

Brian Reidy in typical try-scoring form for Auckland. Too late to stop him is Canterbury centre Brian Langton.
NZ Herald

With the districts scheme having been scrapped, Otahuhu and Mount Albert shared the 1964 Auckland trophies. Fielding virtually the old Southern Districts side, Otahuhu won the minor and major championships, beating Mount Albert 18–5 and 10–5. But Mount Albert struck back to win 15–7 in the Roope Rooster and 19–3 for the Stormont Shield. Otahuhu was the Rothmans representative, beating Ngongotaha (Bay of Plenty) 43–5 in its first match before meeting stiff opposition. Huntly South (Waikato) lost the northern final 15–10 in an even encounter. The final against Hornby in Christchurch was closely contested before Otahuhu got home 10–5 through a try to David Gore and a try and two goals from Ernie Wiggs.

Reidy's treble

Auckland wing Brian (Speedy) Reidy crossed for eight tries in nineteen test matches during an international career that began at fullback in the midweek games of the 1959 tour to Australia and ended back in the No.1 jersey for the only time in a test against Great Britain at Carlaw Park in 1966. His finest day was at Brisbane in 1963, when New Zealand downed a Kangaroos side boasting arguably the fastest three-quarters line of all time, 16–13. Reidy scored the first three of the four Kiwis tries, the fourth going to fellow Aucklander Ken McCracken on the other wing.

Canterbury keeps cup

Hooker Warren Satherley, who raked the ball from twenty-five of the thirty-three scrums, did most to save Auckland's unbeaten home record against Canterbury at the Epsom Showgrounds in 1963. Canterbury retained the Northern Union Cup with a 10–10 draw, after looking the better side for most of the match. The *New Zealand Herald* criticised Auckland's selectors for choosing a mix of experience and youth, and pointed out the home side's second try came when the visitors were down to twelve men because of injury. Canterbury had a late chance to snatch victory, but Pat White was astray with a difficult conversion. Reg Cooke and Ken McCracken were try-scorers in Auckland's only provincial match of the season. In other cup matches, Canterbury beat West Coast twice, Waikato and Otago.

1963: Springboks corralled

Auckland 10 South Africa 4

A South African rugby league side, which included several players with professional experience in Britain and six former Springboks rugby union stars, made an ill-fated tour of Australasia in 1963. The league 'Boks were mauled twice by the Kangaroos and suffered such a physical battering that Newtown second-rower Graham Wilson and Canterbury-Bankstown hooker Fred Anderson were enlisted to accompany them to New Zealand.

It was the presence of the two guest players that cost South Africa the distinction of causing the biggest upset in test history. They beat New Zealand 4–3 (two penalty goals to one try) in an unofficial test, capitalising on their kicking skills on a typically wet and muddy day at Carlaw Park. The South Africans benefited from the coaching assistance of former Kiwis captain Maurie Robertson during their stay in Auckland. In their other fixtures, South Africa beat Wellington but lost to South Island and Auckland.

Because eleven of its players had been called into the Kiwis camp, Auckland had to settle for a virtual B team for its game on the preceding Wednesday. Carlaw Park was muddy even before the onset of torrential August rain, which fell throughout the game. It was a matter of Auckland defending stoutly to win 10–4 after leading 10–2 at the interval because the cagey Anderson gave the visitors an 18–15 scrummaging advantage and they received fifteen of the twenty-four penalties from Waikato referee Roly Avery.

'Under the conditions both teams handled extremely well, but players had little control as they slithered and fell to the ground every time they tried to sidestep or change direction,' reported the *New Zealand Herald*. But the writer was disappointed with the overall effort of the young Auckland side. Fullback Chris Smith, who 'featured in some good breaks', was the most penetrative back, while Graham Mattson and Hoppe Baker were named as the most effective forwards.

Roy Christian, who was to go on and play thirty-two test matches from 1965 to 1972 and captain New Zealand on its most celebrated tour, was then a young and speedy right wing from Otahuhu. Even the quagmire could not dull his pace enough to prevent him opening the scoring. Auckland's other try went to left wing Graham Anderson. Captain Roger Tait did well to convert both tries and complete Auckland's scoring.

South Africa had assembled its strongest pack on tour with famous rugby union forward Martin Pelser back from injury. But it wasted two scoring opportunities in the second spell, when Fred Griffiths lost control as he dived for the line, and Pelser dropped the ball at close range. South Africa had to be satisfied with two penalty goals by Griffiths, who was then captain-coach of North Sydney. Three days later another two Griffiths goals would be enough to beat New Zealand.

Ray Fenton (headband) and Roy Christian move across to cover South African playmaker Ontie Odendaal.
NZ Herald

CHAPTER SEVEN

Auckland team: fullback, Chris Smith; three-quarters, Roy Christian, Ray Townsend, Doug Ellwood, Graham Anderson; halves, Roger Tait (captain), Paul Schultz; forwards, Roy Roberts, Warren Satherley, Hoppe Baker, Jeff Satherley, Graham Mattson, Ray Fenton.

Districts down Eels

District clubs Eastern United and Southern Districts bade farewell to Carlaw Park by beating Parramatta with identical scores of 20–13 after the Eels had opened their three-match visit by edging out Glenora 13–11. Arthur Carson scored Glenora's only try, and Roger Tait and Chris Smith kicked two goals apiece. Loose forward Bob Best was labelled as Glenora's most incisive player. Ernie Wiggs contributed a try and four goals to Southern's success, with centre Clive Neary (two) and wing Roy Christian being the other try-scorers. A bruising encounter included the ordering-off of rival forwards Ewan Moore (Southern) and Noel Dolton (Parramatta) on a touch judge's report after what the *Auckland Star* called 'the tamest incident of the match'.

Well beaten in the scrums, Eastern typically prospered in the loose. Ron Ackland ran the show, mobile packmen Ray Sinel, Jeff Satherley, Gene Woolsey and Kevin Spooner ran wide to link with the backs, and Reg Cooke, Doug Ellwood, Phillip Rowe and Ken McCracken crossed for tries. Cooke added four goals in a powerful centre display. Although Parramatta was without touring Kangaroos

Glenora's Arthur Carson tries to break clear of the Parramatta defence. In support at left is Graham Mattson.
NZ Herald

Ken and Dick Thornett, Ron Lynch and Brian Hambly, it was well served by former Australian half Bob Bugden, English centre Derek Hallas, hooker Bill Rayner, fullback Ron Willey and South African wing Ken Foord, who scored five tries over the three matches.

Back at the top

Auckland regained the Northern Union Cup and undisputed top provincial ranking in 1964 by beating Canterbury 13–7 in Christchurch. With John Lasher decisively out-hooking fellow Kiwi Gary Blackler in the scrums, Auckland never lacked possession. But it took a late converted try to settle the issue. Doug Ellwood, Reg Cooke and Roger Bailey were try-scorers and Jack Fagan kicked two goals. Auckland was the decisive winner of its other games, beating West Coast 44–2 at home and 31–2 in Greymouth – when Fagan contributed sixteen points from two tries and five goals – and outclassing Rest of North Island 29–7 on Carlaw Park. In the latter game Ken McCracken and Roger Bailey recorded try-scoring doubles. On the club scene, three players registered double centuries: Ernie Wiggs 218 for Otahuhu, Reg Cooke 205 for City-Newton, and Roger Tait 203 for Glenora.

1964: Opportunity lost

France 13 Auckland 10

Having beaten France in 1960, Australia in 1961, Great Britain in 1962 and South Africa in 1963, Auckland had the opportunity to restart that cycle when the French returned in 1964. Captained by Bernard Fabre, the Tricolours lost all six test matches in Australasia. But, despite suffering a further setback when star centre Claude Mantoulan broke a leg in the first test, Fabre's men ended Auckland's sequence of success by winning 13–10 for their most significant win of the entire tour.

With the French itinerary covering four weekends, the Auckland match was restored to the Saturday between the second and third tests. If the French were downcast at losing the series in Christchurch seven days earlier there was scant sign of their depression as they recovered from a 5–7 halftime deficit. The flair of outside backs Michel Boule and Andre Bourreil and a determined defensive display carried them home.

'Both players had too much pace for their counterparts, Rowe and Bailey, and between them scored three tries,' reported the *New Zealand Herald*. 'Besides these two grand attacking players the Frenchmen also had far the better defensive

Reg Cooke (Eastern United) fends off Parramatta opponent Kerry Burke during the win over the Eels. At back is Eastern's Keith Wright.
Fairfax Media

Joe Gwynne (Otahuhu) pierces the Mount Albert defence to set up the first try for Ernie Wiggs in the 1964 Roope Rooster final. Mount Albert won 15–7. Mount Albert also won the Stormont Shield after Otahuhu claimed the Fox Memorial and Rukutai Shield.
Fairfax Media

CHAPTER SEVEN

The ever-scheming Cyril Eastlake has Frenchman Andre Bourreil (left) guessing as Roger Bailey accelerates to offer support.
Fairfax Media

backline. The tourists always looked more dangerous when in possession and they made what was a near-Kiwi backline look ordinary at times with their flawless tackling.'

The home side was without original selections John Lasher, Don Hammond (both injured) and Ken McCracken (through illness) but drew severe criticism from the *Auckland Star*. 'Auckland was so poor you had to wonder what was happening,' wrote Brian Doherty. 'France was not particularly good. It was hesitant, threw wild passes and didn't handle as well as in previous matches. Yet Auckland, except for brief periods, was scrambling around like a bunch of novices.'

Auckland was rocked onto its heels in the second minute when Bourreil broke clear and gave Boule an unhindered run to the corner, his try embellished by Roger Garnung's fine conversion. Soon after halftime Boule evaded Rowe and fullback Chris Smith for his second try, and four minutes later Bourreil sprinted eighty metres to score. Only Boule could keep up with his fellow flying Frenchman.

Fabre, at stand-off half, set his players an outstanding tackling example by bottling up the wily Cyril Eastlake, who was then nearing his thirty-fourth birthday and playing his fourth game for Auckland against France over a thirteen-year period. Eastlake, however, marked his representative swansong with a try after a long cut-out pass from Ron Ackland. Rowe was Auckland's other try-scorer and Ernie Wiggs kicked two penalty goals.

Auckland team: fullback, Chris Smith; three-quarters, Roy Christian, Brian Campbell, Roger Bailey, Phillip Rowe; halves, Cyril Eastlake, Eric Carson; forwards, Sam Edwards, Bill Schultz, Graham Mattson, Ernie Wiggs, Don Mann, Ron Ackland (captain).

Frenchman Jean Graceit surrounded by Aucklanders Ernie Wiggs, Graham Mattson and tackler Eric Carson.
NZ Herald

'Taken off the street'

Ivan Stonex and Ted Knowling

Prominent officials become involved in the game from all directions, as veteran Auckland and New Zealand secretary-treasurer Ted Knowling revealed at a national conference in early 1972. Knowling interrupted a serious discussion as to how more people could be encouraged to become involved at club and provincial levels by commenting, 'Goodness me. They're not that hard to find. Ivan Stonex and I were taken off the street and brought into rugby league in 1932'.

Knowling, an imposing character whose speciality was finance, was first enlisted as assistant treasurer of the Auckland Rugby League. In 1933 he succeeded Fred Ellis as treasurer, a position he filled before and after war service until 1947. A year later Knowling began a stint as New Zealand Rugby League secretary which extended until 1966, and from 1951 he combined that with the duties of treasurer, extending the latter through to 1977. He subsequently served a two-year term as Auckland president.

Ted Knowling in 1936.
Auckland City Libraries

The equally hard-working Stonex contented himself with staying at provincial level after first being elected to the new Auckland junior control board. His more than twenty-year association with that body culminated with eight years as its chairman through to 1953.

'In his years with the Board he has shown a selfless devotion to the game that has been an inspiration to all who have worked with him,' said the *League News* of 10 October 1953. 'He has been particularly active as chairman and has played a major part in the post-war development of junior football.'

Speculation that he would retain his interest in the game by taking on something less onerous proved to be unfounded. Stonex became a club delegate on the senior control board, also served as chairman of the officers' association, and in 1964 succeeded Ken Gillam as Auckland Rugby League chairman.

During his time in office he was also ground superintendent at Carlaw Park, working hard to improve the condition of the playing field. Stonex was made an Auckland life member in 1959 and a New Zealand life member on his retirement from office in 1972, the latter fittingly being presented by his alleged 'street pal' of forty years earlier, Ted Knowling.

Ivan Stonex in 1969.
Fairfax Media

Groundhog day

Wellington's representatives in the late 1960s must have suffered from repetitive nightmare syndrome. The Rothmans tournament was changed to a provincial competition in 1965, and in each of the first four seasons a much-improved Wellington side fought its way through to the final, only to be decisively beaten

CHAPTER SEVEN

by Auckland. Fielding star-studded teams, Auckland was held scoreless for long periods in the first and last of those encounters, but only while it wore down Wellington's resistance and loaded up its attacking ammunition. Forwards Victor Yates (1966) and Ernie Wiggs (1967) kicked eight goals in finals, while scrum-half Eric Carson ran in two tries in 1967 and three in 1968. Results were:

1965: Auckland 11 (Tony Kriletich two, Pat Hanna tries; Ernie Wiggs goal) beat Wellington 4 (Finlay Rasmussen, Neil Beri goals).

1966: Auckland 37 (Lester Mills two, Len Morgan two, Billy Harford, Paul Schultz, Victor Yates tries; Yates eight goals) beat Wellington 21 (Gary Smith, John Lafrentz, Barry Drake tries; Neil Beri four, Pat Hanna two goals).

1967: Auckland 39 (Eric Carson two, Phillip Rowe, Victor Yates, Paul Schultz, Bill Schultz, Bing Gascoigne tries; Ernie Wiggs eight goals; Doug Ellwood field goal) beat Wellington 13 (Ron Wood try; Tuhoea Wātene five goals).

1968: Auckland 28 (Eric Carson three, Robert Orchard, Kerry Dines, Tony Kriletich tries; Doug Ellwood five goals) beat Wellington 4 (Peter Simmons two goals).

Auckland loose forward Ray Sinel has the Wellington defence stretched during the 1968 provincial final.
NZRL Year Book 1969

Boys from the bush

New South Wales Country sent three teams to New Zealand between 1965 and 1968 as part of its preparations for the annual City v Country games. In an era when Kangaroos and Kiwis were regularly chosen from the country groups and the provinces, respectively, the short tours aided the national selectors of both countries.

Hooker Alan Buman, second-rower Barry Beath and loose forward Terry Pannowitz used the 1965 Country visit to earn a second trip to New Zealand as members of the Australian team later in the season. Captain and scrum-half Arthur Summons, prop Ron Crowe and stand-off Earl Harrison had already been Kangaroos and second-rower Barry Beath made it in 1967. But after beating Canterbury 32–10, a morning flight and a resilient Auckland team proved too much at Carlaw Park next day. Auckland won 18–5 through tries to Brian Reidy and Bill Snowden and six goals from Jack Fagan.

A year later Country, including Buman and Pannowitz plus future internationals in second-rower Allan Thomson, wing Les Hanigan and stand-off Gary Banks, returned with similar results. The tourists beat Northland 13–0 and Canterbury 21–12 but again fell to Auckland, 23–2. Wing Bob Mincham scored three tries, Roger Bailey and Roger Tait one each, and there were goals from Ernie Wiggs (three) and Tait.

The opposition changed in 1968, and Country's results worsened. Despite the presence of international forwards Buman, Crowe, Thomson, Pannowitz and Ron Costello, Country lost to Southern Zone 12–10, Northern Zone 13–5 and New Zealand Māori 18–12.

1965: Kangaroos too strong

Australia 18 Auckland 2

Stung by the concession of a freak try to Kiwis centre Roger Bailey in the second test, which meant they had to settle for a tied two-match series, the 1965 Kangaroos struck back to decisively beat Auckland 18–2 two days later. Tour manager Arnold Stehr told the *New Zealand Herald* it was being treated as a third test, and Australia would be fielding a side to suit such an occasion. Meanwhile Auckland was weakened by the withdrawals of Kiwis Bill Snowden, Roger Bailey, Paul Schultz, Don Hammond and Ray Sinel.

Auckland had opted for a big pack of forwards, including massive props Roy Roberts and Albie Wiggs. Kiwis front-rower Eddie Moore was slotted into the second-row, and Ernie Wiggs dropped back to loose forward. Only Moore had played in the tests, and it was expected the Auckland forwards would be fresh for the occasion.

CHAPTER SEVEN

But the *Herald* next day reported the Auckland forwards were outclassed. Not for most of the first half, though, as the rival packs slugged it out before Australia managed a 7–2 halftime lead. The *Herald* might have been more forgiving if it had considered the casualties suffered by the home side. Moore had his nose broken and was replaced by loose forward Tony Kriletich at halftime, and Ernie Wiggs suffered a severe head gash in a collision with his brother that left Auckland down to five forwards for the last twenty-four minutes.

It was a tough game for both teams. Giant Kangaroos prop Lloyd Weier needed stitches in a deeply cut chin, and opposing scrum-halves Johnny Gleeson (Australia) and Billy Harford (Auckland) were knocked unconscious. The *Herald* accused Australian forward Brian Hambly of delivering the knockout blow to Harford, who 'recovered after receiving medical attention for a few minutes and

Jack Fagan, the Auckland and Kiwis fullback, practising his goalkicking under the eye of Kiwis coach Maurie Robertson.
NZ Herald

played a courageous game'. That incident sparked rugged exchanges, but football took over from fouling in the second spell. Kangaroos wing Mick Cleary was named by *The Press* as the culprit when Moore's nose was broken.

Graham Mattson was singled out by the *Herald* as Auckland's outstanding forward, with Ernie Wiggs next best until his premature departure. 'In the backs it was the powerfully built Otahuhu wing Christian who stood out. He simply burst past the opposition with his crashing runs and left his opposite, Cleary, standing dazed with his beautifully executed runs.'

According to the *Auckland Star*, Gary Bailey tackled well against the dangerous Graeme Langlands, and Reg Cooke and Doug Ellwood played solid all-round games. Jack Fagan's penalty goal was Auckland's only reply to Australia's four tries and three goals.

Auckland team: fullback, Jack Fagan; three-quarters, Roy Christian, Gary Bailey, Reg Cooke, Brian Campbell; halves, Doug Ellwood, Billy Harford; forwards, Roy Roberts, Len Morgan, Albie Wiggs, Eddie Moore (replaced by Tony Kriletich), Graham Mattson, Ernie Wiggs.

Tough at the top

Marist enjoyed its best season for nearly two decades by winning the Fox Memorial and sharing the Stormont Shield in a 15–15 draw with Otahuhu in 1965. It went even better the next year, conceding the Rukutai Shield to Otahuhu but winning the Fox Memorial, Roope Rooster and Stormont Shield. Coached by former Kiwis wing Neville Denton, Marist was captained by Auckland scrum-half Billy Harford in 1965 and Kiwis wing Brian Reidy in 1966. Kiwis Reidy, Oscar Danielson, Tony Kriletich and brothers Bill and Paul Schultz featured strongly in both seasons, and Sam Edwards joined them in 1966.

Competition was tough, however. In 1967, and despite the off-season losses of Kiwis Jack Fagan, Bill Snowden (both retired) and Gary Bailey (in Australia), Ponsonby claimed all the major trophies except the Roope Rooster. The squad boasted such notables as current Kiwis Roger Bailey and Rick Carey, former Kiwi Ken McCracken, future internationals Mike McClennan, Don Mann and Brian Tracey, and former All Black Victor Yates. The coach was former Kiwis utility Ian Grey. But Ponsonby's reign lasted just one year before Mount Albert triumphed in the 1968 and 1969 Fox Memorials, and Ellerslie, Otahuhu, Ponsonby and Richmond shared around the other three major trophies in those two seasons.

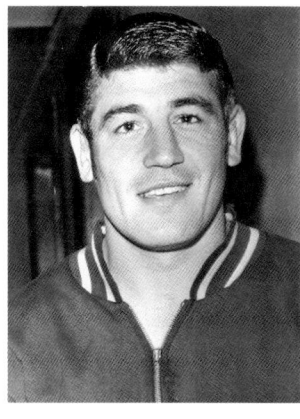

Tony Kriletich.
Christchurch Star

Bill Snowden.
Fairfax Media

CHAPTER SEVEN

Ken McCracken, drawing and passing for Ponsonby.
NZ Herald

Hookers collide as Auckland's Bill Schultz tackles Britain's Colin Clarke as Victor Yates and Roger Tait move in at right.
NZRL Year Book 1967

1966: Last minute loss

Great Britain 12 Auckland 11

The 1966 Great Britain Lions saved their unbeaten eight-match record in New Zealand at the last gasp when fullback Arthur Keegan kicked a penalty goal for a 12–11 victory over Auckland on a firm Carlaw Park. The penalty was awarded by local referee Alan Taylor after British wing Berwyn Jones was obstructed by Auckland fullback Roger Tait after chipping ahead. The penalty was given where the ball landed, twenty-five yards from the goal-line and wide out. Keegan showed no nerves and was on target.

It was the only time on tour that any side had got within range of the tourists. Their next closest victory was by 22–14 in the second test match played two days earlier, when Auckland forward Ernie Wiggs kicked seven penalty goals to provide all of New Zealand's points. Auckland selectors Des Barchard, Bruce Robertson and Gary Phillips left Wiggs out of their team, preferring fresh forwards. Indeed, the only second-test Kiwis called up were fullback Brian Reidy and centre Roy Christian, who were slotted onto the Auckland wings. Injured test centre Roger Bailey was replaced by his brother, Gary.

'The tourists led 5–2 at halftime and 10–4 seven minutes after halftime, but a clever try by Auckland, when [Paul] Schultz and [Bruce] Castle combined, changed the whole complexion of the game,' reported the *New Zealand Herald*. 'There was still 30 minutes of play left at this stage and the game became torrid. A midfield brawl broke out after Castle had scored and it took some minutes to separate fighting players. Auckland could not take their attempt at conversion until the brawl had been ended.

'Great Britain kept play in their forwards for the remainder of the second half and found it hard to penetrate the Auckland defence. However, they later appeared assured of the try when Jones was obstructed and would have been unlucky to have lost on the run of play.'

'Castle led the Auckland team by example and his try was a just reward for splendid backing up and solid tackling,' said the *Auckland Star*. 'Doug Ellwood, like Castle, was close to all the action. Victor Yates and Eddie Moore made some barging runs down the middle and both worked hard on defence.' Auckland's other points resulted from three goals by Yates and one by Ellwood.

Auckland team: fullback, Roger Tait; three-quarters, Brian Reidy, Gary Bailey, Lester Mills, Roy Christian; halves, Doug Ellwood, Paul Schultz; forwards, Roy Roberts, Bill Schultz, Oscar Danielson, Eddie Moore, Victor Yates, Bruce Castle (captain).

Bruce Castle, Auckland captain against Great Britain. *NZRL Year Book 1967*

CHAPTER SEVEN

University returns

University returned to the Auckland inter-club scene in 1967 when a sixth-grade side was coached by former Kiwis captain Bill Snowden. Granted senior status in 1968, University blossomed under the coaching of another international, Jack Fagan. In its third season it fielded senior, reserve, third- and sixth-grade teams, before relegation from senior A to senior B in 1972 led to some talented players moving on. The senior B squad performed with credit under the coaching of Jack Wright through to 1976, but from 1977 to 1980 only a sixth-grade team survived.

Having several school teachers in its ranks encouraged University to establish an annual secondary schools tournament in the early 1970s. The event was funded by the Auckland Rugby League and was well supported by the referees association. Although University has not featured in inter-club competitions since 1980, an Auckland team has always competed in the annual New Zealand Universities winter tournament. Players who went on to become Kiwis include Kevin Barry, Chris Jordan, and Iva and Tea Ropati.

Backward step

Kiwis officials caused a shock by naming Auckland forwards Ernie Wiggs at wing and Ray Sinel in the centres for the 1968 World Cup tournament, held in Australia and New Zealand. They had signalled the move by playing them in those roles in lead-up trials, obviously eager to utilise Wiggs' kicking prowess and Sinel's size and mobility. But the experiments were not successful. Sinel played centre in the opening match against France before reverting to the second-row against Great Britain. Wiggs played on the wing in all three games, kicking five goals against France (lost 15–10), three against Australia (31–12) and four against Great Britain (38–14) for twenty-four of his team's thirty-six points. Auckland centre Paul Schultz scored three of the Kiwis' four tries in what was a disappointing campaign.

Cup goes west

Although Auckland dominated the Rothmans championship, it made the tactical error of taking the Northern Union Cup down to Greymouth's Wingham Park during the 1968 World Cup tournament when ten of the nineteen Kiwis were Aucklanders.

However, with quality players such as captain Roger Bailey, Mike McClennan, Dennis Key, Ken McCracken, John Sparnon, Gary Woollard, Victor Yates and future

Kiwis forwards Bill Burgoyne, Doug Gailey and Ray Williams available, Auckland was confident of keeping the cup. But the *Greymouth Evening Star* reported West Coast 'tackled hard and treated the ball like a gold nugget' to win 16–3 in heavy conditions. Down by ten points at halftime, Auckland's only reply was a Key try.

The next day, Queen's Birthday Monday, Auckland beat Canterbury 29–15 in Christchurch, having led 23–0 at one stage. Key claimed two more tries but only one of Auckland's seven tries was converted – by front-rower Albie Wiggs. Auckland did not see the cup (by then renamed the Rugby League Cup) again until 1986 as Canterbury, West Coast, Wellington, Waikato and Taranaki took turns, most more than once, at having possession of the symbol of inter-provincial supremacy.

Centre Ray Wilson scores for Auckland against Canterbury at Christchurch.
Christchurch Star

Souths the champs

South Sydney rightfully proclaimed itself Australasian club champion in 1968. Having beaten Manly-Warringah 13–9 in the Sydney grand final, the Rabbitohs crossed the Tasman for an unbeaten three-match visit to Auckland. The victims were Auckland champion Mount Albert by a convincing 27–13, Ponsonby 31–3 and Auckland Māori 33–14. Upon returning home, Souths accepted a challenge from Brisbane title-winner Brothers, and promptly annihilated the northern upstart by 55–15. Bob McCarthy, the rampaging second-rower, scored eight tries in the four games at Auckland and Brisbane and Aboriginal fullback and goalkicker Eric Simms totalled fifty-one points. The *1969 New Zealand Rugby League Annual* advocated the introduction of an annual Australasian club championship, with top teams from other provinces being invited to challenge Auckland's best to take on the Sydney and Brisbane winners.

Ponsonby fullback Mike McClennan has Roger Bailey in support as he attempts to fend off South Sydney's Paul Sait.
NZ Herald

CHAPTER SEVEN

Mincham's five-try feast

Auckland won a fifth consecutive Rothmans title in 1969 when it beat first-time finalist Canterbury 48–16 at Carlaw Park, after the visitors had surprisingly led 14–13 at halftime. Such was Auckland's increasing dominance that the *Christchurch Star* questioned the value of staging competitions between Auckland and other individual provinces. (Years later there were to be formats such as the inter-districts, which combined several provinces against Auckland, or franchises, which split Auckland into various regions.) Len Morgan won the hooking duel 23–9 against Kiwis utility forward Bill Noonan. Props Oscar Danielson and Henry Tatana blasted holes in a weakening Canterbury defence for their loose forwards and backs to prosper. Wing Bob Mincham was the major beneficiary with all three of Auckland's first-half tries and two more in the second. Captain Roger Bailey contented himself with a couple. Ernie Wiggs, Paul Schultz and the entire front-row of Morgan, Tatana and Danielson got one try apiece and Wiggs kicked six goals.

Bob Mincham takes to the air to score one of his five tries against Canterbury in 1969.
NZ Herald

1969: Referee, and Kangaroos, crash

Auckland 15 Australia 14

Carlaw Park was the stage for many dramatic scenes, but few topped the later stages of Auckland's 15–14 defeat of Australia in 1969. Kangaroos forward John Wittenberg (who fractured a cheekbone when tackling John Sparnon) and Wellington referee Earle Pilcher (knocked unconscious in a collision with an Australian player) were both carried off by stretcher between the seventieth and seventy-third minutes. As Pilcher lay prone, Auckland scored what would have been a match-clinching try, but there was no-one to award it!

Only the previous weekend the Kiwis had achieved a sensational 18–14 second test victory to tie the two-match series. Bay of Plenty wing Phillip Orchard's try-scoring run down the grandstand touchline provided an indelible memory for the ecstatic fans who cheered his every powerful stride. The tour-ending Auckland encounter, which was Australia's sixth game in fourteen days, did not reach the same heights but the closeness of the scores and the mishaps to Wittenberg and referee Pilcher when Auckland led 13–9 made it memorable.

Pilcher had crashed to the ground after colliding with Australian forward Col Weiss, who was in pursuit of Auckland prop Doug Gailey. Weiss told reporters he accidentally struck Pilcher with his right shoulder, but other players thought the referee was also knocked into the path of Auckland forward Eddie Moore. As Pilcher lay prone just inside Australian territory on the grandstand side several of the Auckland players, unaware of what had happened, were celebrating fullback John Young's 'try' at the Stanley Street end. The other players stood in a stunned group around the fallen referee.

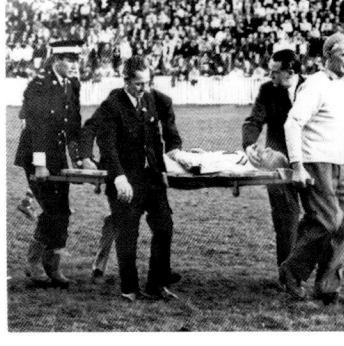

Referee Earle Pilcher carried unconscious from the field after being knocked out in Auckland's game with Australia. Holding his jaw is New Zealand Rugby League president Dr Leo Cooney.
Christchurch Star

Jubilant Auckland stand-off Gary Woollard (right) looks in vain for referee Earle Pilcher to award a try to fullback John Young, who is being helped up by hooker Bill Burgoyne. Australian centre Father John Cootes holds the ball and Auckland forward Tony Kriletich stands next to the upright.
NZRL Year Book 1970

CHAPTER SEVEN

Ernie Wiggs kicks one of his six goals against the 1969 Kangaroos. Referee Earle Pilcher looks on.

Fairfax Media

The hectic last seven minutes were controlled by touch judge Ron Caddy. Within seconds of accepting the whistle Caddy awarded Auckland the penalty from which Ernie Wiggs kicked a forty-yard goal for a 15–9 advantage. Australia replied immediately with a converted try to advance within one point. That was as close as it got, though a desperate field goal attempt by Bob McCarthy seemed on target until the ball cannoned into the face of an Auckland forward.

Earlier in the game Pilcher had allowed Wiggs a second chance at a penalty goal when he spotted one of the Australians moving as the first kick was taken. Both attempts missed, but Wiggs' kicking prowess still had much to do with the outcome. His five penalty goals and conversion of Eric Carson's try were just enough to head off Australian tries to John Cootes and Dennis Manteit, Cootes' penalty and conversion, and Dennis Ward's two field goals.

'The high spot for Auckland was the try scored by scrum-half Carson, after he had moved inside Moore, the second-row forward, who had made a dashing break,' reported the *New Zealand Herald*. Forwards Moore, Wiggs and Ray Sinel earned praise in the *Auckland Star* – "All three hurt the Australians when they ran, often pulling in two men for the tackle.' The *Herald* writer expressed some sympathy for the Australians, who had players 'not really in shape for such hard opposition' and 'seemed unlucky not to be awarded a try' by Pilcher, who ruled McCarthy's pass to Ron Costello was forward.

Auckland team: fullback, John Young; three-quarters, John Sparnon, Roy Christian, Paul Schultz, Mike McClennan; halves, Gary Woollard, Eric Carson; forwards, Doug Gailey, Bill Burgoyne, Victor Yates (replaced by Tony Kriletich), Eddie Moore, Ernie Wiggs, Ray Sinel.

Referee's neck was broken

Referee Earle Pilcher, who now lives in Christchurch, has revealed that the injury he suffered at Carlaw Park in 1969 was far worse than originally diagnosed. In company with Australian forward John Wittenberg, he was taken by ambulance to Auckland Hospital. After four days of diagnosis and treatment he was released, returned to Wellington and resumed his job of driving buses for New Zealand Railways Road Services.

But three months later he felt an alarming 'jolt' in his neck as he was driving his car home from work, and another when playing with his young daughter. Pilcher consulted his doctor and then a specialist, who sent him to Wellington Hospital, where he waited another week for the necessary equipment to be repaired. Only then was it discovered that Pilcher had suffered a compound fracture of his neck. He belatedly underwent a bone graft and was restored to full fitness. He spent ten weeks in hospital and was grateful to the New Zealand Rugby League for paying his wages over that period.

Pilcher led a full rugby league life as work promotion transfers took him from Wellington, where he guided the Wainuiomata club out of recess, to Greymouth, and more refereeing, then Dunedin, where he was president of the Otago Rugby League, and on to Christchurch in 1986. He controlled other international matches, including South Island's victory over the 1980 Australians, and retired from refereeing in 1987. His last game was between Randwick, the club he had played for, and a Kiwis XIII.

Despite being knocked out, Pilcher has a clear recollection of the 1969 incident. He is adamant Weiss was the only player who struck him, sure he did not take any backward steps that might have brought them onto a collision course, and certain he was not propelled into the path of any Auckland player. Pilcher said Weiss 'took exception' when he penalised him for not packing properly into a scrum a few minutes earlier. When Weiss returned to Wellington with the 1972 Queensland team Pilcher telephoned him and they 'had a discussion'. Pilcher would not comment on whether he thought the incident was an accident.

When Raper played for Auckland

An Auckland team, reinforced by Kangaroos loose forward legend Johnny Raper and dual Australian rugby internationals Phil Hawthorne and Dick Thornett, beat the triumphant Kiwis second test team 18–10 in late September 1969 in a special fixture to mark the New Zealand Rugby League's diamond jubilee. While it was a festive occasion, the match was played in all seriousness on a hard and fast Carlaw Park.

'This game might be remembered as Johnny Raper's match, so profound was his influence on many phases of the play,' said the *New Zealand Herald*. 'It was his first appearance at Carlaw Park and even though he is now 30, many of the 12,000 who were there yesterday will hope that more will be seen of his wonderful talents on the same ground. It must not be thought that the Auckland victory was a one-man show, for all, including the two other Australians, Thornett [second-row] and Hawthorne [stand-off half], played a noble part in the victory.'

History was served when Ernie Asher, whose association with the game extended back to the 1908 and 1909 Māori tours to Australia and New Zealand's first home test match in 1910, carried out the ceremonial kick-off. Auckland handled better than the Kiwis, proving correct pre-match concerns that the southern members of the New Zealand squad had been out of football for some weeks.

From the start, Auckland set the pace with Ernie Wiggs kicking two penalty goals and Hawthorne landing a field goal. As halftime neared, the Kiwis clicked into gear and slippery scrum-half Graeme Cooksley crossed for the first try. A Don Ladner penalty goal cut Auckland's lead to 6–5 early in the second spell, before Auckland made its winning break through a Wiggs penalty, tries to Bob Mincham

CHAPTER SEVEN

and Thornett, and two Wiggs conversions. The Kiwis made the final score more respectable via a Brian Clark try and Ladner penalty.

'Apart from Raper, heroes in the Auckland team were Liles, a daring running fullback, Carson, an enterprising scrum-half, Wiggs, Dick at prop, and Morgan, who only went down by one scrum to the Kiwi captain, O'Neil,' said the *Herald*. Dick played at prop after Thornett stated his preference for the second-row. In a late forward reshuffle, Dick came into the front-row and second-rower Ray Sinel was shunted to the reserves.

Auckland team: fullback, Bland Liles; three-quarters, Bob Mincham, Roger Bailey (captain), Paul Schultz, Mike McClennan; halves, Phil Hawthorne (Australia), Eric Carson; forwards, Henry Tatana, Len Morgan, Gary Dick, Dick Thornett (Australia), Ernie Wiggs, Johnny Raper (Australia).

New Zealand: fullback, Don Ladner (West Coast); three-quarters, Phillip Orchard (Bay of Plenty), Roy Christian (Auckland), Brian Clark (Auckland), Mocky Brereton (West Coast); halves, Gary Woollard (Auckland), Graeme Cooksley (Canterbury); forwards, Oscar Danielson (Auckland), Colin O'Neil (Wellington, captain), Doug Gailey (Auckland), Bill Deacon (Waikato), Bill Noonan (Canterbury), Tony Kriletich (Auckland).

Dick Thornett, wearing his borrowed boots, in rampaging form for Auckland against New Zealand.
NZRL Year Book 1970

'Boot-less' Dick Thornett

Auckland coach Don Hammond recalled that big Dick Thornett caused a stir before playing against New Zealand. The Australian forward left his saturated football boots in the boiler room at Carlaw Park to dry after training, only to find them shrivelled and useless on match day. Because Thornett could fit into nothing less than a size thirteen, his situation would normally have been serious. But former Kiwis forward Ray Cranch worked in the footwear industry and came to the rescue with a new pair of boots. Thornett was a multi-skilled sportsman in a talented sporting family. Dick represented Australia at both rugby codes and in water polo at the 1960 Rome Olympics. One brother, John, captained the Wallabies, and another, Ken, played fullback for the Kangaroos.

CHAPTER 08

AUCKLAND'S GRAND SLAM
1970–1979

CHAPTER EIGHT

Auckland's Grand Slam 1970–1979

1970: Magical Millward
Great Britain 23 Auckland 8

Roger Millward was too quick for Auckland forward Brian Lee when scoring his third try.
Fairfax Media

Stand-off half Fred Schuster enjoyed a golden year in 1970, playing for Auckland and New Zealand against Great Britain.
Christchurch Star

Dramatic changes took place during the 1970s. Floodlights were installed at Carlaw Park in 1975, enabling the scheduling of night matches against overseas teams. Traditional Kiwis tours largely took a back seat to world tournaments, which brought more international sides to play Auckland. Australia, Great Britain and France were all beaten twice within the decade, including an incredible triple grand slam in June 1977. Closer ties developed with Australia. The player drain across the Tasman began as a trickle, and the midweek Amco Cup was Auckland's first foray into an Australian professional competition.

First though, Auckland was the last side to be given a lesson in excellence from the 1970 Lions. Captained by Frank Myler, this was undoubtedly one of the greatest of all touring teams. It lost only once in Australia, in the first test match, and was seldom extended on a seven-match visit to New Zealand. The three games against the Kiwis were won by ever-increasing margins, and a side comprised mostly of non-test players comfortably accounted for Auckland 23–8 on the Monday afternoon after the third test.

Kiwis centre Roger Bailey was to have captained Auckland, but the leadership passed to loose forward Tony Kriletich when Bailey withdrew. Local referee Alan Taylor was severely criticised by British management after Auckland benefited from a lopsided twenty-five to seven penalty count. Its only points came from four penalty goals kicked by Ernie Wiggs, while the Lions made reasonably light work of the difficult conditions to score five tries. Three of them went to brilliant young stand-off half, Roger Millward, one of the stars of the tour.

'Twenty-six mud-covered figures skated, slipped and slogged away at Carlaw Park,' reported the *New Zealand Herald*. 'Even in the conditions of yesterday, when the rain of the previous twelve hours turned the ground into a soggy strip, the visitors tried to play the bright open game of the hard surface. It was a tribute to their perseverance that they were able to touch down five times.' Britain led

15–4 at the break, and even Millward and classy three-quarters Alan Hardisty, Syd Hynes and John Atkinson struggled to handle the ball in the second spell. Wiggs place-kicked the ball for touch to achieve more control and accuracy.

'The catching of the Auckland fullback McClennan was bravely done,' said the *Herald*. 'Carson was a lively figure behind the scrum, and the young centres, Redmond and Matete, were keen to chance their arm. The kicks ahead by the forwards, Moore and Morgan, were upsetting for the tourists in the early minutes. Kriletich led his scrum by example rather than word and Wiggs, the power of his boot later reduced to impotence, still had a good game.'

Auckland team: fullback, Mike McClennan; three-quarters, Roy Christian, Wayne Redmond, Paul Matete, John Dagg; halves, Fred Schuster, Eric Carson; forwards, Eddie Moore, Len Morgan, Brian Lee, Ray Williams, Ernie Wiggs, Tony Kriletich (captain).

Walloped by Waikato

Less than two weeks after losing to Great Britain, Auckland suffered a 36–11 semi-final hiding from Waikato at Huntly to abruptly end its five-year reign as national Rothmans champion. Even more remarkable was Waikato's scoring breakdown, with only four tries in its total. The other twenty-four points came from goals by Don Parkinson (ten) and Bill Deacon (two). Wellington referee Jim Campbell also ordered off Auckland captain Roger Bailey. The Rothmans title actually went to Wellington, which beat Waikato 27–21 in the final. Earlier in the season an Auckland B side had downed Waikato 19–11 at Carlaw Park while the A team was away winning against Wellington (30–8) and Canterbury (42–17). The *1971 New Zealand Rugby League Annual* placed Auckland first and Waikato second in its provincial rankings.

Roger Bailey receives his marching orders from referee Jim Campbell at Huntly.
NZRL Annual 1971

Liles led the way

Scores of young Auckland players now stream across the Tasman every year seeking fame and fortune in Australia. But for many years international transfer bans prevented such movement. From the 1960s, experienced Kiwis, such as Aucklanders Ron Ackland, Reg Cooke, Oscar Danielson, Doug Ellwood, Henry Maxwell, Rex Percy, Jim Riddell and Bill Sorensen, qualified for clearances to play and coach in the Australian country districts. In the early 1970s the Sydney clubs became more active in signing New Zealanders, and the player drain had begun.

Bland Liles, the Auckland fullback in the 1969 end-of-season festival game against the New Zealand second test side, never wore the blue and white jersey

CHAPTER EIGHT

Bland Liles in his only appearance for Auckland before joining Parramatta.
NZRL Year Book 1970

Mike McClennan, Auckland's fullback, runs the ball back after an Australian clearing kick. Tony Kriletich provides back-up.
Fairfax Media

again. Parramatta signed him during the off-season, and over the next three years he played sixteen first-grade games for the Eels, scoring three tries, twenty-nine goals and one field goal. Where Liles went, others were to tread in increasing numbers.

By 1972, Otahuhu prop Brian Anderson was playing for North Sydney. Anderson was ruled out of the 1970 New Zealand World Cup team because of a knee injury and never played for his country. Instead, he made forty appearances for the Bears and was joined at North Sydney in 1973 by rangy loose forward Eddie Heatley. Another Otahuhu product, Heatley had ironically replaced Anderson at the 1970 World Cup and played in the thrilling test victory over Australia at Carlaw Park in 1971 before injury cost him a tour to Britain and France later that year. Heatley made twenty-seven appearances for Norths.

Centre Bernie Lowther and prop Henry Tatana, both stand-out performers with the 1971 grand slam Kiwis, were contracted by Canterbury-Bankstown soon after their return from Britain and France. Lowther played ninety-eight first grade fixtures for the Bulldogs and South Sydney before moving to Brisbane. Tatana totalled ninety-five matches for the Bulldogs and St George and was later captain-coach and president of the Cessnock club near Newcastle.

It took some years before the floodgates opened fully – Kiwis forward Kurt Sorensen sat out the 1978 season so he could join elder brother Dane at Cronulla-Sutherland – but in an increasingly professional era it became clear that transfer bans and restrictions would not stand up in court when players or clubs challenged them.

1971: Doing the double

Auckland 15 Australia 14

Auckland completed a double-double when it nudged out Australia on yet another sodden, muddy Carlaw Park day in 1971. The 15–14 scoreline was the same as in 1969, and the victory followed the Kiwis' remarkable 24–3 win in a one-off test match at the same venue three days earlier. Beating the Aussies twice was a perfect prelude to New Zealand's grand slam tour of Britain and France, when test series were won in both countries.

Coach Neville Denton lost test forwards Eddie Heatley and Robert Orchard through injuries but replacements Ray Williams and Don Mann did enough to earn Kiwis tour selection. Gene Woolsey was preferred as hooker, ahead of Bill Burgoyne, to add size to the Auckland pack. Unfortunately for Woolsey, he was the only one of Auckland's starting thirteen not to tour Britain and France. The Auckland backs included seventeen-year-old centre Dennis Williams.

Ellerslie second-rower Murray Eade produced one of the finest games of his career. The *New Zealand Herald* described Eade as the pick of an impressive Auckland forward pack, 'even though Kriletich played not much below his magnificent test form. Eade, who scored two tries, survived a fearful blow in the mouth and continued to play with almost the polish of a McCarthy'. That was high praise, for second-rower Bob McCarthy, along with centre Bob Fulton, was outstanding in the Australian team.

'Tatana can take some of the credit [for the result] again because it was his three conversions that allowed Auckland to get by with three tries [to Australia's

Tony Kriletich, with Ken Stirling looming up in support, against the 1971 Australians.
NZRL Annual 1972

CHAPTER EIGHT

four]. In the forwards he had solid support from the whole pack, including the newcomers Mann, [Ray] Williams and Woolsey, who was almost square in the hooking duel with Fitzsimons.

'Of the Auckland backs, halfback Stirling was once more probably the most valuable player, largely because his cover tackling continued to be almost superhuman. He is an amazing young man. He did not, however, leave all his team-mates far behind because [Dennis] Williams, Lowther and Christian all looked thoroughly at home at this level,' said the *Herald*.

Ray Williams opened the scoring after thirteen minutes, and Eade got his first try fourteen minutes later, both converted by Tatana. Tries to Lionel Williamson and Fulton had Australia back to 10–6 by halftime. Eade's second try was scored soon after the restart for 15–6 and Auckland rode out an Australian storm which led to tries by Bob O'Reilly and Fulton and Ray Branighan's only goal.

Auckland team: fullback, Mike McClennan (replaced by Fred Schuster); three-quarters, Bob McGuinn, Bernie Lowther, Dennis Williams, Roy Christian; halves, Gary Woollard, Ken Stirling; forwards, Henry Tatana, Gene Woolsey, Don Mann, Murray Eade, Tony Kriletich, Ray Williams.

Grand slam Kiwis

Nineteen Auckland players shared in New Zealand's great 1971 grand slam year when Australia was beaten 24–3 at Carlaw Park, the Kiwis won their first test series on British soil since the 1907–08 All Golds, and France was beaten two tests to nil with the other match drawn. Of the nineteen, only Otahuhu backrow forward Eddie Heatley, who suffered a hairline fracture during the Australian test, did not go on the tour.

Those who did tour were: centre, Roy Christian (Otahuhu, captain); loose forward, Tony Kriletich (Marist, vice-captain); backs, Mike McClennan (Mount Wellington), John O'Sullivan (Ponsonby), Bob McGuinn (Otahuhu), Bernie Lowther (Richmond), Dave Sorensen (Otahuhu), Dennis Williams (Te Atatu), Gary Woollard (Mount Albert), Shane Dowsett (Otahuhu) and Ken Stirling (Ellerslie); hooker, Bill Burgoyne (Marist); and forwards Doug Gailey (Ellerslie), Robert Orchard (Ellerslie), Henry Tatana (Mount Albert), Don Mann (Ponsonby), Murray Eade (Ellerslie) and Ray Williams (Richmond)

Christian, Kriletich, Stirling, Orchard and Tatana – along with Canterbury wing Mocky Brereton and Wellington second-rower Garry Smith – played in all seven tests. Dennis Williams provided the single most memorable moment when, a day after his eighteenth birthday, he scored a dazzling try the first time he handled the ball in a test match, against Great Britain at Salford. Dowsett was the unluckiest of the Kiwis, severely damaging his knee soon after arriving in England, undergoing surgery, and displaying immense courage to get back on the field in France.

Auckland prop Henry Tatana crashes into Rest of New Zealand stand-off half Trevor Patrick during the 1971 Kiwis trial. Behind them are John Greengrass (Rest) and Bill Burgoyne.
Fairfax Media

CHAPTER EIGHT

Undisputed champion

Auckland made no race of the 1971 Rothmans championship, comfortably seeing off Waikato 44–9 in a semi-final and Wellington 26–12 in the final. That was the culmination of an unbeaten season which included earlier wins over Waikato 48–5, Rest of New Zealand 33–17, Wellington 60–4, West Coast 37–2, Australia 15–14 and Canterbury 28–15. It was the first of four consecutive Rothmans successes. In 1972 Auckland won the round-robin finals, beating Waikato 20–11 and Wellington 41–13 and drawing 16–16 with Canterbury; in 1973 Auckland beat Wellington 29–13 in the final after previously accounting for Northland 33–2 and Wellington 34–14 and losing to West Coast 14–25; and in 1974 Auckland was unbeaten in the finals against Canterbury 23–0, Wellington 47–12, West Coast 46–0 and Waikato 14–7. There was one totally unexpected loss during that period – by 3–2 to an emerging Taranaki side on a very wet Pukekura Park in New Plymouth in 1972. Auckland returned in 1973 and won 28–17.

Eddie Heatley clears the ball for Auckland against Canterbury at Carlaw Park in 1971.

Fairfax Media

Auckland, the 1973 inter-provincial champion.

Back row: Les Beehre, Bob Jarvis, Tom Conroy, Dave Sorensen, Kevin Barry.

Middle row: Ray Cranch (selector), Ashley McEwen, Wayne Robertson, Lyndsay Proctor, Steve Brewster, Travers Hardwick (selector).

Front row: Neville Denton (selector-coach), Len Hall, Dennis Williams (captain), Des Jenkinson (manager), Murray Eade (vice-captain), Brian Tracey, Stan Turner (masseur).

In front: Warren Collicoat.

Absent: Doug Gailey, Peter Gurnick, John O'Sullivan, Don Mann.

Warren Collicoat collection

CHAPTER EIGHT

Aussie visitors

Auckland and Queensland met again after thirty-seven years at Carlaw Park in 1972. Whereas they had drawn 18–18 in 1925, this time the Queenslanders got home by 18–17. The visitors included notable future coaches Wayne Bennett (wing) and John Lang (hooker) and were captained by Kangaroos loose forward Col Weiss. Auckland needed Warren Collicoat's seven goals to stay in contention, having conceded four tries to one by Dave Sorensen, although it lost Ken Stirling (broken nose and double vision) and Ray Williams (dislocated shoulder) during the game. Auckland recorded mixed results against two more New South Wales Country teams, winning 20–12 in 1970 (tries by Roger Bailey, John Dagg, Eddie Heatley and Bernie Lowther, and four Henry Tatana goals) but losing 21–6 (three Collicoat goals) to the 1974 side which included great Kangaroos centre and goalkicker Mick Cronin. Bailey was talked out of representative retirement against Brisbane in 1974 but his presence could not prevent a 10–4 loss at Carlaw Park.

George Rainey: 'Mr Auckland Rugby League'

One of Ivan George Rainey's death notices in 2003 paid tribute to the assistance he had rendered a club chairman who wrote 'as far as I am concerned you will always be Mr Auckland Rugby League'. Rainey had become Auckland's longest-serving chairman during a term which lasted from 1972 to 1985 and only ended when he began a seven-year stint as president and chairman of the New Zealand Rugby League.

It was more by accident than design that a young George Rainey found rugby league. The first decade of his life was spent at Horeke, a hamlet on the southern side of the Hokianga harbour, and he was not introduced to the game until his family moved to Glen Eden in time for the 1940 season.

During the next eight years Rainey played through the grades with Glenora until, again by chance, he discovered there was more to rugby league than the on-field activities. Having just left Mount Albert Grammar, he went along to his club's annual meeting and left as its newly elected secretary-treasurer. Rainey played on, winning the J S W Dickson Medal as the most sportsmanlike junior player, and playing for Auckland against Waikato at second division level.

But the strong-minded Rainey was destined to attain much more prominence in the boardroom. He managed the first Glenora team to win a major trophy, the Roope Rooster in 1962, helped the club grow into the largest in Auckland, and was suitably surprised when life membership was bestowed upon him by his club-mates.

George Rainey receives his New Zealand Rugby League life membership from Trevor Maxwell, his successor as chairman.
Bernie Wood collection

In 1969 Rainey received a telephone call from Gus Malam, a former Glenora club chairman who was then a member of the Auckland Rugby League board of control, asking him to accept a nomination as vice-chairman. Rainey was elected in a six-sided ballot, and at the beginning of the 1972 season succeeded the retiring Ivan Stonex as chairman. Malam became his deputy. Rainey's greatest achievement was in making Carlaw Park freehold, an investment that should pay dividends forever.

The 'Mr Auckland Rugby League' title was hard-earned. Rainey put his province first and foremost in many contentious issues that pitted Auckland against the rest of the country. During the 1977 World Championship home games, he severely criticised the national selectors, believing that they took too little notice of Auckland's victories over Australia, Great Britain and France.

When Ron McGregor retired as New Zealand Rugby League president and chairman in 1986, Rainey was persuaded to succeed him. To many it was a case of gamekeeper turning poacher, but Rainey argued on behalf of his country at international level as strongly as he had done for his province and, before that, for his club.

Rainey also had a soft spot. The battle over player transfers to overseas clubs hit its peak when Junior Kiwi Tony Kemp went to the Supreme Court to seek a release so he could join the Newcastle Knights on a lucrative contract. The New Zealand Rugby League opposed Kemp's move but Rainey's heart was not in it. He was heard to ask: 'How can we stop a freezing worker from Hawera taking up a deal to earn himself $74,300 a year?'

Rainey was a life member of the Auckland and New Zealand leagues and served on both of their judiciary and appeals committees. He was on the Warriors management board during the club's formative years. Initially Rainey was keen for the Warriors to base themselves at a redeveloped Carlaw Park. When he realised that was not practicable and that the park's days were numbered, he consoled himself by saying, 'It's all part of the cycle of how the game moves forward'.

George Rainey started his own nursery business in 1959 and in 1972 began the first of three terms as president of the New Zealand Nurserymen's (now New Zealand Garden Industry) Association. After more than twenty years on the executive he was made a life member in 1990. He was also a life member of the Friends of the Botanic Gardens.

CHAPTER EIGHT

Otahuhu and Kiwis legend Roy Christian, leading by example for Māori against Pākehā in 1972. Māori won 18–13.
Fairfax Media

Otahuhu the club of the '70s

Although Ponsonby stole the limelight in 1972 and 1973, and Ellerslie (1974), Mount Wellington (1976) and Richmond (1979) also had their names inscribed on the Fox Memorial Shield, there can be no argument that Otahuhu was the top club of the 1970s. The Rovers won five championships, and in 1975 and 1977 made a clean sweep of the Fox Memorial, Rukutai Shield, Roope Rooster and Stormont Shield.

Otahuhu had great leaders in its championship years: coaches such as Simon Yates in 1970 and 1971, Joe Gwynne in 1975 and Graham Lowe in 1977 and 1978, and inspiring captains Eddie Moore, Roy Christian, Shane Dowsett and Mark Graham. Otahuhu methods also worked overseas. In 1980 Lowe coached and Graham and prop Stan Napa starred in the Norths team which won the Brisbane club premiership.

Fourteen Otahuhu players represented New Zealand in the 1970s: Christian, Dowsett, Graham, Bob McGuinn, Eddie Heatley, Dave Sorensen, Paul Matete, Peter Gurnick, Bob Jarvis, Murray Wright, John Wright, Nick Wright, Glenn Taylor and Gary Prohm. Injury prevented prop Brian Anderson from being the fifteenth.

So dominant was Otahuhu that the *1979 New Zealand Rugby League Annual* advocated a return to district football because Otahuhu was 'making a mockery

Otahuhu coach Joe Gwynne and captain Shane Dowsett with the Stormont Shield in 1975.
NZRL Museum

of the club competition structure'. It pointed out that Graham, Prohm, Taylor, Nick Wright and John Wright toured Australia with the 1978 Kiwis, Roger Rota, Terry Whittle, Ken Andersson, William Tonga-Tama, Neville White and Owen Wright played for Auckland, Dowsett was a former Kiwi, and Bob Ofsoski and Napa had previously represented Auckland. To top it off, Otahuhu beat Sydney club Cronulla-Sutherland 8–2 in a late-season attraction at Carlaw Park.

Ironically, it took an Otahuhu man to beat Otahuhu. Gwynne switched his coaching talents to Richmond in 1979 and led the blue and maroons to their first Fox Memorial title since 1956. Otahuhu retained the Rukutai Shield for a third year, but Richmond beat it in the Fox final 16–15 and later accounted for Roope Rooster winner Manukau in the champion of champions.

These ponies were thoroughbreds

Ponsonby won three of the four major trophies in 1972 (Ellerslie took the Rukutai Shield) and 1973 (Mount Wellington claimed its first Roope Rooster), but the highlight of its two-year reign was a sensational 27–21 victory over Sydney club Cronulla-Sutherland at Carlaw Park on 30 September 1973. It has been hailed as the greatest club match seen at the park.

Ponsonby's favourite son, Roger Bailey.
Fairfax Media

Much of the pre-match publicity for the Four Roses $1,000 match centred around two men who had already fashioned long and distinguished careers, Ponies centre Roger Bailey and Cronulla's English scrum-half Tommy Bishop. And, almost inevitably, it was Bailey who dominated the headlines the next day. By then Bailey had been off the international scene for three years, but he had a legion of followers in Auckland and was a promoter's dream.

Bailey was accidentally kicked in the head as he scored Ponsonby's first try and later had little memory of a frantic match which thrilled 15,000 fans. He rejected medical advice not to return after halftime and, as the *Auckland Star* reported, Bailey 'played strictly by instinct, but a groggy Bailey is still a far better centre than most with two clear eyes and steady feet'. In fairy-tale fashion, Bailey also scored Ponsonby's last try, racing onto a deft pass from prop Don Mann.

After the Cronulla–Sutherland battle. Famed coach Bill Telford congratulates Roger Bailey and John O'Sullivan in the Ponsonby dressing room.
Fairfax Media

John O'Sullivan scored the second try from a passing rush and Wayne Robertson, brushing aside tacklers with contemptuous ease, laid on a try for Don Rota. Brian Tracey kicked a conversion and two penalty goals, and Ponsonby was up 15–2 at halftime. Wing Tom Hill scored soon after the break and two more Tracey penalties spurted Ponsonby ahead by 22–2. But Cronulla launched a rousing comeback, which produced tries for Fred Dennehy (two), Bob Wear and Peter O'Brien to trail by just 22–18.

With the game seemingly sliding out of Ponsonby's reach, Bailey, playing almost by instinct, sent the crowd into an uproar. With typically brilliant anticipation,

CHAPTER EIGHT

he dashed into the line to take Mann's pass twenty metres out and score the try which sank the Sharks. Tracey converted, and Cronulla's late try could only reduce the margin to six points.

There were other outstanding displays from second-rower Robertson, who was the *Star*'s choice as man of the match, props Mann and Joe Cowan, the tough-tackling Tom Conroy and Don Rota, and hooker Warren Satherley. An early hit by Mann on Bishop's former Great Britain test team-mate, prop Cliff Watson, set the standard for a day of tough tackling. Cronulla's backs were also subdued by an uncompromising Ponsonby defence led by Bailey, O'Sullivan and Hill.

Junior tourists

In 1973 the Auckland Rugby League supported the efforts of junior board chairman Sel Bennett to send an under-twenty-three side on a three-match tour of New South Wales. Officials resisted the temptation to include premier grade players and ensure better results and were satisfied with what was achieved. The *1974 New Zealand Rugby League Annual* accurately predicted the benefits would become evident in future years. Among the players were future Kiwis Dane O'Hara, John Smith and John Wright, and budding coach Stan Martin. The juniors lost to Cronulla-Sutherland 20–8 at Endeavour Oval, beat an Australian Aboriginal side 23–5 in an electrical storm under the Redfern Oval lights, and lost to Australian Capital Territory 14–11 in a night game at Queanbeyan. Three more tours were held at two-yearly intervals, the 1975 under-twenty-one team featuring Graham Lowe in his first representative coaching role and future Kiwis Owen Wright and Glenn Taylor. Another under-twenty-one side toured in 1977, and the under-nineteens crossed the Tasman in 1979.

Inter-city clash

Brisbane City beat Auckland 10–4 in a penalty-ridden clash at Carlaw Park in May 1974. Frustrated referee Dave Sargeant blew thirty-five penalties, twenty-seven of them to Auckland and mostly against Brisbane prop and captain Greg Veivers for boring in on Auckland hooker Tom Conroy or stealing the loose head from Tony Kriletich. 'What could you do short of sending the whole Brisbane front-row off?' asked Sargeant in the *Auckland Star*. Auckland was hit by the late withdrawals of Ken Stirling and Murray Eade, with Stirling's replacement, Shane Dowsett, not being able to train with the side. Captain Roger Bailey did his utmost to spark the home team, but to no avail. The match disappointed a bumper 12,000 crowd. Warren Collicoat's two penalty goals were all Auckland managed in reply to tries by John McCabe and John Grant and two Wayne Stewart goals.

The lights of Leichhardt

Auckland made its Australian Amco Cup midweek knockout debut against country team Western Division in the second round of the 1974 competition. There was widespread disappointment that a seemingly favourable draw should end with a 13–7 defeat on a wet and muddy Sydney night. But those part-time 'Westies' went on to beat professional city rivals Canterbury-Bankstown, Manly-Warringah and, in the final, Penrith to cause one of the greatest upsets in the game's history.

The Amco Cup, with most games played at Balmain's Leichhardt Oval, was an instant hit with television viewers. Auckland, and other New Zealand sides who competed in midweek competitions under various sponsors through to 1985, struggled to make an impact against well-prepared and fully primed sides that were waiting for them to cross the Tasman.

The closest Auckland went towards making a final was in 1975, when it beat Manly on a penalty count-back after they were tied 14–14 at fulltime. Ponsonby wing Colin Andrews was the only non-international in an Auckland line-up that included Dennis Williams as captain, Fred Ah Kuoi and brothers Dane and Kurt Sorensen. Its tries were scored by prop Lyndsay Proctor and scrum-half Kevin Barry, and Warren Collicoat kicked four goals.

Auckland's dream stayed alive when traditionally strong country district Newcastle, in the days before the Knights, was knocked over by 26–16 in a quarter-final. Ken Stirling, Mark Graham and Murray Eade had joined the all-star Auckland combination, which had recently beaten France and Wales at

Murray Eade (right) farewells son Antony before leaving for an Amco Cup match in 1975. Team-mates, from left, are Dennis Williams, Bob Jarvis, John O'Sullivan, Ken Stirling, Lyndsay Proctor and coach Bill Sorensen.

Fairfax Media

CHAPTER EIGHT

home. Collicoat, Graham, Ah Kuoi, Eade, Stirling and John O'Sullivan were try-scorers, and Collicoat kicked another four goals.

But Auckland was eliminated, 23–10, by Eastern Suburbs in a semi-final. Tries to Stirling and replacement Warren Winter and two Collicoat goals were nowhere near enough to beat classy Easts, which went on to win the Amco Cup final 17–7 over Parramatta and, a few months later, thrash St George 38–0 in the Sydney grand final.

In 1976, the Amco Cup was expanded, and Brisbane clubs were among the newcomers. Auckland welcomed that move by running over the top of Redcliffe 30–5 at Lang Park. Fred Ah Kuoi (three), Dave Lepper, Dennis Williams and

Prolific Amco Cup points-scorer Warren Collicoat playing for Mount Albert in the 1973 Roope Rooster final.
NZ Herald

Kurt Sorensen touched down and Joe Karam kicked six goals. But two months later Balmain was too good at 21–8. Lepper and Kurt Sorensen scored again and Bill Sorensen junior kicked the only goal. Balmain went on to win the final over North Sydney.

Two New Zealand entrants were invited in 1977, only for Northern Division to beat Auckland 23–2 and Brisbane Souths to knock out Canterbury 20–12. An air traffic controllers' strike had caused the Northern Division game to be postponed, and the new date clashed with a Kiwis trial that involved fourteen of Auckland's top players. It was tough enough tackling the Aussies without encountering handicaps such as that.

Wellington was hammered 63–5 in the 1978 opening match, when Auckland was seeded through to the fourth round. There it beat country division Riverina 39–3, Olsen Filipaina being judged man of the match for a rampaging two-try display. Nick Wright contributed eighteen points from two tries and six goals, and Roger Rota, Jeff Grainger, Murray Netzler, Terry Whittle and Kevin Hughes also scored tries. Unfortunately, the quarter-final against Cronulla-Sutherland clashed with the Kiwis tour of Australia and, despite Auckland's pleas, only Filipaina and Nick Wright were released to play. Adding insult to injury, expatriate Aucklander Dane Sorensen was man of the match in Cronulla's 22–6 victory.

The format changed in 1979, with four groups of four teams playing for semi-final berths. Auckland failed to flatter, losing to Penrith by 12–5, to Canterbury-Bankstown by 12–3 and to Cronulla-Sutherland by 30–10. The competition was a triumph for Cronulla and the Sorensens, Kurt having sat out the 1978 season to obtain a clearance and join Dane at the Sharks. Cronulla beat Brisbane 22–5 in the final, and Kurt Sorensen was named player of the series, collecting several television sets and video recorders along the way.

New sponsors did not help Auckland's, or New Zealand's causes. In the 1980 Tooth Cup, Auckland lost to Western Suburbs (40–14) and South Sydney (47–5) and in 1981 Central Districts was just as comprehensively beaten by Manly (51–11) and Penrith (31–5). It became the KB Cup in 1982 and South Island lost to Canberra (47–15) and Brisbane (34–3). In 1983 Central was a 50–0 loser to Newtown. Auckland qualified for the National Panasonic Cup in 1984, losing to Queensland Country 25–18 at Lang Park, and 1985, when beaten 32–10 by Western Suburbs at Leichhardt Oval. No New Zealand teams competed in subsequent midweek competitions through to 1989.

CHAPTER EIGHT

1974: Britannia rules no more

Auckland 11 Great Britain 2

Auckland began what was to be a sequence of five wins in six matches against Great Britain touring teams with its 11–2 success at Carlaw Park in 1974. It was the obvious high point of a season which had previously included losses to Australian opponents New South Wales Country, Brisbane and Western Division and some questioning of coach Neville Denton using former Kiwis loose forward Tony Kriletich as a prop and second-rower Tom Conroy at hooker.

Denton was vindicated when Auckland handled another muddy occasion with far more confidence than the British side which had won the test series by two

Auckland hooker Tom Conroy breaks away from Britain's Steve Norton and team-mate Peter Gurnick.
NZ Herald

matches to one at the same venue four days earlier. Kriletich was always going to play at prop, but Conroy was again switched to hooker when Brian Donnelly (along with backrow forwards Murray Eade and Wayne Robertson) withdrew before the game. Kriletich seamlessly adjusted to his new role and Conroy won the scrums 18–16.

The reshuffle of the Auckland pack benefited those who were belatedly included. Second-rowers Josh Liavaa and Peter Gurnick and loose forward Barrie Dyer all went into the notebooks of the New Zealand selectors for the 1975 season. Bob Jarvis had made his Kiwis debut as a replacement during the third test three days earlier, and he not only reprised that role for Auckland, but also scored the only try of the match.

Jarvis made his entry when Ken Stirling damaged a hamstring after fifty-two minutes. Six minutes later Jarvis was diving under the crossbar at the end of a sparkling reply to a British goal-line drop-out. Warren Collicoat fielded the ball and moved it to his left, for Graham Smith, John O'Sullivan and Colin Andrews to handle before Andrews turned back infield and found captain Don Mann and Jarvis outnumbering the last defender. Collicoat kicked four goals to just one by British forward John Gray.

Diminutive but speedy Auckland wing Len Hall stood out in conditions hardly suitable for a player in his position. He was recalled by referee Bob Cooper for a marginal forward pass in a move which would have produced another

The joys of a winter's afternoon at Carlaw Park seem to be lost on Lions front-rowers Terry Clawson, John Gray and Jim Thompson.
NZ Herald

splendid team try, kept Britain guessing with his short kicking game, and found the acceleration to cut down Allan Bates and David Redfearn when British tries looked likely.

'Instead of resigning themselves to sharing an 80-minute wallow in the mud, the Aucklanders produced a surprisingly fluent pattern which severely shook, and once shattered, the British defence,' reported *The Press*. Mann announced his retirement later in the week, after what the media described as 'the greatest success of his long career'.

Auckland team: fullback, Warren Collicoat; three-quarters, Len Hall, John O'Sullivan, Dennis Williams, Colin Andrews; halves, Graham Smith, Ken Stirling (replaced by Bob Jarvis); forwards, Tony Kriletich, Tom Conroy, Don Mann (captain), Peter Gurnick, Josh Liavaa (replaced by Doug Gailey), Barrie Dyer.

1975: Out of the shadows

Auckland 9 France 3

The understudies emerged from the chorus line and filled starring roles when Auckland beat France 9–3 in the first of its three 1975 international matches at Carlaw Park, also the first to be held under the new floodlights. Both France and Wales met Auckland in mid-season and Australia dropped by in October as subsidiary matches to the five-nation home and away World Championship.

The French fixture occurred while the Kiwis were in camp, and Auckland coach Bill Sorensen was effectively deprived of his first-choice team. Undaunted, he expressed confidence in the best of the rest, predicting a win in the *New Zealand Herald* on match morning. The French had been given permission to use four substitutes to combat travel fatigue, but Sorensen stuck rigidly to the international rules and used no replacements.

'Auckland played the French at their own passing game and came out the masters,' reported the *Herald*. 'The Aucklanders were as quick as the French but far more reliable in their ball handling and cover defence. France, apart from their speed, were uncertain in many aspects of their play.'

Backrower Barrie Dyer, named as the player of the night, Graham Price, Doug Taurua and Alby Hansen 'excelled' in the forwards, while Warren Winter 'played another brilliant game, comparable with his efforts as fullback in the earlier Kiwi trials.'

There was also praise for Dave Sorensen's leadership, for scrum-half Stewart Norton and three-quarters Ken Andersson, Colin Andrews and Fred Ah Kuoi, who 'deserve mention for displays which were a treat to watch'. This was the only appearance by Price, Norton and stand-off half Chris Jordan in Auckland's ten-match season.

Barrie Dyer scores Auckland's only try in the victory over France. Defenders Jean-Marie Imbert (left) and Rene Terrats cannot hold Dyer.
NZ *Herald*

Auckland led 7–0 at halftime, thanks to a Dyer try in the fortieth minute, and a penalty goal and conversion from Jordan. At that stage Auckland led the penalties 8–0 and hooker Murray Wright held a 10–9 advantage in the scrums. But France received much more ball after the break, gaining seven penalties to five, and winning eight of the thirteen scrums.

Against the run of play, and on the back of solid Auckland tackling, Jordan kicked another goal. The only French points came from a late try to wing Elie Bonal as they finally found a way around the Auckland defensive line. Even then, the *Herald* claimed Bonal 'appeared to be pushed out by Winter' over the grandstand touchline, regained his balance and ran on.

Auckland team: fullback, Warren Winter; three-quarters, Fred Ah Kuoi, Ken Andersson, Dave Sorensen (captain), Colin Andrews; halves, Chris Jordan, Stewart Norton; forwards, Alby Hansen, Murray Wright, Doug Taurua, Mark Graham, Graham Price, Barrie Dyer.

1975: Too tough for Wales

Auckland 31 Wales 5

The big boys were back from Kiwis duty, and the Welsh were required to return to Carlaw Park while still feeling the mental and physical bruises of having lost a hard-fought 1975 World Championship game to New Zealand 13–8. The test

Rising stars. Dane Sorensen passes to younger brother Kurt in a 1975 match for Mount Wellington against Otahuhu. They played alongside their uncle, Dave, in the big win over Wales. The Otahuhu defenders are Neville White and Glenn Taylor.

Fairfax Media

CHAPTER EIGHT

was too rough in the opinion of some, for the Welsh management was required to give an assurance to the New Zealand Rugby League that the incidents which marred the test match would not be repeated.

Before the year was out, notorious Welsh forward Jim Mills would be barred from playing again in New Zealand as a result of incidents on the tour and the shameful stomping of Kiwi John Greengrass in Swansea. Against Auckland, Wales was strangely lifeless, its limp display being described by coach Les Pearce as a disgrace. But the visitors still managed to concede fourteen of the seventeen penalties awarded by West Coast referee Ted Gutberlet.

Only wing Clive Sullivan and captain for the night Kel Coslett escaped the *New Zealand Herald's* condemnation of the Welsh lack of effort. Auckland was lauded. 'Once again, they rose to the occasion. Even the inept display by the Welsh could not detract from the way the fifteen – Dave Sorensen and Doug Taurua, who came on as replacements, included – played as a team. They supported each other not only in running but also as they went for the tackle.' Many times the ball was jolted from Welsh hands.

Stand-off half Bob Jarvis was named player of the match and especially impressed with his play-making. Captain Dennis Williams added to the Welsh discomfort with his kicking, launching bombs that were seldom defused confidently and gaining plenty of territory with his long punts. Front-rower Alby Hansen, a pre-match replacement for the injured Lyndsay Proctor, was also outstanding.

'All the Sorensens [prop Dane, second-rower Kurt and replacement Dave] had good games, as did John O'Sullivan, Murray Eade, Tom Conroy and Ken Stirling. But it was a Kiwi effort once again, with every man contributing to the win. Auckland won the game because their backs and forwards were able to move the ball almost without opposition. They checked almost every movement by the Welsh before they were started,' said the *Herald*.

Hansen scored two of Auckland's tries, with one each from Fred Ah Kuoi, Warren Collicoat and John O'Sullivan. Collicoat kicked eight goals. The Welsh try went to Colin Dixon and Coslett kicked one goal. Auckland scored all twenty-one points in the first half, by which time the result was beyond doubt.

Auckland team: fullback, Warren Collicoat; three-quarters, Fred Ah Kuoi, John O'Sullivan, Dennis Williams (captain), Colin Andrews; halves, Bob Jarvis (replaced by Dave Sorensen), Ken Stirling; forwards, Dane Sorensen, Tom Conroy, Alby Hansen, (replaced by Doug Taurua), Mark Graham, Kurt Sorensen, Murray Eade.

1975: Kangaroos restore order

Australia 17 Auckland 6

The Kangaroos were well on their way to another world title when they beat Auckland by 17–6, scoring three tries to none, at Carlaw Park in October 1975. Those looking for positives noted that Auckland did better than the Kiwis in their 24–8 loss to Australia the previous weekend. But it was disappointing that fullback Warren Collicoat was the only point-scorer for both home teams with four goals for New Zealand and three for Auckland.

Coach Bill Sorensen was already without Ken Stirling and Bob Jarvis and later lost Murray Eade, Tom Conroy and Dane Sorensen from his original side, replacing them with Alby Hansen, Murray Wright and Doug Taurua. Among the Kiwis backing up for Auckland were nineteen-year-old wing Fred Ah Kuoi and eighteen-year-old second-rower Kurt Sorensen, who had just become New Zealand's youngest test forward.

Forwards Hansen, Peter Gurnick and, especially, Wayne Robertson were credited by the *Auckland Star* with firing up an Auckland side 'which delighted in knocking down the Australians and in powerhouse running. And no-one was better at it than prop Wayne Robertson. His tackling was strong and clean and he tackled more often than anyone else, and his attack bothered the Australians.

Mark Graham cannot prevent Mick Cronin scoring a try for Australia. Auckland's Alby Hansen (left) and Australia's Ray Higgs look on.
NZ Herald

CHAPTER EIGHT

Gurnick was tireless on attack and defence. Hansen made mistakes, a couple of them costly, but it took five Australians to halt him.'

However, coach Sorensen was not happy that Auckland's effort waned in the second half. Auckland had been close to scoring at least two tries before the interval and Sorensen felt his players should have made better use of Wright's 17–9 scrummaging superiority over makeshift Australian hooker Ray Higgs and sixteen to seven penalty advantage from referee Neville Kesha.

'Instead of improving on the first half, they went backwards,' Sorensen lamented. 'We were unlucky to miss two tries in the first half and Australia scored one against the run of play. I thought the second half was going to be a grand finale. Instead we went back to running in ones and not using the ball. Slowly we died.'

Auckland appeared likely to lead at halftime when Collicoat kicked two penalty goals against one by Mick Cronin for the Kangaroos. But scrum-half Tommy Raudonikis came up with a try, converted by Cronin, and Cronin added another penalty to make it 9–4. After Collicoat kept local hopes alive with his third goal, Australia moved out of range courtesy of tries from Cronin and Allan McMahon and a final penalty goal by Cronin.

Auckland team: fullback, Warren Collicoat; three-quarters, Fred Ah Kuoi, Paul Matete (replaced by Barrie Dyer), Dennis Williams (captain), Bill Sorensen junior; halves, John Smith, Shane Dowsett; forwards, Alby Hansen, Murray Wright, Wayne Robertson, Kurt Sorensen, Peter Gurnick, Mark Graham (replaced by Doug Taurua).

Southern raiders

On the day of Auckland's match with Australia in late 1975, news came out of Christchurch that the Hornby club was in the process of signing former Kiwis Wayne Robertson and Wayne Redmond from Auckland and that current international Bob Jarvis had expressed an interest in joining them. It was the start of a mini-migration of leading Auckland players to Canterbury and Wellington.

Redmond actually stayed put with Glenora and Auckland. But Robertson (from Ponsonby) and Jarvis (Otahuhu) were accompanied to Hornby by representative hooker Murray Wright (Otahuhu) and Mangere East second-rower Wayne Bunn. International backs Warren Collicoat (Mount Albert) and John O'Sullivan (Ponsonby) and one-game Auckland prop Brian Jolley (Ellerslie) took up positions with Wellington clubs.

A massive transfer wrangle erupted, whipped along by Auckland chairman George Rainey. The New Zealand Rugby League altered its constitution to increase transfer fees where it could be established that 'poaching' had occurred.

Bob Jarvis playing for Hornby against Graeme Cooksley's Eastern Suburbs team.
Christchurch Star

Bob Jarvis (left) and Wayne Robertson at the Islington freezing works in Christchurch.
Christchurch Star

Hornby recruit Wayne Robertson runs away from Papanui defenders Haydon Moore and Norm Geddes.
Christchurch Star

Canterbury was ordered to pay $1,000 each for Robertson, Jarvis and Wright and Wellington $1,000 for Collicoat. It was successfully argued O'Sullivan had moved on a legitimate job transfer. Bunn and Jolley did not attract transfer fees.

Hornby rose from ninth to third in the 1976 club competition, but Canterbury hardly prospered from the influx of talent. Robertson felt Canterbury should assist Hornby with the $3,000 fees and made himself unavailable for provincial duty. Jarvis was plagued by head injuries and appeared only once in red and black, but Wright and Bunn had mighty games against Auckland in the national Rothmans final. Collicoat, O'Sullivan and the unheralded Jolley were all regular Wellington representatives.

It was a severe test of Auckland's depth, one which it passed with flying colours, at least on a domestic level. Auckland accounted for Midlands-Bay of Plenty 51–26, Waikato 34–18, Wellington 36–23 – when new hooker Murray Netzler scored three of the eight tries – and deterred a stern Canterbury challenge 29–22 in the Rothmans final. Against overseas rivals it fell to Balmain at the second Amco Cup hurdle, beat St Helens, lost to Eastern Suburbs and beat Sydney Metropolitan.

Speed bump

After twenty games over fifty-nine years, and nothing more than three draws to show for it, Canterbury at last broke through for its first away victory over Auckland at Carlaw Park in October 1975. Auckland had previously lost 20–17 to West Coast at Greymouth, and the 15–14 defeat by Canterbury interrupted its proud sequence as Rothmans provincial champion from 1973 through to the last competition in 1979.

CHAPTER EIGHT

While dropping decisions at Wingham Park, Greymouth, was nothing new, it would have come as a shock to another outstanding group of international players. Captained by Dennis Williams, the Auckland team also included Ken Stirling, Mark Graham and Kurt Sorensen. The only non-Kiwis among the fifteen players were wing Bill Sorensen junior and rugby union recruit Alby Hansen at prop. Replacement Paul Matete (two) and Stirling scored tries and Warren Collicoat kicked four goals.

It was a different story for Auckland coach Bill Sorensen against Canterbury. The match was played the same night the Kiwis left for World Championship matches in Europe, taking fourteen Aucklanders and two Cantabrians. None of the starting backs had appeared in Auckland's nine previous games, including up-and-coming scrum-half Shane Varley, but the pack contained Graham, Wayne Robertson, Ian Bell and Murray Wright. Wing David Kerr (two), centre Neville White and Robertson scored tries and Phillip Dryland kicked a goal before Canterbury's discarded Kiwis wing Mocky Brereton surged away for the match and Rothmans championship winning try.

Auckland extracted its revenge in the four remaining Rothmans finals:

1976 (coach, Bill Sorensen): beat Canterbury 29–22 at Christchurch. Kurt Sorensen two, Dennis Williams, John Smith, Stewart Norton tries; Chris Jordan seven goals.

1977 (coach, Bill Sorensen): beat Wellington 36–22 at Carlaw Park. Dane O'Hara two, Warren Winter two, Dennis Williams two, John Smith, Mark Graham tries; Joe Karam six goals.

1978 (coach, Don Hammond): beat Canterbury 20–13 at Carlaw Park. Olsen Filipaina, Fred Ah Kuoi, Gary Hooker, Stewart Norton tries; Nick Wright four goals.

1979 (coach, Don Hammond): beat West Coast 43–19 at Carlaw Park. Gary Kemble three, Olsen Filipaina two, Shane Varley two, Alan McCarthy, Toa Fepuleai tries; Tangi Raumati eight goals.

Jumping (codes) Joe

No signing of a rugby union player caused more publicity than that of All Blacks fullback Joe Karam by Auckland club Glenora before the 1976 season. Auckland sports fans poured into Parnell to watch the new attractions of Karam and a floodlit Carlaw Park. Karam kicked some great goals that night and was rushed into coach Bill Sorensen's Auckland team. In six representative appearances he scored fifty-three points. Karam's 160 club points helped Glenora reach the Fox Memorial grand final, where it lost 20–12 to Mount Wellington.

But by the end of his three-year contract, Karam was not able to hold a place in the Glenora team, having been succeeded as fullback and goalkicker by Warwick Freeman. Karam had played one game for Auckland in 1977, kicking six goals against Wellington, but that was to be his lot. The *New Zealand Rugby League Annual* explained he found his tackling work-rate far more demanding than in rugby union, and he lacked any conviction on attack. Ironically, had Karam stayed in his former code he would probably have kicked the All Blacks to victory over the Springboks in 1976.

Glenora recruit Joe Karam.
Fairfax Media

Graham Whiting on debut for Maritime against Marist.
Fairfax Media

CHAPTER EIGHT

> Several others jumped codes about the same time. Powerful forward Alby Hansen joined Mount Albert and represented Auckland. When the Maritime club burst onto the Auckland scene in 1975, enlisting former Kiwis Roger Bailey and Rick Carey plus future Kiwi Kevin Potter, it also poached All Blacks forward Graham Whiting plus Tony (Tank) Gordon and Wayne Marsh from rugby union in King Country. Whiting was a flop, but Gordon played as a wing and goalkicker for the 1975 New Zealand World Championship team and later led a rugby league renaissance in Bay of Plenty and coached the Kiwis from 1987 to 1989.

World 'club' challenge

Auckland compensated for a 1976 season without any official international fixtures by inviting British champion St Helens and reigning Sydney champion Eastern Suburbs to Carlaw Park. There was also a late-season visit from a predominantly youthful Sydney Metropolitan side chosen from clubs not involved in the premiership play-offs.

St Helens had already lost to Easts in a forerunner to the World Club Challenge and to Queensland before coming on to Auckland. Josh Liavaa produced a barnstorming game in the forwards as Auckland won 20–13, through tries scored by Joe Karam, Fred Ah Kuoi, Kurt Sorensen and Bill Sorensen junior, and Karam adding four goals.

But an Easts side determined to prove it was indisputably the best club team in the game (ignoring the fact that Auckland is a province) was a far more difficult proposition. Coached by Jack Gibson and captained by another legend, Arthur Beetson, the Roosters also boasted Russell Fairfax, Ian Schubert, Mark Harris, John Brass, Royce Ayliffe and Elwyn Walters in its ranks.

Easts recovered from a first-minute Dave Lepper try to lead 20–3 late in the first half. Kurt Sorensen scored just on halftime, Auckland conceded another try soon after the restart and then got as close as 23–14 before Beetson claimed a try for himself. At fulltime Auckland was behind only 26–22, rueing the inability of its various goalkickers to land more than two conversions. Young Ellerslie fullback Gary Kemble signalled his arrival in the big time.

But Gibson suffered a rare loss in a pre-match joust with the equally formidable Auckland chairman George Rainey. The dispute was over the international rule that permitted only two replacements. Gibson wanted a four-man bench. Rainey said no. Gibson threatened to pull out of the game. Rainey still said no. The game went on.

Coached by former Kangaroos hooker and noted hard man Noel Kelly, and captained by former test scrum-half Tommy Raudonikis, the Sydney Metropolitan tourists thrashed Waikato and a North Island XIII but lost 18–5 to a New Zealand XIII, 18–17 to South Island and, in their final appearance, 17–7 to Auckland.

Sydney led 7–3 at halftime but had no answers to Auckland in the second spell. Dennis Williams (two) and John Smith scored tries, and Karam kicked four goals. Alan McCarthy, who had replaced Alby Hansen early in the match, was credited with 'turning on one of the most blistering tackling displays of the season in the first half' by the *New Zealand Rugby League Annual*, and Dane and Kurt Sorensen were also in top gear.

Not quite a Kiwi

Had an official New Zealand team been selected in 1976, the celebrated Sorensen family would probably have had a fifth Kiwi. Bill Sorensen junior's form for Auckland earned him the reserve back position in the New Zealand XIII that beat Sydney Metropolitan 18–5 at Carlaw Park. Sorensen was one of six players chosen by New Zealand selectors Ron Ackland, George Menzies and Morrie Church who had not worn the Kiwis jersey. While Chris Jordan (Auckland), Kevin Fisher (Waikato), Whare Henry (Wellington) and Bruce Gall (Taranaki) later became Kiwis, centre or wing Sorensen and Canterbury prop Terry Gillman never did take that final step. The Sorensen Kiwis were Bill Sorensen senior, his brother Dave, and their nephews Dane and Kurt.

1977: Grand slam – strike one
Auckland 19 Australia 15

Only supreme optimists would have predicted the remarkable grand slam that Auckland achieved in June 1977. Australia was beaten on 1 June, Great Britain fell on 14 June, and France crashed on 21 June, all under the Carlaw Park lights. It was a case of rags to riches, for a weakened Auckland side had been summarily dismissed from the Amco Cup by country team Northern Division the previous week. The Kangaroos, meanwhile, had beaten New Zealand 27–12 in their opening World Cup fixture.

'Auckland took only 80 minutes to convince 9000 Carlaw Park fans how wrong the Kiwis selectors had been with their selection for the international championship match against Australia three days earlier,' wrote Richard Becht in the *New Zealand Rugby League Annual*. 'After Auckland's marvellous performance under lights most of the crowd, in fact, could see no reason why nearly all of the Auckland team could not play for the Kiwis.

Dennis Williams, Auckland captain for its 1977 international grand slam.
Fairfax Media

CHAPTER EIGHT

'And on at least three counts they were right: loose forward Mark Graham, a stupendous game on attack and defence, winger Warren Winter, who made Mark Harris' life a misery, and prop Lyndsay Proctor, all gusto up front, proved they deserved to be among the first three picked for a Kiwi team. Yet only [one national selector] Ron Ackland saw the match – and the Kiwi team for the second international against Great Britain amazingly did not include Graham or Winter.'

At halftime it was 14–7 to Auckland, thanks to tries by centre Olsen Filipaina, from a Graham break, and hooker Glenn Taylor, who was well positioned to capitalise on a midfield surge by fullback Gary Kemble. Those efforts were complemented by Chris Jordan's four goals. Australia predictably fought back to 14–12, but a fine Dennis Williams try, converted from the sideline by Jordan, kept the home side out of range.

The Kangaroos were not at full-strength, fielding rangy second-rower Rod Reddy in the centres in place of injured backs Mick Cronin and Allan McMahon, but were still a formidable unit. Utility back John Smith was retained in his Kiwis role of scrum-half by Auckland coach Bill Sorensen, despite the availability of highly promising Shane Varley. The *New Zealand Herald* reported that Kiwis Jordan, Williams and Kurt Sorensen were much more effective than in the test match.

Auckland team: fullback, Gary Kemble; three-quarters, Warren Winter, Olsen Filipaina, Dennis Williams (captain), Chris Jordan; halves, Dave Sorensen, John Smith; forwards, John Wilson, Glenn Taylor, Lyndsay Proctor, Kurt Sorensen, Alan McCarthy, Mark Graham. Reserves: Dave Lepper, Mark Lowe.

1977: Grand slam – strike two

Auckland 14 Great Britain 10

Auckland hackles, particularly those of chairman George Rainey, bristled again when the Kiwis were beaten 30–12 by Great Britain at Christchurch, and coach Ron Ackland announced there would be no changes for the final World Cup game against France. That Ackland released Auckland's Kiwis to play for the provincial team against the British midweek did not appease the critics.

'Again Auckland produced what the Kiwis had no idea of doing – imaginative, positive play and, with it, a sticking, courageous defence,' said Richard Becht in the *New Zealand Rugby League Annual*. 'It was too much for the Kangaroos and the British faltered to the same approach.' Becht pin-pointed the performance of twenty-year-old fullback Gary Kemble as the feature of the match.

'Kemble's game had everything,' he wrote. 'He took the high kicks with the calmest efficiency, while his moves into the backline on attack always stunned the British. The tourists found out all about Kemble's smooth attack when he roared into the line outside centre Fred Ah Kuoi, made a thrilling 50-metre break to within metres of the British line before drawing fullback George Fairbairn and in-passing to Ellerslie club-mate, winger Chris Jordan, who scored the try and converted.

'Again Lyndsay Proctor had a driving game at prop as did his front-row partner Mark Lowe while Alan McCarthy was all-guts on defence. Jordan scored all of Auckland's first half points with a try, conversion and penalty to give Auckland a 7–5 edge at the break. Jordon retired hurt then and the second half produced a snorting try from discarded Kiwi winger Dane O'Hara, who crashed through two tackles for the touchdown, while Kemble kicked two important penalties.' O'Hara had been a pre-match replacement for Warren Winter.

British coach David Watkins, still fit and full of tricks, captained the Lions from the centres in place of tour captain Roger Millward and test centre Les Dyl. He also rested several forwards for the World Cup clash with Australia the following weekend. It was Watkins who put up the bombs that Kemble countered so expertly.

The *New Zealand Herald* pondered why Auckland was performing so much better than the Kiwis, deciding 'a possible answer could be that the intensive training sessions before the tests were a case of too much hard work too soon'. But that did not explain why the Auckland Kiwis looked so much fresher and better in blue and white than in black and white.

Auckland team: fullback, Gary Kemble; three-quarters, Dane O'Hara, Dennis Williams (captain), Fred Ah Kuoi, Chris Jordan (replaced by Olsen Filipaina); halves, Dave Sorensen, John Smith; forwards, Lyndsay Proctor, Glenn Taylor, Mark Lowe, Kurt Sorensen, Alan McCarthy, Mark Graham. Reserve forward: Stan Napa.

John Smith, the Auckland scrum-half, breaks free of Britain's Phil Hogan.
NZ Herald

CHAPTER EIGHT

1977: Grand slam – strike three

Auckland 17 France 0

'This was the icing on the cake for the magnificent Bill Sorensen-coached Auckland side. The treble against international sides had been completed,' wrote Richard Becht in the *New Zealand Rugby League Annual* about Auckland's shut-out of France. The only unfortunate aspect of the occasion was the wretched Tuesday night weather and playing conditions, cold and windy and Carlaw Park at its muddy worst.

On the previous Saturday an unconvincing Kiwis team had beaten the French 28–22 to avoid the World Cup wooden spoon. During that week the Auckland Rugby League had repeated its call for a sole New Zealand selector-coach. It demanded the Kiwis captaincy be passed from West Coaster Tony Coll to Aucklander Dennis Williams, that the test team be named earlier and that Auckland receive a game against the World Cup winner. It was essentially told by the New Zealand Rugby League to go through the correct channels.

'The 17–0 victory by [Auckland] was decisive enough but it in no way indicated the gruelling effort needed for it to be achieved,' said the New Zealand Press Association. 'For thirty-eight minutes the match was precariously poised with neither side being able to dominate. Certainly, Auckland had a 4–0 lead but the points were gained from penalties.

Second-rower John Wilson pushes off an attempted tackle by Jean-Jaques Cologni.
NZ Herald

Auckland's 1977 international champion team.
Back row: Dave Lepper, Alan McCarthy, Dane O'Hara, Mark Lowe, Dave Sorensen.
Middle row: George Rainey (chairman), Luther Toloa, Gary Kemble, Kurt Sorensen, Lyndsay Proctor, Mark Graham, Stan Napa, Bill Nesbitt (manager).
Front row: Graham Coutts (masseur), John Smith, Fred Ah Kuoi, Dennis Williams (captain), Chris Jordan, Warren Winter, Bill Sorensen (coach).
In front: Glenn Taylor.
Absent: Olsen Filipaina, John Wilson.
NZRL Museum

CHAPTER EIGHT

'Then in the thirty-ninth minute the brilliant action of Fred Ah Kuoi in accelerating to gather in a Dennis Williams kick through centre-field allowed the Kiwi centre to make ground before unloading to Dave Sorensen for a try under the post. That try, converted by Chris Jordan, was the turning point of the match.'

In the second spell Auckland maintained the intensity of its tackling, which had been the most notable aspect of that less than brilliant first half. Although the French were providing more opposition than many expected, Auckland ran in further tries in the last ten minutes to Dane O'Hara and Williams, a long-range individual effort which clinched him the man of the match award. Jordan finished with three goals, and John Wilson one. Another glaring statistic was the 17–3 penalty count to Auckland from referee Neville Kesha.

'Auckland, after peaking for the more difficult Australia and Great Britain clashes, was not at its best. Injuries did not help, though, with loose forward Mark Graham and prop Mark Lowe both out [Richmond's Luther Toloa made his sole appearance for the season] and Lyndsay Proctor and Alan McCarthy being replaced at halftime because of injury. But the most unsettling factor for the locals was a tenacious French defence which did not know when to let up,' wrote Becht.

Auckland team: fullback, Gary Kemble; three-quarters, Dane O'Hara, Fred Ah Kuoi, Dennis Williams (captain), Chris Jordan; halves, Dave Sorensen, John Smith; forwards, Lyndsay Proctor (replaced by Stan Napa), Glenn Taylor, Luther Toloa, John Wilson, Alan McCarthy (replaced by Olsen Filipaina), Kurt Sorensen.

Bill Sorensen, who gave great service to Auckland as a player, coach and selector, was made a New Zealand Rugby League life member in 1991. Fittingly, it was presented by former Auckland (then NZRL) chairman George Rainey.
Bernie Wood collection

Unexpected bonus

Brian Doherty revealed in the *Auckland Star* that the Auckland players received a double bonus – modest by today's standards – for beating Australia in the first leg of their grand slam. As the team filed out for the second half, leading 14–7, coach Bill Sorensen learnt that a sponsor would give the side a bonus of $500 if it won. He told second-rower Kurt Sorensen, the last man out, and the word spread quickly through the team, which was on a $20 a head bonus from the Auckland league for a victory. 'It put a lot of keenness into everybody', captain Dennis Williams said afterwards. Such was the near-amateurism of New Zealand rugby league in that era.

Auckland takeover

The severe criticisms made by Auckland chairman George Rainey of New Zealand's poor 1977 World Cup performance appeared to have some effect on the Kiwis team that toured Australia and Papua New Guinea the following year. Retiring Auckland sole selector-coach Bill Sorensen joined fellow Aucklander Ron Ackland (who continued as Kiwis coach) and Canterbury newcomer Harry Walker on the national selection panel.

Ellerslie scrum-half Ken Stirling returned to international football after three years to captain the tourists. He took over from West Coast's Tony Coll, who had relinquished the job during the off-season. Eighteen Auckland players were included among the original twenty-four chosen, with loose forward Mark Graham becoming the nineteenth when Canterbury's Barry Edkins was injured on debut.

The 'bolter' in most minds was North Shore stand-off half Steve McGregor, who was plucked from virtual third division football and scored six tries in eight minor games. Centre Olsen Filipaina was the individual star, but all three tests were lost by wide margins. Stirling retired permanently after the tour, and in 1979 Ackland was succeeded as Kiwis coach by West Coast-born, Auckland-resident, former Wigan star Ces Mountford.

CHAPTER EIGHT

Fullback Warwick Freeman scores for Auckland despite the arrival of St George defender Jack Jeffries.
NZ Herald

Try-scoring feast

One scribe described it as a 'try-scoring feast' when Sydney club St George – then between its 1977 and 1979 premiership triumphs – scored five tries to four in beating Auckland 27–18 in September 1978. It was indisputably a spectacular encounter, though some of the Aucklanders were short of match fitness because their club seasons were finished. Warwick Freeman, Dennis Williams, Olsen Filipaina and Gary Prohm touched down for Auckland, and Freeman, who had replaced original fullback choice Nick Wright, kicked three goals.

A week later there was a near try-scoring famine when Otahuhu beat another Sydney club, Cronulla-Sutherland, by 8–2 in what was billed as a trans-Tasman championship. Otahuhu coach Graham Lowe had no shortage of talent in his pack, which consisted of John Wright, Glenn Taylor, Stan Napa, Owen Wright, Terry Whittle and captain Mark Graham. The only tries of the match went to Graham and fullback Nick Wright, who also added a goal.

Inter-districts shock

An inter-districts competition was introduced by the New Zealand Rugby League in 1979 and produced a staggering result. Central Districts, with rising stars such as cousins Howie and Kevin Tamati, Graeme West and Bruce Gall in the pack, and Wellington-based former Kiwi Warren Collicoat kicking the goals, went through unbeaten from wins over Auckland (26–18 at Wellington), South Island (21–16 at Christchurch) and Northern Districts (32–7 at Upper Hutt). Auckland also lost to South Island 11–10 at Carlaw Park and beat Northern 22–12 at Huntly. South overpowered Northern 42–8 at Christchurch to finish runner-up. It was 1983, at the fifth attempt, before Auckland topped an inter-districts points table, but it then won five in succession before the series ended in 1987.

Thirty seconds of fame

Surely there has never been a shorter representative debut than that of Mangere East forward Clarrie Paul in the 1979 Amco Cup match against Cronulla-Sutherland in Sydney. Paul was sent onto Leichhardt Oval as a halftime replacement, but his enthusiasm unfortunately got the better of him. Within thirty seconds Paul had felled Cronulla and former Auckland second-rower Kurt Sorensen with a badly misdirected tackle and was promptly sent from the field.

1979: Last battle to Britain

Great Britain 18 Auckland 10

The final match of the 1979 Lions tour was a battle between two desperate teams. Great Britain for the first time lost all three tests in Australia and, though it had sewn up the New Zealand series within two matches, the Kiwis had fought back for an 18–11 victory in the third. The Lions did not want to finish off with another defeat. Auckland had failed dismally in the Amco Cup and the inter-districts competition. Its pride was severely dented.

There was almost a Hollywood ending, but not for the home side. Veteran forward Brian Lockwood was prevailed upon to lead the Lions after trying to cry off through injury. He went out in a blaze of glory, scoring the try – his first on the entire tour – that put Britain ahead and on the way to its eventual 18–10 success. But this was also Auckland's best performance of the season and much of their lost pride was restored.

'The Auckland dressing room looked like a casualty clearing station last night after the team had valiantly but unsuccessfully tried to hold on to a two-point lead,' reported the *New Zealand Herald*. 'The Aucklanders held the lead until the seventy-first minute when they went from a lead of 10–8 to finish eight points

Olsen Filipaina is too late to prevent Lions wing David Barends from claiming his try.
NZ Herald

CHAPTER EIGHT

behind after two converted tries were scored against them. Fred Ah Kuoi, the Auckland captain, described the match as much harder than the test the Kiwis won on Saturday.

'Afterwards, Doug Gailey, Gary Kemble, Olsen Filipaina, Wayne Robertson, Fred Ah Kuoi and Murray Netzler all sported facial cuts and Toa Fepuleai was limping badly.' Scrum-half Shane Varley, the player of the match, quipped: 'If we got a point for every stitch, we would have won.' Some of the physical damage was inflicted during a brawl which erupted from a scrum. More than 12,500 fans enjoyed an exceedingly entertaining match.

Auckland completely dominated a scoreless opening quarter, before a Fepuleai try and two Filipaina goals created a seven-point advantage. But it was only 7–6 at the break, Britain having closed the gap through tries to David Barends and David Topliss. Props Gailey and Wayne Robertson reignited Auckland in the second spell with punishing centre-field runs, and Gary Kemble tested the Lions defence from fullback.

Filipaina stretched the lead to 10–6 with a typical try but the conversion attempt was one of his four costly goalkicking misses. John Woods kicked a penalty for Britain before the balding Lockwood scuttled through to touch down under the crossbar. Woods converted for 13–10 and converted again when Peter Glynn claimed the final try of the tour.

Auckland team: fullback, Gary Kemble; three-quarters, James Leuluai, Olsen Filipaina, Ken Andersson, Toa Fepuleai; halves, Fred Ah Kuoi (captain), Shane Varley; forwards, Wayne Robertson, Murray Netzler, Doug Gailey, Alan McCarthy, Owen Wright, Gary Prohm.

CHAPTER 09
CHANGING TIMES
1980–1989

CHAPTER NINE

Changing Times
1980–1989

1980: No pressure? Not much

Australia 21 Auckland 7

As if defending a record of three wins in four matches against Australian teams since 1965 was not enough, Auckland Rugby League chairman George Rainey piled more pressure upon his 1980 representatives. He told the *New Zealand Herald* on match morning that the Auckland forwards were stronger than those fielded by the Kiwis in two losing test teams and had been given a 'raw deal' by the national selectors.

Auckland stand-off half Ron O'Regan eludes Ray Price (left) and Greg Brentnall to score the only try for the New Zealand XIII against the 1980 Kangaroos in Christchurch.

Christchurch Star

'We'll be out to prove a point,' said Rainey. 'We have in our clubs forwards who can match players like Barry Edkins, Kevin Tamati, Graeme West and Mark Broadhurst any time. But while those players have been chosen for the Kiwis, Tom Conroy, Gary Prohm, John Gordon and Alan McCarthy, to name a few of our representatives, have been ignored.' Rainey was critical that only the three Auckland-based selectors, and not all six, would attend the match.

Auckland was beaten 21–7 by the Frank Stanton-coached Kangaroos, who completed an unbeaten seven-match record. But the home side did have one consolation. Centre Dave Lepper, who had replaced original selection James Leuluai before the game, succeeded where the Kiwis had failed by scoring the only try against Australia in three games at Carlaw Park. Fullback Gary Kemble created the opportunity with a timely run and pass.

The Australians might have won the tests, but they had suffered physically. Forwards Les Boyd (left wing) and Jim Leis (stand-off half) started in the backs, and when centre Chris Close was injured he was replaced by combative scrum-half Tommy Raudonikis. The *Herald* reported that opposing fullbacks Kemble and Greg Brentnall at one stage engaged in an old-style kicking duel, punting high and long four times each before Kangaroos half Steve Martin fielded the ball and kicked for his outside backs.

'Generally, the lack of speed of the Aucklanders and the many gaps they provided proved their undoing,' said the *Herald*. 'The best back for Auckland was John Smith, who had such a grand game. It was a pity he was not chosen for the Autex International test series. Pat Poasa had a narrow lead over Alan McCarthy for the best forward.

'Winning praise were Tom Conroy for his tackling, Dennis Williams for his generalship and Kemble for settling down to a solid game after a nightmarish first quarter when he could not field a high ball.' In what was described as 'a tough battle', Australian centre Mick Cronin shone with a try and six goals. Rod Reddy and Martin were the other try-scorers. It was 9–4 at halftime, and Lepper's try was Auckland's only highlight after that.

Auckland team: fullback, Gary Kemble; three-quarters, Chris Jordan, Dave Lepper, Dennis Williams (captain), Dane O'Hara; halves, Ron O'Regan, John Smith; forwards, Doug Gailey, John Gordon, Pat Poasa, Tom Conroy, Alan McCarthy, Gary Prohm. Reserves: Peter Simons, Ian Bell.

Of the four Auckland forwards mentioned by Rainey, only Prohm was chosen for the Kiwis tour to Britain and France. He was to develop into one of this country's most versatile footballers. The other Auckland-based Kiwis were backs Kemble, O'Hara, Leuluai, Fred Ah Kuoi and Shane Varley. Significantly, the tourists were captained by former Otahuhu loose forward Mark Graham, who was then with Brisbane Norths. The professional era was just around the corner.

Gary Prohm, on the cusp of an illustrious and versatile career.
Fairfax Media

CHAPTER NINE

Referee John Percival makes his point.
Christchurch Star

'Percy' hangs up the whistle

Auckland's most celebrated referee John Percival blew the final whistle on his international career in 1980, the second test between New Zealand and Australia at Carlaw Park being his twenty-sixth at that level. To put his achievement into context, no other New Zealand referee had then reached double figures in test appointments. Fellow Aucklander Dennis Hale later refereed thirteen tests between 1990 and 1995.

Percival dominated the international scene from his debut in the first test of the 1964 French tour at Carlaw Park. Wellington referee Earle Pilcher controlled the second test of that series before Percival returned for the third. Over the next sixteen years the only other officials to get a turn were Peter Yaxley (Canterbury, one 1974 test), Bob Cooper (Waikato, one 1975 World Championship fixture) and Kevin Steel (Auckland, one test each in 1979 and 1980).

As a youngster playing for Point Chevalier, Percival harboured lofty aspirations. He was a Schoolboy Kiwi in 1947 and an Auckland junior representative before injuries persuaded the slightly built second-rower to become a 'rookie ref' in 1956. Three years later he was in charge of senior club games and in 1960 controlled France's tour match against Taranaki. Vic Belsham (Auckland) was then New Zealand's top-ranked referee. Waikato's Roly Avery succeeded Belsham in 1961, before Percival became the undisputed number one.

The shrill blast of Percival's whistle instilled fear into the hearts of even the toughest overseas professionals and frequently had their coaches and managers venting their anger when he strictly enforced the laws of the game as they were interpreted in New Zealand.

'Control was the essence of my game,' Percival told the *1988 New Zealand Rugby League Annual*. 'When they lined up for internationals you could feel the tension. It was quite frightening. They had been wound up by their coaches. I felt it was my job to take control of them in the first ten minutes and bring them back to earth. I would always find penalties early in the match, get command and then back off as they settled down.'

Percival was never hesitant to dismiss players who warranted it. In 1965 he sent off renowned Kangaroo Graeme Langlands for attacking the head of Kiwis fullback Jack Fagan. When the St John Ambulance attendant confirmed Fagan had been seriously injured – the wound required seven stitches – Percival sent Langlands to the showers. He was not reluctant to adopt an 'if he goes, you go' policy. He signed off his test career by sending off notorious Australian forward Les Boyd for persistent infringements.

Backchatting was another of Percival's pet hates. The Australians dubbed him 'Ten yards Jack' for taking penalties ten yards further upfield for dissent. He once walked a British team forty yards for chipping him. Although his actions were then deemed to be controversial, the awarding of a second penalty for dissent was subsequently added to the rule book.

The first test of the 1974 British tour was described by Percival as his 'most difficult'. 'It was an atrocious day and the Poms didn't even want to take the field,' he recalled. 'They disputed every ruling and when I sent Colin Dixon off [for a high tackle on John Greengrass] they threatened to walk off en masse. It was an unpleasant situation.' The Lions management insisted on a different referee being assigned to the other two tests. But after Yaxley had refereed the second match in Christchurch, coach Jim Challinor and manager Reg Parker relented at the New Zealand Rugby League meeting which appointed Percival to the third test.

Carlaw Park was Percival's second home, but he also became the first New Zealand official to travel extensively. Four matches in Australia during the 1968 World Cup tournament included the final between Australia and France at Sydney, and he officiated in 1975 World Championship matches in Brisbane, Sydney, Bordeaux, Swansea and Wigan.

After his retirement from the big time Percival continued to referee age-grade football and hold administrative positions in the Auckland referees association. He was a popular leader of Kiwis supporters groups on overseas tours run by travel agent and fellow referee Dave Sargeant and in 1995 became the only non-player to be elected into the New Zealand Rugby League Legends of League.

Taming the districts

Seldom has Auckland's supremacy within New Zealand been so extensively challenged as during the early seasons of the inter-districts championship. The inaugural victory by Central Districts in 1979, with South Island the runner-up, was to be no fluke. Central won again in 1980, South took the trophy on scoring percentages in 1981, and Central regained the title in 1982. Auckland had suffered four consecutive losses to Central, by 26–18, 22–13, 19–10 and 10–9. The combined side, drawing most of its players from Wellington and Taranaki, was clearly superior over that period.

But all that changed from 1983, appropriately starting with a 52–2 thrashing of Central at Carlaw Park. Ron O'Regan, Dean Bell, Daryl Morrison and James Leuluai touched down twice apiece in a ten-try blitz of a Central side which was only a shadow of its predecessors. Auckland then overpowered South 34–22 at Christchurch, with Owen Wright and Mark Bourneville crossing for two tries each, and routed Northern Districts 68–12 at Carlaw Park. Nick Wright enjoyed a points feast of four tries and eight goals, while O'Regan scored another three tries and Bell two. It could hardly have been more emphatic.

CHAPTER NINE

Auckland fullback Nick Wright has too much pace for South Island forward Barry Edkins in Christchurch.
Christchurch Star

In the five seasons from 1983, Auckland never lost a game under the coaching of Bob Bailey. The only hiccup was a 12–12 draw with South Island at Greymouth in 1985, but, as Auckland Rugby League chairman George Rainey remarked as he left Wingham Park, 'a draw is as good as a win here'. Indeed it was, for Auckland topped the table ahead of South on a points count-back. South had emerged as Auckland's strongest challenger, but Auckland still won 22–18 at home in 1984, 38–8 at home in 1986, and 26–24 back at Greymouth in the final inter-districts competition of 1987 before it was discontinued.

1981: French under fire

Auckland 20 France 10

The 1981 French tour was the first such venture for seventeen years, coming after they had beaten the 1978 Kangaroos in a home series and only months after drawing one-all with the 1980 Kiwis. It was also the first time that France visited New Zealand before going on to Australia. Despite the impressive form and new itinerary, the Tricolours were well beaten in all four test matches.

France gained some consolation in the other tour fixtures in New Zealand, heading off a South Island XIII, Central Districts, New Zealand Māori and Northern Districts. But it was no match for Auckland, which scored four tries to two in winning 20–10 in a Monday night match at Carlaw Park, and it was all downhill across the Tasman.

This was the last of seven matches between France and Auckland, and the home team's fifth victory. Only the 1951 and 1964 touring sides had beaten the blue and whites. Auckland had won in 1955, 1960, 1975 and 1977. When France returned to New Zealand in 1995, it was matched against Bartercard Cup champion North Harbour.

'The Auckland team, with four current Kiwis, six former Kiwis and two New Zealand Maori representatives, was very strong,' noted the *New Zealand Herald*. 'They had been drilled to spin the ball out wide and they did this admirably with strong support for the backs from Ian Bell, who scored two tries.

'Captain Shane Varley again played intelligently and skilfully, often nipping any chance of an attack by the French in the bud. Deservedly, he was named man of the match for Auckland. James Leuluai carried on from his good work in the second test and Marcus Pouesi was impressive until he was substituted in the second half by Gary Kemble.

'In the last eight minutes of the first half the French could not score even when Auckland were down to 11 men. Lyndsay Proctor had been sent to the sin-bin after an earlier warning for dangerous tackles and Kevin Schaumkel was on the ground injured.'

Bell scored first in the thirteenth minute, Leuluai sprinted from near halfway for his try from a clever Varley cut-out pass, Ron O'Regan and Varley set Dane O'Hara up for a try soon after halftime, and Bell capitalised on good work by Gary Prohm and Varley to complete the scoring. Nick Wright kicked four goals. The French points came from Guy Lafforgue and Guy Alard tries and two Andre Perez goals.

Auckland team: fullback, Nick Wright; three-quarters Gary Prohm, Marcus Pouesi, James Leuluai, Dane O'Hara; halves, Ron O'Regan, Shane Varley (captain); forwards, Lyndsay Proctor, Les Beehre, Pat Poasa, Kevin Schaumkel, Tom Conroy, Ian Bell. Reserves: Gary Kemble, Mark Gillespie.

The player drain

The proliferation of New Zealand players, particularly from Auckland, in the British and Australian professional competitions can be traced back to 1981. Mark Graham moved from Brisbane to join Norths in the Sydney premiership and showed club scouts what talent could be plucked from across the Tasman. Meanwhile, officials of the Hull club, inspired by the stylish manner in which the 1980 Kiwis performed at the Boulevard, led the charge to attract top-class players to Britain.

Guy Alard reaches out in the tackle of James Leuluai to score a try for France.
NZ Herald

CHAPTER NINE

Hull director Dick Gemmell travelled to Auckland and signed outside backs James Leuluai and Dane O'Hara to three-year deals. Fullback Gary Kemble also agreed to an off-season contract, which later became full time. Gemmell was keen to bag stand-off half Fred Ah Kuoi as well, but Hull had to wait for the skilled playmaker. Ah Kuoi first spent three seasons with North Sydney before completing the Kiwis quartet at Hull.

It was inevitable that other British clubs would follow the highly successful Hull's lead. Neighbour and fierce rival Hull Kingston Rovers responded by signing Auckland utility Gary Prohm and West Coast scrum-half Gordon Smith for the 1982–83 northern season. Canterbury and Kiwis prop Mark Broadhurst, who had been with Manly-Warringah and Illawarra, joined them a year later. The Hull derbies were clashes to behold.

Wigan, of course, will long be the British club most associated with New Zealand imports, extending back to Auckland's Lance Todd after the 1907–08 All Golds tour. Among the Aucklanders to feature in Wigan's golden era were Dean Bell, who appeared in the first seven of eight consecutive Challenge Cup triumphs from 1988, Kevin Iro, who scored two tries in three consecutive Wembley finals between 1988 and 1990, Sam Panapa, Henry Paul and rugby union recruits Frano Botica and Va'aiga Tuigamala. Former Otahuhu mentor Graham Lowe was one of three New Zealanders to coach Wigan.

Kemble, Leuluai and O'Hara were true pioneers of the player drain. The British playing register for 1981–82 included Auckland representatives Ron O'Regan at Barrow and Shane Varley at Workington Town among a handful of New Zealanders, most of them on off-season stints. Eight years later the list had grown to sixty-two names, almost half of them having international experience.

Hull trio: Dane O'Hara, Gary Kemble and James Leuluai in 1982.
NZ Herald

Rugby league was then a winter game in Britain and it was customary for New Zealanders to return to their homeland in the northern summer and play a few games for their clubs and provinces in a bid to earn Kiwis selection against touring Lions teams and the Kangaroos at home and away. They were also eligible for test matches in Britain and France when the Kiwis mounted northern tours in 1985, 1989 and 1993. That all changed when the British Super League became a summer sport in 1996, running parallel to the Australian National Rugby League and ending traditional tours.

The McClennan factor

Mount Albert dominated the Auckland club scene from 1981 to 1986, appearing in all six Fox Memorial grand finals and winning five of them. Coach Mike McClennan was the master tactician behind all that success. His son, Brian, was an influential on-field force alongside Shane Cooper among the inside backs.

While McClennan was expert at peaking his teams on the biggest day of the club season, when up to 12,000 fans packed into Carlaw Park to admire the Mount's triumphant march, he also guided his players to successes with the Rukutai Shield in 1981 and 1983, the Roope Rooster in 1984, and the Stormont Shield in 1981 and 1985.

The only grand final defeat was by 14–11 to Otahuhu in 1983, when Owen Wright and Hugh McGahan demonstrated their burgeoning potential in the Otahuhu pack. Even then it took a late try to deny Mount Albert fans another celebration. They might reflect that the 1982 and 1984 victories at the expense of Otahuhu were ample compensation.

New challengers emerged after that. Mount Albert, with Paddy Tuimavave scoring two tries, denied first-time grand finalist Manukau 24–19 in the 1985 decider. Te Atatu reached the grand final for the first time in 1986, only to be blitzed 31–4 by Mount Albert.

By winning a third consecutive outright championship, Mount Albert had emulated the feats of Ponsonby from 1917 to 1919 and City between 1921 and 1923. It had taken sixty-three years to find a third treble title-winner. (Eastern United, which plundered so many trophies during the districts era, shared two of its four Fox Memorial wins.)

Mike McClennan.
Fairfax Media

CHAPTER NINE

The McClennans moved to Northcote and in 1989 claimed another Fox Memorial. In February 1990, Mike McClennan was appointed coach of proud Lancashire club St Helens, linking up again with Cooper. The high points of his four-year stay were Premiership finals in 1992 and 1993. Saints lost to Wigan the first time but gained sweet revenge in 1993 when Cooper was loose forward and captain and fellow Aucklander Tea Ropati was the stand-off half.

Brian McClennan famously followed his father into coaching. He took Hibiscus Coast from obscurity to a national Bartercard Cup title, won two more with Mount Albert and another with the Auckland Lions, plotted New Zealand's amazing 24–0 victory over Australia in the 2005 Tri-Nations final, and was headhunted by powerful British club Leeds. The McClennan magic was evident as Leeds won the 2008 World Club Challenge and Super League grand final in his first season.

John Ackland was a try-scorer and player of the match when Mount Albert beat Glenora in the 1981 Fox Memorial grand final.
Fairfax Media

Wellington shut-out

A national inter-club competition introduced in 1982 as the Wrangler Cup proved to be a benefit for Wellington clubs Petone and Randwick. Neither Otahuhu nor Glenora reached the final. Otahuhu beat Addington (Canterbury) and Western Suburbs (Taranaki) before falling 9–8 to Petone in a semi-final. Randwick eliminated Glenora 8–5 in the first round. Petone won the all-Wellington final 16–14. In 1983 the name was changed to the Tusk Cup.

Tusk Cup treble

Otahuhu (1983), Mount Albert (1984) and Manukau (1985) kept the Tusk Cup in Auckland for all three years of the national knockout competition's existence under that name. In all cases Wellington's Randwick was the runner-up. Finals were televised live and proved to be popular viewing throughout the country.

Giant prop Frank Tinitelia's spectacular try from seventy metres out, when he broke two tackles and fended off three more, was the highlight of Otahuhu's 30–22 victory in the 1983 decider. Owen Wright, Peter Simons, John Zwart and Daryl Morrison contributed the other Otahuhu tries and Bob Croawell kicked five goals. Otahuhu had been a 14–8 winner over Mount Albert in its quarter-final.

Mount Albert gained vengeance in 1984, eliminating Otahuhu 24–16 in a semi-final and accounting for Randwick 24–10 in the final. Tries for the winners were scored by Cedric Lovett, who also kicked four goals, John Ackland, Michael Moorwood and Ricky Cowan. In its opening match Mount Albert had pounded Gisborne club AML by 104–4. Mount Albert's closest encounter was an 8–4 win over Hornby in near-unplayable Christchurch weather.

Poor Randwick had to settle for second best again in 1985, crushed 34–13 by Manukau, when the winner received $15,000 and the runner-up $5,000. Kelly Shelford provided two tries and three goals, Peter Rewha, Chappie Pine, Richard Rawiri and Kennedy Toagaga one try each, and Terry Rawiri two goals. Pine became the first double winner of national club titles, having been among Petone's 1982 Wrangler Cup champions. Mount Albert's Tusk Cup defence had ended with a 24–10 semi-final loss to Manukau.

(1) Otahuhu prop Frank Tinitelia, scorer of the most spectacular try in a Tusk Cup match.

(2) Shane Cooper (Mount Albert) holds the Tusk Cup triumphantly aloft in 1984 as Rodney Rasmussen (Randwick) contemplates the result.

Fairfax Media

CHAPTER NINE

Hull of a draw

Auckland referee Kevin Bailey awarded British club Hull a penalty try just before fulltime to complete the scoring in an exciting 28–28 draw with Auckland at Carlaw Park in 1983. Bailey ruled that young scrum-half Tony Collinson had been impeded when chasing a kick into the Auckland in-goal area. Both coaches felt their players had frittered away winning leads, Hull at 16–6 in the first half and Auckland at 28–16 with thirteen minutes remaining.

Hull came to New Zealand as first division champion, Yorkshire Cup winner and Challenge Cup runner-up. It was not at full-strength without Lions Steve Evans, Steve Norton and Lee Crooks, and Dane O'Hara did not play against Auckland. O'Hara's fellow Kiwis, James Leuluai and Gary Kemble, lined up against their old province and Leuluai scored a try.

Auckland coach Bob Bailey surprised commentators by retaining Otahuhu scrum-half Daryl Morrison for his entire five-match campaign even when Kiwis Clayton Friend and Gary Freeman were available. The Ackland brothers, John and Geoff, packed down in the second-row, with Geoff scoring two tries against Hull. Ron O'Regan also scored twice, Dean Bell's try resulted from a John Ackland bomb, and Nick Wright kicked four goals.

Geoff Ackland was then in the midst of a representative try-scoring spree. He did not play against Northern Districts but touched down once against South Island, twice against Hull, once against Central Districts and capped it all off with three tries in a 44–2 victory over New Zealand Māori.

Owen Wright on the charge for Auckland against Hull.
Fairfax Media

Gary Kemble playing for his professional club against his old province.
Fairfax Media

Six of the best

Otahuhu loose forward Hugh McGahan rewrote the world test try-scoring records when he touched down an incredible six times in the Kiwis' 60–20 victory over Papua New Guinea at Carlaw Park in 1983. The value of tries had that season been raised to four points, enabling McGahan to also exceed Des White's New Zealand test record of twenty-two points against Australia at Brisbane in 1952.

McGahan was aided by another change introduced in 1983 – the stopping of the clock for kicks at goal. This resulted in the match lasting almost 100 minutes, so it was hardly surprising that the stopped-clock rule was discarded. An even bigger help to McGahan was Kiwis second-rower Kurt Sorensen, who featured in ten of New Zealand's eleven tries and shared the man of the match award.

In future years McGahan was to fashion an outstanding career with Eastern Suburbs in Sydney, captain the Kiwis to victory over Australia at Brisbane, and be joint winner with star Kangaroos scrum-half Peter Sterling of the Golden Boot Award as the world's best player. But in 1983 he had been left out of the home and away tests against Australia, so when Kiwis coach Graham Lowe told him to 'be a finisher not a setter-up' against the Kumuls he followed his instructions to the letter.

The next most tries scored by Kiwis at test or World Cup level is four, by Brian Jellick against Tonga at Carlaw Park in 1999 and by Manu Vatuvei against England in a 2008 World Cup pool game at EnergyAustralia Stadium in Newcastle.

Hugh McGahan.
Fairfax Media

CHAPTER NINE

1984: Cedric's clincher

Auckland 18 Great Britain 16

Auckland wing Cedric Lovett clinched an 18–16 victory over the 1984 Great Britain Lions with one of the finest pressure goals seen at Carlaw Park. Moments earlier Lovett had made a sideline break and, when cornered, punted infield. Had the British contented themselves with fielding the ball and taking a tackle the match would have ended at 16–16. But forward Andy Goodway needlessly sent Lovett sprawling and was penalised by local referee Ray Shrimpton.

Lovett lined up the kick from twenty-five metres out and a couple of metres in from touch. To the delight of the 7,000 fans who had braved a wet Tuesday night, and to the relief of Auckland coach Bob Bailey, who could not watch, the ball flew straight and true. Though beaten in all six test matches in Australasia, the Lions' only loss in seventeen other fixtures had been to Toowoomba. Plenty of pride was at stake in the tour finale.

Bailey remained loyal to his regular provincial side, resisting any temptation to stack his team for the occasion. But when Hugh McGahan withdrew through injury, Bailey called in rugged test prop Kevin Tamati as his only overseas-based player. Fullback Darrell Williams, centre Dean Bell and halves Shane Cooper and Clayton Friend were then on the brink of illustrious professional careers.

Lions coach Frank Myler fired a verbal broadside at Shrimpton after the match, not for the whistle-blower's decision to penalise Goodway for pushing Lovett, but for allowing Cooper to get across for his second try from a tap penalty when he caught the defence unawares. Myler claimed Shrimpton had penalised British loose forward Mick Adams for doing the same thing during the Ashes test series in Australia.

There was no disputing Cooper's first try after ten minutes. A bomb was hoisted, British fullback Mick Burke misfielded and the alert Cooper was on hand to score. Lovett's conversion edged Auckland 6–0 ahead at halftime. A combined passing rush led to a Lovett try, but Britain temporarily led 14–10 after a Keith Mumby try and two more to Goodway. Cooper's disputed second try, Lovett's conversion and a penalty goal by David Hobbs for the visitors set the scene at 16–16 for Lovett's eleventh-hour heroics.

The least affected individual after the match appeared to be Lovett himself. 'I wasn't really under pressure,' he told the media. 'I just kicked it. Naturally I was rapt when it went through.'

Auckland team: fullback, Darrell Williams; three-quarters, Cedric Lovett, Dean Bell, Ron O'Regan (captain), Joe Ropati; halves, Shane Cooper, Clayton Friend; forwards, Kevin Tamati, Lindsay Hooker, Ricky Cowan, John Ackland, Steve Howells, Owen Wright. Replacements: Afi Ah Kuoi, John Zwart.

Cedric Lovett, kicker of the winning goal against the 1984 Lions.
Fairfax Media

A friend in need

Clayton Friend could not quite spur Manukau to a Fox Memorial triumph in his last season before taking up a contract with North Sydney. But Manukau, coached by Friend's uncle, Cameron Bell, did carry off the Rukutai Shield and the Roope Rooster and made its season even more memorable by convincingly beating top British club St Helens 26–10. Manukau earned the right to play the Saints by leading after seven competition rounds and was a worthy representative. The combative Friend got under the skin of his rivals in more ways than one. At one stage St Helens captain Harry Pinner spent ten minutes in the sin-bin for head-butting the Kiwis scrum-half. Just before fulltime, Friend anticipated an inside ball from Pinner, intercepted the pass and scampered forty-five metres to score.

Manukau scrum-half Clayton Friend leaves St Helens defenders Shaun Allen (left) and Paul Round in his wake.
Fairfax Media

CHAPTER NINE

Cup cliff hanger

Only forty-eight hours after Auckland had drawn its 1985 inter-districts match with South Island at Greymouth, it reverted to being a provincial team and challenged Canterbury for the Rugby League (formerly Northern Union) Cup at the Addington Show Grounds in Christchurch. Several reinforcements had been flown in to bolster coach Bob Bailey's team but players from both sides were still feeling the effects of their showdown in Greymouth. That did not prevent them from producing another thriller. Incredibly, the cup stayed with Canterbury after another draw, 22–22. More remarkably, half of those points were rattled on in the last nine minutes. In that time Auckland led twice, Canterbury once and they were level on two occasions. Just on time Canterbury forward Paul Truscott crashed over for the try which, with replacement Phil Bancroft's conversion, prevented the cup from going north. Ron O'Regan (two), Mark Elia and Sam Panapa scored Auckland's tries and Nick Wright (two) and Paddy Tuimavave kicked goals. Truscott, Adrian Shelford, Mike Kerrigan and Brent Todd were Canterbury's try-scorers, with two goals to Bancroft and one to Marty Crequer.

1985: Kangaroos kick back

Australia 50 Auckland 10

Auckland wore the backlash of one of Australia's most humbling rugby league occasions, the 18–0 defeat by the Kiwis at Carlaw Park in the third test of a fiercely contested series. The Kangaroos had won the first test with a late converted try at Brisbane, and the second with an even later converted try at Carlaw Park. Australian coach Terry Fearnley made several controversial changes which ignited inter-state rivalries within his camp, while the Kiwis used their disappointment and the public's encouragement to inspire them to their third test shut-out.

Joe Ropati (hand injury), Clayton Friend (neck) and Owen Wright (ankle) withdrew from the Auckland side after having taken knocks in the test two days earlier. Friend and Wright were 'late scratchings' and it was not until two hours before kick-off that coach Bob Bailey was able to finalise his side. The Australians, meanwhile, brought back the Queenslanders who were still seething at missing the test team.

One of those jilted Queenslanders, centre Chris Close, made his point by scoring three of Australia's eight tries against Auckland. Co-centre Michael O'Connor enjoyed a points-scoring picnic with a try and nine goals from eleven attempts. By halftime it was 20–0 and that quickly increased when rampaging forward Noel Cleal scored the first of his two tries. Garry Jack and Des Hasler were Australia's other try-scorers.

Auckland's first points did not come until the forty-eighth minute, when wholehearted forward Dennis Stewart crossed from a tap penalty. Nick Wright added the conversion for 6–26 but Close soon completed his try-scoring treble and the margin continued to grow. The Australian dominance was interrupted only by a Mark Bourneville consolation try.

Several flare-ups marred the match, though did not diminish the entertainment for an estimated 15,000 fans, and local referee Dennis Hale sin-binned rival forwards James Goulding and Peter Tunks in the first half and Auckland prop Frank Tinitelia after a brawl just before fulltime.

Stewart was judged to be the best Auckland player, not only for his strong burst to score but for his non-stop tackling against the waves of Australian attacks. Goulding, who had been named Junior Kiwis captain but was to be promoted into the full New Zealand team to tour Britain and France, and Sam Panapa, diligently filling in for Friend at scrum-half, were others singled out for praise.

Auckland team: fullback, Nick Wright; three-quarters, Mark Bourneville, Darrell Williams, Ron O'Regan (captain), Mark Elia; halves, Kelly Shelford, Sam Panapa; forwards, Ricky Cowan, Tracey McGregor, Frank Tinitelia, Dennis Stewart, James Goulding, Dean Lonergan. Reserves: Paddy Tuimavave, Ian Bell.

Auckland second-rower Dennis Stewart is out-jumped by Kangaroos forward Peter Tunks. Nick Wright can't bear to look.
NZ Herald

CHAPTER NINE

Back where it belongs

Coach Bob Bailey admitted in the aftermath of Auckland's 16–14 Rugby League Cup win over Canterbury at Christchurch in 1986 that his fingernails had been nervously gnawed during the tense final few minutes. Canterbury staged a late attack, prop Ross Taylor was dragged down just short of the goal-line and then prevented from playing the ball quickly. But West Coast referee Paddy Byrne ruled no infringement had occurred and the local fans' call for the penalty, which might have drawn the game and retained the cup, fell on deaf ears.

When the symbol of inter-provincial supremacy, presented to the New Zealand Rugby League by the managers of the first British touring team in 1910, had last been in Auckland in 1968 it was known by its original name of Northern Union Cup. Although Auckland had not seriously pursued the prize over the ensuing eighteen years, it sent a powerful line-up to Christchurch. Only hooker Tracey McGregor was not a former, current or future Kiwi.

Bob Bailey in 1990.
Fairfax Media

Wings Marty Crequer (from Canterbury) and Shane Horo (from Waikato) had transferred to Auckland, joining Darrell Williams, Mark Elia, Tea Ropati, Shane Cooper and Gary Freeman in a talented backline. McGregor packed down with props Peter Brown and George Mann and backrowers Owen Wright, Dean Lonergan and captain Ron O'Regan. The reserves were Paddy Tuimavave and James Goulding. Canterbury fielded seven internationals in halves Brendon Tuuta and Phil Bancroft and forwards Taylor, Brent Todd, Wayne Wallace, Esene Faimalo and Barry Edkins.

Auckland led 6–0 at halftime thanks to a Ropati try just before the break. Williams and Goulding scored the other tries which, with Brown's two goals, nudged the challenger out to 16–8 well into the final quarter. Todd had gained Canterbury's first try and when Edkins scored and converted (his third goal) the margin was reduced to two points to start Bailey's nerves jingling.

When the provinces met again at Carlaw Park three months later, with the Cup again at stake, Auckland was without twelve Kiwis who were touring Australia and Papua New Guinea. Canterbury had lost only Wallace and Todd. Of the side which had won the cup in Christchurch only Horo, Tuimavave, McGregor and Mann defended it.

But Auckland's new-look combination of Kevin Teague, Shane Horo, Peter Kelly, Tuimavave, Mark Bourneville, Dave Watson, Brian McClennan (captain), Craig Coyle, McGregor, Mann, Chappie Pine, Peter Ropati, Mark Horo and reserves Dennis Stewart and Sam Panapa was more than up to the task.

The Horo brothers, Watson and Tuimavave scored tries, and Teague kicked three goals in a 22–8 victory. McClennan earned the award as the best player on the night. The Rugby League Cup stayed in the Carlaw Park trophy cabinet for three more years.

Cup-winning captain Brian McClennan.
Fairfax Media

Te Atatu at the top

In 1986 Te Atatu had the distinction of winning the renamed Lion Red League Nationals knockout title before claiming its first Auckland championship. Te Atatu won the Rukutai Shield as Auckland's minor premier, only to be routed 31–4 by Mount Albert in its first Fox Memorial grand final. But the positions were reversed in the Lion Red final, with Te Atatu running away to a 36–10 victory. Te Atatu had eliminated the invariably strong Wellington clubs, Randwick and Upper Hutt, before overpowering hot favourite Mount Albert in the final. Peter Brown, Mark Horo, Craig Coyle and Terry O'Shea took charge of the forward battle, Ron O'Regan was a skilful playmaker and outside backs Shane Horo and Mark Elia capitalised. Brown and Horo each scored two of Te Atatu's seven tries.

CHAPTER NINE

Elated Te Atatu captain-coach Ron O'Regan holds the Fox Memorial Shield aloft at Eden Park in 1988.
Fairfax Media

Te Atatu forward Peter Brown breaks away from Mount Albert's Cedric Lovett and Shane Cooper in the 1986 grand final.
Alex Jacob

Two years later, with O'Regan making his debut as player-coach, Te Atatu won a Lion Red League Nationals and Fox Memorial double at the expense of Glenora. Te Atatu advanced from third qualifier to beat minor premier Glenora 22–16 in the Fox showdown despite being reduced to eleven men for part of the last quarter, when Sam Panapa was sin-binned and then Brown sent off for a high tackle. O'Regan superbly organised Te Atatu's defences in that time of need. The national final was held at Eden Park as curtain-raiser to the World Cup final and in front of a crowd building to more than 48,000. Brown, Elia and Mark Horo were committed to the Kiwis, but Te Atatu recovered from an eight-point deficit to win 18–8 thanks to two tries by Carl Magatogia, another by Panapa and three O'Shea goals.

Dean Bell a southerner?

There is no family in Auckland more synonymous with rugby league than that which encompasses the Bells and the Friends. Dean Bell, who captained the Kiwis, achieved fame with British glamour club Wigan and led the Auckland Warriors in their inaugural Winfield Cup season in 1995, was a sparkling jewel in the family crown. Yet he once lined up for South Island against Auckland and all but inspired his unfamiliar team-mates to victory.

The occasion was the final 1987 inter-districts clash at Wingham Park, Greymouth. With Auckland having a settled line-up, Bell was drafted into the South squad as a guest player so that he would get some match practice between his return from Wigan and upcoming test matches in Papua New Guinea and Australia.

It was a move welcomed by South coach Ray Haffenden. South had already lost to Central Districts and Northern Districts, while Auckland had scored sixty-two points against Northern and fifty-eight against Central. Auckland coach Bob Bailey was stepping down from the position and was keen to break a Wingham Park hoodoo extending back nearly twenty years.

Within sixteen minutes Auckland led 18–0, before South cut into that deficit so steadily that it drew level soon after halftime. Bell's astute marshalling of his midfield troops limited the effectiveness of the Auckland backs but tries to Shane Horo (two), Mark Horo and Gary Freeman and five Peter Brown goals finally exorcised the ghosts of Wingham Park by 26–24.

CHAPTER NINE

Ropati quartet

Four Ropati brothers, John, Joe, Tea and Peter, were in the Auckland starting teams which thrashed Northern 62–6 and Central 58–14 at Carlaw Park during the 1987 inter-districts championship. John was the Auckland fullback in eight of the nine representative fixtures, Joe played on the wing three times, Tea appeared in all nine while switching between stand-off half, centre, and reserve back, and Peter was ever-present at prop, second-row or on the bench. Tea and Peter were in good company. Only hooker Rene Nordmeyer and captain and loose forward Ron O'Regan also played in every game of an unbeaten campaign. The Ropati family was by no means finished. Another brother, Iva, was then advancing through the grades towards Auckland and higher honours.

Darrell Williams in action for Manly.
Fairfax Media

Williams first winner

Auckland centre Darrell Williams became the first New Zealander to taste success in a Winfield Cup premiership when his Manly-Warringah side beat Canberra 18–8 before 50,201 fans in what was to be the last grand final at the Sydney Cricket Ground. The other Kiwis to have played in Sydney Cricket Ground grand finals were Canterbury prop Bill Noonan (for Canterbury-Bankstown in 1974) and Auckland prop Henry Tatana (for St George in 1975). Both of their teams lost to the great Eastern Suburbs side of their era. But in 1987 there had to be a New Zealander stepping up to receive a winner's medal, with Williams opposed by Canberra's former Canterbury prop Brent Todd. Although a loser at the Sydney Cricket Ground, Todd played in three more grand finals at the Sydney Football Stadium, for two wins and a loss.

Fox crosses the harbour

The Fox Memorial Shield crossed Auckland harbour for the first time since North Shore had won the 1941 club championship when Northcote achieved a hard-earned 12–8 victory over Mangere East in the 1987 grand final at Carlaw Park. In front of 14,000 spectators, Northcote battled through with only twelve men for sixty minutes after captain Jeff Clarke was ordered off for a high tackle on Mangere East prop Peter Neilson. New coach Graeme Birch received great service from Kiwis Gary Freeman, Marty Crequer and Shane Horo, the fearsome Fue brothers, John and Peter, Dean Birch and Shane Hansen. With only eight teams, the minor premiership was intense. After conceding two points on protest for using an ineligible player, Northcote finished just one point behind Mangere East and ahead of Te Atatu and Otahuhu on count-back, with Mount Albert one point out of the top four. John Fue scored Northcote's only try in the grand final, Birch kicked three goals, and both Birch and Freeman landed field goals.

Northcote farewelled Freeman to a professional career with Sydney club Balmain by beating Mangere East in the Lion Red League Nationals knockout final at Carlaw Park. The two Auckland sides had roared through the earlier rounds, Northcote eliminating Hornby (Canterbury) 30–4 and Mangere East beating Randwick (Wellington) 48–12 in the semi-finals. Once again, there was little between them in the final, with Shane Horo and Robert Moimoi scoring tries for Northcote, Geoff Hindman and John Ropati replying in kind for Mangere East, and the Tigers getting home on the back of Birch's three goals against two by Robert Pera. It did not help Mangere East's chances that key players George Mann and Dave Townsend were injured in a car accident on the eve of the game. Northcote forward Chappie Pine received his third winners' medal, having previously been with Petone in 1982 and Manukau in 1985.

Northcote captain Jeff Clarke walks from Carlaw Park after being sent off in the 1987 grand final.
Fairfax Media

Less than ninety minutes later he was lifting the Fox Memorial Shield after Northcote's 12–8 victory over Mangere East.
Fairfax Media

New Zealand XIII

It was the season before the birth of the Brisbane Broncos, so when Queensland brought a Residents team to Auckland in 1987 it included Gene Miles, Wally Lewis, Allan Langer, Greg Dowling, Greg Conescu and Mark Hohn. The New Zealand XIII it beat 18–14 at Carlaw Park was also without any Sydney-based professionals but – wearing white jerseys with black vees – it fielded future professionals Kevin Iro, Gary Mercer, Tea Ropati, Sam Panapa, Gary Freeman, Adrian Shelford, Sam Stewart and Mark Horo. Two Auckland families enhanced proud records when Warren Mann lined up on one wing and Peter Ropati packed down in the second-row. They were the only non-Kiwis in the team but their selection showed how close they came to full international honours. The New Zealand tries were scored by Panapa and Tea Ropati, and Tea Ropati (two) and Peter Brown kicked goals. Queensland slaughtered Bay of Plenty 72–6 in its other game.

Battle of the bears

Glenora might not have won its $20,000 winner-take-all challenge to North Sydney in their 1987 match at Carlaw Park, but the club emerged smiling financially when the promotion attracted 12,000 spectators. Norths brought Mark Graham and Clayton Friend back to their home town, and Glenora bolstered its ranks with several invitation players, notably Auckland captain Ron O'Regan. The sizeable prize money ensured the validity of the contest. Only one try was scored by each side in Norths' 11–8 victory, Steve Hanson for the winners and Dave Watson for Glenora.

Taking on the Brits:
1987 Auckland tour of Britain

A 10–6 victory over world club champion Wigan at Central Park was the highlight of Auckland's ambitious six-match tour of Britain in 1987. Coached by expatriate Aucklander Graham Lowe, Wigan had beaten Sydney champion Manly-Warringah for the world title just before the Auckland squad arrived. Auckland also beat Leeds 29–25 and Warrington 22–16 and lost to St Helens 52–26, Hull 26–24 and a test-standard Chairman's XIII 12–6.

Coached by Bob Bailey, managed by Peter McLeod and Bill Nesbitt, and with Graeme Coutts as the travelling physiotherapist, the team was: backs, Shane Cooper, Marty Crequer, Gary Freeman, Clayton Friend, Shane Horo, Kevin Iro, Warren Mann, Sam Panapa, Michael Patton, John Ropati, Tea Ropati, and Paddy Tuimavave; forwards, Peter Brown, James Goulding, George Mann,

Lindsay Hooker, Mark Horo, Steve Kaiser, Dean Lonergan, Rene Nordmeyer, Ron O'Regan (captain), and Peter Ropati.

The thirty-two-year-old Kaiser, a front-rower from Te Atatu, was regarded as the surprise selection because he had not played for Auckland since a midweek match in 1979. But Bailey had no qualms at recalling Kaiser, describing him as 'the best open side prop in Auckland'. Apart from Kaiser and North Sydney scrum-half Friend, all of the selected players had been involved in the province's unbeaten nine-match domestic programme.

Many of the Aucklanders were having their first game for several weeks when they took on Leeds, and it showed as the home team raced twenty points clear. However, a superb all-round second-half performance from 24–10 down limited Leeds to a solitary field goal and enabled Auckland to get home 29–25 thanks to a last-minute Lonergan try. Crequer was named as Auckland's best player, and there were particularly strong games from Panapa, Lonergan, Friend and O'Regan. Kaiser celebrated his belated comeback with a try.

Two days later Auckland was opposed by Warrington, then unbeaten and regarded as the most physical side in Britain. Warrington justified that reputation, but Auckland led by six points at halftime before going on to win 22–16. Freeman starred and second-rowers Lonergan (two) and Mark Horo took the scoring honours with all three of Auckland's tries.

AUCKLAND RUGBY LEAGUE
1909–2009

The 1987 Auckland team which toured Britain.

Back row: Shane Cooper, Rene Nordmeyer, Paddy Tuimavave, George Mann, Marty Crequer, Shane Horo, Mike Patton, Warren Mann, Peter Ropati.

Middle row: Steve Dodds (promoter), James Goulding, Dean Lonergan, Kevin Iro, Peter Brown, Steve Kaiser, Lindsay Hooker, Sam Panapa, Bill Shrimpton (referee), Graeme Coutts (physiotherapist).

Front row: Bill Nesbitt (manager), John Ropati, Mark Horo, Ron O'Regan (captain), Bob Bailey (coach), Clayton Friend, Gary Freeman, Tea Ropati, Peter McLeod (chairman).

Peter Brown collection

CHAPTER NINE

Legendary coach Alex Murphy and his potent St Helens side were poised to pounce when Auckland lined up for its third game in a week at Knowsley Road. The heavy travelling and playing toll counted against the visitors, though sparkling displays by Friend and Iro added to the overall spectacle. The Saints produced a high standard of attacking football to score nine tries against Auckland's five in a 52–26 result.

Hull's golden era had passed, but it matched Auckland's five tries and kicked three goals to two in a 26–24 boilover. Auckland officials were disappointed with the manner in which tries were frittered away by poor finishing and concluded it was a game their players should have won comfortably. Instead, Hull prevailed with a late try. Former Kiwi James Leuluai captained Hull from stand-off half and maintained his reputation as a big match try-scorer.

The Wigan fixture had always been tagged as one which would make or break the on-field success of the tour. Wigan went into the match a warm favourite after its triumph over Manly and because of Auckland's consecutive losses. If anything, Auckland's 10–6 success flattered Wigan.

'Auckland dominated the game with a strong defensive effort that kept Wigan tryless throughout the 80 minutes and only goalkicking kept the locals in the game,' said the *1987 Auckland Rugby League Year Book*. Auckland's tries came from Cooper and Shane Horo and big games were turned in by Peter Brown [player of the day] and the halves, Clayton Friend and Gary Freeman. Overall, however, it was a superb team effort that secured the victory.'

Tea Ropati tackled by Garry Schofield with Sam Panapa in close attendance during the Leeds match.
Peter Brown collection

Injuries forced rearrangements to the Auckland side for the unofficial test against a Chairman's XIII coached by Malcolm Reilly which included such lauded internationals as Garry Schofield, Martin Offiah, Shaun Edwards, Deryck Fox, Lee Crooks, Roy Powell and Andy Platt. Auckland fielded John Ropati, Panapa, Tea Ropati, Tuimavave (replaced by Patton), Shane Horo, Cooper, Freeman, Brown, Hooker, Goulding, Kaiser, Peter Ropati and Mark Horo.

'Despite the injury toll and the strength of the opposition Auckland could be considered unlucky not to win,' said the *Year Book*. 'Auckland were by far the more enterprising team and had much of the territorial advantage but a lack of finishing at crucial times and some bad luck saw the Great Britain selection win 12–6. Only a disputed try separated the teams. Gary Freeman was named player of the day.'

Five players were sent off during the tour – Mark Horo and Leeds' Kevin Rayne in the first match, Kaiser at St Helens, and Brown and Crooks in the tour finale. Suspensions for two matches were imposed on all except Rayne, who was sidelined for four games. Brown, Shane Horo and Panapa appeared in all six fixtures, Brown scoring most points (thirty-two) and goals (fourteen) and Horo most tries (six).

Opinions were divided as to the respective merits of the tour from playing and financial perspectives. It was generally agreed that Auckland's players – and the Kiwis, who were due to tour Britain in 1989 – would benefit from the experience. But there was criticism of the poor promotion by the Rugby Football League and the host clubs. Attendances varied from 10,743 for the Wigan game down to a

Clayton Friend kicks downfield and Gary Freeman chases after it against Wigan.
Peter Brown collection

mere 1,921 spectators at Hull. Business manager McLeod and promoter Steve Dodds were resigned to the bold venture suffering a financial loss.

Tour results:

Sunday, October 25: Auckland 29 (Panapa, Kaiser, Crequer, Brown, Tuimavave, Lonergan tries; Brown two goals; Lonergan field goal) beat Leeds 25 (Schofield two, Spencer two tries; Creasser four goals; Crooks field goal). Halftime: 24–10.

Tuesday, October 27: Auckland 22 (Lonergan two, M Horo tries; Brown five goals) beat Warrington 16 (Roberts, Drummond tries; Turner four goals). Halftime: 14–8.

Sunday, November 1: St Helens 52 (Quirk three, Platt two, Veivers, Evans, Bailey, Ledger tries; Tanner eight goals) beat Auckland 26 (S Horo two, Iro two, Friend tries; Brown three goals). Halftime: 28–16.

Wednesday, November 4: Hull 26 (Ellis two, Windley, Leuluai, Patrick tries; Pearce three goals) beat Auckland 24 (S Horo two, Iro, Cooper, Freeman tries; Brown two goals). Halftime: 16–6.

Sunday, November 8: Auckland 10 (S Horo, Cooper tries; Brown goal) beat Wigan 6 (Stephenson two, Lydon goals). Halftime: 10–0.

Tuesday, November 10: Chairman's XIII 12 (Offiah, Ford tries; Whitfield two goals) beat Auckland 6 (S Horo try; Brown goal). Halftime: 2–6.

Auckland's tour followed that of the Junior Kiwis, who accumulated 323 points and conceded only thirty-six in seven matches against the best British junior amateur players. Aucklanders on that tour were David Marsh, Jarrod McCracken, Kevin Iro, David Bailey, Thom Perenara, Dean Clark, Todd Price, Carl Hall, Carl Findlay, Jason Lowrie, Terry Cuthbert, Tame Tagaloa, Tony Tuimavave, Mike Setafano and Pecham Murray.

1988: New team tames Lions

Auckland 30 Great Britain 14

New coach Cameron Bell and a radically revised Auckland team enjoyed a decisive 30–14 victory over the 1988 Great Britain Lions at Carlaw Park. Only wings Mark Bourneville and Marty Crequer (a pre-match replacement for Shane Horo) and prop Peter Brown were Kiwis and only fullback Paddy Tuimavave and centre Mike Patton were other survivors of Auckland's tour of Britain a few months earlier. Tuimavave was promoted to captain in the absence of Shane Cooper and Mark Horo.

The Lions had come to New Zealand fresh from a big win over Australia in the third test at Sydney. They beat Wellington in a midweek match, but lost

Kelly Shelford about to score one of his two tries against Great Britain.
NZ Herald

12–10 to the Kiwis on a wintry Christchurch afternoon. That result catapulted New Zealand into the World Cup final against Australia later in the year. Britain named nine test players against Auckland, eager to at least finish its tour on a positive note.

Making his debut for Auckland was twenty-two-year-old hooker Duane Mann, preferred ahead of Glenora club-mate Greg Hiley. Cooper, Kevin Iro and the Horo brothers were out with injuries. Bell settled on a new halfback combination of former Canterbury representative Phil Bancroft and Kelly Shelford, brought Nahu Timoko into the second-row and switched Shane Hansen to loose forward.

Hansen was given the task of covering wily British scrum-half Andy Gregory and carried out his role so successfully that the *New Zealand Herald* reckoned most of his thirty-eight tackles were made on Gregory. Mann even topped that tackle count by six and was chosen as player of the match for a tremendous first-up display. Tuimavave was twice beaten by impressive Lions wing Henderson Gill, but those were his only blemishes in an inspiring captain's example.

'If Tuimavave, Hansen and Mann were the outstanding players, not far behind were Peter Brown, with another hard-working performance, halfback Phil Bancroft,

CHAPTER NINE

and Kelly Shelford with his charging runs and fine kicking,' said the *Herald*. 'David Watson, Se'e Solomona, Francis Leota and Mark Bourneville never let up.'

Britain led only when Paul Loughlin opened the scoring with a penalty goal. It was 14–4 to the home side by halftime. Brown, backing up from the test match in Christchurch, scored a try and three goals and Tuimavave was also a try-scorer. Any chance of Britain recovering went when Shelford scored early in the second spell. He was to add a second try, Leota grabbed another, and Bancroft kicked two goals. Britain's points came from Gill's two tries and Loughlin's three goals.

Auckland team: fullback, Paddy Tuimavave (captain); three-quarters, Mark Bourneville, Mike Patton, Dave Watson, Marty Crequer; halves, Kelly Shelford, Phil Bancroft; forwards, Peter Brown, Duane Mann, Se'e Solomona, Nahu Timoko, Francis Leota, Shane Hansen. Replacements: Dean Birch, Greg Hiley.

Queensland hammered

A Queensland Residents team played three matches on a May 1988 New Zealand tour, seeking to create player depth in the first Winfield Cup season of the Brisbane Broncos. The Residents beat West Coast 24–12 and Canterbury 26–22 but had no answers to Auckland when suffering a 70–12 hiding. Young Manukau centre Dave Watson had been elevated to partner Kevin Iro in the centres, and both thoroughly enjoyed themselves. Watson scored four tries and Iro two. Iva Ropati (two), Andrew Ah Kuoi, Paddy Tuimavave, Greg Hiley, Dean Birch, Se'e Solomona and Peter Brown were also try-scorers and Brown (six) and Birch (one) kicked goals. In the second half Auckland rattled on forty-four unanswered points.

By the time Auckland played Winfield Cup champion Canterbury-Bankstown in a September $30,000 challenge match, Bell had problems. Watson and Shane Cooper had departed for England, while top clubs Te Atatu and Glenora were engaged in the national knockout competition. He called in fullback Tom Sutton, stand-off Brian McClennan, hooker Rene Nordmeyer, young loose forward Tony Tuimavave, and new reserves Darryl Henare and Darren Harris. Front-rower George Mann was back from a season with Newcastle.

Bell was proud of the manner in which his makeshift team extended the Bulldogs, who just held on to win 20–16. Shane Horo and Tony Tuimavave scored Auckland's tries and Birch kicked four goals. Bulldogs coach Phil Gould was particularly impressed with Auckland props Solomona and Mann, while Tuimavave and Hansen were the other forwards to stand out. Down by four points with time running out, Auckland launched one last raid, only for captain and centre Paddy Tuimavave to be held up over the goal-line and the ball to spill loose.

Kevin Iro clashes with opposing Canterbury-Bankstown centre Andrew Farrar.
Fairfax Media

First division champion

Although Auckland won the inaugural provincial first division championship, which replaced the inter-districts competition in 1988, it also suffered its first loss to Wellington for seventy-five years. Only three provinces competed, and Auckland had the title in safe keeping after wins over Canterbury (30–21 in Christchurch and 20–4 at Carlaw Park) and Wellington at home (22–18). Canterbury and Wellington had shared a win and a loss against each other.

Inevitably, it was Wellington's 18–10 victory at the Hutt Recreation Ground which grabbed the biggest headlines. Wellington coach Howie Tamati was confident enough to ask Auckland to bring the Rugby League Cup south, but his request was not granted. The on-field inspiration was former Aucklander James Leuluai, engaged by Wellington after finishing up at English club Hull. Big men Robert Piva and Kelly Makoare and hooker Daryl Rolleston, who took four tight heads, ruled around the rucks. Kevin Iro and Shane Horo scored Auckland's tries, and Dean Birch kicked a goal.

CHAPTER NINE

'The pressure of having to keep up an unbeaten record against Wellington for 75 years is now over,' said Auckland coach Cameron Bell. 'Gone too is the pressure of not having been beaten by a New Zealand side for five years. The pressures were beginning to tell and if they were not obvious they would have been by next year.'

Bell and his players rectified the situation in 1989, when Bay of Plenty became the fourth first-division province. Auckland was extended only in its opening game against Wellington at Carlaw Park. Reduced to twelve men early in the second half when Dave Watson dislocated an elbow after both replacements had been used, Auckland stuck to its task to win 12–6. Dean Clark, back from a rookie season with Eastern Suburbs in Sydney, and Mark Horo scored the tries, and Phil Bancroft kicked two goals.

Auckland would go on to humble Canterbury 50–12 at home, Bay of Plenty 88–14 at Rotorua (Bancroft two tries and fourteen goals), Canterbury 38–4 at Christchurch, Wellington 32–10 at home and Bay of Plenty 62–6 at home (Tea Ropati two tries and nine goals). The only setback was a 38–30 loss to Rest of New Zealand, which included Aucklanders Shane Cooper, George Mann, Tea Ropati and Se'e Solomona.

Auckland loose forward Neville Ramsay keeping his attacking options open against Wellington at Carlaw Park in 1988.
Fairfax Media

1989: Carlaw Park cheers

Auckland 26 Australia 24

Kelly Shelford's winning penalty goal in Auckland's 26–24 defeat of the 1989 Kangaroos was from a far easier position than those of Des White for the 1951 Kiwis against France and Cedric Lovett for Auckland against Great Britain in 1984. But the cheers erupting from the Carlaw Park crowd has become an indelible memory for those who were there. New Zealand, with the Kiwis one down in the test series and well beaten in the 1988 World Cup final at Eden Park, was in serious need of a major victory and Auckland provided it.

It was all the more welcome because it was totally unexpected. Auckland coach Cameron Bell lost Kevin Iro, Phil Bancroft, Duane Mann and Mark Horo to the Kiwis squad and Paddy Tuimavave and Peter Brown through injury. Seven of his men had been in the President's XIII overrun 50–12 by Australia a week earlier, prop Mike Thomson was debuting in place of Brown, and fellow prop George Mann and wing Kevin Pulieata were playing their first games of the season. It seemed to be no contest.

But Auckland hinted at an upset when Mike Patton scored in the fourth minute from a Kelly Shelford chip kick. Australia claimed the next ten points from Michael Hancock and Dale Shearer tries and a Michael O'Connor goal. Auckland levelled 10–10 by halftime when Shelford deftly put Dave Watson into a gap and then converted the Watson try. It was game on, and the packed terraces were simmering with excitement.

AUCKLAND RUGBY LEAGUE
1909–2009

Shane Hansen comes to grips with Kangaroos scrum-half Greg Alexander.
Fairfax Media

The after-match scene in the Auckland dressing room leaves no doubts as to the outcome of a rousing encounter.
NZ Herald

CHAPTER NINE

A Shelford penalty goal and conversion of Francis Leota's try made it 18–10. Could the unthinkable happen? Australia regathered its composure to put on consecutive tries by Tony Currie, Shearer and Greg Alexander and suddenly it was 24–18 to the tourists. Did Auckland have anything left?

'When we were down (18–24) we just got together behind the goal-line and said "let's keep this ship together",' hooker Peter Ropati told the *New Zealand Herald* afterwards. 'We could have been content with just closing up and keeping it down to a close score. But we went back and attacked. It shows there are good footballers in New Zealand – you don't have to go to Sydney to make it.'

From a tap penalty, Watson darted across field and found loose forward Shane Hansen storming up to crash through for a try which Shelford converted. It was 24–24. Referee Bill Shrimpton penalised Australian prop Martin Bella for stomping, and replacement Tea Ropati's long-range kick had the height but was wide. Shrimpton then penalised Alexander for flicking the ball away when caught on the sixth tackle in front of the posts. Shelford was on target, it was 26–24, and Auckland's defence held firm against the desperate Australians.

'Halfback Neville Ramsay turned in a lionhearted display and was on to any loose ball, Shelford set the backs going and his tactical approach was superb, and Watson repeatedly tested the Australian defence,' said the *Herald*. 'Hansen and Leota tackled superbly and debutant prop Mike Thomson took it to the Australians. But it was not really the time to pick out special heroes. It was a dazzling match in which both sides had provided sporting entertainment of the highest order.'

Auckland team: fullback, Carl Magatogia; three-quarters, Sam Panapa, Mike Patton, Dave Watson, Kevin Pulieata; halves, Kelly Shelford (captain), Neville Ramsay; forwards, Mike Thomson, Peter Ropati, George Mann, Tawera Nikau, Francis Leota, Shane Hansen. Replacements: Tea Ropati, Taime Tagaloa.

Roosters plucked

Paul Vautin, the Australian captain against Auckland, and fellow Kangaroos forward David Trewhella returned to Carlaw Park with Eastern Suburbs later in the 1989 season. They brought Kiwis Hugh McGahan and Kurt Sherlock with them, but the result was still the same. Auckland, though unable to call on players from Fox Memorial finalists Northcote and Mangere East, dominated the second half to win 26–12 after consecutive tries to Nahu Timoko, Mike Patton and Greg Hiley. Tawera Nikau and Neville Ramsay also scored tries and Phil Bancroft kicked three goals. Front-rower Hiley, rated by the *New Zealand Rugby League Annual* as the stand-out player, and replacements Timoko, Rusty Matua and Terry O'Shea made their only appearances of the season. Coach Cameron Bell used the growing demand for an Auckland team in the Winfield Cup as motivation for his players.

Northcote double

Northcote won the Auckland Fox Memorial championship and Lion Red national knockout title under new coach Mike McClennan and captain Brian McClennan in 1989. The opponent which suffered most was Mangere East, beaten 30–8 in a Fox semi-final, 30–14 in the Fox grand final and 48–24 in a Lion Red semi-final. In the national final, Northcote held out Wellington champion Wainuiomata 10–4. The Northcote squad included established and rising stars such as Marty Crequer, Sean Hoppe, Robert Moimoi, Paddy Tuimavave, Stuart Galbraith, Jason Lowrie, Shane Hansen and Tony Tuimavave. After a scoreless first half, centres Moimoi and Paddy Tuimavave pierced the Wainuiomata defence for tries, and Crequer kicked one goal. Wainuiomata's reply was two Jason Gilbert penalty goals.

CHAPTER NINE

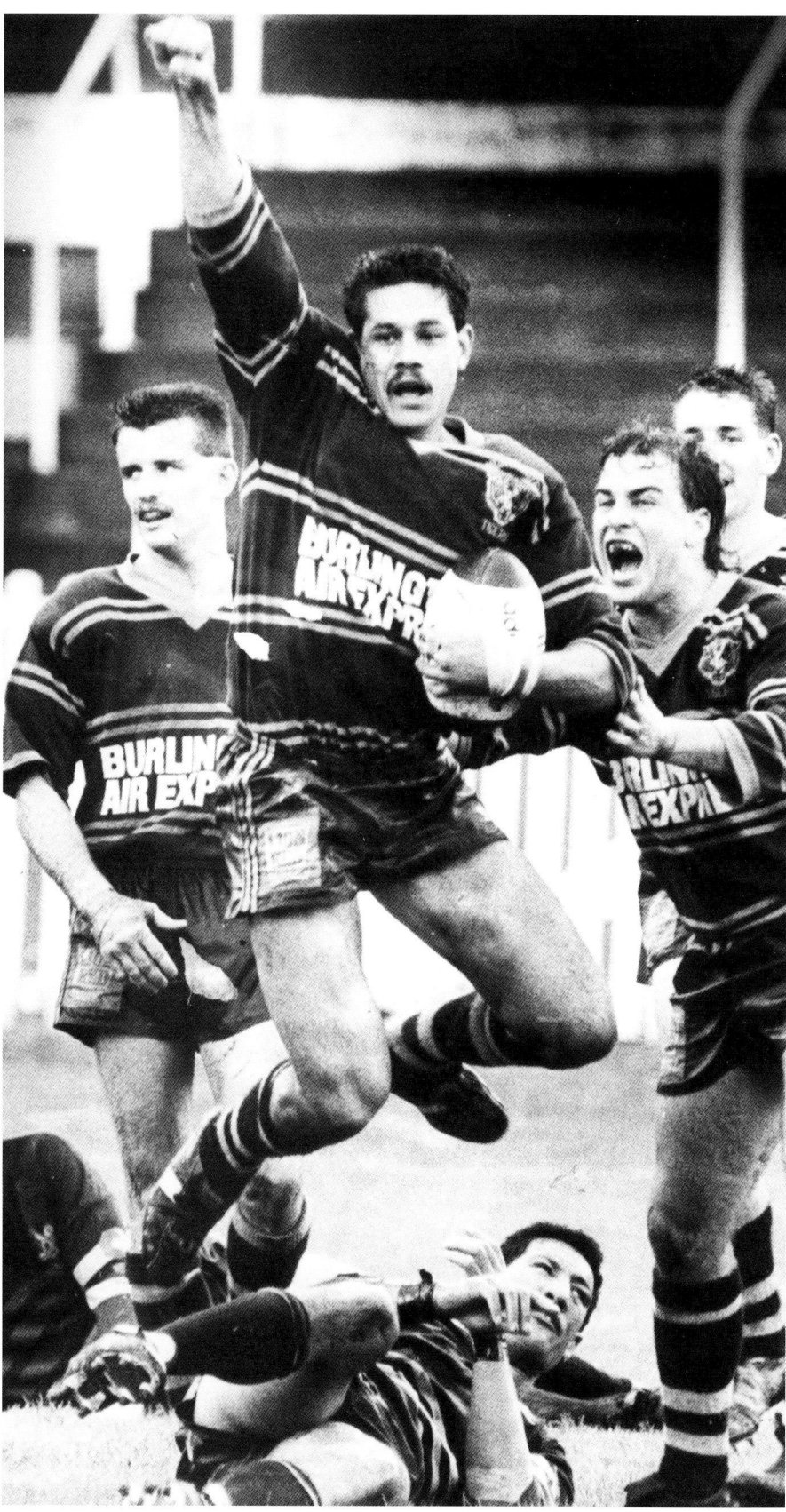

Paddy Tuimavave salutes his try, which clinched the 1989 national club final against Wainuiomata. Captain Brian McClennan (right) rushes to congratulate him.
Fairfax Media

CHAPTER 10

THE NERVOUS NINETIES
1990–1999

CHAPTER TEN

The Nervous Nineties 1990–1999

Decade of constant drama

Rugby league in New Zealand changed forever in the 1990s, and more so in Auckland than anywhere else. All levels of the game were affected. The first half of the decade was filled with excited speculation and then near frenzied anticipation as Auckland lobbied for and succeeded in having a team accepted into the 1995 Australian Winfield Cup premiership. No sooner did the Auckland Warriors become reality than they, and the New Zealand Rugby League, deserted the Australian Rugby League and aligned with the breakaway Super League organisation.

In preparation for the Warriors, the New Zealand Rugby League introduced the national Lion Red Cup franchise competition in 1994. Extending over the full season and with extensive playoffs, the ambitious and very expensive format used the Winfield Cup as its blueprint. It not only impacted on traditional inter-provincial rivalry, but also drained players from local inter-club competitions in all participating leagues. The Lion Red Cup lasted only three years but was a forerunner to the equally extensive but more frugal Bartercard Cup, which existed from 2000 to 2007.

The old order of the Kiwis topping the rugby league pyramid, above inter-provincial and senior inter-club layers and then junior and schoolboy levels, had gone forever. Even the Kiwis tended to take second place behind the Warriors in many minds. Traditional tours stopped in 1996 when rugby league in Britain adopted the Super League concept and switched to a summer sport. It was no longer possible for the Kiwis and Kangaroos to make full post-season tours of Britain and France, nor for the Lions to reciprocate during their off-seasons. New Zealand players who signed for British clubs were gone for good.

Because they played every week, and the Kiwis generally had to be content with one-off test matches, the Warriors assumed top position in the new pyramid. The Lion Red Cup reduced serious inter-provincial football to irregular contests – the Rugby League Cup even became the plaything of the minor leagues early in the twenty-first century – and club competitions had fallen to level five. The news media, especially in Auckland, was infatuated with the Warriors at the expense of all else.

All of that was ahead of the game when the 1990s dawned. The then unnamed Warriors were just a dream harboured by a group of far-sighted Auckland enthusiasts, the Auckland representative team encountered a new challenger in Canterbury, the Northcote juggernaut was about to start rumbling in Auckland, and Great Britain was poised to make its only tour of New Zealand without first visiting Australia. Carlaw Park lost its test match status to bigger and more modern venues such as Mount Smart Stadium and North Harbour Stadium, but was still headquarters for all other important games.

1990: Play it again Sam

Auckland 24 Great Britain 13

A dazzling try by centre Sam Panapa swung the 1990 match against Great Britain firmly in Auckland's favour. With Britain having edged out to a 13–12 lead early in the second half, Panapa carved through from sixty metres out and ran around, past and away from the cover defence to put his side on the path to an eventual 24–13 victory. It was Auckland's third consecutive defeat of the Lions and seventh win in eleven matches dating back to 1954.

Tawera Nikau against Great Britain.
Fairfax Media

Peter Ropati about to be sandwiched between Chris Bibb (No.1) and another British player.
Fairfax Media

CHAPTER TEN

This British tour was unlike any of those that preceded it. It was the only time the Lions did not go to Australia. They started out rather rockily in Papua New Guinea, stacking up three victories over regional sides but only sharing the honours in a two-test series. In New Zealand, they scraped to a one-point win over a President's XIII at Napier and lost to Canterbury before meeting Auckland in a rare Sunday fixture.

Panapa had already been a try-scorer at wing for the President's men in the tour-opener and touched down twice for Auckland. He continued his scoring sequence in the first test but the British were to continue on their roller-coaster ride, losing to Wellington but narrowly beating the Kiwis in the first two tests before losing the third in Christchurch. They also beat the Kiwi Colts, New Zealand Māori and a Taranaki Invitation XIII.

Auckland coach Graham Mattson had the satisfaction of watching his positive tactics produce the biggest winning margin over the Lions. 'We figured that we could try to run them all over the park and the gaps would come in the end,' he told the *New Zealand Herald*. 'They have some big forwards and were pretty strong up the middle, especially in defence. In fact we were losing ground when we tried to take it up the middle.'

Pivotal to the plans were halves Stuart Galbraith and captain Brian McClennan, who said Britain had 'run out of petrol' in the final stages. 'We made a lot of splits out wide and by the last twenty minutes they were feeling the pinch.' Auckland's fine finish came after a first half when niggly play sometimes flared into open warfare and rival scrum-halves Galbraith and Bobbie Goulding spent time in the sin-bin. Britain lost influential forward Kelvin Skerrett at halftime through injury, and Auckland was temporarily without prop Se'e Solomona while he had a head cut stitched.

Wing Mike Patton opened Auckland's account with a try, and Tawera Nikau superbly set up Panapa's first try for a 12–12 halftime scoreline. After Panapa's second try, Peter Brown kicked a penalty goal and converted a seventy-fifth minute try by Nikau which sealed the issue. Skerrett and Graham Steadman scored tries for Britain, Jonathan Davies kicked two goals, and Goulding kicked a field goal.

Auckland team: fullback, Paddy Tuimavave; three-quarters, Warren Mann, Iva Ropati, Sam Panapa, Mike Patton; halves, Brian McClennan (captain), Stuart Galbraith; forwards, Peter Brown, Peter Ropati, Se'e Solomona (replaced by Francis Leota), Tawera Nikau, Taime Tagaloa, Tony Tuimavave. Reserves: Dean Clark, Vila Matautia, George Mann.

Winfield Cup closer

Another milestone towards breaking into the Winfield Cup was reached in 1990 when the previously lukewarm New Zealand Rugby League gave its full support to Auckland's bid. New Zealand Rugby League president George Rainey said a number of perceived problems had been solved. The International Board had ruled overseas-based Kiwis would in future be available only for tests and not tours, the Auckland Rugby League reported an increase of fifty-four junior and schoolboy teams because of the interest sparked by the Winfield Cup on television, and other provinces had been 'generally supportive' while expressing 'concern about transfer fees and the possible gravitation of players towards Auckland'. Rainey said the major advantage would be enabling New Zealand's best players to have professional careers without going overseas.

One slip-up

While beating the British was the obvious highlight, Auckland slipped up only once in its seven-match 1990 representative campaign. That was at the Addington Show Grounds in late April, when Canterbury caught Graham Mattson and his players by surprise. Auckland had opened the national first division competition with a 64–0 whitewash of Bay of Plenty on a day that Canterbury lost 42–2 to Wellington. Mattson felt it was a chance to give other members of his squad a run, and it was to be the only game when Brian McClennan was not wearing the Auckland number six jersey.

Auckland had given Canterbury more incentive by taking the Rugby League Cup south and, after running with a strong wind, the locals shocked by leading 21–2 at halftime. Auckland came back so strongly that it got ahead at 22–21 with fifteen minutes remaining, but a series of fumbles, missed tackles and poor goalkicking halted its advance. Two minutes from fulltime loose forward Logan Edwards evaded two desperate tackles to give Canterbury its 25–22 victory. Both teams scored four tries, Taime Tagaloa, Tawera Nikau, Sam Panapa and Warren Mann touching down for Auckland.

By season's end Canterbury's trophy cabinet was empty. It lost the Rugby League Cup to Wellington and had to settle for third in the national championship. Auckland recovered its commanding form to beat Wellington 38–18 at Wellington, Bay of Plenty 62–8 and Canterbury 40–18 at home, thus setting up a virtual final against Wellington at Carlaw Park. With Peter Brown leading the way up front and the backs eagerly grabbing their chances, Auckland won 24–4 through tries to Warren Mann (two), Iva Ropati, Peter Ropati and Panapa and one goal each by Brown and McClennan.

CHAPTER TEN

Changing sides. Phil Bancroft, a Cantabrian playing for Auckland, caught in a bear hug by Ricky Cowan, an Aucklander playing for Canterbury, at Christchurch in 1990. Canterbury's Logan Edwards looks on.
Christchurch Star

Carlaw's days numbered

Rugby league in Auckland was looking for a new home before 1990 and believed it had found one in Western Springs. 'In considering the promotional aspect of our game, we need to determine the standards that we require for the home of rugby league,' said Auckland Rugby League general manager Brian Mills in the year book. 'The ARL board has been grappling with this problem over a number of years now. Western Springs appeared to be the ideal solution until its rejection by the Auckland City Council. The fact is that Carlaw Park, although adequate in the interim, is a sub-standard facility when considering the facilities that are provided by other sporting organisations. For example, individual plastic seating, VIP boxes, catering and refreshment lounges, convenient parking. Redevelopment of Carlaw Park is not a realistic alternative without a massive injection of capital that the game just does not have. We need to look to a facility such as the proposed Superdome or an existing facility such as Mount Smart Stadium.' Chairman Peter McLeod, who called the city council's decision not to support a move to Western Springs 'an astonishing turn around', stressed the matter was becoming urgent. The 1990 Auckland test match was held at Mount Smart.

Peter McLeod.
NZ Herald

Never say die – Otahuhu

On the eve of the last 1990 Rukutai Shield round, the Joe Gwynne-coached Otahuhu was fourth-equal and in danger of missing the Fox Memorial playoffs. But Otahuhu beat Mount Albert 28–10 and rivals Glenora and Richmond failed to win their games. A week later Otahuhu was trailing 18–9 to Glenora at halftime in the sudden-death semi-final, yet won 37–18 with a stunning second half that set the standard for the rest of its season. Minor premier Northcote was despatched 26–8 in the preliminary final, and Te Atatu was swept aside 28–14 in the grand final. Vila Matautia, Dean Clark, Rusty Matua and Mark Riley scored tries and Clark kicked six goals. Inspirational figures Clark and Tawera Nikau set up two tries each. Northcote won the Rukutai and Stormont shields and Richmond the Roope Rooster. Otahuhu reached the Lion Red League final but failed to maintain its second half heroics. It lost 34–12 to Wellington club Wainuiomata, despite leading 12–4 at the break.

CHAPTER TEN

Rusty Matua takes the field for Otahuhu on grand final day.
Photosport

The Ropati brothers, from left, Iva, Joe, Peter, Romi, John, Feu and Tea, pictured in 1986.
Fairfax Media

Five into one

Five Ropati brothers, Peter, John, Joe, Tea and Iva, twice made appearances together for Mangere East during the 1991 season. The *Lion Red Rugby League Annual* reported that Peter (Leigh), Joe (Swinton) and Tea (St Helens) had returned from their respective English clubs. John, Iva and Tea were among the try-scorers in a 37–14 win over Te Atatu. Former Kiwis wing Joe impressed in the second-row. By the time the Fox Memorial playoffs began the Ropatis had again scattered to many parts of the rugby league world, and Te Atatu gained revenge in the sudden-death semi-final. When Iva played four tests on the 1993 Kiwis tour of Britain and France he, along with Joe (a 1983–87 Kiwi) and Tea (1986–97), made their family the first to provide three test-playing brothers. In the 1930s, three Brimble brothers had represented New Zealand but only one of them played in a test match.

Northcote supreme

Northcote, coached by astute tactician Graeme Norton, would have needed a sizeable truck to transport all of its trophies in 1991. It made a clean sweep of the Fox Memorial, Rukutai Shield, Roope Rooster and Stormont Shield in Auckland and was an emphatic winner of the Lion Red League. In the latter it stormed through the early rounds before beating Halswell (Canterbury) 26–12 in a semi-final and perennial Wellington runner-up Randwick 30–12 in the final. Speedy young wing Sean Hoppe scored two tries in both games.

CHAPTER TEN

The champion 1992 Northcote team.

Back row: Fa'ausu Afoa, Vae Afoa, Geoff Morton, Phill Filipo.

Third row: Ritchie McIntosh (medic), Casper Ioani, Jason Lowrie, Michael Davies, Loi Machee, Don Stewart, Mark Elia, Francis Delia (photographer).

Second row: Trevor McLeod (cleric), Robert Hall (co-coach), Jason Kaulima, Logan Campbell, Ted Dalton (club captain), Patrick Hellesoe, Jonaree McIntyre, Graeme Norton (coach), Steve Culpan (doctor).

Front row: Dave Mackintosh, Dennis Good (manager), Richard Greer, Murray Orr (manager), Tony Tuimavave, Don Hickey (chairman), Ken McIntosh, Gary Cooksley (manager), Sean Carey.

In front: John Lepper (ball boy), Kalem Good (ball boy). Absent: Stuart Galbraith, Troy Stewart, Richard Stewart.

Graeme Norton collection

Only Mangere East beat Northcote during the entire Auckland season. But Northcote had faltered after winning the 1990 minor premiership and the playoffs were to be the true test. A 24–8 success over defending champion Otahuhu in the major semi-final installed Northcote as a warm favourite for the Fox grand final. Its opponent was again Otahuhu, which wrested a 14–10 lead at halftime. However, tries to Stuart Galbraith, who became the first recipient of the Doug Price Memorial Medal as man of the match, and Hoppe sent Northcote clear before a late Otahuhu try reduced the difference to 23–20. In other finals Northcote beat Richmond for the Stormont Shield and Te Atatu for the Roope Rooster.

It was the start of the longest Fox Memorial dynasty as Northcote became the first club to win four consecutive championships outright. Despite losing Hoppe and Gene Ngamu to Australian clubs before the start of the 1992 season, farewelling Galbraith to Sydney in mid-May, and supplying twelve players to Auckland representative duty, Northcote also retained the Roope Rooster and Stormont Shield. To cap it off, the Tigers beat Rukutai Shield winner Mount Albert 11–6 in the Fox grand final, scoring two tries – by Vae Afoa and Logan Campbell – to one and defending strongly to the finish. But the Tigers failed to become the first back-to-back national club title-winner, and went down 25–18 to Wellington champion Wainuiomata at Carlaw Park in the last Lion Red League knockout.

Only the Stormont Shield (won by Mount Albert in the first game of the season) eluded Northcote in 1993. Gary Kemble succeeded the retired Norton as coach and steered the Tigers to a seven-point advantage in the minor premiership. Northcote held the Roope Rooster for a third consecutive year by beating Manukau 14–0, and the Fox grand final was won 29–10 against Te Atatu. Although the try-scoring margin was four (Mark Elia two, Jonaree McIntyre and Willie Poching) to two, the Tigers led 24–4 at halftime and won decisively thanks to six Dave Mackintosh goals and a Ken McIntosh field goal.

Incredibly, of that winning team, fullback-turned-centre Mackintosh, prop Mike Davies and wing-to-reserve McIntyre were all that remained when Otahuhu was beaten 32–12 in the 1994 Fox grand final. The club scene had undergone a complete makeover in personnel because of the national Lion Red Cup competition. Kemble relocated to Hawke's Bay and David Harding coached the Tigers. But Northcote easily completed its 'quaddie' thanks to three tries to future test and Australian NRL front-rower Paul Rauhihi, two by Mackintosh and another to Cory Jamieson. Although the Tigers regained the Stormont Shield, 30–18, at the expense of Manukau, strong rival Otahuhu snaffled the Rukutai Shield and Roope Rooster.

Northcote's Mark Elia has Mount Albert's Noora Samuela wrong-footed in the 1992 Fox Memorial grand final won by the Tigers 11–6.
NZ Herald

CHAPTER TEN

Crises in Christchurch

Former Kiwis forward Owen Wright enjoyed a mostly successful term as Auckland coach from 1991 to 1993 – but matches against Canterbury at the Addington Show Grounds proved to be an itch that he could not eradicate any more than predecessor Graham Mattson or successor Dominic Clark. While maintaining Auckland's outstanding home record against the southerners, Wright's teams lost in Christchurch to the Frank Endacott-inspired Cantabrians 33–24 in 1991, drew 8–8 in 1992, and were well beaten 40–12 in a 1993 round-robin game and 36–12 in the national first division final.

It was the first-division final that captured most media attention, particularly as it was also the last significant inter-provincial clash before the introduction of the season-long Lion Red Cup. Wright called in a group of professional players who had returned from their overseas clubs, Tawera Nikau (as captain), Duane Mann, Se'e Solomona, Tea Ropati, Craig Innes and Iva Ropati. That fired up Canterbury, whose only professional returnee was Brendon Tuuta. Before a capacity crowd, Canterbury scored seven tries to two (by Mann and Tea Ropati). Auckland had also previously lost 27–22 at Wellington.

Auckland won the first division championship in 1991, when it edged Wellington 25–24 in a Rugby League Cup challenge at Wellington, before again leaving the cup behind in Christchurch. In its 1992 provincial season Auckland remained unbeaten despite drawing at Christchurch and just fending off Wellington 24–23 at Carlaw Park. A Vila Matautia try, two Patrick Hellesoe goals and a Dave Townsend field goal were sufficient to beat Canterbury 9–6 at Carlaw

Se'e Solomona has Iva Ropati in support in Wellington in 1993. Result: Wellington 27, Auckland 22.

Fairfax Media

Park in 1993 before it all unwound on the road. The two losses at Christchurch and one at Wellington were the most sustained by any Auckland team against other provinces in one season.

'In the three years I have been involved with Auckland, I remain staggered at the number of players who have gone overseas to play,' said Wright in summing up Auckland's 1993 season. 'While it's good for those players, sooner or later the cupboard back home had to become bare. Officials have to realise that eventually you run out of quality players, having to constantly rebuild. That is exactly what happened this year.'

Commenting on his selecting for the final seven English-based professionals (Dean Clark subsequently withdrew because of injury), Wright said: 'I was on a hiding to nothing. Had I gone south without them and lost I would have been flogged by the media, and by including them I was accused of breaching the spirit of the championship.'

Wright, who named the draws with Balmain (1991) and Manly (1993) and winning the Lion Red Showdown final over North Sydney in 1991 as the highlights of his coaching term, was saddened by the demise of inter-provincial football on the eve of the Lion Red Cup. He expressed a hope that both could live side by side.

Trans-Tasman 'title'

Auckland beat North Sydney 8–4 in a try-less trans-Tasman quadrangular final late in 1991. The event, dubbed the $100,000 Lion Red Showdown, also involved Western Suburbs and Canterbury. Phil Bancroft (three) and Dave Mackintosh kicked goals for Auckland and Daryl Halligan replied with two for Norths. Auckland earlier edged out Canterbury 14–13, Norths beat Wests 30–12 and, in a tie for third, Canterbury and Wests drew 18–18.

What was an excellent idea failed to capture the imagination of the public because neither Sydney side was at full-strength, and Auckland and Canterbury were weakened by a clash with the Lion Red National Cup inter-club tournament. Canterbury officials refused to recognise the matches as having full representative status. Former Auckland captain Paddy Tuimavave was drafted into the injury-hit Canterbury squad on his return from Western Australia.

Matches were played Friday night (in front of 5,000 fans) and Sunday afternoon (4,000). Loose forward Neville Ramsay won the award for best Auckland player, and rookie Canterbury forward Quentin Pongia showcased his burgeoning talents. Inside backs Greg Florimo (Norths) and Jason Taylor (Wests) won their teams' awards. Bancroft, Stuart Galbraith, Andrew Ah Kuoi, Peter Ropati and captain Tony Tuimavave were other outstanding Aucklanders.

CHAPTER TEN

In March an Auckland Invitation XIII, including guest players John Lomax, Syd Eru (both Wellington), Brent Stuart and Whetu Taewa (both Canterbury), drew 16–16 with Balmain in an intense encounter which thrilled a 15,000 crowd at Carlaw Park. Auckland tries went to Mike Thomson, from a Kelly Shelford bomb, and Taewa, in support of an angled Iva Ropati run. Bancroft was on target with four goals. Thomson opened the scoring but it took a late penalty goal by Bancroft to secure the draw. The Invitation XIII played a man short for forty-five minutes after Tony Tuimavave's dismissal for a high tackle.

Peter Ropati feels the brunt of the North Sydney defence in the quadrangular final. At right is Tony Tuimavave.
Fairfax Media

Auckland double

Expatriate Aucklanders Dean Bell and Gary Freeman completed a unique New Zealand double in 1992 by respectively winning the most prized individual awards in the British and Australian professional competitions. Bell was a linchpin of the dominant Wigan club, his contribution being recognised by his receiving the prestigious Man of Steel award as the game's best player in Britain. He had captained Wigan to yet more triumphs in the Challenge Cup final at Wembley and the Premiership final at Old Trafford. Only one honour was missing, and Bell rectified that in 1993 by winning the Lance Todd Trophy as man of the match in the Cup final. Freeman, then Kiwis captain, had transferred from Balmain to Eastern Suburbs for the 1992 Australian season. Despite his club narrowly failing to make the playoffs, Freeman was the Dally M player of the year, ahead of two other great inside backs, Terry Lamb (Canterbury-Bankstown) and Allan Langer (Brisbane Broncos). Freeman was also New Zealand's player of the year.

Dean Bell at Wigan.
Photosport

Gary Freeman at Balmain.
John Coffey collection

CHAPTER TEN

> ### Disappearing act
>
> An estimated 17,000 fans could not help but be impressed with wing Sean Hoppe's display in a 1992 pre-season match against the Canberra Raiders at Carlaw Park. So were Canberra officials it seems, for within forty-eight hours the young Northcote flyer had signed for the Raiders and was contemplating a season playing alongside Gary Belcher, Mal Meninga, Laurie Daley and company. That was the beginning of an outstanding career with Canberra, North Sydney, the Warriors and St Helens plus thirty-five tests and seventeen test tries for the Kiwis. The Raiders also went home with a 32–14 win over Auckland after establishing an 18–10 halftime lead.

1992: Lions have last laugh

Great Britain 14 Auckland 8

An eighty-two-year history of rivalry between touring British teams and Auckland ended abruptly in 1992 when the Lions gained their first win in four matches since 1979. Including the double dates involving both Auckland City and Auckland Province in the 1920s, the visitors won sixteen of twenty-four fixtures. But Auckland had held the upper hand over the last two decades, when most of the matches were held under the Carlaw Park floodlights.

British officials reverted to the traditional tour format, reaching New Zealand via Papua New Guinea and Australia. The Ashes battle was hard fought, the Kangaroos winning the first test at Sydney, the Lions pulling off a 33–10 boilover in Melbourne, and Australia keeping the trophy with a 16–10 victory at Brisbane. It was fresh from that disappointment that the midweek Lions held out Auckland 14–8 as a prelude to beating Canterbury and sharing a closely contested two-test series with the Kiwis.

A month had elapsed since Auckland completed its provincial campaign and coach Owen Wright was without Dean Clark (Kiwis duty) and captain Tony Tuimavave (broken arm). Prop George Mann was refused permission to play by his St Helens club. But Iva Ropati joined Mark Elia in the centres, and Tony Tatupu and Francis Leota formed a potent new second-row combination. Scrum-half Clayton Friend took over the captaincy.

The Lions 'midweekers' – a term which hardly applicable to a backline containing Steve Hampson, Alan Hunte, Joe Lydon, Paul Newlove and captain Deryck Fox – kept their unbeaten record intact during a scoreless second half. Auckland spent most of that period in Britain's territory without being able to pierce a stubborn defensive screen.

Auckland was first on the board in the twenty-third minute when fullback Dave Mackintosh scored a try from a dazzling break by loose forward Neville Ramsay. Lions inside backs Fox and Kevin Ellis soon combined to put Hunte across, and when Fox's grubber kick laid on a try for Ellis the tourists led 12–4. Penalty goals by Mackintosh and Fox completed the scoring.

'Auckland centres Iva Ropati and Mark Elia looked dangerous on attack, with both making a number of breaks in the second half. Their efforts came to nothing though, either through a lack of support or the effectiveness of Britain's defence,' said the *Lion Red Rugby League Annual 1992*. 'Others to stand out for Auckland were former test players Mike Patton and Clayton Friend. Among the forwards Ramsay set an example with his high work rate and second-rower Francis Leota was also effective with the ball in hand and in the tackle.'

Auckland team: fullback, Dave Mackintosh (replaced by Matthew Tuisamoa); three-quarters, Mike Patton, Mark Elia, Iva Ropati, Logan Campbell; halves, Ken McIntosh (Mike Kini), Clayton Friend (captain); forwards, Fa'ausu Afoa, Brady Malam, James Pickering (Jason Lowrie), Francis Leota, Tony Tatapu (Phil Robarts), Neville Ramsay.

Hail the referee

Auckland referee Dennis Hale broke one world record and equalled another in 1992, according to the *Lion Red Rugby League Annual*. Hale became the first referee in history to control six test matches in a twelve-month period – between Australia and Papua New Guinea at Goroka and Port Moresby the previous October, the entire Ashes series involving Australia and Great Britain at Sydney, Melbourne and Brisbane in June, and the July test between the Kangaroos and Kumuls at Townsville. When Hale added the World Cup final between Australia and Great Britain at Wembley later in 1992, he equalled Australian Greg McCallum's 1989 record of controlling five internationals in a calendar year.

Hale had made his international debut during the 1990 Great Britain tour of Papua New Guinea. The first test at Danny Leahy Oval in Goroka was literally a riotous occasion, with tear gas and rifle volleys fired by the police to control disturbances from frustrated, stone-throwing fans outside the ground as the Kumuls beat Britain for the first time, 20–18. As the gas wafted over the playing field the players and referee hit the turf in a hurry. But it was not a new experience for Hale, who was the man with the whistle when even more serious ructions disrupted a Papua New Guinea Cambridge Cup final a few years earlier.

The Goroka game was the first of eleven consecutive test appointments for Hale. When the International Board ruled in 1995 that the visiting nation should provide the referees, Hale controlled the first trans-Tasman test in Brisbane

Dennis Hale broke one world record and equalled another in 1992.
Fairfax Media

CHAPTER TEN

before handing over to fellow Aucklander Phil Houston for the other two. Hale's thirteenth and last test was between England and Fiji at Wigan during the 1995 World Cup. He remains second behind the legendary John Percival among New Zealand's test appointees.

The *1990 Auckland Rugby League Yearbook* described Hale as 'a fitness nut' who had played, coached and administered at the North Shore club before turning to refereeing in 1976 and graduating to the senior ranks in 1981. Even five years out from Auckland's entry into the Winfield Cup Hale made the accurate observation: 'I hope that at least one referee from here can become involved, although you would probably have to start at under-21 level. Eddie Ward is the only referee from outside of Sydney who has got Winfield Cup games, and it would be a case of whether they considered we were up to their standard.'

Warriors accepted

In 1992, Auckland's Winfield Cup entry was accepted by the New South Wales Rugby League, and the embryo club was named the Warriors in a nationwide public competition. After years of meetings and negotiations it all hinged on a comparatively brief presentation by bid chairman Peter McLeod and Tony Sernack, chief executive of Dominion Breweries which pledged backing of $10 million over five years. McLeod said Auckland would have been ready by 1994 but was happy to be admitted from 1995. Tom Aldridge was the acting chief executive. Other newcomers to the expanded competition would be the South Queensland Crushers, North Queensland Cowboys and Perth-based Western Reds.

In the *1992 Auckland Rugby League Yearbook*, chairman McLeod predicted the invitation for Auckland to join the Winfield Cup 'will change our game and indeed the entire New Zealand sporting scene. By becoming the first sport to compete in an international competition for the entire season, rugby league has gained the sporting initiative in New Zealand and we cannot afford to surrender that.'

McLeod reported an additional 131 teams being fielded in Auckland in the 1992 season, a growth of about twenty-five per cent and a cumulative growth over three years in excess of fifty per cent. But he was extremely disappointed at the lack of enthusiasm from Auckland clubs leading up to the proposed 1993 national Superleague competition (which became the Lion Red Cup from 1994). He backed Superleague as a means of promoting and televising the game in New Zealand and competing against the overwhelming interest in the Winfield Cup.

Wiki in demand

Young Otahuhu and New Zealand Māori wing Ruben Wiki was the subject of a tug of war when Auckland coach Owen Wright chose him for the pre-season match against Manly-Warringah at Carlaw Park in January 1993. Winfield Cup club Canberra also wanted Wiki to trial against Wellington club Wainuiomata. This time Auckland prevailed, and Wiki was a try-scorer in the 16–16 draw with Manly. But Wiki soon joined the Raiders, who two years later won a court battle with the Warriors to retain Wiki's services.

The Auckland-Manly encounter pitted Wright against his own former Otahuhu mentor Graham Lowe, who brought a strong team across the Tasman. Wright was suffering from his now customary loss of leading players, notably Jason Lowrie to Eastern Suburbs, Mike Patton to France and Dean Clark to Hull Kingston Rovers. The latest new-look Auckland combination was accused of overstepping the mark as Manly stars Geoff Toovey (broken jaw) and Cliff Lyons (medial ligament damage) became casualties of a rugged game.

Ruben Wiki in 1992.
Fairfax Media

But Auckland also demonstrated plenty of skill in coming back from a 12–2 deficit in the second half. Paul Mansson scored an intercept try, Wiki had Fred Robarts to thank for his walk-in try and Auckland led 16–12 after Tony Tatupu scored. In the seventy-fifth minute, when a man short, Manly levelled up through a Danny Moore try. Busy Auckland referee Grant Wallace sin-binned five players, Manly's John Jones (twice), Des Hasler and Ian Roberts and Auckland's Fa'ausu Afoa and captain Tony Tuimavave.

Auckland also played Winfield Cup wooden-spooner Gold Coast twice in 1993, but they were tame and disappointing affairs. Gold Coast won 30–4 at Carlaw Park in late February, with Mark Elia taking over the captaincy from an injured Tuimavave, and 18–10 at Tweed Heads in September, when Dave Townsend was Auckland's skipper.

Kiwis cupboard is bare

In days when Kiwis touring teams were selected exclusively from domestic football it was not unusual for Auckland clubs to provide more than half of the players. Mark Graham, then with Brisbane Norths, became the first overseas-based tourist when he led the 1980 Kiwis to Britain and France, and the number increased with each succeeding tour. But it was still a shock, and one not only felt north of the Bombay Hills, when no Auckland resident players were named for the 1993 northern hemisphere tour.

Even when Jarrod McCracken and Brent Todd withdrew through injuries, the replacements came from Christchurch to increase the Canterbury contingent to eight. There were also four from Wellington and Jason Mackie became Northland's

CHAPTER TEN

fourth Kiwi and first test player. The selectors had obviously been strongly influenced by Canterbury's two big wins over Auckland in the first division championship, while Wellington had shared a win and a loss with Auckland.

Hooker Duane Mann and centre Iva Ropati were back in Auckland by the time of selection. But in both cases that was a recent move after having played extensively in England. Nor could the absence of Aucklanders be explained by the migration of players to Australia. Of the eleven Australian-based players, only captain Gary Freeman, Sean Hoppe, Gene Ngamu and Jason Lowrie had Auckland backgrounds. Those who promoted the theory that 'when Auckland is strong New Zealand is strong' found their argument justified when the Kiwis suffered three decisive test losses to Great Britain.

In contrast, Auckland supplied eleven of the twenty-six Junior Kiwis who made a highly successful tour in tandem with the senior Kiwis. Captain Henry Paul was actually elevated into the seniors, a stepping stone to an outstanding professional career in Britain. The other Junior Kiwis from Auckland were backs Peter Lima, Gus Malietoa-Brown, Meti Noovao, Robert Ofanoa and Willie Swann, and forwards David Fatialofa, Bryan Henare, Jonathan Hughes, Danny Lima and Joe Vagana.

Warriors get (Mount) Smart

Many of the pieces of the Auckland Warriors Winfield Cup jigsaw were put in place during 1993. Or rather from December 1992, when former Parramatta premiership-winning coach John Monie was appointed head coach. A month later another Australian, Ian Robson, became chief executive. The effervescent and media-savvy Robson made such an indelible mark on the New Zealand sporting scene that other codes were soon looking across the Tasman when recruiting officials.

In March the official jersey was released, incorporating the blue and white of Auckland and red and green of main sponsor DB Bitter. On 19 March, the strip was worn for the first time by a scholarship squad against the Northland under-nineteen team in a curtain-raiser to a Brisbane v Canterbury-Bankstown Winfield Cup match at Carlaw Park. Canterbury-Bankstown and Kiwis forward Gavin Hill was the embryo club's first professional signing in June, and two months later great Kiwis and Wigan centre Dean Bell was named as the Warriors' first captain.

Another decision, which would outlast all of the coaching, playing and administrative appointments, remained. Opinion was sharply divided about where the Warriors should make their headquarters – the Auckland Rugby League's preference of Carlaw Park or the Warriors Board's favoured Mount Smart

Stadium, which had been the main venue for the 1990 Commonwealth Games. In October it was resolved, after the Auckland Regional Council promised a major upgrade of Mount Smart.

Polynesian festival

After the outstanding success of the 1992 Pacific Cup, the Auckland Rugby League held an inaugural Polynesian Rugby League Festival at Carlaw Park in October 1993. Teams of Auckland-resident players represented American Samoa, Cook Islands, Fiji, Māori, Niue, Tokelau and Tonga plus an Auckland XIII in two sections. In the final, Auckland Tonga 16 (Willie Wolfgramm, Esau Mann, Mike Veikoso tries, Steven Firth two goals) beat Auckland Māori 8 (Darryl Beazley, Solomon Kiri tries), while the Auckland XIII beat Auckland American Samoa 40–35 in the plate final. A number of women's games held during the nine-day tournament were also well received.

1994 Lion Red Cup

After much fanfare the national Lion Red Cup kicked off in 1994. The Auckland Vulcans, Counties-Manukau Heroes, North Harbour Sea Eagles and Waitakere City Raiders represented Auckland against two teams each from Canterbury and Wellington and one apiece from Bay of Plenty, Hawke's Bay, Taranaki and Waikato. Based on the Winfield Cup, there was a minor premiership comprising twenty-two rounds leading into top-five playoffs.

Five Auckland Vulcans who played in the pre-season final win over Waitakere, Cyril Howard, Una Taufa, Vinnie Weir, David Murray and Eugene Bourneville.

Photosport

CHAPTER TEN

First, though, the Gary Prohm-coached Vulcans beat Waitakere 22–18 after extra time in the pre-season knockout tournament. Down 6–16 at halftime, the Vulcans eventually drew level through a last-minute Jason Mackie try and won in overtime with Andrew Ah Kuoi's second try. Auckland had shaded North Harbour 26–24 in one semi-final, suggesting the Auckland teams would be very prominent in the season proper.

And so it proved. Counties-Manukau was minor premier, one point ahead of Waikato Cougars and two in front of North Harbour and Canterbury Cardinals. Auckland finished fifth and Waitakere City seventh behind Taranaki Rockets. In the playoffs Canterbury eliminated the Vulcans and Waikato before losing the preliminary final to Counties-Manukau. In the major semi-final North Harbour had beaten Counties-Manukau 25–22 to be first into the grand final.

Captained by astute playmaker Duane Mann and coached by Graeme Norton, North Harbour triumphed 24–16 over the Stan Martin-coached Counties-Manukau in the title decider at Carlaw Park. It was virtually all over by halftime, when North Harbour led 20–6. Centre Jason Kaulima scored two tries, Fa'ausu Afoa, Lafaele Filipo and Jason Palmada got one apiece, and Quinten Dane and Latham Tawhai kicked goals.

Tawhai was paired with Ken McIntosh in the halves, Kaulima and Tony Tatupu formed a penetrative centre duo, and an emerging Joe Vagana served a second-row apprenticeship alongside Don Stewart behind powerful props Afoa and Filipo. Clearly, Norton and Mann had plenty of material to work with. Mann was named Lion Red Cup player of the year and captain of the year, and Martin was coach of the year. Wilson Marsh (Counties-Manukau) scored the most points with 223, while Auckland's Phil Houston was referee of the year.

Duane Mann, North Harbour captain, and Joe Vagana.
Graeme Norton collection

The Lion Red Cup divided the rugby league supporter base. Some welcomed the first New Zealand semi-professional competition, others mourned the demise of provincial rivalry and the detrimental effect on the standard of club football around the country. At season's end came the shock disclosure of a million-dollar shortfall due to shortages of projected sponsorships and poor gate receipts. The New Zealand Rugby League in October decided to continue in 1995 provided all participating teams raised a minimum $175,000 to survive.

Mann in charge

Duane Mann, who had returned to Auckland the previous year after playing more than 100 consecutive matches for Warrington in England, had the dual distinction of captaining the Kiwis to Papua New Guinea and the New Zealand Residents to Australia while also leading North Harbour in 1994. Both touring teams were coached by Cantabrian Frank Endacott.

Four of the Kiwis were selected out of the Lion Red Cup – Mann and Tony Tatupu (North Harbour) and Hitro Okesene and Whetu Taewa (Counties-Manukau). There were sixteen from the Winfield Cup plus Kevin Iro (Leeds) and Aaron Whittaker (Wakefield Trinity) from Britain. The Kiwis won both tests and three other games comfortably.

The Residents were also too good in their four fixtures against Australian country and combined sides. Mann's fellow Aucklanders on tour were transplanted southerner Taewa, Okesene, Solomon Kiri, Jason Temu and Des Maea (Counties-Manukau), Henry Paul and David Bailey (Waitakere City), Tatupu and Fa'ausu Afoa (North Harbour) and Aaron Lester (Auckland Vulcans). On their return home the Residents blitzed Western Samoa 64–2 at Carlaw Park, Bailey and Taewa scoring three tries each.

CHAPTER TEN

Wigan's Warriors

The countdown towards Auckland's Winfield Cup entry gathered pace in 1994, with plenty of correspondence between the Warriors and Wigan. The British club accused former coach and Warriors appointee John Monie of breaching an agreement not to approach any Wigan player apart from Dean Bell. Monie denied having made such a commitment and signed seasoned Lions forwards Andy Platt and Denis Betts along with double New Zealand rugby international Frano Botica. Platt was swapped for Junior Kiwis captain Henry Paul when Wigan waived Platt's transfer fee and the Warriors released Paul. Experienced Australians Greg Alexander and Phil Blake and overseas-based professionals Sean Hoppe, Stephen Kearney, Gene Ngamu, Willie Poching, Tea Ropati and Se'e Solomona added to an attractive playing roster. The Warriors also believed they had contracted the best Lion Red Cup players and Junior Kiwis. Frank Endacott was appointed reserve grade coach.

Canterbury holds Cup

Auckland and Canterbury officials were keen to keep their Rugby League Cup rivalry alive and arranged a 1994 Queen's Birthday Monday challenge match in Christchurch. Both teams had new coaches, former Mount Albert mentor Dominic Clark for Auckland and Wally Wilson for Canterbury. But the outcome was unchanged, with Canterbury winning 28–20 despite Wilson losing five players overnight after the two Christchurch-based Lion Red Cup teams refused to rest their provincial representatives. Logan Edwards played a role in five of Canterbury's six tries and Mark Nixon, usually a stand-off or centre, was outstanding at scrum-half in opposition to Auckland youngster Stacey Jones.

Auckland's team was largely representative of its four Lion Red Cup teams, with only Hibiscus Coast stand-off half Brian McClennan called in from the local Rukutai Shield competition. The team featured Wilson Marsh, Solomon Kiri, Andrew Ah Kuoi, Whetu Taewa, Bryan Laumatia, McClennan, Jones, Fa'ausu Afoa, Duane Mann (captain), Lafu Papalii, Tony Tatupu, Jason Palmada and Tony Botica, plus reserves Vinnie Weir, David Murray, Hitro Okesene and Brett Kingham. Original reserve Paul Mansson was a late withdrawal. Kiri, Afoa, Laumatia and Weir scored tries, and Marsh kicked two goals.

The night the world changed

On the night of 10 March 1995, the New Zealand rugby league world changed forever. It was an extraordinary occasion at the renamed Ericsson (Mount Smart) Stadium. Preceded by a breathtaking entertainment package, the Auckland

Warriors and Brisbane Broncos indulged in a thrilling contest, eventually decided by brilliant Broncos scrum-half Allan Langer creating and scoring two tries and kicking a field goal to transform a 10–22 deficit into a 25–22 victory.

The Warriors' first team consisted of Phil Blake, Sean Hoppe, Dean Bell (captain), Manoa Thompson, Whetu Taewa, Gene Ngamu, Greg Alexander, Gavin Hill, Duane Mann, Hitro Okesene, Stephen Kearney, Tony Tatupu and Tony Tuimavave, with interchange players Se'e Solomona, Tea Ropati, Jason Mackie and Martin Moana. Fullback Blake scored the first Warriors try after a break by Taewa down the left wing. Hoppe, Tatupu and Ropati were the other try-scorers, and Ngamu added three goals. The attendance was 31,500.

Ericsson (Mount Smart) Stadium on the Auckland Warriors opening night 10 March 1995.
Auckland Regional Council

Warriors prop Gavin Hill leads the charge into the Broncos defensive line.
Photosport

CHAPTER TEN

But 1995 was to be a season of turmoil for the sport worldwide, no less so than for the Warriors. The Australian Rugby League was isolated internationally when, after half of its clubs aligned themselves with the breakaway Super League movement bankrolled by News Limited and led by former Broncos chief executive John Ribot, the national bodies in New Zealand and Great Britain followed suit. The 'war' raged for several years, led to separate Australian Rugby League and Super League competitions being held in 1997, and left former friends and colleagues feuding into the next century.

On the field the Warriors were to sweep their supporters through a hot and cold campaign. Second-up, they lost to Illawarra at Wollongong. Their first win should have been by 46–12 over Western Suburbs at Ericsson Stadium. In those days of unlimited interchanges any number of players could sit on the bench, but only seventeen in total could take part. When the Warriors sent Joe Vagana on late in the match he was the eighteenth man and the Warriors subsequently lost their points. It ultimately cost them a place in the top-eight playoffs.

The Warriors lost to North Sydney away and Manly-Warringah at home before they achieved their first genuine victory, a 38–12 pasting of Illawarra at Ericsson Stadium in round six. There was another big win at Parramatta a week later, when record-breaking All Blacks wing John Kirwan got his first start and, more significantly, teenaged scrum-half Stacey Jones debuted off the bench. Jones scored a try and kicked a goal, and gave every indication that his would be a great career. Over the next decade or so he lived up to every bit of that promise.

1995: Sea Eagles flying high

North Harbour 40 France 10

North Harbour not only retained the Lion Red Cup in 1995, it also had the distinction of beating a full international team. France was rebuilding after a seventy-four-point hiding from the Kangaroos at home the previous December and played four matches in New Zealand. The tourists started with a 24–2 victory over Waikato, lost the first test match 22–6 at Ericsson Stadium, and then shocked the Kiwis with a 16–16 draw in the second test at Palmerston North. Eccentric French referee Marcel Chanfreau, in charge because the International Board allowed touring teams to bring their own referees, had much to do with that result.

Between the tests, France was humbled 40–10 by North Harbour at Takapuna, conceding eight tries to the soaring Sea Eagles, who were coached by Graeme Norton and captained by wholehearted forward Don Stewart. The North Harbour team for the historic occasion was: Quinten Dane, Steve Barry, Paki Tuimavave, Jason Kaulima, Frank Fuimaono, Aleki Maea, Latham Tawhai, Lafaele Filipo,

Contented North Harbour coach Graeme Norton enjoys the Lion Red Cup and a sample of the sponsor's product in 1995.

Fairfax

Sean Wilson, Ben McLean, Don Stewart, Keneti Asiata, Jason Palmada. Interchange: Cory Jamieson, Auvae Tapuai, Richard Stewart, Mike Setefano.

Tries for North Harbour were scored by Barry, Tuimavave, Fuimaono, Tawhai, Asiata, Setefano, Jamieson and McLean, and goals were kicked by Tawhai (two), Jamieson and Maea. The French replies consisted of tries to Pascal Bomati and Claude Sirvent and a goal to Arnaud Dulac. North Harbour's feat was to remain unique because of the short lifespan of the Lion Red Cup and the approaching demise of international tours.

The triumph over France came in a week when North Harbour also beat the Canterbury Cardinals and Auckland Warriors Colts (who had replaced the Auckland Vulcans) in the Lion Red Cup. Norton said those wins were the turning point of a season that had begun far from promisingly with five successive defeats. The Sea Eagles had suffered more than any of the twelve Lion Red Cup teams from a player exodus. Only eleven of the thirty-two players used in 1994 remained, with Warriors hooker Duane Mann the biggest loss.

Midway through the minor premiership North Harbour was tenth with just nine points from eleven games. But it won nine of its second-round fixtures to eventually finish third behind the Warriors Colts and Counties-Manukau Heroes. There was another setback when North Harbour lost its first playoff match to the Heroes, but it recovered to eliminate Waikato Cougars and then the Heroes, thanks to a remarkable surge from 0–19 down to win 28–19.

Shocked Heroes coach Stan Martin could only shake his head in disbelief.

North Harbour repeated its Houdini act in the grand final, fighting back from 2–15 at halftime to win 28–21 over a Warriors Colts side coached by John Ackland and including such promising types as Nigel Vagana, Bryan Henare, Frank Wātene and the Swanns, Anthony, Logan and Willie. Once again, loose forward Palmada was a dominant figure, and Stewart, Setefano and replacement Filipo also exerted control over the Colts forwards. Centre Tuimavave's try, the start of a comeback which produced twenty-six unanswered points, was crucial. Fuimaono, Wilson and Palmada also scored tries, and Dane kicked six goals. Colts tries went to Vagana, captain Meti Noovao, Willie Swann and Henare. Noovao kicked a goal and a field goal, and replacement Steve Buckingham a goal.

Norton and Stewart were respectively named coach and captain of the year. Norton could now count sixteen trophies in seventeen finals stretching back to his time with Northcote, while Stewart appeared in all twenty-seven of North Harbour's matches and rampaged over for sixteen tries. Throughout the season he led the way to the opposing goal-line and beyond. A transplanted centre, Stewart switched to the forwards in the midst of winning four Fox Memorial titles with Northcote from 1989 to 1993.

North Harbour forwards, Ben McLean, Sean Wilson, Don Stewart, Mike Setefano (partly obscured), Keneti Asiata and Jason Palmada.
Photosport

North Harbour captain Don Stewart.
Photosport

CHAPTER TEN

Auckland teams again had the better of their Lion Red Cup rivals. The Warriors Colts, Counties-Manukau and North Harbour filled the top three placings in the round-robin, with Waitakere City coming home eighth.

Clark captures Cup

Auckland coach Dominic Clark and his players broke the Christchurch jinx in 1995, ending a run of six losses and a draw at the Addington Show Grounds dating back to 1990. First, though, they suffered that sixth loss during a southern tour in early June. In a controversial climax, Wellington referee Stephen Church changed a probable match-winning penalty to Auckland into a Canterbury clearing kick and the locals held on to win 16–15. Auckland's pre-match mood had not been helped when Canterbury declined to put the Rugby League Cup on the line. A 34–10 defeat of West Coast at Greymouth was some compensation.

Clark had the Rugby League Cup very much in his sights during a disrupted preparation for Auckland's second trip to Christchurch. But the timing, just four days after the Lion Red Cup final, caused wholesale defections. Clark dropped those who did not attend training and finished with a nucleus of ten Counties-Manukau players, Waitakere's Willie McLean, and the rest from the Auckland club competition. Ironically, the many established Counties combinations proved decisive in Auckland's 21–18 victory.

The much-revised Auckland line-up comprised Te Manawa Loza, Willie McLean, Paul Heta, Richard O'Connell, Ben Fahey, Shane Edwards, Leroy Joe, Mark Faumuina, Junior Fiu, Gavin Welsh (captain), Steve Ekepati, Gareth Adams and Matthew Sturm. The bench players were Junior Papalii, Malesala Malesala, Lawrence Tagaloa and Jerry Seuseu. The hard working Sturm was the outstanding individual, setting up the first two tries. Adams (two), Fahey and Edwards crossed for tries, Fahey also kicked two goals, and Joe kicked a field goal.

Front-rower Welsh had earlier captained Otahuhu to a blistering 32–0 win over Marist in the Fox Memorial grand final, when Faumuina, Fahey and Heta were again among his team-mates. Though finishing three points behind City-Point Chevalier – which at one stage won seventeen consecutive games – for the Rukutai Shield, Otahuhu marched through the playoffs by beating Marist 24–16 and City-Point Chevalier 25–10 before shutting out Marist in the decider at Carlaw Park. Like Dominic Clark in Christchurch, Otahuhu coach Trevor McLeod found salvation for the previous year's loss to Northcote.

Otahuhu captain Gavin Welsh with the Fox Memorial Shield

Photosport

Women in action

Auckland has been the national, indeed the world, stronghold of women's rugby league since the New Zealand women's federation was formed and the original Kiwi Ferns toured Australia in 1995. New Zealand has relied heavily on its powerful Auckland nucleus to be unbeaten at World Cup tournaments through to 2008. That pattern was established from the inaugural provincial tournament at Nelson when twelve teams from eight districts entered and the two Auckland sides met in the final. It was no surprise that sixteen of the twenty-three players who toured Australia were from Auckland – Luisa Avaiki, Golly Baker, Nadene Conlon, Wendy Cunningham, Michelle Driscoll, Eva Epiha, Juanita Hall (captain), Tania Martin, Therese Mangos, Nicole Presland, Eileen Rankin (vice-captain), Lynley Tierney, Sara White, Rachael White, Tammi Wilson and Leah Witehira.

Nicole Presland.
Photosport

1996 Reserves upstage Warriors

While the Auckland Warriors finished eleventh, three points out of the playoffs, in the 1996 Optus Cup, their reserves went all the way to run Cronulla-Sutherland to a 14–12 grand final decision at the Sydney Football Stadium. The young Warriors, having won seventeen of their previous eighteen games, made too many early errors before a likely title-winning try was ruled out by touch judge Martin Weekes. Dashing centre Nigel Vagana scored three tries against Brisbane in the qualifying final, and was promptly signed by English club Warrington.

The Warriors were given a kick-start when all of the eight Super League-aligned clubs declined to play in the first round of the Australian Rugby League competition. With the Warriors' players and head coach John Monie on strike, reserve grade coach Frank Endacott drew up a list of Otahuhu and Ellerslie club players prepared to travel to Brisbane and take on the Broncos. On hearing that, the Broncos forfeited, and the Warriors were awarded winning points in first and reserve grades.

But the all too familiar roller-coaster was back on the tracks after that – a win over Illawarra at home, a loss to Western Suburbs at Campbelltown, a win over North Sydney at home, a loss at Manly, a rare away victory at Wollongong, then a 28–4 pasting of Parramatta at Ericsson Stadium when Gary Freeman was sin-binned and then sent off for repeated infringements. But there was a mid-season recession and a disappointing final month to produce a 10–11 win-loss record.

Stephen Kearney and Stacey Jones were the stand-out forward and back in a season when the Warriors were still struggling to get their balance right. Those who had served their professional apprenticeships in Australia adjusted more

CHAPTER TEN

easily than the players brought back from Britain. Awen Guttenbeil was the most promising of the young forwards. Imports Andy Platt and Greg Alexander were returning to their homelands after passing their knowledge onto the likes of rampaging prop Joe Vagana and Jones, and Matthew Ridge was the big signing for 1997. Ridge and another Auckland rugby union recruit, Craig Innes, had been Optus Cup winners with Manly.

Third time lucky

Counties-Manukau, having twice bowed to North Harbour, finally got its hands on the Lion Red Cup in 1996 when the Heroes beat top qualifier Waitakere City Raiders 34–22 in the grand final at Carlaw Park. Auckland representation had been reduced to three teams with Manawatu replacing the Warriors Colts and the trio finished comfortably clear of the rest in the minor premiership. But Counties-Manukau never got to defend its prize in 1997. The national competition was canned after continuing to leak money at an alarming rate.

Recently returned from England, Cameron Bell replaced coach Stan Martin, who had gone to Whitehaven. Bell lost outstanding halves Clayton Friend (twice injured) and Dean Clark (signed by Leeds) during the season. He switched Dean Mackwood from hooker to scrum-half and persuaded former Kiwis captain and hooker Duane Mann to don the number six jersey when he offered his services after Clark's departure. The forwards were led by Jerry Seuseu, Matthew Sturm, Frank Wātene and hooker Esau Mann.

Just as impressive was Waitakere's success in winning nineteen of twenty-two round-robin games under new coach Del Hughes. The Raiders actually beat

Counties-Manukau players with the Lion Red Cup, Jerry Seuseu, Te Manawa Loza, Steve Ekepati, Esau Mann, Matthew Sturm and Ray Barchard.

Photosport

Counties-Manukau 26–8 during the playoffs to be first into the grand final, only for Bell's boys to rejoin them with a 22–6 preliminary final victory over Waikato Cougars. North Harbour had been eliminated by consecutive losses to Counties-Manukau and Waikato.

Waitakere led 16–8 at halftime of the grand final and 22–8 soon afterwards thanks to a try-scoring treble by Boycie Nelson, another try to fellow centre David Bailey, and three Ben Lythe goals. But that was to be Waitakere's lot. Esau Mann emerged from the sin-bin to combine with substitute Neville Ramsay and give Counties-Manukau full control for the last thirty minutes. Gus Malietoa-Brown (two), Ramsay, Watene, Charlie Kennedy, Esau Mann and Duane Mann scored the Heroes' tries, and Te Manawa Loza kicked three goals.

Bell was named coach of the year, and Seuseu the player of the year.

St Paul's treble

St Paul's College had been the leading rugby league secondary school in Auckland for several years before it won all of the first three national championships, introduced in 1994. The college which produced Stacey Jones, the Vagana cousins, Joe and Nigel, and David Solomona beat Wainuiomata College (Wellington), New Plymouth Boys' High School and Aranui High School (Christchurch) in the finals. In 1996 New Zealand Rugby League development manager Richard Bolton proudly announced that a total of 126 schools had participated to find twenty-two qualifiers from sixteen regions.

But the eighty-four-game unbeaten record St Paul's had fashioned in Auckland and national competitions was broken in 1997 when Aranui, which had developed a strong sports academy, thumped the perennial champion 48–6 in the final at Christchurch's renamed Rugby League Park. On the previous day, all but two of Aranui's players had been in Invercargill losing the South Island secondary schools' rugby union final to Southland Boys' High School – typical of the dual codes commitments of many competing schools.

Otara's overtime epic

It took Otara thirty-one years, but only two seasons in the top grade, to win the 1996 Fox Memorial Shield. The manner of its 36–28 grand final defeat of Otahuhu ensured it would never be forgotten.

The Scorpions led 24–12 midway through the second half, only for Otahuhu to draw level and almost snatch victory with a field goal before fulltime. The deadlock could not be broken in the first two periods of extra time, and both sides were all but out on their feet before Otara triumphed with two tries in the third.

Player-coach Ronald Kite kicked four goals for Otara in the Fox Memorial grand final.
Photosport

CHAPTER TEN

Otara, Fox Memorial winner.
Photosport

The two Counties-Manukau rivals had already met four times during the season, for two wins apiece, including a one-point margin to each. Club stalwart Ronald Kite was player-coach, the club chose Saulimai Lavea as its player of the year, Andrew Grey was top try-scorer in his first season of rugby league, and Alex Tupou led the points scorers.

Manurewa enjoyed a dream start to its first year of premier football by beating Otara 31–26 in the Roope Rooster final before going on to finish fourth in the fourteen-team round-robin. Otahuhu received its just rewards by carrying home the Rukutai and Stormont shields.

Decade in wilderness

Auckland's Rugby League Cup rivalry with Canterbury continued for two more seasons before the venerable old trophy vanished into the wilderness. In 1996, an Auckland team crammed with players who lifted Counties-Manukau, Waitakere City and North Harbour to the top rungs of the Lion Red Cup almost slipped up at Carlaw Park against a Canterbury side drawn from two Lion Red Cup stragglers. Auckland held on to win 24–20 after leading 24–10 into the final quarter. Te Manawa Loza, Richard Stewart, Cheaf Lee Fakavamoeanga and Steve Ekepati were try-scorers, and Ben Lythe (three) and Loza kicked goals. Dominic Clark stepped down as representative coach at season's end.

In 1997, new coach Brian McClennan suffered the fate of so many of his predecessors on his first visit to Christchurch when Canterbury took the cup 32–26. McClennan's ability to lift his teams before and during matches was already coming to the fore, however. It was all Canterbury at 28–0 and 32–8 before Auckland roared into life and got as close as six points by fulltime. Stewart, Paki Tuimavave, Tama Hohaia, Charlie Kennedy and Boycie Nelson scored tries, and Lythe kicked three goals in that late scoring burst, while young Mangere East wing Lesley Vainikolo gained some valuable experience.

Ironically, both Auckland and Canterbury finished the season empty-handed. Canterbury defended the cup against West Coast (twice), Nelson-Marlborough, Southland and Taranaki before losing it 34–18 to Waikato in the Challenge Cup provincial final. (In 1998 Waikato lost the Rugby League Cup to Taranaki. From there it passed between minor provinces Coastline, Tasman, Otago, Gisborne and Hawke's Bay, before the latter lost to Canterbury B in 2007 and the then ninety-seven-year-old trophy returned to mainstream competition.)

The Challenge Cup had replaced the Lion Red Cup and involved two Auckland teams: the Heroes coached by McClennan and captained by Duane Mann, and the division-two Raiders coached by Clark and captained by John Fuimaono. The Heroes were unbeaten in six round-robin games before losing twice to Waikato in the playoffs, while the struggling Raiders managed just one win before being knocked out by Northland. The cost-conscious Challenge Cup, with its repetitive regional fixtures, was to be a one-year wonder.

Changes for the Warriors in 1997

Decisive action was taken when the Auckland Warriors failed to fire over the first half of the 1997 Super League season. First, chief executive Ian Robson, the man who had sold the team to the New Zealand public, was replaced by Bill MacGowan, and, a couple of months later, reserve grade (and Kiwis) coach Frank Endacott took over the top team from John Monie. By season's end there was promise of better things ahead.

It was a season of universal turmoil. Super League and the Australian Rugby League ran separate competitions, and the former also staged a World Club Challenge which proved little more than the superiority of the Australasian clubs over their British counterparts. The Warriors did particularly well, however, reaching the semi-finals before losing 22–16 to eventual winner Brisbane Broncos in Brisbane. Last in the Super League Telstra Cup after a seven-match losing streak, the Warriors managed to climb only as high as seventh (of ten) and missed the playoffs. Stephen Kearney and Stacey Jones were again the outstanding individuals.

The Warriors reserves reached their second grand final, going down to a slick Canterbury Bulldogs outfit 40–12. Gary Kemble had succeeded Endacott as coach, and front-rower Jerry Seuseu spearheaded a successful season. The Colts

CHAPTER TEN

claimed the minor premiership and beat Penrith 27–12 in the major semi-final, only to lose 22–18 to the same team on grand final day. David Solomona, Ali Lauitiiti and Monty Betham were among the young stars.

General manager Patrick Carthy reported in the *1997 Auckland Rugby League Yearbook* that a change to the Companies Act on 1 June led to the Auckland Rugby League becoming sole shareholder in the company. 'The clubs of Auckland voted to retain full shareholding with a review in July 1998,' wrote Carthy. 'Not all problems have been resolved, but the League, New Zealand Rugby League and the Warriors are working to ensure successful conclusions.'

Glenora glitters

The Glenora Bears did not so much win the last three Fox Memorial grand finals in the 1990s as obliterate their rivals – the Mangere East Hawks by 34–14 in 1997 and 35–6 in 1998 and the Otahuhu Leopards by 24–4 in 1999. While Mangere East was minor premier in the first season, Glenora claimed the Rukutai

Fox Memorial treble for Glenora in 1999.
Photosport

Shield in 1998 and 1999 and added the Roope Rooster to its haul in 1999. Neil Joyce coached the Bears to their first triumph and Del Hughes to the other two. On-field leadership was provided by the durable Duane Mann.

Ten clubs vied for $60,000 prize money in the new 1997 Super 10 competition. But Glenora had only shared (with Eastern United in 1962) and Mangere East had never held the Fox Memorial Shield, so there was much more than money and pride at stake when they ran onto Carlaw Park. It was 20–4 by halftime, and no contest afterwards as loose forward Kosta Malametinos scored two of Glenora's five tries, and Ben Lythe kicked six goals and a field goal. Glenora had finished fifth and last of the qualifiers and eliminated Marist (57–20), Otahuhu (12–8) and Northcote (30–12) en route to the grand final.

In contrast, Glenora won its first sixteen round-robin games in 1998. It blasted Mangere East 38–16 in the major semi-final before the Hawks headed off Northcote 24–16 in the preliminary final. In the grand final Mangere East held Glenora to 10–6 at the break before conceding all twenty-five points in the second spell. Wing Brian Jellick scored two tries, as he had done in the major semi-final, centre Alan Lio also got two, and Lee Tamatoa and Steve Buckingham one each. Sharpshooter Lythe kicked five goals and a field goal to end the season with 324 points.

By 1999, the contest was the Super 12 with the addition of Hibiscus Coast and Eastern Tornadoes, the latter a combination of Mount Wellington, Otara and Pakuranga. A commendable third in the Rukutai Shield, Hibiscus Coast beat Northcote in the playoffs before being crushed 41–6 as Glenora advanced to the grand final. Otahuhu then beat Hibiscus Coast 30–19 to also qualify. The Leopards had been heroic in reaching the grand final from fourth, and they held Glenora to 6–4 at halftime before their resistance was broken. Scrum-half Aaron

Glenora forward Bleu Tamatoa has Ben Lythe in support in 1997.
Photosport

Glenora Bears: Ben Valeni, man of the match in the 1999 Fox Memorial grand final, and Junior Fiu.
Photosport

CHAPTER TEN

Tucker, twice a runner-up with Mangere East before transferring to the Bears, Shannon Lee, Greg Ashby and Ben Valeni's tries were complemented by four Buckingham goals.

Front-rower Valeni, who was man of the match in the grand final, and stand-off half Buckingham were the placegetters behind Te Atatu forward Fred Robarts in the Auckland Referees Association best and fairest player of the year competition. Despite Te Atatu finishing no higher than ninth, Robarts became the first double winner of that award for twenty-one years.

Honeymoon at Carlaw

Auckland captain Ben Lythe had good reason to thank his wife, Mardie, after the 44–8 national provincial final victory over Canterbury at Carlaw Park in 1998. The couple had been married only the previous day and effectively started their honeymoon with Ben helping prove Auckland was a cut above the other provinces. Lythe scored a try and kicked eight goals to complement other tries by Boycie Nelson, Junior Fiu, Cliff Beverley, Keneti Asiata, Lee Tamatoa and Don Stewart. Auckland was always in control, as it had been all season.

In its north zone fixtures, Auckland routed Bay of Plenty 46–4 and 80–4 and thumped Waikato 34–14 and 82–12. Coach Dominic Clark had plenty of talent to pick from in the Fox Memorial and honed his team's sharpness with two early season 26–24 losses to the Auckland Warriors reserves. A third game, in August, also resulted in a Warriors win, by 28–24. Prop Greg Ashby led the way up front and hooker Shane Edwards and halves Lythe and Darryl Beazley were all game-breakers in their own right. The only disappointment was Waikato's refusal to put the Rugby League Cup up for challenge.

Warriors sold

After what was described by one writer in the *1998 New Zealand Rugby League Annual* as 'a year of total non-achievement', the Auckland Warriors were sold by the Auckland Rugby League to a consortium of world-renowned former coach Graham Lowe, company director and former Marist player Malcolm Boyle, and the business arm of the Tainui Māori Trust. The Warriors finished fifteenth in the unified twenty-team National Rugby League competition that emerged from the 'Super League war'.

Graham Lowe and Mark Graham together again in 1998.
Photosport

Lowe and Boyle expressed interest in buying the club in 1997 but had been told then that it was not for sale. 'By 1998 the climate had changed,' said the *Annual*. 'The Auckland Rugby League (ARL) was tired of owning a club that was bringing them no financial return and they badly needed money to inject new life in to the game at grassroots level.

'Initially there were numerous expressions of interest but by the time the company appointed to conduct the sale, Arthur Anderson, became involved the numbers were three. In the end the ARL had two bids to consider, the Lowe-Boyle group and another headed by former Kiwi prop and Warriors board member Dean Lonergan. Enhancing the Lowe-Boyle bid was a superior amount of money up front, and greater resources. They did not take long to receive the necessary backing from the National Rugby League of Australia and the New Zealand Rugby League.'

The financial arrangements included $2 million in cash on settlement, $1.5 million in deferred settlement over three years, a development grant each year to the Auckland Rugby League of $250,000, 350 tickets to home matches, and a corporate box at Ericsson Stadium. While Lowe, who became the club's executive chairman, was involved fulltime, Boyle and the Tainui trust were not, though they had seats on the new board of management.

The *Annual* said the average home attendance had dropped to 8,000, and the club was in debt by at least $3 million. Former New Zealand captain Mark Graham, who had a long association with Lowe at Otahuhu, Brisbane Norths, and the Kiwis, and on the coaching staff at Manly, was appointed head coach, and journalist Trevor McKewen became chief executive. Mike McClennan was Graham's assistant coach, Hugh McGahan the football manager and Bob Hall was responsible for talent identification.

That considerable amount of pooled rugby league knowledge could not lift the Auckland Warriors into contention for the major NRL trophies, or even near the playoffs. They finished eleventh (of seventeen) in 1999 and second-last (of fourteen) in 2000, but severe off-field financial problems overshadowed even those distressing results.

The key assets of the club were eventually purchased by business tycoons Eric Watson and Mark Hotchin, with the Auckland Rugby League forced to write off the $1.5 million deferred settlement. The renamed New Zealand Warriors finally lived up to some of the high expectations they had always carried. Eighth playoff qualifier in 2001, they won the minor premiership and reached the grand final in 2002, and made the preliminary finals in 2003. Three more bleak years preceded a fourth placing in 2007 and a remarkable run from eighth in the regular season to get within one game of the 2008 grand final.

CHAPTER TEN

Auckland cut in half

In yet another attempt to create a viable provincial competition, the New Zealand Rugby League divided Auckland into North and South in 1999 to play Canterbury, Taranaki, Wellington, Northland, Waikato and Bay of Plenty. Auckland South was unbeaten in the round-robin, though held to an 18–18 draw by Taranaki, but Auckland North lost to Canterbury 24–18 in Christchurch and Auckland South 31–20.

Preliminary fixtures were spaced from March to July and the playoffs held in September and October to avoid clashes with club commitments. The national competition therefore had little continuity, and coaches were frustrated. Despite North's hiccup in Christchurch, the two Auckland sides were always on course to meet twice more in the playoffs.

National Provincial Cup champion Auckland South.
Photosport

South beat North 22–0 in the major semi-final, with Henry Fa'afili, Herman Lemafa, Hare Te Rangi and Sinave Faitala scoring tries, and Daniel Mildenhall kicking three goals. Strengthened by three contracted Cronulla Sharks players, Taranaki eliminated Canterbury in the minor semi-final and extended Auckland North to 20–18 in their preliminary final.

The extra game served North well, but South still prevailed, 24–22, in the grand final. Tries for the winners went to Adrian Smith (two), Te Rangi and Ed Toby, with four goals from Mildenhall. North also scored four tries, through Alan Lio, Peter Lewis, Richard White and Harry Kapi, and Lewis kicked three goals.

Stan Martin, back from three years in England, was the successful coach. He based his side around Otahuhu club players Fa'afili, Te Rangi, Faitala, Clinton Toopi, Shane Edwards, Eric Pele and Phillip Leuluai and called up the very experienced Dean Clark from second division to be his on-field general. North coach Dominic Clark was especially well served by loose forward Kosta Malamatenios, who played every match, backs Jarod Trott, Jamie Cook and Aaron Tucker and second-rower Henry Perenara.

Martin also coached a combined Auckland team to beat New South Wales Country 33–6. With club-based Warriors unavailable, he included eight Glenora Bears in his line-up. The Country team warmed up with a 44–10 defeat of Wellington and held Auckland to 16–6 at halftime before Martin's men finished over the top of them. Trott, Lio, Edwards, Boycie Nelson and Junior Fiu scored Auckland's tries and Steve Buckingham kicked six goals and a field goal.

Last test at Carlaw

Carlaw Park hosted the last of its sixty-eight test matches during the inaugural 1999 Tri-Nations series. But New Zealand was not playing Australia or Great Britain. While those two nations were meeting in Brisbane, it was arranged for the Kiwis to play Tonga in a one-off Friday night test.

In contrast to the many dramatic internationals held at the park, and considering Tonga had all but beaten New Zealand at Warrington in their 1995 World Cup encounter, this was an anti-climax. It is not so much remembered for the Kiwis' 74–0 victory, nor the four tries scored by wing Brian Jellick or Henry Paul's prolific scoring, but for the injury suffered by Stacey Jones.

Wounded Warrior Stacey Jones.
Photosport

Jones dislocated an elbow and fractured a wrist when colliding with team-mate Joe Vagana as they tackled Tongan fullback Paul Koloi in the tenth minute. The champion scrum-half had previously emerged unscathed from 100 consecutive Warriors matches and eighteen tests. Warriors officials were far from amused and, more immediately, the Kiwis missed Jones in their 22–20 Tri-Nations final loss to Australia at Ericsson Stadium.

Expatriate Aucklander Jellick was making his test debut from North Queensland Cowboys. The Bradford-based Paul, making a rare appearance in his favourite stand-off half position, totalled twenty-six points from a try and eleven goals. His points and goals respectively set and equalled New Zealand test records. The team score and winning margin were also records. A reported 4,528 spectators attended what became Carlaw's last test.

CHAPTER 11

THE TWENTY-FIRST CENTURY
2000–2008

CHAPTER ELEVEN

The Twenty-first Century 2000–2008

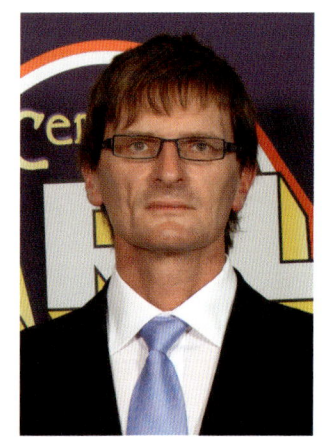

Patrick Carthy.
Farrelly Photos

Juggling the resources

The new millennium was to bring with it new challenges for rugby league in Auckland. Contributing four teams to the Lion Red Cup in the mid-1990s, at a time when the Warriors were about to kick off and the trans-Tasman player drain was bubbling along, had proved a test of Auckland's talent depth. But that depth was tested again in 2000, when the Bartercard Cup was launched with eight Auckland-based sides competing against four from other parts of the country.

Auckland Rugby League general manager Patrick Carthy adopted a positive stance in his annual report: 'There was concern as to the effect it would have on the prestigious Fox Memorial competition and the standard of play in the Auckland premiership. With the loss of 136 regular premier players it was a justified concern. However, this was counteracted by the implementation of a new grading round format. This put all aspiring clubs on an even playing field and gave them the opportunity to play at the highest level.

'One thing that can be said is that a number of clubs and players took the opportunity presented and gave it their best shot, the quality of football not diminishing greatly. We saw the resurgence of clubs such as Richmond, Te Atatu and Bay Roskill through the grading rounds and witnessed the depth of the clubs which had been participating in the Bartercard Cup. These players and team officials would not have had the opportunity if it had not been for the Bartercard Cup introduction. The game is about opportunities and the pressure was on all participating teams from the first week of the season. There was no cruising.'

All was not well with the Warriors. Although no longer owned by the Auckland Rugby League, the highs and lows experienced by the club influenced the public perception of the sport in general. In 2000 the Warriors collapsed financially before New Zealand millionaire businessman Eric Watson purchased the key assets. They were rebranded as the New Zealand Warriors, with new colours of black and grey, and Daniel Anderson, an unknown Parramatta lower grade coach, was given the job of rebuilding from the rubble. Auckland lost its annual development grant of $250,000, which represented a quarter of the league's income.

As if to reflect the woes of the Warriors and uncertainty in the domestic game, a makeshift Kiwis team suffered a record 52–0 loss to Australia in the Anzac test match in Sydney. Later in the year the Kiwis pounded England 49–6 at Bolton to reach the World Cup final. But the Kangaroos proved to be too strong once again, even if the 40–12 scoreline did not reflect the intensity of the first hour.

2000 Bartercard Cup

As opposed to the composite teams that competed in the short-lived Lion Red Cup, the emphasis in the inaugural 2000 Bartercard Cup was on established club teams. Auckland's entrants were Eastern Tornadoes, Glenora, Hibiscus Coast, Manurewa, Mount Albert, Northcote, Otahuhu, and a combination of Marist and Richmond. They came up against Bay of Plenty club Ngongotaha, Wellington's Wainuiomata and Porirua City, and the Canterbury Bulls. Two full rounds of home and away fixtures over twenty-two weeks preceded a top-five playoff culminating in the grand final at Carlaw Park.

The Canterbury Bulls beat the Otahuhu Leopards 38–24 in a thrilling title-decider, one that was much closer than the score would argue. Otahuhu led 8–2 in the early stages and later recovered from an 8–20 halftime deficit to lead again at 24–20. But the southerners mounted a storming four-try finish. The *New Zealand Rugby League Annual* said 'it was a shame there had to be a loser. Otahuhu could find consolation, scant as it might have been, that it contributed fully to a rousing finale. Independent observers claimed it was the best domestic game seen for years, and the intensity was as great as in any NRL match.'

A try for Esau Mann in the inaugural Bartercard Cup grand final.
Photosport

CHAPTER ELEVEN

Otahuhu was the minor premier by four points from Canterbury, losing only four times in the regular season. Eastern finished third, and Wainuiomata and Glenora rounded off the top five. Mount Albert, Manurewa, Hibiscus Coast, Marist-Richmond and Northcote filled the placings from sixth to tenth, with Ngongotaha and Porirua City trailing the field. In the playoffs, Glenora was eliminated by Wainuiomata, and Eastern lost to Canterbury and Wainuiomata. Otahuhu was first into the grand final with a 51–28 rout of the Bulls (32–0 at halftime), but the Cantabrians earned a second chance by thrashing Wainuiomata 34–6.

Aucklanders gained many individual awards. Otahuhu's Esau Mann was captain of the year, and George Tuakura named best and fairest player. The distinction of scoring most tries was shared by Hare Te Rangi (Otahuhu) and Remus Gentles (Eastern). Mount Albert's Carl Doherty was the most prolific scorer with 215 points, and Eastern's Mark Murray kicked the most field goals. Bill Shrimpton was referee of the year. Six former Kiwis coached teams: Gerard Stokes (Canterbury); Dean Clark (Otahuhu); James Leuluai (Eastern); John Ackland (Mount Albert); Duane Mann (Glenora); and Mike Kuiti (Porirua). Clark and Mann played as well as coached.

Otahuhu reversed the roles in the Fox Memorial. After finishing one Rukutai Shield point behind Richmond, the John Clark-coached Leopards completed a 21–14 grand final win over Richmond when Steve McCulloch scored in the last minute. Clark rated captain Mike Annadale, Jason Maera, Kimi Iobu and Paolo Teniseli as among his best players. Otahuhu was also reserve grade champion, testifying to the depth within its ranks and the manner in which it took on the challenge presented by the arrival of the Bartercard Cup.

Representative scene

Bartercard Cup players aspired to earn New Zealand Residents selection, as well as attract the attention of those scouting for professional clubs. Among those original Bartercard Cup players who fashioned successful careers in Australia and Britain were Otahuhu centre and wing George Carmont, Marist-Richmond utility back Motu Tony, and Eastern Tornadoes forward Phillip Leuluai.

Twins and fellow centres David and Paul Fisi'iahi (Eastern) were in the Residents team which made a three-match Australian tour in July 2000. The other Auckland players were Tony, Leuluai, Boycie Nelson (Glenora), Anthony Kiro (Manurewa), Paea Kailea, Peter Lewis, John Vaigafa (all Mount Albert), Anthony Seuseu (Hibiscus Coast), Ben Lythe (New Zealand Warriors), Shane Edwards, Hare Te Rangi, captain Esau Mann, George Tuakura and Jonathan Smith (all Otahuhu).

Fox Memorial winner Otahuhu.
Photosport

Otahuhu and Auckland captain Mike Annadale.
Photosport

Tony scored two tries, Paul Fisi'iahi and Nelson one apiece, and Lythe kicked three goals when the Residents controversially lost 24–22 to Sydney Metropolitan at Wentworthville. Residents officials were adamant they were robbed. Te Rangi appeared to cross for a legitimate match-winning try when, with both touch judges running to the posts, the referee believed he had seen a forward pass and called everyone back. The Residents hammered Victoria 64–0, with Te Rangi claiming four tries, and Dubbo Combined 82–10.

But a weakened Residents side served as sacrificial lambs to the World Cup Kangaroos at Gosford in October. The Bartercard Cup season was well over and New Zealand Māori, Tonga and Western Samoa had first call on players for their World Cup build-ups. In front of 16,200 adoring fans, the Australians won 108–0. Of the sixteen Aucklanders who toured three months earlier, only Edwards, Leuluai and Seuseu remained. They were joined by Alan Lio (Glenora), Paul Ah Kuoi (Marist-Richmond), Tyson Majoribanks (Otahuhu) and Sinave Faitala (Eastern). Edwards, the captain, was an early casualty with concussion.

Player availability also became an issue for Auckland premier coach Dominic Clark in a two–nil series loss to the Cook Islands World Cup team. The short tour to the Cooks and return match at Carlaw Park in October replaced a planned two-match tour of Fiji in June, which was cancelled forty-eight hours before departure because of the political coup there.

At domestic level, an Auckland Fox Memorial team won all six matches in a North Island division two competition against Coastline, Wellington, Manawatu, Taranaki, Northland and Waikato. Only in the last game, with Taranaki at New Plymouth, was Auckland seriously threatened. Taranaki led 24–4 at halftime before being run down and beaten by 34–31. Coach Del Hughes relied largely on Otahuhu and Richmond players, and Otahuhu skipper Mike Annadale also led Auckland. Richmond hooker Tevita Latu later represented New Zealand and Tonga and played professionally in Australia and Britain.

Taking on Sydney

Coached by Stan Martin, an Auckland team of Bartercard Cup players made a two-match trip to Sydney in September 2001. A Northern Māori XIII was beaten 48–6 at Brookvale Oval, but a Sydney Metropolitan combination comprised mainly of former or fringe NRL players dominated early and late to beat Auckland 34–12 at Campbelltown Stadium. Daniel Floyd scored two tries and kicked eight goals from as many attempts in the first game, and Joe Flavell (two) and Joe Galavao crossed for tries against Metropolitan.

Touring team: Daniel Floyd, Karl Te Mata, Tyrone Pau, Jeremy Smith, Brendan Solomon (Hibiscus Coast), Harry Kapi (Northcote), Anthony Kiro, Joe Galavao, Wayne Barnett (Manurewa), Paul Ah Kuoi, Jason Temu (Marist-Richmond), Joe Flavell, Hare Te Rangi, Eric Pele (Eastern), Cliff Beverley (Glenora), Paolo Teniseli, Herman Lemafa (Otahuhu), Junior Fiu (Northcote). Beverley, Galavao and Temu were Warriors contracted players.

But Auckland failed to retain its North Island division two title, named the Super Seven after the addition of Northland. A 44–48 loss to Waikato left Auckland level with Taranaki on top of the minor premiership table, though boasting a superior points differential. In the round-robin Auckland had beaten Wellington by a massive 74–22. When they met again in the semi-final at Wellington, Auckland slumped from a 29–10 halftime lead to suffer a shock 35–40 defeat. Wellington went on to beat Taranaki 30–24 in the final.

Double grand final day

Grand final day at Carlaw Park in 2001 was notable for many reasons: Hibiscus Coast completed a rapid rise through the grades by beating Eastern Tornadoes 28–18 for the Bartercard Cup; Northcote shocked minor premier Richmond 30–29 with a last-minute try in the Fox Memorial decider; the joint promotion between the New Zealand and Auckland leagues was televised live on Sky; and fans were able to back their favourite teams at the TAB. Not Richmond's Marcus Perenara, however, for the younger brother of Melbourne Storm player Henry Perenara ran onto the field at just fifteen years, ten months and fourteen days.

Hibiscus Coast, under the co-coaching of Brian McClennan and Tony Benson, finished the Bartercard Cup round-robin four points clear of Eastern, with Canterbury Bulls, Otahuhu and Manurewa the other qualifiers. Eastern lost to and then beat Canterbury in the playoffs, but Hibiscus Coast was primed for the occasion. A stand-out performer in a champion team was fullback Daniel Floyd, who amassed an astonishing 308 points from twenty-five tries and 104 goals in twenty-one appearances. After leading 18–12 at halftime, Eastern wilted under the sustained pressure of a young Raiders side which included nine Warriors development players.

The Warriors loaned surplus players out to Bartercard Cup teams. Iafeta Paleaaesina, Motu Tony, Clinton Toopi, Shontayne Hapi, Richard Villasanti, Mark Tookey, Nathan Wood, David Myles, Justin Murphy and Cliff Beverley all

Lamond Copestake scored two tries for Northcote in the Fox Memorial grand final.
Photosport

Victorious Hibiscus Coast co-captains Richard White and Anthony Seuseu with the Bartercard Cup.
Photosport

CHAPTER ELEVEN

used the national competition as a stepping stone to or from the NRL, but none featured in the grand final. Hibiscus Coast stand-off half Jeremy Smith was man of the match, Regan Wigg (two), Mikio Filitonga, Shaun Ata and Floyd scored the winner's tries, and Floyd kicked four goals.

Floyd was named best and fairest player over the season, an award he won decisively from future Parramatta front-rower Fuifui Moimoi (Mount Albert), and registered most points and tries. McClennan was coach of the year, and Richard White captain of the year in a Hibiscus Coast clean sweep. Referee of the year was Andy Cook (Auckland).

Richmond clinched the Rukutai Shield thanks to an exciting last-round 18–12 victory over Otahuhu, finishing one point ahead of Northcote. The two clubs were always on course to clash in the Fox Memorial grand final as Manukau, Ponsonby and Otahuhu fell by the wayside in the playoffs.

An 11.50am kickoff did not detract from the occasion, and 6,000 fans were captivated by Richmond's initial ascendancy and Northcote's powerful and ultimately irresistible comeback to get home 30–29. Doug Price Memorial Medal winner Khamal Ganley and Lamond Copestake scored two tries apiece for Northcote. To complete a North Shore title treble, Hibiscus Coast beat City-Newton 39–18 in reserve grade.

Northcote celebrations after edging out Richmond.
Photosport

Farewell to Carlaw

Two appropriately exciting finals featured on Carlaw Park's official closing day, 14 September 2002 – though two minor representative matches were to follow after a hastily arranged tour by Tonga. On the last big day at rugby league's eighty-one-year-old spiritual home, Mount Albert held off Hibiscus Coast 24–20 to win the Bartercard Cup, and Hibiscus Coast needed double extra time to edge out Otahuhu 44–40 in the Fox Memorial grand final.

Mount Albert had fallen on hard times since the last of its three consecutive Fox triumphs in 1986, sinking as low as Auckland's third division in the 1990s. But winning the Phelan Shield in 1998 and the Sharman Cup the following year gave the club's management the confidence to successfully apply for Bartercard Cup inclusion in 2000. A meritorious sixth that season, Mount Albert slumped to tenth in 2001 and even suffered an 86-point loss to the Canterbury Bulls.

But the Lions roared again in 2002 under the astute coaching of John Ackland. They lost only one game in the minor premiership (to Wellington) and finished a remarkable eight points ahead of Hibiscus Coast Raiders, a side they beat 44–0 during the season. Otahuhu, Eastern Tornadoes and Marist-Richmond made it an all-Auckland playoffs series. But Hibiscus Coast was not prepared to relinquish its title without a fight, and upset Mount Albert 26–24 in the major semi-final after scoring the first sixteen points.

Mount Albert regained its poise by eliminating Otahuhu 36–20 in the preliminary final. In a seesawing grand final, the Lions led 10–4 at halftime, the Raiders levelled up, the Lions made their winning break, and then resisted waves of Raiders attacks for the 24–20 victory. Loose forward Sala Fa'alogo, who scored two tries, won the Ken Stirling Shield as man of the match. Kelvin Wright, Hutch Maiava and Duane Bundock got one each and Ben Lythe kicked two goals.

Ackland acknowledged that the signing of influential Glenora halves Lythe and Steve Buckingham was an important factor in Mount Albert's form turnaround. Buckingham played his first game for two months in the grand final after recovering from a knee injury. Hibiscus Coast, on the other hand, lost its own inside backs, Aaron Aspin and Jeremy Smith, during the match through injuries. Sala Fa'alogo, Wayne McDade and Maiava stood out in the Lions pack, and future Kiwis forward David Fa'alogo was solid in the centres. Ackland also praised wing Bundock, a survivor of the dim third division days.

The annual Bartercard Cup awards flowed Mount Albert's way, to Ackland as coach of the year, Lythe as captain of the year, Maiava as best forward and fullback Lee Finnerty as best back. Finnerty and Otahuhu wing Archie Ikihele finished with most tries (twenty-seven), and Otahuhu's Boycie Nelson topped the points scorers with 256. Those individual scoring feats were all the more noteworthy because the minor premiership had been reduced from twenty-two to sixteen rounds.

The curtain falls on Carlaw Park.
Photosport

CHAPTER ELEVEN

Hibiscus Coast used double overtime to deprive Otahuhu of the Fox Memorial.
Photosport

Hutch Maiava (Mount Albert), a try-scorer in the Bartercard Cup grand final victory over Hibiscus Coast.
Photosport

Mount Albert's resurgence prevented Hibiscus Coast from completing a double on Carlaw Park's last finals day. But taking the Fox Memorial Shield home for the first time was the best possible compensation. The Fox team kept its supporters' on the edge of their seats over the closing stages of the season, edging out minor premier Papakura Sea Eagles 40–38 in the major semi-final and then requiring two periods of extra time to overcome Otahuhu 44–40 in the grand final.

Otahuhu led 24–16 at halftime and stayed ahead into the last ten minutes. But Hibiscus Coast scored a converted try on the hooter to tie up the scores. Three penalty goals had Otahuhu in a winning position with only seconds left in the first period of extra time, only for the Raiders to draw level through another converted try. The sudden-death golden point rule was then applied. But it was another ten minutes before Hibiscus Coast clinched victory, the match having lasted a total of 100 minutes.

Ruben Enoka and Robbie Gilmour both scored two tries for the Raiders, and Junior Asiata replied in kind for Otahuhu. Hibiscus Coast's Willie Bishop won the Doug Price Medal as man of the match and was the competition's leading try-scorer and goalkicker.

Though it failed to make the grand final, Papakura had been the form club for most of the season. It won all seven grading games and lost only twice in the fourteen-round minor premiership to win its first Rukutai Shield. But two-point losses to Hibiscus Coast and Otahuhu ended the Sea Eagles' season. Hibiscus Coast trounced Marist 64–4 in the Roope Rooster final.

Carlaw's treasures

Redundant as a rugby league venue after the 2002 season, Carlaw Park continued to fill occasional headlines for almost five years before its redevelopment reached the point of no return. The Auckland Rugby League's administration headquarters remained at the park until 2004, when it moved to larger and more modern facilities in a building shared with the New Zealand Rugby League near Mount Smart Stadium in Penrose.

By then Carlaw Park had become a car park, providing valuable finance while plans for its development were being processed. 'The development has been on the planning board since 2003 after all avenues were exhausted to develop the park into a leading stadium in Auckland with multi functional facilities and amenities,' said the Auckland Rugby League in a news release.

The project included 'a precinct incorporating a business park, serviced and owner occupied apartments, and other residential facilities. Under the development partnership, Auckland Rugby League will maintain ownership of the freehold land (or as much as possible) as well as owning as much of the business park buildings as possible. In the medium term, this development will eventually see the league's income triple from its current $1.2 million per annum and secure the financial future of the game in Auckland. The project is scheduled to commence in late 2006.'

But the awarding of the 2011 Rugby World Cup to New Zealand, and knowledge the final would inevitably be played in Auckland, caused the city's sporting venues to come under the microscope. After a much trumpeted scheme to build a new waterfront stadium was abandoned, it was inevitable eyes would again be cast towards the nearby Carlaw Park.

'The argument to have the Rugby World Cup stadium at Auckland's Carlaw Park is by no means dead,' said a *Newstalk ZB* report in December 2006. 'Funding

Stand-off Willie Bishop (Hibiscus Coast) scored in the Fox Memorial grand final and was judged the 'best and fairest' player for 2002.
Photosport

CHAPTER ELEVEN

company MPI believes it has two private companies willing to pay half of the $400 million it would cost to build.' Director Lloyd Parrant was hoping to stall development of a retirement village on the site and said he had drawings of what would be a 40,000-seat stadium with 20,000 removable seats. But the authorities pressed on with plans to redevelop Eden Park.

In March 2007 the demolition men moved in to flatten Carlaw Park's old wooden Railway Stand and the terraces that had hosted hundreds of thousands of rugby league fans over eighty years. Since the ground's closure the stand had been vandalised, become a home for transients and a target for taggers. However, much of the rimu timber was salvaged by the Auckland Rugby League, which commissioned a limited edition of polished plaques to be made for sale.

Demolition workers were also to knock down the old embankment scoreboard and the ticket booths at the park entrance. Auckland Rugby League spokesman Gordon Gibbons revealed the scoreboard had been transformed into a residence by one homeless man. 'You have to come up through a trapdoor and the place was absolutely immaculate. A guy had his clothes hung up there with a little stove and a bed – absolutely amazing,' he said.

One of the turnstiles was preserved in the new rugby league museum in Penrose; but it was not possible to similarly restore the scoreboard because of its size. Gibbons confirmed the number one ground would be retained to provide an income from the retirement home to be built on it. The number two ground was sold as part of a commercial development which included a hotel, residential apartments, cafes, restaurants and an office park.

First, though, Carlaw Park's past was to take precedence over its future. Under the Historic Places Act 1993, any location where there is evidence of human occupation before 1900 is defined as an archaeological site. This means it requires an authority from the New Zealand Historic Places Trust before works which will modify, damage or destroy the site can begin. While they might have uncovered any number of football boot studs and broken teeth, Carlaw Park's nineteenth-century uses were of prime interest.

Tucked into a gully between the northern slopes of the Domain and the south side of Parnell, the area was, in the 1840s, the location of one of Auckland's first flour mills. Next came a tannery before, in 1882, the land was purchased by Chan Ah Chee and turned into a market garden. It was the latter use which most excited the archaeologists led by Dr Hans Bader, who described it as the first significant Chinese excavation site in the North Island.

'When the mill was built the valley was a swamp which is probably why it was so fertile as market gardens later on,' said Dr Bader. 'The stream that ran across the flats was redirected along the shoulder of the hill, where it fed the millpond, sluicing down from there into the millrace.' Bader suspected that when the

Chinese took over the land the dam from the old mill was still intact and that they had cut it to recreate the stream and irrigate their gardens.

The location and layout of the Low and Motion flour mill was pinpointed and a nearly complete century-old hide was discovered in one of the old tannery's pelt pits.

Brick foundations of Chan Ah Chee's house were located intact under the tarmac of the old car park. Among the discoveries were imported domestic and commercial ceramics, several dozen intact rice wine bottles and some seventeenth-century Chinese coins, which were many sided and with a hole in the middle. Despite colonial Auckland experiencing an economic recession, the Chinese community prospered. Chan Ah Chee went on to own six commercial properties on Queen Street, along with three other market gardens around Auckland and a banana plantation in Fiji.

In late November 2008 the *New Zealand Herald* reported that plans for a $120 million retirement village to be built on the land still owned by the Auckland Rugby League had been unveiled by Vision Senior Living. Described as the most centrally located retirement village in the country, the first fifty-eight of more than 200 apartments were scheduled for completion in the first quarter of 2010. Units of one to three bedrooms would sell for between $489,000 and $1.1 million. Development was already well under way. Carlaw Park had irrevocably moved from the sports section to the business pages.

Bruise brothers

Front-rowers Fuifui Moimoi (Glenora) and Hutch Maiava (Mount Albert) became cult figures in the NRL with their blockbusting hit-ups and uncompromising defence. But in 2002 they were New Zealand A team-mates on tour to France (beating France A 50–28 and France Juniors 30–20 and losing to France 16–19) and the United States (winning 78–4 against the national team). The team was coached by Gary Kemble and captained by Mount Albert scrum-half Ben Lythe.

Such was the Auckland clubs' Bartercard Cup domination that only three 'outsiders' made the touring team, Wellington forwards Chris Faifua and Jonny Limmer and Canterbury wing Eddie Hei Hei. Otahuhu centre George Carmont, Mount Albert centre David Fa'alogo, Marist-Richmond hooker Tevita Latu and Eastern-Manukau prop Phillip Leuluai subsequently joined Australian professional clubs, with Fa'alogo switching to the second-row well before he shared in New Zealand's 2008 World Cup triumph.

Auckland's New Zealand A players were Gavin Bailey, Fuifui Moimoi (Glenora), Wayne Barnett (Manurewa), Steve Buckingham, David Fa'alogo, Lee Finnerty, Ben Lythe, Hutch Maiava (Mount Albert), George Carmont, Archie Ikihele, George Tuakura (Otahuhu), Daniel Floyd, Tyrone Pau, Regan Wigg (Hibiscus

Coast), Karl Guttenbeil, Ricky Henry, Tevita Latu (Marist-Richmond) and Phillip Leuluai (Eastern-Manukau).

Players in the New Zealand Warriors system were not eligible for the tour. But nine who appeared in the 2002 Bartercard Cup had their hour of glory in the last regular NRL round when Warriors coach Daniel Anderson rested experienced and injured regulars. Karl Te Mata and Iafeta Paleaaesina (Hibiscus Coast), eighteen-year-old Evarn Tuimavave (Marist-Richmond), Jeremiah Pai and Logan Swann (Eastern-Manukau), Vinnie Anderson and David Myles (Mount Albert), Henry Fa'afili (Manurewa) and Sione Faumuina (Glenora) had the satisfaction of beating Wests Tigers 28–12 at Ericsson Stadium.

A rich vein of talent had also been unearthed at Junior Kiwis level. Aucklanders Manu Vatuvei, Jerome Ropati, Thomas Leuluai and Evarn Tuimavave were to be in the World Cup-winning New Zealand squad six years later. Other future internationals were Louis Anderson and Epalahame Lauaki. Ropati scored two tries when the Junior Kiwis beat Wests-Tigers Elite in Rotorua and Australian Institute of Sport in Wellington.

Warriors 'fever'

Under coach Daniel Anderson, the New Zealand Warriors were in the midst of their first, albeit brief, golden era. They had finished eighth in 2001, qualifying for their first playoffs, but were eliminated by minor premier Parramatta at Parramatta Stadium. In 2002 they won the J J Giltinan Shield as minor premiers and beat Canberra Raiders 36–20 at Ericsson Stadium and Cronulla Sharks 16–10 at Telstra Stadium to reach the grand final.

Support for the Warriors swept throughout New Zealand, building to their championship match with the Sydney Roosters. But the Brad Fittler-inspired Sydneysiders were too good, winning 30–8 after a brilliant Stacey Jones try had put the Warriors ahead early in the second half. Auckland juniors to appear on that historic night at Telstra Stadium were Clinton Toopi, Francis Meli, Motu Tony, Stacey Jones (captain), Jerry Seuseu, Ali Lauitiiti, Awen Guttenbeil and Logan Swann, plus Lance Hohaia and Wairangi Koopu from Waikato.

The Warriors maintained their fine form in 2003, getting within one game of the grand final before losing to eventual premiers the Penrith Panthers 28–20 at the renamed Stadium Australia. Backed by another wave of national support, which increased as the playoffs advanced, the Warriors had previously beaten the Canterbury Bulldogs 48–22 at the Sydney Showground, with Meli crossing for an amazing five tries, and the Canberra Raiders 17–16 at Sydney's Aussie Stadium, thanks to a match-winning Jones field goal.

St Paul's in Sydney

Perennial schools champion St Paul's College reached the quarter-finals of the highly prestigious Australian Nutri-Grain Cup competition in 2002. First, St Paul's established its top Auckland ranking by beating Kelston Boys High School 20–12 and confirmed its national standing by beating Aranui High School (Christchurch) 16–6. Accepted into the last thirty-two of the Nutri-Grain Cup, St Paul's was too strong for former winner Erindale College (Canberra) 30–10 and eliminated Penrith powerhouse St Dominic's College 13–12 before succumbing to Patrician Brothers (Blacktown) 10–6 in a tight encounter.

Year of the Hawks

It was actually the fortieth year of the Mangere East Hawks in 2003, and they celebrated that anniversary with their first Fox Memorial Shield victory (having been beaten grand finalists in 1978, 1987, 1989, 1997 and 1998). They also had their name inscribed on the Rukutai Shield for the third time. But both contests were close. The minor premiership was won on percentages from Richmond, and the grand final result, a 30–29 win over Hibiscus Coast, said it all.

The Fox Memorial showdown was again held in conjunction with the New Zealand Rugby League's Bartercard Cup finale. But, for the first time, Carlaw Park was not the venue. Instead, the two games were televised live on Sky from Ericsson Stadium. Less satisfactory was the need to play the Sharman Cup and Phelan Shield finals – won respectively by Northcote and East Coast Bays – on an Ericsson Stadium number two field which resembled a sandpit.

Mangere East's first Fox Memorial victory, in 2003.
Photosport

Although top in the round-robin, Mangere East completed the double the hard way after an initial bye in the top-five playoffs. The Hawks were beaten 29–12 by Hibiscus Coast in the grand final qualifier and needed their second life, a 24–19 victory over Richmond. Having accounted for both Richmond (41–28) and Mangere East in its previous games, Hibiscus Coast was favoured to retain the Fox Memorial. But the match went down to the wire and Mangere East just got there on the call of time. Hibiscus Coast had to settle for the Roope Rooster, courtesy of a 22–20 win over Manurewa.

So near for Brothers

The Canterbury Bulls edged out their strongest Auckland rivals in 2003, enjoying a superior points difference after finishing level with Mount Albert Lions in the Bartercard Cup minor premiership, and then finishing with a flurry through two Chris Newton tries in the last seven minutes to beat Marist-Richmond Brothers 32–28 in a memorable grand final at Ericsson Stadium.

Auckland still provided eight teams to the national competition, with Northcote being replaced by North Harbour Tigers representing all of the North Shore clubs. The Auckland teams finished from second to ninth behind the Bulls and ahead of Central Falcons, Wellington Orcas and Taranaki Wildcats.

The Auckland finalists largely eliminated each other in the playoffs. Eastern Tornadoes beat Hibiscus Coast Raiders, the Brothers beat the Lions twice to remove the defending champions from contention, and between those games the Lions eliminated the Tornadoes. Canterbury had trounced Marist-Richmond 40–18 in the major semi-final at Christchurch but the grand final was always scheduled for Ericsson Stadium.

After thirty-eight minutes of the grand final it was 12–0 to the Bernie Perenara-coached Brothers. But that lead was reduced to 12–6 by halftime and, despite skipping clear again at 22–12 and 28–18, Marist-Richmond could not shake off the southerners during a tense and entertaining second spell. The Bulls, coached by Phil Prescott, prided themselves on their fitness and eventually wore down the flagging Brothers defence to go ahead in the seventy-ninth minute.

It hurt Perenara's interchange roster that prop Evarn Tuimavave was sidelined from the fourth minute with a shoulder injury. Jerome Ropati, the Brothers' star stand-off half, had been on stand-by to make his NRL debut in Sydney had Stacey Jones not passed a fitness test. Ropati flew back to Auckland on match morning, the travel seemingly blunting his effectiveness. Best for the Brothers were Glen Rota, Henry Turua, Karl Guttenbeil, Ricky Henry and future Manly and Kiwis centre Steve Matai.

Tough English tour

Thirteen players from Auckland clubs, of a total of twenty-two, toured England with the New Zealand A team in 2003. They were Gavin Bailey, Karl Edmondson, Epalahame Lauaki (Glenora Bears), Steve Buckingham, Wayne McDade, Hale Va'asa (Mount Albert Lions), Sinave Faitala, Paul Fisi'iahi, Tame Tupou (Eastern Tornadoes), Ricky Henry (Marist-Richmond Brothers), Aoterangi Herangi (Manurewa Marlins), Tyrone Pau (Hibiscus Coast Raiders) and George Tuakura (Otahuhu Leopards).

Results-wise, the tour was not a success. After recovering from a twenty-four-point deficit midway through the second half to draw 24–24 with Cumbria at Whitehaven, New Zealand A lost to National League Two 27–8, Warrington 28–26, the full Great Britain test side 52–18 at Headingley and National League One 40–28. The individual highlight was Canterbury Bulls fullback Lusi Sione's three tries against Great Britain.

Start of a dynasty

Mount Albert was to prove a mountain too steep for most opponents to climb at both Bartercard Cup and Fox Memorial Shield levels for five seasons from 2004. The Lions won both the national and local championship grand finals at Ericsson Stadium that season and went on to keep the Bartercard Cup in 2005, 2006 and 2007 – as the Auckland Lions for the last two years – and regained the Fox in 2006 and 2008.

Mount Albert stand-off and captain Steve Buckingham after the 2004 Bartercard Cup victory over Marist-Richmond Brothers.
Photosport

The 2004 Bartercard Cup included a new Counties-Manukau entry in place of Manurewa Marlins. Manurewa became affiliated with Eastern Tornadoes, while Ellerslie left the Tornadoes to become half of Otahuhu-Ellerslie Leopards. Taranaki dropped out and was replaced by Waicoa Bay Stallions, a blending of Waikato, Bay of Plenty and Coastline. When Mount Albert lost two of its first three games, to Otahuhu-Ellerslie and Canterbury Bulls, it was destined to play catch up behind front-runner Marist-Richmond Brothers.

After sixteen rounds Marist-Richmond (twenty-seven points) qualified first for the playoffs ahead of Otahuhu-Ellerslie (twenty-four), Mount Albert (twenty-four), North Harbour Tigers (nineteen) and Canterbury (eighteen). For the first time Auckland teams trailed the field, Glenora Bears finishing eleventh and Hibiscus Coast Raiders last. North Harbour eliminated Canterbury 45–10, and the Auckland clubs settled down to fight it out. The Leopards beat the Tigers, only for the Leopards to lose twice to the Lions in a series of big-cat contests.

CHAPTER ELEVEN

Marist-Richmond had been first into the grand final, having beaten Mount Albert 35–22, and hopes were high the Brothers would clinch the title that so narrowly eluded them the previous year. But the Lions thrived on their heavier workload, established a 20–6 lead by halftime, and ran in seven tries to four in their 40–20 victory.

Gus Malietoa-Brown and Misili Manu scored two tries apiece, Regan Wigg and Rowan Baxter one each, and captain Steve Buckingham contributed a try and six goals. Workaholic second-rower Wigg was awarded the Ken Stirling Medal as man of the match. Manu was the competition's top try-scorer and Buckingham accumulated the most points. Club chairman Tony Sadgrove gave great credit for the result to Bartercard Cup coach of the year Brian McClennan, who, in turn, praised stand-off half Buckingham for his on-field leadership.

Even before the Bartercard Cup kick-off, Lions supporters were celebrating a 14–10 win over defending champion Mangere East Hawks in the Fox grand final curtain-raiser. There were many similarities between the two competitions. Mangere East carried off the Rukutai Shield ahead of Manurewa, Mount Albert, Richmond and Papakura. Despite Mangere East winning the major semi-final over Mount Albert, the Lions predictably roared back to beat Manurewa and then Mangere East when it mattered most. Ellerslie won the Roope Rooster.

Dan Adams (representing the sponsor, Mad Butcher) and Graham Rattenburg with the Fox Memorial Shield after Mount Albert's defeat of Mangere East.

Photosport

A plus and a minus

Mount Albert skipper Steve Buckingham captained New Zealand A teams to a win and a loss against Australian opponents in 2004. New South Wales Country was beaten 36–18 at North Harbour Stadium in mid-season but four months later another Auckland-dominated combination lost 18–6 to the Jim Beam Cup representatives from Sydney.

Halves Buckingham and Aoterangi Herangi and Canterbury interchange forward Chris Newton were the most prominent performers against Country. The teenaged Herangi gained confidence from playing alongside the vastly experienced Buckingham and continued to impress after switching to hooker. Newton scored two tries, as did centre Paul Fisi'iahi. Wing Rowan Baxter and Canterbury hooker Andrew Auimatagi got one try each, and Buckingham kicked six goals.

But New Zealand A failed to capitalise on scoring opportunities against the Jim Beam Cup team. Down by six points at halftime, the chances of a comeback were slim after the Australians increased the lead early in the second spell, just before heavy rain began to fall. Buckingham scored the home team's only try from a tap penalty and kicked the conversion. Coach Phil Prescott lamented the costly handling errors and rated the opposition as much stronger than New South Wales Country.

New Zealand A v NSW Country: Misi Taulapapa (Marist-Richmond), Karl Johnson (North Harbour), Paul Fisi'iahi (Otahuhu-Ellerslie), Ricky Henry (Marist-Richmond), Rowan Baxter (Mount Albert), Steve Buckingham (Mount Albert, captain), Aoterangi Herangi (Counties-Manukau), Kurt Cawdron (Marist-Richmond), Andrew Auimatagi (Canterbury), Jason Duff (North Harbour), Sam Wallace (Canterbury), Henry Turua (Marist-Richmond), Frank-Paul Nuuausala (Otahuhu-Ellerslie). Interchange: Bernard Perenara (Marist-Richmond), Chris Newton (Canterbury), Lee Tamatoa (Glenora), Ben Valeni (Glenora).

New Zealand A v Jim Beam Cup: Paul Atkins (Otahuhu-Ellerslie), David Fisi'iahi (Otahuhu-Ellerslie), Paul Fisi'iahi (Otahuhu-Ellerslie), Ricky Henry (Marist-Richmond), Misi Taulapapa (Marist-Richmond), Steve Buckingham (Mount Albert, captain), Jared Trott (North Harbour), Kane Ferris (Canterbury), Louis Talamavao (Mount Albert), Jason Duff (North Harbour), Henry Turua (Marist-Richmond), Simon Mannering (Wellington), Corey Lawrie (Canterbury). Interchange: Daniel Vasau (North Harbour), Chris Newton (Canterbury), Joe Tau (Mount Albert), Siali'i Tufeao (Otahuhu-Ellerslie).

Auckland senior representative teams also played both Australian visitors, with similar results. Auckland beat New South Wales Country 22–14 but lost to the Jim Beam Cup squad 30–28.

CHAPTER ELEVEN

Bull fighters

Mount Albert Lions won their last Bartercard Cup title under their own name and the first under the Auckland Lions banner by fending off strong Canterbury Bulls charges in 2005 and 2006. On both occasions the Lions had been minor premiers with the Bulls second and they maintained those rankings through to the grand finals, despite the best efforts of Counties-Manukau Jetz and North Harbour Tigers in 2005 and Waitakere Rangers and Tamaki Leopards in 2006.

But Mount Albert head coach Brian McClennan was as much relieved as typically upbeat after the Lions' close call in 2005. The Bulls were actually first into the grand final with a 34–24 victory over the Lions in the major semi-final, and the Bartercard Cup seemed destined to go south for a third time in the final minute of the grand final at Ericsson Stadium.

Just as the scoreboard clock ticked down to 00:00, Mount Albert second-rower Fabian Souter stretched out for the try which gave his side its 24–22 win. The Bulls had led 22–10 after dominating possession in the third quarter, and they went close to adding more points. However, a try and a penalty goal preceded a clever piece of work by injury-hampered Steve Buckingham that put speedy young fullback Patrick Ah Van over for his second try to make it 22–20.

The weight of possession had swung dramatically towards the Lions and, as McClennan observed later, both teams had toiled so hard on defence over the first hour that the team with the ball was destined to score late points. On the last play of the game, Lions scrum-half Bernard Perenara got a pass away to Souter, who had just enough freedom in a tackle to fall forward and touch down. Ah Van (two), Rowan Baxter, Paul Fisi'iahi and Souter scored Mount Albert's tries, but Buckingham (two goals) had an average day with his boot.

McClennan and his men had a little more leeway at the renamed Mount Smart Stadium in 2006, fending off the Bulls 25–18 in the grand final. This time Buckingham's kicking was crucial. Both sides scored three tries – Kelvin Wright, Regan Wigg and Miguel Start for the Lions – but the influential and frequently outstanding Buckingham kicked six goals and the match-clinching field goal. Bulls coach Phil Prescott no doubt had Buckingham in mind when he said the Lions' big-match experience was a telling factor in the outcome.

The Bartercard Cup was reduced from twelve to ten teams in 2006. Harbour League replaced Hibiscus Coast Raiders and North Harbour Tigers, Waitakere Rangers replaced Glenora Bears, Auckland Lions replaced Mount Albert Lions and Marist-Richmond Brothers, Tamaki Leopards replaced Otahuhu-Ellerslie Leopards and Eastern Tornadoes, and Northern Storm was formed to represent Northland. The number of Auckland teams had been reduced from eight to five, clubs giving way to franchises.

AUCKLAND RUGBY LEAGUE
1909–2009

Bartercard Cup champion again. Mount Albert in 2005.
Photosport

Bernard Perenara, the Lions scrum-half.
Photosport

CHAPTER ELEVEN

Rowan Baxter, a try-scorer in the 2005 Bartercard Cup grand final.
Photosport

The Bartercard Cup's most successful combination, Mount Albert playmaker Steve Buckingham and coach Brian McClennan.
Photosport

Marlins land the big one

Manurewa fans became accustomed to cheering their players on in finals from 2005 to 2008. The Marlins landed the big one, the Fox Memorial Shield, at the expense of Papakura Sea Eagles in 2005 and 2007, won the Sharman Cup over Howick Hornets in 2006, but lost out to Richmond Rovers in the 2008 Sharman Cup decider. Manurewa yo-yoed between premier and second division competitions, reflecting the intriguing nature of the club scene in Auckland during and immediately after the Bartercard Cup era.

Veteran Kiwis centre Richard Blackmore had reinvented himself as a second-rower and was a try-scorer and influential figure during the 34–24 defeat of Papakura in the 2005 Fox decider. Blackmore was also co-coach with Rusty Matua before returning to coach former club Otahuhu in 2006. In his absence, Matua not only lifted Manurewa back into the top grade in 2007 but also to a 28–20 extra-time victory over luckless Papakura – runner-up for the third consecutive year – to regain the Fox.

Neither Manurewa nor minor premier Papakura had appeared in a Fox final before 2005, and it was the former that handled the early nerves better. The Marlins scored the first eighteen points of the match, led 18–6 at the break, and got out to 30–6 before a face-saving flurry from the Sea Eagles reduced the eventual deficit to ten. William Heta was another stand-out for the winners. Manurewa had only qualified fifth before dominating the playoffs with half-century scores over Richmond and Mount Albert and a 16–14 victory against Mangere East.

Having lost to Mount Albert by a painful 49–6 in the 2006 Fox final, Papakura regained its consistency, and the Rukutai Shield, in 2007. But Manurewa had recovered from a disastrous start of having won just one of its first seven matches to qualify in fourth place through a streak of ten successes in eleven games. Unfortunately for the Sea Eagles, the grand final was that eleventh game.

Manurewa enjoyed increasingly more convincing wins over Marist, Glenora and Richmond in the playoffs. In the grand final, Papakura again appeared to lack match practice and soon fell twelve points behind. The Sea Eagles soared from that point, were much the better side in the second half and appeared to be deserving champions at 20–16. But a late Vince Fatu try levelled the scores and forced the game into extra time. Manurewa added tries in both five-minute periods as the Papakura effort wilted. Fullback Victor Field was named man of the match.

CHAPTER ELEVEN

Manurewa Marlins, whose first appearance in a Fox Memorial grand final was successful in 2005.
Photosport

William Heta, a stand-out performer for the Marlins.
Photosport

> ## Big turnaround
>
> Auckland achieved a forty-point turnaround in a week against Wellington to win the 2006 national first division championship. After losing 36–14 in their round-robin match, the Sam Panapa-coached Auckland side overcame an early 6–14 deficit to win the final 32–14 at Wise Park, Wainuiomata. Down by eight points early in the second half, desperate Auckland defence just prevented a runaway Wellington try, and the match turned on the resulting penalty for a double movement. For the first time in two matches, Auckland applied pressure and capitalised on Wellington's errors.
>
> Earlier in the competition, Auckland had beaten Waikato and Canterbury, the latter through a late try in Christchurch. The Auckland team was made up of premiership players who had made no more than three Bartercard Cup appearances. Eight of them came from Mount Albert and four from Marist.
>
> The Auckland squad for the final (with scorers in brackets) consisted of Savinata Hafoki, Ben Collins (try), Willy Ale (try), Guenther Schaumkel, Meke Tofu (two tries), Simon Ieremia (six goals), Eddie Leavai, Pena Tuia (captain), Morris Ikeroma, Darren Himiona, Guy McPherson, George Taunga, Jack Noble, Fale Talaepa (try), Gordon Albert, Tony Tuia, T J Aoese, and eighteenth man Jacob Yandall.

Residents in spotlight

New Zealand Residents players have never been so much in the spotlight than when they played the Tri-Nations champion Kiwis at Wingham Park, Greymouth, on 4 November 2006. The match was scheduled to give the Kiwis match practice during their Tri-Nations defence. It was always going to be a major happening with West Coasters starved of big-game attractions, but it also caught the attention of the national news media in the wake of the Nathan Fien eligibility controversy.

The Australian-born Warriors utility had been included in the Kiwis squad on the basis he had a New Zealand-born grandmother. But it was subsequently revealed she was actually his great-grandmother, one generation too far removed for Fien to qualify on hereditary grounds. Fien, who was disqualified from the remainder of the Tri-Nations, was to be a 2008 World Cup winner with the Kiwis, having by then qualified on residential grounds.

Of course, the out-of-season Residents stood no chance against full-time professionals. They did better than expected in holding the Kiwis to a 34–4 result, particularly when conceding only ten first-half points. Residents from Auckland-based Bartercard Cup teams were backs Tui Samoa, David Fisi'iahi,

CHAPTER ELEVEN

Cooper Vuna, William Heta and Kelvin Wright, forwards Julian O'Neill, Sinave Faitala and Sala Fa'alogo, and interchange players Cliff Beverley, George Tuakura and Wayne McDade. Fa'alogo played against his brother and fellow second-rower David for the first time.

Steve Buckingham, the Auckland Lions Bartercard Cup captain, was not available for the Greymouth match. He had been named player of the tournament when the Residents won a quadrangular contest against New South Wales Country, the Jim Beam Cup representatives from Sydney, and the Queensland Rangers at Rotorua in June.

In that tournament, Fisi'iahi and fellow Auckland Lions centre Miguel Start opened the campaign with three tries each, and Buckingham kicked eight goals, in a 52–4 thrashing of the Queenslanders. In the other preliminary games, the Residents beat a Jim Beam Cup team which included expatriates Willie Bishop, Chan Ly and Eddie Leuluai, but lost to Country.

However, they comfortably accounted for Country 32–18 in the final, with tries to Vuna (two), Fa'alogo, Tuakura, Sonny Fai and Canterbury's Lusi Sione and four Buckingham goals. Other Aucklanders in the squad were Faitala, Heta, Samoa, Wright, Paletasala Ale, Dylan Davis, Fabian Souter and Henry Turua. Sam Panapa was assistant coach to fellow former Kiwi David Lomax.

The Stormont Shield.
Auckland Rugby League

Stormont Shield returns

The historic Stormont Shield was reintroduced in 2006 and contested by the Lion Red grading round section winners, with Mangere East beating Papakura. There was also a change in format for the Roope Rooster, the holder defending it against all comers when playing at home. Mount Albert repelled all challenges and by season's end also had the Rukutai Shield and Fox Memorial in its trophy cabinet.

While Marist, Otahuhu and Northcote fell by the wayside during the playoffs, the Lions headed Papakura 26–24 in the major semi-final and created grand final records for highest score and biggest winning margin when disposing of the Sea Eagles 49–6 two weeks later. Centre Guenther Schaumkel scored four of Mount Albert's eight tries.

After being an also-ran among the Sharman Cup second division in 2007, Mount Albert climbed back to the top again in 2008. But this time the grand final was still in the balance three minutes from fulltime as minor premier Otahuhu clung to a narrow lead. The Leopards' defence finally snapped, scrum-half Angus Cameron crossed for the winning try, and Steve Buckingham made no mistake with the conversion for a 24–22 victory.

Buckingham was in his familiar pivot position alongside numerous team-mates who had been stalwarts during the now defunct Bartercard Cup days. The Fisi'iahi twins were still there, as was former Kiwi Anthony Swann and Howie Matthews in the backs. Coach Brent Gemmell was blessed with a seasoned starting pack consisting of Matthew Sturm, Regan Wigg, Sione Pouha, Sala Fa'alogo, Schaumkel and Kelvin Wright. Hooker Wigg was the grand final man of the match.

Match officials for the Fox Memorial grand final in 2008, from left: Vern Nathan, Craig Pascoe (referee), Abel Talamaivao, Hayden Price and Greg McIntyre.
Robin Smith collection

Mount Albert celebrates in 2008, Kelvin Wright and David Fisi'iahi.
Robin Smith collection

CHAPTER ELEVEN

Auckland in the Sydney league

The Auckland Rugby League, in partnership with the Auckland Lions franchise, entered a team in the New South Wales Premier League competition in 2007. Established in 1908 as reserve grade, the Premier League still served Sydney-based NRL clubs in that capacity. The Warriors were also able to keep their surplus players match-fit via the Auckland Lions, renamed the Auckland Vulcans in the restyled 2008 NSW Cup. The Lions played home curtain-raisers to the Warriors, but the Vulcans used Mount Smart number two and suburban grounds after the NRL Toyota Cup under-twenty competition came into being.

Graeme Norton coached the Lions to a stunning first-up victory over reigning premier (and eventual 2007 winner) Parramatta 27–8 and there was also a highly commendable early win over a strong St George-Illawarra team. A costly six-match losing streak in mid-season was broken with a 10–8 victory over Manly. Two more games were lost before the Lions made an unlikely playoffs bid by winning five from six. However, a loss to Canberra in the penultimate game evaporated those hopes. The Lions finished tenth of thirteen teams with nine wins and thirteen losses, but they were only two wins outside the top eight.

In October 2007, the Auckland Rugby League agreed to keep the venture alive despite the financial burden of having to pay for the travel and accommodation of visiting Australian teams in addition to their own trans-Tasman costs. The

Ruben Wiki was a one-game Vulcan in 2008.

Photosport

Mount Albert (Lions) connection was severed and the Vulcans name adopted in the off-season. Preparations were delayed when original coaches Gary Kemble and Norton became unavailable. Former New Zealand A and Marist-Richmond coach Bernie Perenara was appointed a month out from the first game.

The Vulcans were in contention for the top-eight playoffs throughout a topsy-turvy season, eventually having to settle for tenth (of twelve) with eight wins and fourteen losses. One more win would have lifted them above Central Coast and Balmain Ryde and extended their season. They received unprecedented publicity when Ruben Wiki, whose form had been affected by a long-term rib cartilage injury, played against Western Suburbs. Wiki returned to the NRL the following week, but Warriors-contracted players such as Ryan Shortland, Wairangi Koopu, Herman Retzlaff and Michael Crockett were regulars.

Samoan international forward Wayne McDade, from Mount Albert, was the Vulcans player of the year after an exceptional season of clocking up the metres with forceful hit-ups and his uncompromising defence. Captain, playmaker and goalkicker Aaron Heremaia, from Manurewa, was runner-up, earning a train-on invitation from the Warriors, while ever-present half and hooker Pita Godinet, from Richmond, was named rookie of the year. After a review of the 2008 season, the Auckland Rugby League successfully applied for financial assistance from Australia to alleviate some of the burden.

The longest game

What was to be the third-last Bartercard Cup game, before that competition's demise, is also believed to have been the longest rugby league match played in New Zealand. The Auckland Lions and Harbour League took 107 minutes and 16 seconds to decide the outcome of the 2007 major semi-final at Waitemata Stadium. Eventually Paul Fisi'iahi got across for his second try, and the Lions won 44–40 to advance directly to the grand final.

It had been 40–40 after eighty minutes, the Lions having salvaged the draw in regular time thanks to a converted try in the final seconds. Until then the two sides had indulged in a free-flowing affair which produced a point a minute. But the scoring dried up in extra time. After five minutes each way it was still 40–40, and it stayed that way for another seventeen minutes and sixteen seconds of golden point time until Fisi'iahi scored.

National television viewers looked on in amazement as players dropped to the ground with cramps and near-exhaustion, and ball-carriers and tacklers summoned their last reserves of energy. The mistake rate understandably increased, making it difficult for either side to mount the attack that would have decided the issue. But there was no noticeable drop in intensity or pace as the support staff worked overtime to keep players on their feet.

CHAPTER ELEVEN

Harbour coach Ken McIntosh could see beyond the disappointment of defeat and recognise the significance of the marathon performance by two courageous teams. 'It was a great game of football, great for rugby league,' McIntosh told the *New Zealand Herald*. 'It was a credit to the players, all of them. It's heartbreaking for us but I can't be disappointed. It could have gone either way. Mount Albert are a class side, they know how to win these games because they've been there, done that.'

New Zealand Rugby League competitions manager Kevin Bailey admitted to being concerned about the players' welfare. 'I don't remember a game going that long,' he said. 'There was a lot of running in the game. It was full-bore for the first eighty minutes and they didn't let up. There was no provision for a replay so we had to get a result.'

Neither team deserved to lose. The only saving grace was the loser being guaranteed a second life. Harbour utilised that to beat Canterbury Bulls 28–24 at Waitemata Stadium a week later and earn a rematch with the Lions in the grand final. Maybe the combatants had seen too much of each other, for the Lions cruised home 28–4 after leading 8–0 at halftime.

McIntosh was not alone in referring to the Auckland Lions as Mount Albert. The *Herald's* report of the longest game also called the winning team Mount Albert. The Lions had won the minor premiership by two points from Harbour, losing only one of their eighteen games and drawing another, with seven points back to Canterbury and one more to Waitakere.

A Saturday double-header was held every weekend, with one game screened live on Māori Television and the other shown the next day, replacing Monday Night Football. Few Warriors featured in the Bartercard Cup because of the Auckland Lions entry into the New South Wales Premier League.

Papakura pipped

Wellington champion Wainuiomata unleashed too much passion and precision at its Wise Park home ground for Manurewa and Papakura in the 2007 national club competition. Fifteen years after brothers John and David Lomax steered their club to win the last national Lion Red Cup knockout title, they were involved in the coaching of a new generation who beat Manurewa 40–18 in their semi-final and Papakura 48–26 in the final. John Lomax was the regular Wainuiomata coach, and David acted as caretaker coach when his brother was not available for the Manurewa match. Wainuiomata scrum-half Quentin Kepa's five tries in the final matched the entire Papakura team effort. In its semi-final, Papakura beat Canterbury champion Kaiapoi 48–22.

Rivalry resumes

Auckland's traditional rivalry with southern provinces resumed when coach Sam Panapa took a squad on an old-style trip to Greymouth and Christchurch during Queen's Birthday weekend 2007. The Auckland and Canterbury teams were chosen from their domestic club competitions below the Bartercard Cup, while West Coast, no longer the force of previous decades, fielded an Invitation XIII which included some expats. Auckland won 26–20 in Greymouth but lost 28–24 in Christchurch.

The tour was mounted to mark 100 years since the formation of the original All Golds and Auckland almost returned home undefeated. After leading Canterbury 8–2, Auckland fell 12–8 behind by halftime. The deficit blew out to 22–8 before burly ball-running forward Tony Tuia sparked an Auckland revival, which led to tries to Alan Lio, Marvin France and Francis Leger. That put the visitors 24–22 ahead with time running out. But Canterbury had one trick left, and centre Kasi Leka crashed over for the match-winning try.

Team of the century

Nine Aucklanders were included in the New Zealand Rugby League's team of the century, announced late in 2007 to commemorate 100 years of international football since the original All Golds had travelled to Britain and Australia. To cap it off, 1980s second-row star Mark Graham was named as the individual player of the century, and 1950s prop Cliff Johnson as the captain of the century.

The team, chosen by an independent panel, was: fullback, Des White (Auckland); three-quarters, Tom Hadfield (Auckland), Tommy Baxter (Auckland), Roger Bailey (Auckland), Phillip Orchard (Bay of Plenty); halves, George Menzies (West Coast), Stacey Jones (Auckland); forwards, Cliff Johnson (Auckland), Jock Butterfield (West Coast), Ruben Wiki (Auckland), Mark Graham (Auckland), Ron Ackland (Auckland), Mel Cooke (Canterbury).

Of note, Baxter, Bailey, Menzies, Jones, Johnson, Wiki, Graham, Ackland and Cooke all captained New Zealand in test matches, while White, Menzies and Ackland coached the Kiwis and Graham coached the Auckland Warriors.

CHAPTER ELEVEN

An Immortal, Ruben Wiki.
Auckland Rugby League

Auckland Immortals

World test match appearance record-holder Ruben Wiki was inducted as an Immortal at the Auckland Rugby League's annual premier awards dinner in September 2008, joining nine other distinguished players and one referee in receiving that accolade. It coincided with his retirement as this country's most capped NRL player.

Unlike the New Zealand Rugby League Legends of League, which covers the entire history of the game, the Auckland Immortals receive their recognition in their own lifetimes and can even be elevated immediately after, or in one case during, their playing careers.

The foundation members, chosen in 1990, included true Auckland legends from the past in Ron Ackland, Roger Bailey, Tommy Baxter, Mark Graham and Des White, plus Kevin Tamati, who had only a brief association with the blue and whites. Significantly, when the New Zealand Rugby League Legends were introduced five years later, they were all among the original inductees.

So, too, was John Percival, the renowned Auckland and international referee. Percival became an Auckland Immortal in the mid-1990s, as did Dean Bell and Gary Freeman, who were stamped with immortality even as they were hanging up their boots in retirement.

Stacey Jones achieved so many extraordinary and unique feats that it was no surprise he should be made an Auckland Immortal while still in his prime in 2003 – two years before he proved to be an inspiring figure in New Zealand's Tri-Nations victory at Leeds, and six years before he made a surprise comeback to the Warriors' playing ranks.

Inaugural Auckland Immortals, Mark Graham, Des White, Roger Bailey, Tommy Baxter, Ron Ackland and Kevin Tamati.
Bernie Wood collection

Cup, championship double

Auckland won the new 2008 Bartercard Premiership inter-provincial championship and, as a welcome bonus, regained possession of the Rugby League Cup with a 38–18 victory over Canterbury in the final at Mount Smart number two ground. The match was not without its controversy, both before and after the kickoff.

Canterbury, unbeaten in the round-robin, was unhappy about having to travel for the final and even less enthusiastic at carrying the cup to foreign fields. New Zealand Rugby League general manager Peter Cordtz told *The Press* the final was held in Auckland because of Māori Television requirements, yet Māori Television had broadcast boxing from Christchurch the previous night.

The New Zealand Rugby League also ruled the cup, which the Canterbury B team had won from Hawke's Bay in 2007 and had been defended by the Cantabrians throughout the Bartercard preliminary rounds, must be at stake whenever the holder met another province, home or away. Neither finalist was impressed with the sandy nature of the playing surface, a problem Auckland had encountered in the past when staging club finals on the Mount Smart number two ground.

Before the competition started, the Auckland Rugby League successfully appealed against a New Zealand Rugby League decision that its representatives must have appeared in at least four of the last seven club rounds to be eligible. That would have ruled out most of those involved with the Auckland Vulcans in the New South Wales Cup.

Auckland was under pressure to qualify for the final. It beat Bay of Plenty 70–0 at home, when centre Sione Tongia contributed four tries and William Heta a try and seven goals, but was held to a 30–30 draw by Wellington at Porirua. Sunita Laiseni's try-scoring treble was vital to Auckland sharing the points. Auckland next beat Waikato 34–10 at Huntly, but lost 36–30 to Canterbury in Christchurch, conceding a last-minute converted try.

That left Auckland not only needing to beat Taranaki at New Plymouth in the last round, but also relying on Canterbury not to slip up at home against Waikato. Auckland did its bit, Nathaniel Neale scoring three tries in a 40–16 victory. But Auckland nerves were frayed when Waikato led Canterbury 16–8 at halftime. Any conspiracy theories were extinguished when Canterbury scored thirty-two unanswered points in the second half.

Inevitably, more southern grumblings about Auckland using Vulcans players were heard before the final. But there were no complaints from Canterbury about which was the better team on the day. From 8–6 at halftime and 18–12 after fifty-five minutes, Auckland dominated possession and points over the last quarter to win 38–18.

CHAPTER ELEVEN

Tongia, described in The Press as 'a mini Manu Vatuvei', charged over for three tries, while Jeremiah Pai earned the Ken Stirling Trophy man of the match award as Auckland's captain, stand-off half, and creator of several tries. Auckland's other scorers were Laiseni, Raymond Ioane, Pita Godinet, Wayne McDade and Monikura Tikinau, while Pai (two) and Heta kicked goals. Sam Panapa was the winning coach.

Warriors: Four from fourteen

Since 1995 the Warriors have cast an enormous shadow over Auckland sport, and not just rugby league. They have dominated media coverage of the code and caused extreme highs and lows in the emotions of their fans and fair-weather friends alike. Winning the minor premiership and reaching the grand final in 2002 was the obvious highlight, but it has been disappointing that they were involved in playoffs only four times (2001, 2002, 2003 and 2008) in their first fourteen seasons. In 1995 and 2007 they missed out after being penalised competition points.

As they looked towards 2009, the Warriors had the encouragement of a stunning end to their 2008 campaign, when they became the first team to qualify eighth and then upset the minor premier (Melbourne Storm at Olympic Park). The Warriors then beat Sydney Roosters at Mount Smart Stadium before being eliminated by eventual champion Manly-Warringah. Seven Warriors also shared in New Zealand's World Cup triumph, six of them playing in the 34–20 final victory over Australia at Brisbane in November.

The Warriors year began tragically when rising star Sonny Fai drowned while assisting his younger brother to safety in the surf at Bethell's Beach on the eve of the first 2009 training session. The twenty-year-old Fai, who alternated between loose forward and centre in his burgeoning career, played Bartercard Cup for Counties-Manukau, was one of the most prominent performers in the inaugural NRL Toyota Cup under-20 competition, and made fifteen first grade appearances in 2008.

Between 1995 and 2008 the Warriors played 341 games, winning 161, drawing five and losing 175. They scored 7,358 points and conceded 7,595. A total of 143 players pulled on the club jersey, just over half of them from Auckland.

In their formative years the Warriors brought home renowned New Zealand players such as Dean Bell, Stephen Kearney, Sean Hoppe, Kevin Iro, Richard Blackmore, Mark Horo, Quentin Pongia and Terry Hermansson. There have been many popular Australians, none more so than current captain Steve Price. Others include Brent Webb and Nathan Fien, who both qualified on residential grounds to play for the Kiwis, current coach Ivan Cleary, plus Kevin Campion, Micheal Luck and Wade McKinnon.

AUCKLAND RUGBY LEAGUE
1909–2009

Auckland juniors who went on to make more than a century of appearances were Stacey Jones (the holder of multiple records with 238 games, seventy-five tries, twelve field goals and 654 points), Logan Swann, Awen Guttenbeil, Jerry Seuseu, Clinton Toopi, Joe Vagana, Ali Lauitiiti, Francis Meli and Monty Betham. Evarn Tuimavave began the 2009 season on ninety-nine, Jerome Ropati on ninety-one and Manu Vatuvei on seventy-five, while Ruben Wiki made eighty-seven appearances in four seasons after returning 'home' from Canberra. Waikato provided Wairangi Koopu (159 games), Lance Hohaia (120) and Sam Rapira (sixty-three). Simon Mannering (seventy-six) has been a stellar recruit from Nelson, via Wellington.

Six All Blacks, Matthew Ridge (signed from Manly), Frano Botica (from Wigan), John Kirwan, Mark Ellis, Mark Carter and Mark Robinson, played for the Warriors with mostly moderate effect. Ridge (thirty-seven) registered most games, ahead of Ellis (thirty-six).

Promising youngsters such as brothers Henry and Robbie Paul and Lesley Vainikolo slipped through the Warriors' net before making first grade, while Shontayne Hape and Thomas Leuluai were among those who went overseas to establish themselves. Current rookie of the year Ben Matulino carried huge expectations into 2009.

The word 'roller-coaster' has surely been used about the Warriors more than any other New Zealand sports team. However, the club has built up a solid fan base, one which is often doubled or trebled at matches when the team is riding high. The Warriors might not be universally popular because they have pushed traditional domestic rugby league from centre stage, but there is no doubt they have raised the sport's profile in the national mindset.

Stacey Jones, multiple record holder.
Photosport

CHAPTER ELEVEN

The World Cup.
Auckland Rugby League

Auckland, home of the World Cup

On a brilliant Brisbane night, the Kiwis surprised most of their own supporters, delighted the thousands of British fans in attendance, and shocked the Australians by beating the Kangaroos 34–20 in the 2008 World Cup final. Down 10–0 after missing an early try-scoring opportunity, the Kiwis were behind 16–12 at halftime before dominating the second spell to score four more tries and concede only one.

The original World Cup trophy, first contested in 1954 and reinstated after being lost for some years, was carried home to Auckland in triumph. Previous Kiwis teams had reached finals in 1988 and 2000, but were comfortably beaten by the Kangaroos on both occasions. Australia had dominated the international scene for thirty years – losing only the 2005 Tri-Nations final to New Zealand at Leeds – and were expected to extend that record at home.

A first-up 30–6 beating of the Kiwis and an even bigger thrashing of England served to reinforce that opinion, and the Kangaroos were unbackable favourites for the Suncorp Stadium showdown. The Kiwis had fought their way back into the final by disposing of England in a round-robin game in Newcastle (36–24) and in their semi-final in Brisbane (32–22). Australia had an easier (52–0) path to the final against surprise qualifier Fiji.

Australians might not agree, but there is no more appropriate home for the World Cup than Auckland. A perusal of the Kiwis and Kangaroos squads revealed that there were eleven players born in Auckland (including Australian interchange player Karmichael Hunt), five born in Sydney (including Kiwis Nathan Cayless and Jason Nightingale) and four born in Brisbane.

The ten Auckland-born Kiwis, with their listed junior clubs, were Greg Eastwood (Manurewa Marlins), David Fa'alogo (Mount Albert Lions), Bronson Harrison (Leichhardt Wanderers, Sydney), Krisnan Inu (Cabramatta, Sydney), Thomas Leuluai (Otahuhu Leopards), Steve Matai (Ponsonby Ponies), Sam Perrett (Burleigh Bears, Gold Coast), Jerome Ropati (Marist Saints), Evarn Tuimavave (Richmond Rovers) and Manu Vatuvei (Otara Scorpions). Vatuvei's four tries at Newcastle were a New Zealand record against England or Great Britain.

Warriors to play in the final were fullback Lance Hohaia, wing Vatuvei, centres Ropati and Simon Mannering, Australian-born scrum-half Nathan Fien and interchange forward Sam Rapira. Tuimavave made his Kiwis debut against England at Newcastle. Leuluai, who played hooker in the final, and head coach Stephen Kearney were former Warriors players. The Warriors also provided Steve Price and Brent Tate to the Australian squad, but both missed the final because of injuries.

In good hands

The current Auckland Rugby League administration inherited a situation unknown to its predecessors – what to do with an historic but ageing and costly inner-city stadium that had been built in the 1920s and remained unchanged for several decades as other venues were developed in suburban Auckland.

That Carlaw Park's lifespan did not end in a pile of rubble, a fire sale and a frittering away of the proceeds on spur-of-the-moment projects is due to the Auckland Rugby League board, under the chairmanship of Cameron McGregor and administered from day to day by general manager Patrick Carthy.

Heavy tackles were replaced by heavy machinery in early 2008 when the first stage of development began on the old number two ground. In 2009 construction of a retirement village will begin on the former number one ground. This land is still owned by the Auckland Rugby League, which leased it out to developers for $1 million a year from November 2008. These assets are held in the Carlaw Heritage Trust and assure the Auckland Rugby League of long-term financial stability.

'From an Auckland Rugby League perspective, to be able to have this sort of income coming in is huge for us,' McGregor, chairman since 2001, told the *East and Bays Courier* in January 2009. 'A lot of us would have liked to have a stadium there but that was not possible when the Warriors committed to Mount Smart. It was a great asset sitting there, but with no money. Now, as far as the ARL is concerned, our future is secure.'

Rugby league and Carlaw Park have been major features of the McGregor family history. Like his father Ron before him, Cameron McGregor has the game's best interests close to his heart. His earlier memories include playing in the halftime midget matches at Carlaw Park.

But he also followed his father's career path as a chartered accountant and was aware the Auckland Rugby League needed a financial as well as a football future. For this, he deserves to be ranked alongside renowned former chairmen such as James Carlaw, after whom the park was named, and George Rainey, who purchased it on behalf of the league. Only Rainey's 1972 to 1985 chairmanship was longer than that of Cameron McGregor.

Patrick Carthy succeeded Brian Mills as general manager in 1994, when the game was undergoing dramatic changes because of the advent of the Auckland Warriors and Lion Red Cup. Of all the secretaries and treasurers who preceded him, only Ivan Culpan (secretary from 1918 to 1948) served a longer term.

Although only thirty-four years of age when taking over from Mills, Carthy already had an extensive grounding in rugby league administration with the Auckland schoolboys board and junior management committee and as business manager of Counties-Manukau Heroes. He was also a popular and extremely efficient business manager of the Kiwis from 2002.

CHAPTER ELEVEN

In March 2007 the demolition of Carlaw Park became a reality.
NZ Herald

AUCKLAND RUGBY LEAGUE
STATISTICS

Statistics

Auckland Rugby League office holders

President

1909–1910	C D Grey
1911–1913	J S Dickson
1914–1926	Hon A M Myers MP
1927	G Baildon
1928–1935	J Carlaw
1936–1941	J A Lee MP
1942–1944	G Grey Campbell
1945–1955	E J Osborne
1956–1960	J A Redwood
1961–1963	J W Watson
1964–1987	Sir D M Robinson
1988–1991	J E Knowling
1992–1997	A A Malam
1998–2008	G S Whittle

Chairman

1909–1910	D W McLean
1910–1913	B Brigham
1914	W Roope
1914–1917	R Benson
1918–1930	J Carlaw
1921–1926	W J Hammill
1927–1932	G E Rhodes
1933–1941	G Grey Campbell
1942–1947	J W Watson
1948–1956	D A Wilkie
1957–1963	K L G Gillam
1964–1971	H I Stonex
1972–1985	I G Rainey
1986–1989	A A Malam
1990–1993	P J McLeod
1993–1995	S K Shanks
1996–1997	G Ryan
1997–1998	S L Bennett
1998–2001	S M Pearson
2001–2008	C W McGregor

Secretary

1909–1910	E W Watts
1910	A J Powley
1911–1912	H B Oakley
1913	G Hunt
1914–1917	R A Spinley
1918–1948	I Culpan
1949–1961	R G McGregor
1962–1968	G W Batchelor
1969	R W Appleby
1969–1975	T Hammill
1975–1979	N W Jones
1980–1981	B J M Scott
1982	W J McNamara
1983–1988	D V Jenkinson

General Manager

1989–1994	B N Mills
1994–2008	P J Carthy

Treasurer

1909–1910	W T Wynyard
1910–1911	P S Ussher
1912	C Liversidge
1913	A Murdock
1914–1918	N Culpan
1919–1932	F Ellis
1933–1947	J E Knowling
1948–1955	A E Chapman
1956	K L G Gillam
1957–1960	G N Hall
1961–1968	M A Gore
1969–1973	O Mooney
1973–1976	R G Penney
1976–1978	R I Forsyth
1978–1994	T J McKeown
1995–1997	M T Tolich

Life members

The following list of eighty-six life members (in alphabetical order) was compiled from those named in the Auckland Rugby League's fiftieth anniversary publication in 1959 and from the honours board which for many years graced the Carlaw Park boardroom wall.

- C Adamson
- A Ansell
- E K Asher
- A Ball
- J Ball
- D Bankier (Mrs)
- G W Batchelor
- R J Best
- S Billman
- L Binns
- D G Blake
- B Brigham
- R T Brown
- L Bull
- T Carey
- Mr and Mrs J Carlaw
- O Chalmers
- A E Chapman
- E Chapman
- F H Chapman
- G Chapman
- W C Christian
- J Clark
- W F Clarke
- E C Cooper
- R J Cranch
- I Culpan
- B W Davis
- T Davis
- W R Dick
- R Doble
- L A Drake OBE (Dr)
- J Endean
- T Fielding
- E Fox
- C E Friend QSM (Mrs)
- M A Gore
- W J Grieve
- C Hall
- W A Hiley
- C Howe
- G Hunt
- D V Jenkinson
- J Johansson (Mrs)
- L Johnstone
- G Kelly
- J E Knowling
- K T Lawson
- P C Leitch QSM
- C Liversedge
- T A McClymont
- R A MacDonald
- E C McEwan
- R G McGregor OBE
- T J McKeown
- D W McLean
- D McLeod
- O McManus
- A A Malam
- W E Mincham
- C G Mitchell
- W L Nesbitt
- A J O'Shanassy
- G W Pearson
- E Phelan
- G G Plant
- A E Powell
- E D Price
- J W Probert
- I G Rainey
- M N Ritchie
- P W Rogers
- W R Seagar
- S K Shanks
- W Sorensen
- H I Stonex
- F Thompson
- H Tito
- P S Ussher
- A Walding
- E W Watts
- M C Wetherill
- G Whitley
- G S Whittle
- D A Wilkie

STATISTICS

Edith Wood Memorial Honours Board

The original fourteen names engraved on the Edith Wood Memorial honours board in 1939, to recognise those who had given twenty-five years service, had grown to 114 by February 2009. In the order that they appear on the board, they are:

D W McLean
J Carlaw
E K Asher
R Benson
A Ferguson
I Culpan
E J Phelan
C Raynes
A Campny
F Thompson
W Liversidge
W E Mincham
M J Hooper
J Clark
A W Asher
E Chapman
G Stevens
A Rae
G Hunt
B W Davies
L Bull
J Rukutai
T Fielding
B Longbottom
M Wetherill
J W McGregor
W A Swift
J O'Sullivan
P W Rogers
A E Humphries
C J Moore
F H Chapman
H J Mann
J G McCowatt
T R Davis
W F Clarke
G Whaley
S Billman
A E L Rout
A R Sanders

J J Davison
J P Kirwan
J Duffy
C G Howe
H L Gedye
T Tracey
F Ellery
A G Daniels
W Glover
J B Chalmers
G W Batchelor
G Kelly
A Kirkland
L A R Johnston
J T Hill
W F Lauder
J McInnarney
E R Boss
W R Dick
A J O'Shanassy
R T Otto
F Harris
H G Arthur
R I Plumber
A J Taylor
H R Thomas
G T McLeod
R K McLeod
K H Pittman
H E Hobman
A E Mitchell
A Lennie
M G Wetherill
W J Grieve
A Frost
W H Bisman
A F Walding
J D Neal
W L Nesbitt
D Alder

W A Anderson
I M Anderson (Mrs)
J Grieve
D Bankier (Mrs)
T Andrews
C O Harford
J Gallagher
M N Ritchie
E Neal
E G Tod
R Lipscombe
K Hughes
D Sargeant
L Cassie (Mrs)
J Brown
F R A Stonex (Mrs)
C G Mitchell
P G Rattray
J Shelley
J Shelley (Mrs)
T Ryan
N Bunt
J Courtnay
J Courtnay (Mrs)
J Field (Mrs)
T Casey
G Breckon
A A Malam
I G Rainey
J W Percival
W C Christian
A Olsen
A A Humby
C K Steele-Shanks MNZM (Mrs)

AUCKLAND RUGBY LEAGUE
1909–2009

Current clubs

The thirty-two Auckland Rugby League clubs in 2009 are:

Bay Roskill	Marist	Point Chevalier
City	Mount Albert	Ponsonby
East Coast Bays	Mount Wellington	Pukekohe
Ellerslie	New Lynn	Richmond
Glenfield	Northcote-Birkenhead	Rodney
Glenora	North Shore/Navy	Te Atatu
Hibiscus Coast	Otahuhu	Tuakau
Howick	Otara	Waiheke
Mangere East	Pakuranga	Waitemata
Manukau	Papakura	Waiuku
Manurewa	Papatoetoe	

Affiliates

Current Auckland Rugby League affiliates are:

- Auckland Maori Rugby League Inc
- Auckland Rugby League Referees Association Inc
- Auckland TAG Inc
- Clubs of Auckland Inc
- Masters of Rugby League Auckland Inc
- Papakura Rugby League Foundation Inc
- Rugby League Development Foundation Inc

Former clubs

Past clubs which competed in Auckland Rugby League competitions include:

Akarana	Greenlane	Panmure
Avondale	Grafton Athletic	Parnell
Blockhouse Bay	Kaipara	Remuera
City-Newton	Kingsland	Rugby League North Shore Normans Sports Association (2007)
City-Point Chevalier	Manukau-Greenlane	
Devonport	Maritime	
Eastern Suburbs	Mount Roskill	Sunnyside-Stanley Bay
Eden Ramblers	Newton	University
Eden Roskill	North Shore Albions	Wesley
Glen Eden	North Shore Rugby League & Sports Association (2005)	Zora
Glen Innes		

STATISTICS

Major inter-club trophies

The premier championship Fox Memorial Shield succeeded the original Myers Cup and Monteith Shield as the symbol of Auckland club supremacy in 1931. Since 1940 the Rukutai Shield has been awarded to the minor premier at the end of the regular season. Donated in 1915, the Roope Rooster was traditionally a pre-season knockout competition until changed to a challenge format in 2006. From 1925 to 1997 the Stormont Shield was at stake in a champion-of-champions playoff between the championship and knockout winners, but returned from recess in 2006 to be contested between the two top grading round qualifiers.

Year	Fox Memorial (and predecessors)	Rukutai Shield	Roope Rooster	Stormont Shield
1910	City			
1911	City			
1912	Newton			
1913	North Shore			
1914	North Shore			
1915	Grafton		North Shore	
1916	City		City	
1917	Ponsonby		Ponsonby	
1918	Ponsonby		City	
1919	Ponsonby		Newton	
1920	Maritime		Newton	
1921	City		City	
1922	City		Ponsonby	
1923	City		Ponsonby	
1924	Marist		City	
1925	City		Ponsonby	Ponsonby
1926	Ponsonby		Richmond	Ponsonby
1927	Newton		Richmond	Newton
1928	Devonport		Marist	Marist
1929	Ponsonby		Marist	Marist
1930	Ponsonby		Ponsonby	Devonport
1931	Marist		Devonport	Devonport
1932	Devonport		Marist	Marist
1933	Devonport		Richmond	Devonport
1934	Richmond		Richmond	Richmond
1935	Richmond		Newton	Richmond

1936	Manukau		Manukau	Richmond
1937	Richmond		Marist	Marist
1938	Marist		Richmond	Richmond
1939	Mount Albert		Marist	Mount Albert
1940	Richmond	North Shore	Richmond	North Shore
1941	North Shore	North Shore	Manukau	Manukau
1942	Manukau	City-Otahuhu	Richmond	Manukau
1943	Manukau	Manukau	Manukau	Manukau
1944	City	City	Ponsonby	City
1945	Otahuhu	Otahuhu	North Shore	North Shore
1946	Richmond	North Shore	Marist	Richmond
1947	Mount Albert	Marist & Richmond	Mount Albert	Mount Albert
1948	Marist	Marist & Richmond	Mount Albert	Mount Albert
1949	Richmond	Richmond	Richmond	Richmond
1950	Mount Albert	Mount Albert	Mount Albert	Marist
1951	Richmond & Mount Albert	Mount Albert & Richmond	Point Chevalier	Point Chevalier
1952	Ponsonby	Ponsonby	Ponsonby	Ponsonby
1953	Point Chevalier	Mount Albert	Ponsonby	*Not played*
1954	Ponsonby	Ponsonby & Mount Albert	North Shore	North Shore
1955	Richmond	Richmond & North Shore	Ellerslie	Ellerslie
1956	Richmond	Richmond & Point Chevalier	Ellerslie	Richmond
1957	Ellerslie	Ellerslie & City-Newton	Otahuhu	*Not played*
1958	Ponsonby	Ponsonby	Marist	Marist
1959	Western United	Western United	Ellerslie	Ellerslie
1960	Eastern United & Southern Districts	Eastern United	Glenora	Eastern United & Glenora
1961	Eastern United	Eastern United	Eastern United	Eastern United
1962	Eastern United & Glenora	Eastern United	Eastern United	Glenora
1963	Eastern United	Southern Districts	Eastern United	Eastern United
1964	Otahuhu	Otahuhu	Mount Albert	Mount Albert

STATISTICS

1965	Marist	Ponsonby	Otahuhu	Marist & Otahuhu
1966	Marist	Otahuhu	Marist	Marist
1967	Ponsonby	Ponsonby	Otahuhu	Ponsonby
1968	Mount Albert	Ponsonby	Ellerslie	Ellerslie
1969	Mount Albert	Otahuhu	Richmond	Mount Albert
1970	Otahuhu	Mount Albert	Otahuhu	Mount Albert
1971	Otahuhu	Otahuhu	Marist	Otahuhu
1972	Ponsonby	Ellerslie	Ponsonby	Ponsonby
1973	Ponsonby	Ponsonby	Mount Wellington	Ponsonby
1974	Ellerslie	Ellerslie	Otahuhu	Ellerslie
1975	Otahuhu	Otahuhu	Otahuhu	Otahuhu
1976	Mount Wellington	Mount Wellington	Richmond	Richmond
1977	Otahuhu	Otahuhu	Otahuhu	Otahuhu
1978	Otahuhu	Otahuhu	Glenora	Otahuhu
1979	Richmond	Otahuhu	Manukau	Richmond
1980	Richmond	Richmond	Manukau	Manukau & Richmond
1981	Mount Albert	Mount Albert	Otahuhu	Mount Albert
1982	Mount Albert	Glenora	Otahuhu	Otahuhu
1983	Otahuhu	Mount Albert	Manukau	Manukau
1984	Mount Albert	Otahuhu	Mount Albert	Otahuhu & Manukau
1985	Mount Albert	Manukau	Manukau	Mount Albert
1986	Mount Albert	Te Atatu	Manukau	Manukau
1987	Northcote	Mangere East	Otahuhu	Mount Albert
1988	Te Atatu	Glenora	Northcote	Otahuhu
1989	Northcote	Northcote	Mangere East	Northcote
1990	Otahuhu	Northcote	Richmond	Northcote
1991	Northcote	Northcote	Northcote	Northcote
1992	Northcote	Mount Albert	Northcote	Northcote
1993	Northcote	Northcote	Northcote	Mount Albert
1994	Northcote	Otahuhu	Otahuhu	Northcote
1995	Otahuhu	City-Point Chevalier	*Not played*	Otahuhu
1996	Otara	Otahuhu	Manurewa	Otahuhu
1997	Glenora	Mangere East	Marist	Otara
1998	Glenora	Glenora	Mangere East	*Not played*

1999	Glenora	Glenora	Glenora	Not played
2000	Otahuhu	Richmond	Not played	Not played
2001	Northcote	Richmond	Not played	Not played
2002	Hibiscus Coast	Papakura	Hibiscus Coast	Not played
2003	Mangere East	Mangere East	Hibiscus Coast	Not played
2004	Mount Albert	Mangere East	Ellerslie	Not played
2005	Manurewa	Papakura	Mount Albert	Not played
2006	Mount Albert	Mount Albert	Mount Albert	Mangere East
2007	Manurewa	Papakura	Papakura	Richmond
2008	Mount Albert	Otahuhu	Mount Albert	Richmond

Winners and co-winners

Winners (with shared successes in brackets) of the major trophies:

Fox Memorial (25 clubs have won or shared 99 championships): Mount Albert 13 (1), Ponsonby 12, Otahuhu 11, Richmond 10 (1), City 8, Northcote 7, Marist 6, Glenora 3 (1), Devonport 3, Manukau 3, North Shore 3, Eastern United 2 (2), Ellerslie 2, Manurewa 2, Newton 2, Grafton 1, Hibiscus Coast 1, Mangere East 1, Maritime 1, Mount Wellington 1, Otara 1, Point Chevalier 1, Te Atatu 1, Western United 1, Southern Districts 0 (1).

Rukutai Shield (22 clubs have won or shared 69 round-robin competitions): Otahuhu 13, Mount Albert 7 (2), Ponsonby 6 (1), Richmond 4 (5), Glenora 4, Mangere East 4, Northcote 4, North Shore 3 (1), Eastern United 3, Papakura 3, Ellerslie 2 (1), Manukau 2, City 1, City-Otahuhu (wartime amalgamation) 1, City-Point Chevalier 1, Mount Wellington 1, Southern Districts 1, Te Atatu 1, Western United 1, Marist 0 (2), City-Newton 0 (1), Point Chevalier 0 (1).

Roope Rooster (20 clubs have won 91 knockout finals): Otahuhu 11, Richmond 11, Marist 10, Ponsonby 9, Manukau 8, Mount Albert 8, Ellerslie 5, City 4, Northcote 4, Eastern United 3, Glenora 3, Newton 3, North Shore 3, Hibiscus Coast 2, Mangere East 2, Devonport 1, Manurewa 1, Mount Wellington 1, Papakura 1, Point Chevalier 1.

Stormont Shield (17 clubs have won or shared 74 matches): Richmond 11 (1), Mount Albert 10, Otahuhu 8 (2), Marist 7 (1), Ponsonby 6, Manukau 5 (2), Northcote 5, Ellerslie 4, Devonport 3, North Shore 3, Eastern United 2 (1), Glenora 1 (1), City 1, Mangere East 1, Newton 1, Otara 1, Point Chevalier 1.

STATISTICS

Fox Memorial grand finals

Fox Memorial grand finals were introduced in 1958 and have been held every year since then with the exception of 1964, when there were no playoffs. Titles were shared in 1960 and 1962 when there was a draw after eighty minutes and no extra time was played. Extra time was played in 1996, 2002 and 2007.

Grand final results

Year	Winner	Runner-up
1958	Ponsonby 18	Otahuhu 7
1959	Western United 15	Richmond 0
1960*	Eastern United 7	Southern Districts 7
1961	Eastern United 24	Glenora 7
1962*	Eastern United 17	Glenora 17
1963	Eastern United 8	Southern Districts 0
1964	No grand final (Otahuhu champion)	
1965	Marist 19	Glenora 6
1966	Marist 24	Ponsonby 7
1967	Ponsonby 12	Otahuhu 9
1968	Mount Albert 12	Ponsonby 7
1969	Mount Albert 20	Marist 0
1970	Otahuhu 10	Mount Albert 5
1971	Otahuhu 25	Mount Albert 12
1972	Ponsonby 14	Ellerslie 12
1973	Ponsonby 15	Otahuhu 5
1974	Ellerslie 16	Ponsonby 8
1975	Otahuhu 22	Northcote 8
1976	Mount Wellington 20	Glenora 5
1977	Otahuhu 11	Richmond 3
1978	Otahuhu 18	Mangere East 4
1979	Richmond 16	Otahuhu 15
1980	Richmond 21	Otahuhu 15
1981	Mount Albert 18	Glenora 7
1982	Mount Albert 18	Otahuhu 8
1983	Otahuhu 14	Mount Albert 11
1984	Mount Albert 25	Otahuhu 6
1985	Mount Albert 24	Manukau 19
1986	Mount Albert 31	Te Atatu 4
1987	Northcote 12	Mangere East 8
1988	Te Atatu 22	Glenora 16
1989	Northcote 30	Mangere East 14
1990	Otahuhu 28	Te Atatu 14
1991	Northcote 23	Otahuhu 20
1992	Northcote 11	Mount Albert 6

1993	Northcote 29	Te Atatu 10
1994	Northcote 32	Otahuhu 12
1995	Otahuhu 32	Marist 0
1996+	Otara 36	Otahuhu 28
1997	Glenora 34	Mangere East 14
1998	Glenora 35	Mangere East 6
1999	Glenora 24	Otahuhu 4
2000	Otahuhu 21	Richmond 14
2001	Northcote 30	Richmond 29
2002+	Hibiscus Coast 44	Otahuhu 40
2003	Mangere East 30	Hibiscus Coast 29
2004	Mount Albert 14	Mangere East 10
2005	Manurewa 34	Papakura 24
2006	Mount Albert 49	Papakura 6
2007+	Manurewa 28	Papakura 20
2008	Mount Albert 24	Otahuhu 22

* championship shared

+ extra time played

Lion Red Cup grand finals

1994	North Harbour 24	Counties-Manukau 16
1995	North Harbour 28	Warriors Colts 21
1996	Counties-Manukau 34	Waitakere City 22

Bartercard Cup grand finals

2000	Canterbury Bulls 38	Otahuhu Leopards 24
2001	Hibiscus Coast Raiders 28	Eastern Tornadoes 18
2002	Mount Albert Lions 24	Hibiscus Coast Raiders 20
2003	Canterbury Bulls 32	Marist-Richmond Brothers 28
2004	Mount Albert Lions 40	Marist-Richmond Brothers 20
2005	Mount Albert Lions 24	Canterbury Bulls 22
2006	Auckland Lions 25	Canterbury Bulls 18
2007	Auckland Lions 28	Harbour League 4

National club knockout finals

Rothmans £1,000 tournament

1962	Eastern United 25	Hornby (Canterbury) 2
1963	Southern Districts 15	Linwood (Canterbury) 2
1964	Otahuhu 10	Hornby (Canterbury) 5

STATISTICS

Wrangler Cup

| 1982 | Petone (Wellington) 16 | Randwick (Wellington) 14 |

Tusk Cup

1983	Otahuhu 30	Randwick (Wellington) 22
1984	Mount Albert 24	Randwick (Wellington) 10
1985	Manukau 34	Randwick (Wellington) 13

Lion Red League Nationals

1986	Te Atatu 36	Mount Albert 10
1987	Northcote 14	Mangere East 12
1988	Te Atatu 18	Glenora 8
1989	Northcote 10	Wainuiomata (Wellington) 4
1990	Wainuiomata (Wellington) 34	Otahuhu 12
1991	Northcote 30	Randwick (Wellington) 12
1992	Wainuiomata (Wellington) 25	Northcote 18

Auckland's best and fairest

In 1979 the Auckland Rugby League Referees Association introduced an inter-club best and fairest award which quickly became the most sought-after individual players' prize. Since 2007 it has been known as the Lion Red Fox Memorial Player of the Year, with coaches voting for their best player and the best opposing player in each game. Winners:

1979	Wayne Robertson (Te Atatu)
1980	Darryl Morrison (Otahuhu)
1981	Mark Tavai (Mount Albert)
1982	Paul Bridges (City-Newton)
1983	Owen Wright (Otahuhu)
1984	Dave Sefuiva (Richmond)
1985	Dean Lonergan (City-Newton)
1986	Terry O'Shea (Te Atatu)
1987	Neville Ramsay (Manukau)
1988	Arthur Clark (Otahuhu)
1989	Tawera Nikau (Otahuhu)
1990	Mark Riley (Otahuhu)
1991	Aaron Palelei (Otahuhu)
1992	Tony Botica (City-Point Chevalier)
1993	Roy Tusa (Mangere East)
1994	Sean Wilson (Northcote)
1995	Junior Pumipi (Otara)
1996	Jason Arama (Manurewa)
1997	Tukere Barlow (Mangere East)

1998	Fred Robarts (Te Atatu)
1999	Fred Robarts (Te Atatu)
2000	Daniel Vasau (Richmond)
2001	John Teina (Manukau)
2002	Willie Bishop (Hibiscus Coast)
2003	Corey Wetini (Ellerslie)
2004	Clayton Rogers (Papakura)
2005	Eliakim Fononga (Mangere East)
2006	Darren Himiona (Northcote)
2007	Eddie Leavai (Marist)
2008	Suaia Matagi (Te Atatu)

Inter-provincial competitions

Rugby League Cup

The most enduring inter-provincial trophy is the Rugby League Cup (formerly Northern Union Cup), presented in 1910 by the management of the first British touring team. For most of its lifespan it was contested on a challenge basis. Holders:

1910–21	Auckland
1922–24	South Auckland
1925–26	Auckland
1927	South Auckland
1928–29	Auckland
1930	South Auckland
1931	North Auckland
1932	South Auckland
1933	West Coast
1934–35	Canterbury
1936–46	West Coast
1947–49	Wellington
1950–59	Auckland
1960	West Coast/Auckland
1961	Auckland
1962–63	Canterbury
1964–67	Auckland
1968	West Coast/Canterbury
1969	West Coast
1970	Canterbury
1971	Wellington
1972–73	West Coast
1974	Canterbury
1975–76	Waikato

STATISTICS

1977–79	Taranaki
1980	Wellington/Canterbury
1981	Canterbury
1982–84	Wellington
1985	Taranaki/Canterbury
1986–89	Auckland
1990	Canterbury/Wellington
1991	Auckland/Canterbury
1992	Canterbury/Wellington/Canterbury
1993–94	Canterbury
1995–96	Auckland
1997	Canterbury/Waikato/Taranaki
1998–99	Taranaki
2000	Coastline
2001	Tasman
2002–04	Otago
2005	Gisborne
2006	Hawke's Bay
2007	Canterbury
2008	Auckland

Rothmans Tournament

The longest lasting inter-provincial championship was the Rothmans tournament, which changed from a club basis in 1965 and was overtaken by the inter-districts competition after 1979. The Rothmans was variously contested with a final or on a round-robin basis.

1965 final	Auckland 11	Wellington 4
1966 final	Auckland 37	Wellington 21
1967 final	Auckland 39	Wellington 13
1968 final	Auckland 28	Wellington 4
1969 final	Auckland 48	Canterbury 16
1970 final	Wellington 27	Waikato 21
1971 final	Auckland 26	Wellington 12
1972	Auckland won four-team round-robin	
1973 final	Auckland 29	Wellington 13
1974	Auckland won five-team round-robin	
1975	Canterbury won five-team round-robin	
1976 final	Auckland 29	Canterbury 22
1977 final	Auckland 36	Wellington 22
1978 final	Auckland 20	Canterbury 13
1979 final	Auckland 43	West Coast 19

Inter-districts championship

The inter-districts championship was contested by Auckland, Central, Northern and South Island on a round-robin basis with no final. Winners

1979	Central on count-back from South Island
1980	Central Districts
1981	South Island on triple count-back
1982	Central Districts
1983	Auckland
1984	Auckland
1985	Auckland on count-back from South Island
1986	Auckland
1987	Auckland

National first division

The national first division championship succeeded the inter-districts and preceded the Lion Red Cup. Canterbury and Wellington were the other teams in 1988 and Bay of Plenty joined them from 1989. Only in 1993 was a final played after the round-robin. Winners:

1988	Round-robin	Auckland
1989	Round-robin	Auckland
1990	Round-robin	Auckland
1991	Round-robin	Auckland
1992	Round-robin	Auckland
1993	Final	Canterbury 36 Auckland 12

Australian midweek competitions

New Zealand teams competed in Australian midweek competitions from 1974 to 1985. Some were played on a knockout basis, while others grouped three or four teams in preliminary rounds. In the early 1980s the inter-districts winner represented New Zealand.

Amco Cup

1974	Auckland lost to Western Division 13–7
1975	Auckland beat Manly 14–14 on count-back of penalties
1975	Auckland beat Newcastle 26–16
1975	Auckland lost to Eastern Suburbs 23–10
1976	Auckland beat Redcliffe (Brisbane) 30–5
1976	Auckland lost to Balmain 21–8
1977	Auckland lost to Northern Division 23–2
1978	Auckland beat Riverina 39–3

STATISTICS

1978	Auckland lost to Cronulla-Sutherland 22–6
1979	Auckland lost to Penrith 12–5
1979	Auckland lost to Canterbury-Bankstown 12–3
1979	Auckland lost to Cronulla-Sutherland 30–10
1980	Auckland lost to Western Suburbs 40–14
1980	Auckland lost to South Sydney 47–5
1981	Central Districts lost to Manly 51–11
1981	Central Districts lost to Penrith 31–5

KB Cup

1982	South Island lost to Canberra 47–15
1982	South Island lost to Brisbane 34–3
1983	Central Districts lost to Newtown 50–0

National Panasonic Cup

| 1984 | Auckland lost to Queensland Country 25–18 |
| 1985 | Auckland lost to Western Suburbs 32–10 |

International matches

Auckland v Great Britain

1910	England 52	Auckland 9
1914	England 34	Auckland 12
1920	Auckland 24	England 16
1924	England 24	Auckland City 11
1924	England 28	Auckland Province 13
1928	England 14	Auckland Province 9
1928	England 26	Auckland City 15
1932	England 19	Auckland 14
1936	England 22	Auckland 16
1946	England 9	Auckland 7
1946	England 22	Auckland 9
1950	Great Britain 26	Auckland 17
1954	Auckland 5	Great Britain 4
1958	Great Britain 24	Auckland 17
1962	Auckland 46	Great Britain 13
1966	Great Britain 12	Auckland 11
1970	Great Britain 23	Auckland 8
1974	Auckland 11	Great Britain 2
1977	Auckland 14	Great Britain 10
1979	Great Britain 18	Auckland 10

1984	Auckland 18	Great Britain 16
1988	Auckland 30	Great Britain 14
1990	Auckland 24	Great Britain 13
1992	Great Britain 14	Auckland 8

Played 24, Great Britain won 16, Auckland won 8.

Auckland v Australia

1919	Australia 32	Auckland 8
1935	Australia 16	Auckland City 8
1935	Australia 36	Auckland Province 18
1949	Australia 36	Auckland 18
1953	Australia 26	Auckland 4
1961	Auckland 13	Australia 8
1965	Australia 18	Auckland 2
1969	Auckland 15	Australia 14
1971	Auckland 15	Australia 14
1975	Australia 17	Auckland 6
1977	Auckland 19	Australia 15
1980	Australia 21	Auckland 7
1985	Australia 50	Auckland 10
1989	Auckland 26	Australia 24

Played 14, Australia won 9, Auckland won 5.

Auckland v France

1951	France 15	Auckland 10
1955	Auckland 17	France 15
1960	Auckland 14	France 5
1964	France 13	Auckland 10
1975	Auckland 9	France 3
1977	Auckland 17	France 0
1981	Auckland 20	France 10

Played 7, Auckland won 5, France won 2.

Auckland v New Zealand

1911	New Zealand 16	Auckland 14
1912	New Zealand 38	Auckland 16
1925	New Zealand 41	Auckland 17
1948	Auckland 30	New Zealand 9

In 1969 an Auckland Invitation team beat the Kiwis 18–10

Auckland v Wales

| 1975 | Auckland 31 | Wales 5 |

Auckland v South Africa

| 1963 | Auckland 10 | South Africa 4 |

Auckland v United States All Stars

| 1953 | Auckland 54 | United States 26 |

Auckland v New South Wales

1912	Auckland 10	New South Wales 3
1912	New South Wales 25	Auckland 2
1913	New South Wales 27	Auckland 2
1922	New South Wales 40	Auckland City 25
1922	New South Wales 21	Auckland Province 20

Auckland v Queensland

1925	Auckland City 25	Queensland 25
1925	Queensland 54	Auckland Province 14
1972	Queensland 18	Auckland 17

Kiwis from Auckland clubs

Players selected from Auckland clubs for the Kiwis or the 1907–08 All Golds (total 353).

Name	Usual position(s)	Kiwis debut*	Career tests
ACKLAND, Richard John	Second-row	1983	1
ACKLAND, Ronald Charles	Centre/second-row	1954	18
AH KUOI, Freddie	Stand-off	1975	28
ANDERSON, Harry Douglas	Centre	1947	3
ANDERSON, John	Loose forward	1938	0
ASHER, Arapeta Paurini (Opai)	Wing	1910	1
ASHER, Ernest Te Keepa	Centre	1910	1
AUSTIN, James David	Wing	1954	2
AVERY, Herbert	Loose forward	1919	13
BAILEY, Gary Roland	Centre	1961	0
BAILEY, Roger Wayne	Centre	1961	29
BAKALICH, Vernon Andrew Neville	Wing	1953	13

BANCROFT, Philip William	Scrum-half	1989	1
BANHAM, John Robert	Stand-off	1939	0
BARCHARD, Desmond Alfred	Scrum-half	1947	10
BARCHARD, Leonard	Second-row	1930	0
BARRY, Kevin Edward Anthony	Scrum-half	1975	0
BASS, Nelson Charles	Loose forward	1919	4
BAXTER, Thomas Owen	Centre	1949	29
BEEHRE, Leslie John	Hooker	1975	0
BELL, Dean Cameron	Centre	1983	26
BELL, Ian Cranham	Second-row	1978	4
BELL Keith, George	Centre	1957	0
BELSHAM, Selwyn Eric	Scrum-half	1955	10
BELSHAM, Victor Colin	Stand-off	1948	0
BENNETT, Eric Joseph	Second-row	1920	2
BICKERTON, Stephen Noel	Stand-off	1937	2
BLACKMORE, James Richard	Wing/centre	1991	25
BOLTON, Richard Keith	Loose forward	1972	1
BOURNEVILLE, Mark Trevor	Wing	1985	0
BRIMBLE, Edward Pierrepont	Stand-off	1932	1
BRIMBLE, Walter Pierrepont	Stand-off	1938	0
BRIMBLE, Wilfred Pierrepont	Scrum-half	1938	0
BRISBANE, Hector William	Centre	1924	11
BRODRICK, John Purewa	Second-row	1937	2
BROWN, Graham Stewart	Scrum-half	1967	0
BROWN, Louie Ernest	Wing	1925	9
BROWN, Peter Michael Gordon	Prop	1986	16
BURGOYNE, Graham John	Second-row	1951	0
BURGOYNE, William John Edward	Hooker	1970	4
CAMPBELL, Brian Malcolm	Stand-off	1959	2
CAMPBELL, Gordon	Hooker	1932	2
CAMPBELL, Norman	Fullback	1932	1
CAREY, Richard Lawrence	Stand-off	1967	0
CARLAW, Arthur Edward	Utility back	1909	2
CARSON, Eric Morris	Scrum-half	1968	3
CASTLE, Bruce Eric	Loose forward	1961	2
CHASE, Rangitawhana	Wing	1937	2
CHASE, Thomas	Centre	1939	0

STATISTICS

CHORLEY, Alfred	Fullback	1910	1
CHRISTIAN, Fletcher Roy	Centre	1965	32
CLARK, Brian Robert	Centre	1969	2
CLARK, Dean Gordon	Stand-off	1989	7
CLARK, James	Second-row	1913	0
CLARK, Roy James	Centre	1946	3
CLARK, Stanley	Second-row	1930	1
CLARKE, Alan	Loose forward	1932	1
CLARKE, Warwick Selwyn	Fullback	1946	11
CLOKE, William Ernest	Wing	1919	0
COLE, Hector Stanley Esmond	Stand-off	1926	2
COLLICOAT, Warren Rea	Fullback	1972	16
CONROY, Thomas Harley	Utility forward	1975	8
COOK, George Gray	Wing	1912	0
COOKE, Albert Edward	Utility back	1932	5
COOKE, Reginald Stewart	Centre	1961	7
COOPER, Shane David	Stand-off	1985	12
COWAN, Areariki Arthur (Riki)	Prop	1984	6
CRANCH, Raymond James	Prop	1951	0
CREQUER, Martin Paul	Wing	1986	3
CUNNINGHAM, Rex	Scrum-half	1946	4
CURRAN, William	Centre	1912	0
DANIELSON, Oscar Gustav	Prop	1967	5
DAVIDSON, Benjamin Alfred	Centre	1925	4
DAVIDSON, William George	Hooker	1947	17
DAVIDSON, William John	Fullback	1919	2
DELGROSSO, Frank August	Utility back	1921	9
DEMPSEY, Claude	Fullback	1936	1
DENTON, Neville Leon	Wing	1954	13
DERVAN, William Edward	Loose forward	1912	0
DIXON, Horace William Oscar	Second-row	1925	0
DOWSETT, David Shane	Scrum-half	1971	1
DUFFY, Ronald Harold George	Second-row	1961	0
DUFTY, Calvin Thomas Craddock	Fullback	1919	12
DUNNING, Charles	Prop	1907	2
DYER, Barrie Edward	Second-row	1975	0
EADE, Murray Keith	Loose forward	1971	16

EASTLAKE, Cyril Aston	Utility back	1951	28
EDWARDS, Robert James	Wing	1951	17
EDWARDS, Samuel Kingi	Prop	1962	18
ELIA, Mark Wycliffe	Centre	1985	10
ELLWOOD, John Douglas	Fullback/standoff	1963	6
EMERY, Hone Komanga (Maunga)	Prop	1961	23
ERIKSEN, Leonard Alfred	Scrum-half	1954	3
FAGAN, John Edward	Fullback	1961	17
FEPULEAI, Gasetoa (Toa)	Wing	1978	0
FILIPAINA, Olsen Orekewa	Stand-off	1977	29
FLETCHER, Eric	Scrum-half	1935	1
FORD, James Patrick	Wing	1961	0
FRANCIS, Arthur Reginald Howe	Loose forward	1911	0
FREEMAN, Gary Ross	Scrum-half	1986	46
FRIEND, Clayton Ivan	Scrum-half	1982	24
GAILEY, Douglas James	Prop	1969	19
GARDINER, George	Wing	1926	1
GAULT, Angus Tait	Prop	1937	2
GEORGE, Kenneth Frederick	Prop	1963	0
GILLESPIE, Mark John	Loose forward	1982	0
GILLETT, George Arthur	Utility back	1911	0
GORDON, Anthony Ralph	Wing	1975	3
GOULDING, James Wayne	Prop	1985	5
GRAHAM, Albert Henry (Abbie)	Stand-off	1947	3
GRAHAM, Mark Kerry	Second-row	1977	29
GRAHAM, Ngaroma Romeo (Lummy)	Fullback	1970	3
GRAHAM, Robert Bruce	Prop	1946	1
GREGORY, Charles Edward	Fullback	1925	3
GREY, Eric Charles	Wing	1920	2
GREY, Ian Neville	Loose forward	1954	3
GRIFFEN, James	Prop	1910	1
GROTTE, Robert	Scrum-half	1938	0
GURNICK, William Peter	Loose forward	1972	7
HADDON, Thomas	Second-row	1919	2
HADFIELD, Bernard Tom	Wing	1956	17
HAGGIE, Richard	Fullback	1955	4
HALL, Ernest Trevor	Second-row	1928	2

STATISTICS

HALL, Wilson	Scrum-half	1925	2
HALLORAN, Richard Francis	Scrum-half	1937	2
HAMMOND, Roger Donald	Second-row	1959	20
HANCOX, Claud Charles John	Second-row	1947	0
HARDGRAVE, Arthur	Fullback	1912	1
HARDGRAVE, Roy Arthur	Wing	1928	3
HARDWICK, Travers Harry	Loose forward	1946	14
HARRIS, Clifford Sidney	Centre	1952	0
HARRISON, Rata William	Prop	1961	2
HASSAN, Wilfred Thomsen	Stand-off	1932	1
HATTAWAY, Leonard Vincent (Bill)	Second-row	1959	0
HAYWARD, Harold Owen	Loose forward	1913	0
HEATLEY, Edward Duncan	Loose forward	1970	3
HELANDER, Keith Ervid	Prop	1919	1
HEMI, Jack Raharuhi	Fullback	1936	1
HERRING, Desmond Joseph	Prop	1938	0
HERRING, Ernest	Hooker	1919	7
HORO, Mark Gregory	Second-row	1987	16
HORO, Shane Heta	Wing	1987	3
HOUGH, William Bevin Keith	Wing	1950	9
HOUGHTON, Thomas Herbert	Scrum-half	1909	1
HURNDELL, Clarence Alfred	Second-row	1947	5
HUTT, Louis Stanley George	Utility forward	1928	8
IFWERSEN, Karl Donald	Centre	1913	7
ILES, George Frederick	Wing	1919	4
IRO, Kevin Leslie	Centre	1987	34
JACKSON, Alfred Edward	Scrum-half	1913	0
JACKSON, Frederick Stanley	Prop	1910	1
JARVIS, Robert John	Stand-off	1974	9
JOHNSON, Clifford Raymond	Prop	1950	34
JOHNSON, Joffre John	Prop	1947	4
JONES, Ross Darroch	Second-row	1939	0
JORDAN, Christopher Mark	Fullback	1977	5
JORDAN, Leonard Roy	Centre	1946	8
KAY, Arthur Greig	Centre	1935	6
KEAN, Sydney	Scrum-half	1911	0
KEMBLE, Gary Edward	Fullback	1980	19

KENEALY, Donald James	Wing	1912	0
KEY, Dennis Anthony	Wing	1969	1
KIRWAN, John Patrick	Centre	1925	3
KRILETICH, Anthony Peter	Loose forward	1967	22
LAING, Albert	Fullback	1932	1
LAING, Henry Bircher (Bert)	Stand-off	1919	1
LAIRD, Allan	Loose forward	1948	0
LAIRD, James	Prop	1932	4
LANG, John Henry	Stand-off	1919	1
LASHER, John Dufty	Hooker	1956	0
LAWLESS, Raymond Victor	Second-row	1932	3
LEATHERBARROW, Albert	Hooker	1939	0
LEE, Brian Stanley	Second-row	1961	9
LEOTA, Francis Poipoi	Prop	1989	3
LEULUAI, A'au James	Centre	1979	29
LIAVAA, Siosiua Tu'one (Josh)	Second-row	1975	0
LIST, Victor Claude Wilchefski	Centre	1928	4
LITTLEWOOD, Inglis Ivan Irvine	Wing	1925	0
LONERGAN, Dean Robert	Second-row	1986	11
LOVERIDGE, Norman William	Fullback	1920	1
LOWRIE, Samuel Arthur	Hooker	1919	6
LOWTHER, Bernard Ross	Centre	1970	8
McCLENNAN, Michael James	Fullback	1971	1
McCLYMONT, Thomas Allen	Utility back	1919	4
McCRACKEN, Kenneth Robert	Wing	1961	7
McDONALD, Hector	Loose forward	1924	1
MacDONALD, Ronald Amelioran	Scrum-half	1909	4
McGAHAN, Hugh Joseph	Loose forward	1982	32
McGREGOR, Alwin John (Dougie)	Wing	1919	1
McGREGOR, Ronald George	Wing	1947	5
McGREGOR, Stephen	Stand-off	1978	0
McGUINN, Robert Christopher	Wing	1970	3
McINNARNEY, Arthur James	Wing	1939	1
McKAY, Ronald John	Centre	1954	17
McLEOD, John	Second-row	1937	1
McNEIGHT, William John	Second-row	1938	2
McNEIL, Clarence Alexander	Wing	1938	0

STATISTICS

MACKRELL, William Henry Clifton	Prop	1907	2
MACRAE, Duncan Ross	Second-row	1956	3
MANN, Donald Keio	Prop	1971	4
MANN, Duane Darrin	Hooker	1989	29
MANN, George William	Prop	1989	9
MATAIRA, Hawea Kareha	Prop	1939	0
MATETE, Paul Kehoma	Wing	1975	1
MATTHEWS, Arthur Crook	Centre	1919	0
MATTSON, Graham Victor	Loose forward	1964	2
MAXWELL, Henry Dudley	Prop	1955	20
MEADOWS, Joseph	Second-row	1921	0
MIDGLEY, Gordon Taylor	Wing	1938	0
MILLIKEN, Harold Maurice	Second-row	1939	0
MILLS, Laurence Douglas	Wing	1939	0
MILLS, Lester Bernard	Centre	1967	1
MINCHAM, Edward Thomas	Wing	1935	3
MINCHAM, Robert Andrew Arnold	Wing	1966	4
MITCHELL, Alfred Charles	Wing	1935	1
MITCHELL, George Gordon	Second-row	1939	0
MITCHELL, Robert	Second-row	1912	1
MONCUR, Gordon Edward	Wing	1956	0
MOORE, Edward	Second-row	1964	7
MOORE, Roy Lance	Fullback	1952	6
MORGAN, Leonard Seddon	Hooker	1967	0
MORSE, Francis Sydney	Stand-off	1911	0
MURRAY, Mauriohooho Allen John (Joe)	Second-row	1956	0
NEAL, George	Scrum-half	1919	1
NEPIA, George	Fullback	1937	1
NIKAU, Tawera Nui Eia	Loose forward	1989	19
NURSE, Roydon Frederick	Wing	1946	1
O'BRIEN, Andrew James	Prop	1924	5
O'BRIEN, James Lawrence	Second-row	1925	0
O'HARA, Dane Bradford Mark	Wing	1977	36
OKESENE, Haitrosene	Second-row	1994	5
OLLIFF, Lawrence John	Loose forward	1960	1
ORCHARD, Robert Ian	Prop	1967	18
O'REGAN, Ronald Philip	Centre	1983	8

ORR, Dean	Wing	1983	1
O'SULLIVAN, John Charles	Centre	1971	10
PAKI, George Hori	Second-row	1921	0
PANAPA, Samuel Lameka	Wing	1987	8
PARKES, James	Wing	1926	1
PATERSON, Hugh Murray	Wing	1959	0
PATTERSON, James Gordon	Hooker	1961	3
PATTON, Michael Patrick	Stand-off	1990	6
PAUL, Henry Rangi	Utility	1993	24
PECKHAM, William Frederick	Scrum-half	1928	2
PERCY, Rex William	Loose forward	1955	9
PHILLIPS, Gary Raymond	Fullback	1959	8
PICKRANG, Francis John	Second-row	1936	2
POLSON, Clarence Percival	Scrum-half	1920	4
POTTER, Kevin Bruce	Centre	1975	0
POWELL, Royden Henry Samuel	Scrum-half	1935	4
PRENTICE, Stanley Miller	Stand-off	1928	5
PROCTOR, Lyndsay John	Prop	1974	13
PROHM, Gary John	Utility	1978	24
PYE, Leslie Robert	Prop	1947	2
RATIMA, Joseph Hohepa	Prop	1952	4
REDMOND, David John Stanley Walker	Wing	1948	4
REDMOND, Wayne Stanley Walker	Wing	1970	1
REID, Tom	Prop	1961	2
REIDY, Brian Thomas	Wing	1959	19
RICH, Morris Kenneth	Fullback	1948	0
RICHARDS-JOLLY, Douglas	Second-row	1951	2
RIDDELL, Charles James	Second-row	1955	9
RIECHELMANN, Alan Arthur	Centre	1952	0
RILEY, Brian	Centre	1935	2
RIRINUI, Pita Riwaru	Second-row	1939	0
ROBERTSON, Bruce Edward	Centre	1951	5
ROBERTSON, Maurice Hunter Winsor	Centre	1946	18
ROBERTSON, Wayne Robert	Second-row	1974	3
ROFF, Roy Douglas	Hooker	1952	1
ROPATI, Iva Lewis	Centre	1993	4
ROPATI, Joseph	Wing	1983	9

STATISTICS

ROPATI, Tea Fa'atea	Centre	1986	7
ROWE, Harold Francis	Fullback	1907	8
RUKUTAI, Puhipi James	Loose forward	1911	0
RUSSELL-GREEN, John Henry Edward	Scrum-half	1949	2
SATHERLEY, Clifford Allan Martin	Second-row	1935	3
SATHERLEY, Leslie Charles John Manson	Hooker	1937	1
SAVORY, Charles	Prop	1911	1
SCHULTZ, Paul Joseph	Stand-off	1965	9
SCHULTZ, William Thomas	Hooker	1959	4
SCHUSTER, Frederick Gordon	Stand-off	1970	1
SCOTT, Leonard	Wing	1928	5
SCOTT, Verdun John	Centre	1939	0
SEAGAR, Allan Wilfred	Stand-off	1930	0
SEAGAR, George Bradley	Fullback/loose forward	1910	1
SHELFORD, Kelly	Stand-off	1989	9
SINEL, Harold Raymond	Loose forward	1963	10
SINGE, Arthur Percy	Second-row	1925	1
SMITH, Charles Ernest (Jack)	Fullback	1938	0
SMITH, George William	Wing	1907	4
SMITH, John David	Utility back	1975	12
SMITH, Richard Walton	Wing	1932	1
SNOWDEN, William Leonard	Scrum-half	1959	18
SOLOMON, David	Stand-off	1939	0
SOMERS, Walter Thomas	Hooker	1919	6
SORENSEN, Dane Hans Ivan Peter	Prop	1975	18
SORENSEN, David	Stand-off	1971	1
SORENSEN, Kurt John	Second-row	1975	27
SORENSEN, William	Centre	1951	22
SPARNON, John Edward	Centre	1963	0
STANAWAY, Alexander William	Prop	1911	0
STEWART, Ivan	Stand-off	1919	1
STEWART, Lyle Michael	Centre	1924	1
ST GEORGE, Neville Leonard	Hooker	1925	1
STIRLING, Ivor Gerald	Scrum-half	1939	0
STIRLING, Kenneth Lorrie	Scrum-half	1971	22

STORMONT, William Devanney	Prop	1920	3
TAEWA, Whetu	Wing	1994	6
TAIT, Roger Bruce	Fullback	1965	11
TANCRED, Henry Eugene	Second-row	1919	0
TATANA, Henry Nardy	Prop	1967	10
TATUPU, Kuripitone (Tony)	Second-row	1994	3
TAYLOR, Glenn Royston	Hooker	1978	1
TE WHATA, William	Second-row	1924	1
TETLEY, Harold Gill	Loose forward	1935	4
TINITELIA, Frank	Prop	1983	1
TITTLETON, Walter Harry	Stand-off/centre	1936	4
TODD, Lancelot Beaumont	Stand-off	1907	4
TRACEY, Brian John	Scrum-half	1972	3
TREVARTHAN, Thomas	Stand-off	1936	2
TREVARTHEN, William MacVay	Prop	1907	9
TUIMAVAVE, Paddy	Centre	1990	2
TURNER, George Puhoi	Centre	1957	13
TYLER, William Thomas	Utility	1907	6
VARLEY, Shane	Scrum-half	1978	11
WADDELL, Archibald Thomas	Second-row	1919	0
WALSH, William George	Scrum-half	1919	1
WALTERS, Stanley Charles	Second-row	1913	8
WĀTENE, Puti Tipene (Steve)	Utility	1930	5
WATSON, David Thomas	Centre	1989	15
WEBB, Charles Albert Edward	Scrum-half	1912	0
WEBB, Stanley George	Scrum-half	1925	0
WESTON, Stanley James	Wing	1912	1
WETHERILL, Maurice Charles	Centre	1924	4
WHITE, Desmond Henry	Fullback	1950	21
WIGGS, Ernest David	Second-row/wing	1964	5
WILES, Allan Victor	Centre	1948	1
WILLIAMS, Darrell Christopher	Wing/fullback/centre	1985	21
WILLIAMS, Dennis Arthur	Stand-off	1971	31
WILLIAMS, Raymond Francis	Loose forward	1970	1
WILLIAMS, William	Prop	1919	4
WILSON, Johnnie	Fullback	1972	2

STATISTICS

WILSON, Raymond William John	Centre	1969	1
WINTER, Warren	Wing	1978	1
WOOLLARD, Gary John	Stand-off	1967	10
WOOLLEY, Charles Alexander	Centre	1920	3
WRIGHT, Adrian Henry (Nick)	Fullback	1978	3
WRIGHT, Murray Thomas	Hooker	1975	0
WRIGHT, Owen Grant	Second-row	1982	16
WRIGHT, Wayne John	Prop	1975	0
WYNYARD, John Richard	Scrum-half/stand-off	1907	8
WYNYARD, William Thomas	Utility back	1907	3
YATES, John Edward	Prop	1954	6

* Note: debut year for Kiwis from Auckland club or All Golds.

Kiwis from Warriors

Players selected for the Kiwis from the Auckland-based Warriors (total 48).

Name	Usual position(s)	Kiwis debut*	Career tests
ANDERSON, Louis Manu	Hooker/loose forward	2004	17
ANDERSON, Vincent Manase Mohenoa	Centre	2003	6
BETHAM, Montgomery Junior	Hooker	2001	9
BLACKMORE, James Richard	Wing/centre	1995	25
EDWARDS, Samuel Logan	Loose forward	1995	5
ELLIS, Marc Christopher Gwynne	Wing	1996	5
ERU, Sydney Wiremu	Hooker	1995	18
FA'AFILI III, Henry Aau	Wing	2001	10
FAUMUINA, Sione Vili	Utility	2003	2
FIEN, Nathan Leigh	Hooker	2006	8
GUTTENBEIL, Awen John	Second-row	2002	10
HERMANSSON, Terry Brian	Prop	1999	4
HOHAIA, Lance Kovo	Stand-off	2002	16
HOPPE, Sean Edward	Wing	1995	35
HORO, Mark Gregory	Second-row	1996	16
IRO, Kevin Leslie	Centre	1998	34

JONES, Stacey William Potu	Scrum-half	1995	46
KEARNEY, Stephen Peter	Second-row	1995	45
KOOPU, Dane Wairangi Manuera	Second-row	2004	3
LATU, Tevita Pakai Leo	Hooker	2004	1
LAUAKI, Epalahame Vea Loloko	Second-row	2006	2
LAUITIITI, Alaimatagi	Second-row	1998	19
LEULUAI, Thomas James	Scrum-half	2003	18
MAFI-VATUVEI, Manu (Manu Vatuvei)	Wing	2005	16
MANNERING, Simon Alexander	Loose forward/centre	2006	18
MELI, Francis	Wing	2001	14
NGAMU, Gene Robert	Stand-off	1995	23
OKESENE, Haitrosene	Second-row	1995	5
PALEAAESINA, Iafeta Iakopo	Prop	2005	3
PONGIA, Quentin Lee	Second-row/prop	1998	35
RAPIRA, Sam Tana	Prop	2007	11
RIDGE, Matthew John	Fullback	1997	25
ROPATI, Jerome Piper Leitu	Centre/stand-off	2005	10
ROPATI, Tea Fa'atea	Centre	1997	7
SEUSEU, Jeremy	Prop	2001	11
SWANN, Anthony Gilbert	Centre	1996	1
SWANN, Logan Douglas	Second-row	1996	29
TAEWA, Whetu	Wing	1995	6
TATUPU, Kuripitone (Tony)	Second-row	1995	3
TONY, Iosefo Motu	Utility	2001	13
TOOPI, Clinton James Te-Whata	Centre	2001	22
TUIMAVAVE, Anthono Emil (Tony)	Second-row	1995	1
TUIMAVAVE, Evarn	Prop	2008	1
VAGANA, Joseph Sonny	Prop	1996	25
VAGANA, Nigel Faletoese	Centre	1998	38
WEBB, Brent Douglas	Fullback	2004	17
WIKI, Ruben James	Centre/loose forward//prop	2005	55
YOUNG, Grant Edward	Prop	1997	6

* Note: this is the player's debut year for the Kiwis while at the Warriors. Seven players (Blackmore, Horo, Iro, Okesene, Tea Ropati, Taewa and Tatupu) had previously made their debuts from Auckland-based clubs, and they appear on this list and the list of Kiwis from Auckland clubs. All out-of-town or overseas players signed by the Warriors are aligned with Auckland clubs.

STATISTICS

International records

Auckland players have established world records and dominated the Kiwis test match records.

World records

Most test appearances
Ruben Wiki played in fifty-five test matches from 1994 to 2006.

Most tries in a test match
Hugh McGahan scored six tries against Papua New Guinea at Auckland in 1983.

Most goals in a test match
Des White kicked eleven goals against Australia at Brisbane in 1952, a record broken since test and World Cup status was awarded to developing nations.

New Zealand test records

Most test appearances
Ruben Wiki, as above.

Most consecutive test appearances
Gary Freeman with thirty-seven from 1986 to 1993.

Most test matches as captain
Gary Freeman, nineteen times from 1990 to 1995.

Youngest back
Dennis Williams (eighteen years, one day) against Great Britain at Salford in 1971.

Youngest forward
Sonny Bill Williams (eighteen years, 264 days) against Australia at Newcastle in 2004.

Oldest player
Alf Chorley (thirty-six years, ten months) against England at Auckland in 1910.

Longest career
Kurt Sorensen, whose career spanned fifteen seasons from 1975 to 1989

Most career points
Matthew Ridge scored 168 points (six tries, seventy-one goals, two field goals) from 1990 to 1998.

Most points in a series
Des White scored thirty-six points (eighteen goals) against Australia in Australia in 1952.

Most career tries
Nigel Vagana scored nineteen tries between 1998 and 2006.

Most tries in a match
Hugh McGahan, as above.

Most career goals
Matthew Ridge with seventy-three, including two field goals, from 1990 to 1998.

Note: The above players were registered with Auckland clubs or played for the Auckland-based Warriors. The records for most points in a test match (thirty-two) and most goals in a test match (twelve) were set by Tasesa Lavea against Cook Islands at Reading during the 2000 World Cup. Lavea was born in Auckland but played only rugby union in his home city, before and after his brief rugby league career in Australia.

New Zealand all-match records

Most career points
Des White scored 467 points (seven tries, 223 goals) from 1950 to 1956.

Most points on one tour
Des White scored 202 points in Britain and France in 1951–52.

Most goals on one tour
Des White kicked ninety-five goals in Britain and France in 1951–52.

Most points in a non-test match
Cyril Eastlake scored twenty-five points (three tries, eight goals) against Ipswich at Ipswich in 1959.

Most tries in a non-test match
Rex Percy scored six tries against Central Queensland at Rockhampton in 1956.

Most goals in all matches
Des White kicked 223 goals from 1950 to 1956.

Most goals in a non-test match
Phil Bancroft kicked eleven goals against Selection de l'Aude at Carcassonne in 1989, and Des White against Northern Division at Tamworth in 1952.

The best of the rest
Kiwis records not held by Aucklanders, and the best Auckland performances, are:

Most appearances in all matches
Jock Butterfield (Canterbury and West Coast) played ninety-nine games from 1954 to 1963. Next best is Tommy Baxter, with ninety-four from 1949 to 1956.

Most appearances on one tour
Hubert Turtill (Canterbury) played thirty-three (of thirty-five) games on the 1907–08 tour of Britain. Next best are Bill Sorensen (thirty-three of thirty-seven) in Britain and France in 1955–56 and Des White (thirty-three of forty) in Britain and France in 1951–52.

STATISTICS

Most tries in all matches

Phillip Orchard (Bay of Plenty and Wellington) scored forty tries from 1969 to 1975. Next best is Roger Bailey, with thirty-seven from 1961 to 1970.

Most tries on one tour

Phillip Orchard (Bay of Plenty) scored twenty-seven tries in Britain and France in 1971. Next best is Vern Bakalich (twenty-six) in Britain and France in 1955–56.

Kiwis captains

Auckland resident and Auckland-aligned players to have captained the Kiwis or the All Golds in test matches or on tours are:

1907–08	George Smith
1910–11	Charles Dunning
1912	Arthur Francis
1913	Harold Hayward
1919	Karl Ifwersen
1920	Stan Walters
1921	Henry Tancred
1924	'Scotty' McClymont
1924	Frank Delgrosso
1925	Bert Laing
1926–27	Bert Avery
1928	Maurice Wetherill
1930	Charles Gregory
1932	Hec Brisbane
1935	Bert Cooke
1935	Lou Brown
1936–37	Steve Wātene
1937	Harold Tetley
1938	Bill McNeight
1946	Roy Clark
1950–52	Maurie Robertson
1952	Travers Hardwick
1954	Cyril Eastlake
1955–56	Tommy Baxter
1957–60	Cliff Johnson
1961	Ron Ackland
1961	Don Hammond
1965	Bill Snowden
1967	Bruce Castle
1967	Roger Bailey
1970–72	Roy Christian

1974–75	Ken Stirling
1975	Dennis Williams
1978	Ken Stirling
1979	Fred Ah Kuoi
1980	Dane O'Hara
1980–83	Mark Graham
1984	Fred Ah Kuoi
1985	Mark Graham
1985	Olsen Filipaina
1985	Hugh McGahan
1986	Mark Graham
1986	Ron O'Regan
1986–87	Hugh McGahan
1987–88	Dean Bell
1989–90	Hugh McGahan
1990–93	Gary Freeman
1994	Duane Mann
1995	Gary Freeman
1995–98	Matthew Ridge
1999	Jarrod McCracken
1999–00	Richard Barnett
2002	Stacey Jones
2003–05	Ruben Wiki
2006	Nigel Vagana
2006	Stacey Jones
2006	Ruben Wiki
2007–08	Roy Asotasi

Kiwis coaches

Aucklanders to have coached the Kiwis in test matches or on tours are:

1912	George Gillett
1921	Jim Rukutai
1928	'Scotty' McClymont
1938	'Scotty' McClymont
1946–52	'Scotty' McClymont
1955	'Snow' Telford
1955–56	Harold Tetley
1956–58	'Snow' Telford
1959–60	Travers Hardwick
1961	Des White
1961–63	'Snow' Telford
1964–65	Maurie Robertson

STATISTICS

1965	'Snow' Telford
1968	Des Barchard
1972	Des Barchard
1977–78	Ron Ackland
1979–82	Ces Mountford
1983–86	Graham Lowe
1990–91	Bob Bailey
2001–02	Gary Freeman
2005–07	Brian McClennan
2007	Gary Kemble

Auckland clubs with most Kiwis

Ponsonby, Richmond, Otahuhu and Marist have provided most players directly into the Kiwis. Now that players use professional clubs as stepping stones to international football the following tables (which include the year of their Kiwis debut from that particular club) are likely to remain unchanged.

Ponsonby (44)	Year
CARLAW, Arthur Edward	1909
MacDONALD, Ronald Amelioran	1909
CHORLEY, Alfred	1910
DUNNING, Charles	1910
GILLETT, George Arthur	1911
SAVORY, Charles	1911
HARDGRAVE, Arthur	1912
WEBB, Charles Albert Edward	1912
CLARK, James	1913
LOWRIE, Samuel Arthur	1919
McCLYMONT, Thomas Allen	1919
WALSH, William George	1919
DELGROSSO, Frank August	1921
MEADOWS, Joseph	1921
LITTLEWOOD, Inglis Ivan Irvine	1925
COLE, Hector Stanley Esmond	1926
GARDINER, George	1926
HUTT, Louis Stanley George	1928
PECKHAM, William Frederick	1928
KAY, Arthur Greig	1935

RILEY, Brian	1935
HALLORAN, Richard Francis	1937
HARDWICK, Travers Harry	1946
JORDAN, Leonard Roy	1946
NURSE, Roydon Frederick	1946
WHITE, Desmond Henry	1950
RICHARDS-JOLLEY, Douglas	1951
SORENSEN, William	1951
RATIMA, Joseph Hohepa	1952
ERIKSEN, Leonard Alfred	1954
PERCY, Rex William	1955
BELL, Keith George	1957
SNOWDEN, William Leonard	1959
BAILEY, Roger Wayne	1961
FAGAN, John Edward	1961
LEE, Brian Stanley	1961
MATTSON, Graham Victor	1965
CAREY, Richard Lawrence	1967
MANN, Donald Keio	1971
O'SULLIVAN, John Charles	1971
TRACEY, Brian John	1972
ROBERTSON, Wayne Robert	1974
CONROY, Thomas Harley	1975
ROPATI, Joseph	1986

Richmond (41)	Year
PARKES, James	1926
PRENTICE, Stanley Miller	1928
COOKE, Albert Edward	1932
LAWLESS, Raymond Victor	1932
FLETCHER, Eric	1935
MINCHAM, Edward Thomas	1935
MITCHELL, Alfred Charles	1935
POWELL, Royden Henry Samuel	1935
SATHERLEY, Clifford Allan Martin	1935
TETLEY, Harold Gill	1935

STATISTICS

TITTLETON, Walter Harry	1936
BICKERTON, Stephen Noel	1937
McLEOD, John	1937
SATHERLEY, Leslie Charles John Manson	1937
MILLS, Laurence Douglas	1939
MITCHELL, George Gordon	1939
SOLOMON, David	1939
ROBERTSON, Maurice Hunter Winsor	1946
GRAHAM, Albert Henry (Abbie)	1947
HURNDELL, Clarence Alfred	1947
McGREGOR, Ronald George	1947
LAIRD, Allan	1948
REDMOND, David John Stanley Walker	1948
BAXTER, Thomas Owen	1949
HOUGH, William Bevin Keith	1950
JOHNSON, Clifford Raymond	1950
BURGOYNE, Graham John	1951
ROBERTSON, Bruce Edward	1951
BAKALICH, Vernon Andrew Neville	1953
BELSHAM, Selwyn Eric	1955
RIDDELL, Charles James	1955
LASHER, John Dufty	1956
MURRAY, Mauriohooho Allen John (Joe)	1956
BAILEY, Gary Roland	1961
SPARNON, John Edward	1963
LOWTHER, Bernard Ross	1970
WILLIAMS, Raymond Francis	1970
AH KUOI, Freddie	1975
FEPULEAI, Gasetoa (Toa)	1978
VARLEY, Shane	1978
GOULDING, James Wayne	1985

Otahuhu (34)	Year
HANCOX, Claud Charles John	1947
JOHNSON, Joffre John	1947
YATES, John Edward	1954

HAGGIE, Richard	1955
HATTAWAY, Leonard Vincent (Bill)	1959
FORD, John Patrick	1961
GEORGE, Kenneth Frederick	1963
MOORE, Edward	1964
WIGGS, Ernest David	1964
CHRISTIAN, Fletcher Roy	1965
SINEL, Harold Raymond	1969
HEATLEY, Edward Duncan	1970
McGUINN, Robert Christopher	1970
DOWSETT, David Shane	1971
SORENSEN, David	1971
GURNICK, William Peter	1972
JARVIS, Robert John	1974
MATETE, Paul Kehoma	1975
WRIGHT, Murray Thomas	1975
WRIGHT, Wayne John	1975
GRAHAM, Mark Kerry	1977
PROHM, Gary John	1978
TAYLOR, Glenn Royston	1978
WRIGHT, Adrian Henry (Nick)	1978
McGAHAN, Hugh Joseph	1982
WRIGHT, Owen Grant	1982
ROPATI, Joseph	1983
TINITELIA, Frank	1983
ROPATI, Tea Fa'atea	1986
CLARK, Dean Gordon	1989
LEOTA, Francis Poipoi	1989
NIKAU, Tawera Nui Eia	1989
BLACKMORE, James Richard	1991
SHELFORD, Kelly	1991

Marist (32)	Year
STORMONT, William Devanney	1920
BRISBANE, Hector William	1924
O'BRIEN, Andrew James	1924

STATISTICS

GREGORY, Charles Edward	1925
KIRWAN, John Patrick	1925
SINGE, Arthur Percy	1925
CAMPBELL, Gordon	1932
CAMPBELL, Norman	1932
CLARKE, Alan	1932
HASSAN, Wilfred Thomsen	1932
LAIRD, James	1932
LIST, Victor Claude Wilchefski	1932
ANDERSON, John	1938
GROTTE, Robert	1938
MIDGLEY, Gordon Taylor	1938
BARCHARD, Desmond Alfred	1947
DAVIDSON, William George	1947
EDWARDS, Robert James	1951
HARRIS, Clifford Sydney	1952
RIECHELMANN, Alan Arthur	1952
ANDERSON, Harry Douglas	1954
DENTON, Neville Leon	1954
McKAY, Ronald John	1954
PATERSON, Hugh Murray	1959
REIDY, Brian Thomas	1959
SCHULTZ, William Thomas	1959
DUFFY, Ronald Harold George	1961
EDWARDS, Samuel Kingi	1962
SCHULTZ, Paul Joseph	1965
DANIELSON, Oscar Gustav	1967
KRILETICH, Anthony Peter	1967
SCHUSTER, Frederick Gordon	1970

Representation records

Club with most players in one test team: six by Richmond in both the first test (Bert Cooke captain, Ted Mincham, Ray Powell, Stan Prentice, Cliff Satherley, Harold Tetley) and third test (Eric Fletcher, Ray Lawless, Alf Mitchell, Prentice, Satherley, Tetley) of the 1935 series against Australia; and by Marist in the third test against England in 1932 (Hec Brisbane captain, Alan Clarke, Gordon Campbell, Norm Campbell, Jim Laird, Claude List).

Club with most players in a test series: nine by Richmond in the 1935 series against Australia (as above).

Related Kiwis from Auckland

Three family members in one test team (1): Ian Bell and his nephews Dean Bell and Clayton Friend.

Three brothers to represent New Zealand (2): Ted, Walter and Wilfred Brimble; Joe, Tea and Iva Ropati.

Two brothers to represent New Zealand (20): Louis and Vinnie Anderson; Albert and Ernie Asher; Gary and Roger Bailey; Sel and Vic Belsham; Rangi and Tom Chase; Bill and Ben Davidson; Mark and Shane Horo; Kevin and Tony Iro; Bert and Albert Laing; Alf and George Mitchell; Henry and Robbie Paul; Bruce and Maurie Robertson; Cliff and Jack Satherley; Bill and Paul Schultz; Dick and Jack Smith; Bill and Dave Sorensen; Dane and Kurt Sorensen; Paddy and Tony Tuimavave; Nick and Owen Wright; Dick and Billy Wynyard.

In addition, Rata Harrison, Harold Hayward, Robert Orchard and Walter Tittleton were Kiwis from Auckland clubs who had brothers represent New Zealand from other provinces, respectively Bill Harrison (Wellington), Morgan Hayward (Thames), Phil Orchard (Bay of Plenty and Wellington) and George Tittleton (Waikato).

The Anderson, Asher, Horo, Iro, Paul, Robertson, Schultz, Sorensen (Dane and Kurt), Wright and Wynyard brothers played test matches together, as did the Harrisons and Orchards.

Fathers and sons to represent New Zealand (9): Eric and Ian Grey; Arthur and Roy Hardgrave; Len and Chris Jordan; James and Thomas Leuluai; Don and Duane Mann; Ken and Jarrod McCracken; Ted and Bob Mincham; Dave and Wayne Redmond; Ivor and Ken Stirling.

Brothers to referee and play at same World Cup (1): Vic Belsham was the referee and Sel Belsham the Kiwis scrum-half when New Zealand met Australia in Brisbane during the 1957 World Cup.

STATISTICS

Auckland's test referees

Twenty Auckland referees controlled a total of ninety-two test or World Cup matches between 1910 and 2008. They were, in order of most appointments:

John Percival, 28 (1964–80)
Dennis Hale, 13 (1990–95)
Vic Belsham, 8 (1957–60)
Maurice Wetherill, 5 (1935–37)
Neville Kesha, 5 (1986–88)
Phil Houston, 5 (1995–97)
Dave Pakieto, 5 (1999–2000)
Leon Williamson, 4 (2007–08)
Kevin Steel, 3 (1980–81)
Arch Ferguson, 2 (1914–19)
W Murray, 2 (1919–24)
P W Rogers, 2 (1935–36)
George Kelly, 2 (1955)
Ray Shrimpton, 2 (1984)
Bill Shrimpton, 2 (2000)
Jack Stanaway, 1 (1910)
A Ball, 1 (1920)
L Bull, 1 (1928)
Ted Seagar, 1 (1954)
Andy Cook, 1 (1999)

The most test matches controlled by a referee from outside Auckland is eight by Roly Avery (Waikato) between 1949 and 1962.

Note: Jack Donovan, who played and refereed in Auckland, had transferred to Huntly before being chosen to referee the 1946 test between New Zealand and England.

Bibliography

E Bennetts, 1933, *New Zealand Rugby Football League Annual 1933*, NZ Newspapers, Auckland.

J Coffey, 1987, *Canterbury XIII*, Canterbury Rugby League, Christchurch.

J Coffey, 1991, *Modern Rugby League Greats*, Moa Publications, Auckland.

J Coffey & B Wood, 2007, *The Kiwis: 100 Years of International Rugby League*, Hodder Moa, Auckland.

J Coffey & B Wood, 2008, *100 Years – Māori Rugby League 1908–2008*, Huia, Wellington.

W Davidson, 1948–49, *New Zealand Rugby League Annuals*, self-published, Auckland.

R Davis, 1985, *Great Britain Rugby League Tours*, BRL Lions Association, England.

E Gibson, 1948, *Kiwis 1947–1948*, Wright & Jacques, Auckland.

J Haynes, 1996, *From All Blacks to All Golds: New Zealand Rugby League's Pioneers*, Ryan & Haynes, Christchurch.

T Hyland, 1969, *Marist Memories 1919–1969*, Marist Brothers Old Boys Rugby League Club, Auckland.

L Knight, 2002, *The Shield: A Century of the Ranfurly Shield*, Celebrity Books, Auckland.

T McLean, et al, 1983, *100 Years of Auckland Rugby*, Auckland Rugby Football Union, Auckland.

D Middleton, various years, *Australian Rugby League Yearbook*, HarperSports, Sydney.

B Montgomerie, 2004, *Those Who Played*, Montgomerie Publishing, Sydney.

G Moorhouse, 1995, *People's Game*, Hodder & Stoughton, London.

G Morris and J Huxley, 1983, *Wembley Magic*, Evans Brothers Ltd, London.

P Neazor, 1999, *Ponsonby Rugby Club: Passion and Pride*, Celebrity Books, Auckland.

A Whiticker and G Hudson, 2002, *Encyclopaedia of Rugby League Players*, Gary Allen, Smithfield.

BIBLIOGRAPHY

B Wood (ed.), 1977–2002, *New Zealand Rugby League Annuals*, Wellington.

Other references included Gordon Nuttall's New Zealand rugby league statistics, *Rothmans Rugby League Yearbooks* (Great Britain), *Green and Gold Heroes* (Australia), newspaper files from the *New Zealand Herald* (Auckland), *Auckland Star*, *Auckland Star Sports*, *Waikato Times* (Hamilton), *Havera and Normandy Star*, *Taranaki Herald* (New Plymouth), *The Dominion* (Wellington), *Evening Post* (Wellington), *The Christchurch Star*, *The Press* (Christchurch), *Weekly Press and Referee* (Christchurch), *Evening Star* (Greymouth), *Otago Daily Times* (Dunedin), *Otago Witness* (Dunedin), *The Observer* (Auckland), *New Zealand Free Lance* (Wellington), various Auckland suburban newspapers, the weekly *Auckland Rugby League Gazette* and *League News* match programmes, the *Papers Past* website, Auckland Rugby League annual reports, and anniversary publications produced by many clubs, including Marist, Northcote, North Shore, Otahuhu, Ponsonby, Point Chevalier and Richmond, and by the Auckland Rugby League.

Index

Numbers in italics refer to pages with photographs and information in captions.

A

Abbott, Edwin 99
Ackland, Geoff 260
Ackland, Jim 166, *166*
Ackland, John 258, 259–60, 262, 311, 328, 333
Ackland, Ron 160, *160*, 162, 167, 173, 176, 181–4, 186–9, *189*, 192, 194, 213, 355–6, *356*
    as New Zealand coach 239–40, 245
Adams, Gareth 312
affiliates of ARL 367
Afoa, Fa'ausu 294, 301, 303, 306–8
Afoa, Vae 294
Ah Kuoi, Afi 262
Ah Kuoi, Andrew 278, 297, 306, 308
Ah Kuoi, Fred 225–6, 230–4, 236, 238, 240–1, *243*, 244, 248, 251, 256
Ah Kuoi, Paul 330
Ah Loo, John 160, 172
Ah Van, Patrick 344
Albert, Gordon 349
Aldridge, Tom 302
Ale, Paletasala 350
Ale, Willy 349
Alexander, Greg 308–9, 314
All Golds xii, 3–7, *5*
Allen, Teddy 139
Amco Cup 225–7, 239, 377–8
American All Stars *see* United States All Stars
Amos, Jim 80, 99, 136, 156
Anderson, Brian 214, 222
Anderson, Daniel 326, 338
Anderson, Doug 137, 140, *140–1*, 146, 153, 162
Anderson, Graham 191–2
Anderson, John 118, *118*
Anderson, Louis 338
Anderson, Vinnie 338
Andersson, Ken 223, 230–1, 248
Andrews, Colin 225, 229–32
Andrews, Ron *178*
Annadale, Mike 328, *329*, 330
Aoese, T J 349
Armitage (1910 Newton) 33
Arndt, W 63
Ashby, Greg 320
Asher, Albert (Opai) (Arapeta Wharepapa) xii, 5, 7, 12–16, 25–6, 31, 33–7, *34*, 51
Asher, Ernie (Te Keepa Pouwhiuwhiu) 7, 16, 26, 33–4, *34*, 37–8, *38*, *41*, 47, 51, 207
    as administrator 26, 89, 120, 136
Asiata, Junior 335
Asiata, Keneti 311, *311*, 320
Aspin, Aaron 333
Ata, Shaun 332
Athletic club 173
Atkins, Paul 343
Auckland Lions 352–4
Auckland Māori 203, 305
Auckland North (1999 provincial team) 322
Auckland Rugby League *xiv*, 326, 335–7, 361
    formation 18–19
    first club games 24–5
    first representative games 28–31, *29–30*
    executive disqualified (1913) 44–6
    board established (1931) 67, 97
    dispute with NZRL over Kiwis (1977) 242, 245, 250–1
    life members 365
    office holders 364–5
    ownership of Warriors 318, 320–1
    Sydney venture 352–3
Auckland Rugby Union xii, 15
'Auckland Rules' (rugby union) xii, 54
Auckland South (1999 provincial team) 322–3, *322*
Auckland Tonga team 305
Auckland Vulcans 305–6, *305*, 311, 352–3, 357
Auckland Warriors *see* Warriors
Austin, Jim 160, 162
Australasian teams, Aucklanders in 21, 39, 73
Australia, games against xii
    1919: 57–8, *58*
    1935: 109–12, *110–11*
    1949: 145–7
    1953: 157–8, *158*
    1961: 183–4, *183*
    1965: 197–9
    1969: 205–6, *205–6*
    1971: 214–16, *214–15*
    1975: 233–4
    1977: 239–40, 245
    1980: 250–1, *250*
    1985: 264–5, *265*
    1989: 280–2, *281*
    list of results 379

INDEX

Australian midweek competitions 225–7, 377–8
Australian Rules 69
Australian University teams 74, 77
Avaiki, Luisa 313
Avery, Bert 56–8, 60–1, 70, 76, 79, 80, 82, 87–8, 88, 120
Avery, Roly 191–2, 252
Avery, T 33, 34, 37, 38

B

Baildon, G 76
Bailey, Bill 147, 153
Bailey, Bob 185, 254, 260, 262, 264, 266, 266, 269, 272–3, 273
Bailey, David (1) 185
Bailey, David (2) 307, 315
Bailey, E 33, 56
Bailey, Gary 184–5, 185, 199, 201
Bailey, Gavin 337, 341
Bailey, Kevin 185, 260, 354
Bailey, Roger 184–8, 185–6, 193–4, 194, 199, 201–2, 203, 204, 208, 212–13, 213, 220, 223–4, 223, 238, 394
    honours 355–6, 356
Bakalich, Vern 157–9, 163–5, 165, 167, 169, 170, 394
Baker (1910 North Shore) 33
Baker, Golly 313
Baker, Hoppe 191–2
Ballantyne (1921 Maritime) 63
Balmain 109, 136, 227, 235, 297–8
Bancroft, Phil 277–8, 280, 283, 290, 297–8, 393
Banham, Bob 119
Barber, James 9, 13
Barber, Mal 170
Barchard, Des 137, 141–2, 151, 156, 158–9, 166
    as selector and coach 168, 201
Barchard, Len 99
Barchard, Ray 314
Barchard, Vic 147
Barclay (1908 player) 12
Barnett, Wayne 330, 337
Barry, Kevin 202, 219, 225
Barry, Steve 310–11
Bartercard Cup 286, 326–8, 327, 331, 331, 333, 334, 340, 341–2, 341, 344, 345–6, 353–4
    grand final results 373
Bartercard Premiership 357–8
Baskerville, Albert xii, 3–6, 20
Bass, Nelson 58, 61, 76, 78, 79, 80, 89
Batchelor, George 92, 93, 168
Baxter, Rowan 342–4, 346

Baxter, Tommy 109, 142, 145–6, 151, 153–6, 158–9, 162–5, 167, 168, 177, 178, 355–6, 356, 393
Bay of Plenty 280, 289, 320
Bay Roskill 326
Beattie (1927–28 player) 80, 90
Beazley, Darryl 305, 320
Beehre, Les 219, 255
Beetson, Arthur 238
Bell, Cameron 263, 276–7, 280, 283, 314–15
Bell, Dean xi, 253, 256, 260, 262, 269, 299, 299, 356
    as Warriors captain 304, 308–9, 358
Bell, Frank 121
Bell, Ian 236, 251, 255, 265
Bell, Keith 166, 166, 170, 171, 172
Belsham, Sel 164–5, 167
Belsham, Vic 140–1, 168, 169–70, 172–3, 182, 252
Bennett, J 37, 38, 49, 49
Bennett, Sel 224
Bennett, Wayne 220
Benson, R 120
Benson, Tony 331
Best, Bob 192
best and fairest award 320, 374–5
Betham, Monty 318, 359
Bettis, A 33
Bettis, H 33
Betts, Denis 308
Beverley, Cliff 320, 330–1, 350
Bickerton, Noel 108
Billington, Rex 167, 171
Bint, Graham 170, 172
Birch, Dean 271, 278, 278–9
Birch, Graeme 271
Bishop, Willie 335, 335, 350
Blackball 125, 127, 154
Blackmore, Richard 347, 358
Blake, Phil 308–9
Blakey, Alan 41, 89
Blucher (1910 City) 33
Bolton, Richard xiv, 315
Bonner, J 18, 33
Bonner, W 37, 38
Botica, Frano 256, 308, 359
Botica, Tony 308
Bourneville, Eugene 305
Bourneville, Mark 253, 265–6, 276, 278
Boyd, Les 252
Boyle, Malcolm 320–1
Bradburn (1909–10 player) 30, 33
Brady, H 128
Brady, Phil 92, 93, 98
Bramley (1938 Richmond) 107
Bramley, Trevor 133, 135, 135

Breed, Bill 114–15
Brett, C 33
Brewster, Steve *xiv, 219*
Brien, J *44,* 63
Brigham, Barry 19, 23, 24, *45,* 46, 74
Bright, R 115
Brimble, Edward 112–13, *112*
Brimble, Walter 112–13
Brimble, Wilfred 112–13, *112,* 119
Brimble brothers 112, 293
Brisbane, Hec 79–80, *79,* 85, 92, 93, 94, 98, 99, 101, *102,* 103–5, 120
Brisbane Broncos 309
Brisbane City 224
Britain, 1987 Auckland tour of 272–6, *273–5*
Brockliss, C 37, 38
Brockliss, Morrie 143
Brodrick, J 116–17
Brooker, Evelyn *xiv*
Brooking, Bill 147
Broughton, Joe 116–17
Brown, Dave 100–1, 110, *110*
Brown, Lou 77–8, *77,* 82, 87, 109–15, *113,* 120
Brown, Peter 266–7, *268,* 269, 272, 273, 274–8, 280, 288–9
Buckingham, Steve 311, 319–20, 323, 333, 337, 341–4, *341, 346,* 350
Buick, S 19
Buller 89–90
Bundock, Dwayne 333
Bunn, Wayne 234–5
Burge, Frank 57, 58, 77
Burgoyne, Bill 203, *205,* 206, 214, 216, *217*
Burgoyne, Graham 143, 146, 153, 156
Butler (1943 Manukau) 127
Butterfield, Jock *182,* 183, 355, 393
Byrne, Con 5, 9

C

Cadman, A *44*
Cadman, I *43, 44*
Cameron, Angus 350
Campbell, Brian 166, *166,* 173, 176, *186,* 194, 199
Campbell, G Grey 70, 97, 115–16
Campbell, Gordon (Stump) 92, 93, 103–5, *105*
Campbell, Jim 213, *213*
Campbell, Logan *294,* 301
Campbell, Norm 92, 93, *102,* 103–5
Campbell (unspecified) 75, 98
Campion, Kevin 358
Campny, A 120
Canberra Raiders 300, 303
Canterbury xii, 21–2, 43–4, 189–90, 234–5
    games against
        1910s–20s: 39, 70, *71,* 75, 86, *86,* 89
        1930s–40s: 96, 109, 119, 134–5, *135,* 139–41, *148*
        1950s: 152–3, 157, 160, 162–3, 166, *171*
        1960s: *182, 182,* 186, *186,* 190, *190,* 193, 203–4, *203–4*
        1970s–80s: 213, 218, *218,* 235–6, 264, 266, 279–80
        1990s: 289, *290,* 296–7, 304, 308, 312, 316–17, 320, 322
        2000s: 349, 355, 357
Canterbury Bulls 327, 340, 344
Canterbury-Bankstown 227, 278, 279
Carey, Rick 199, 238
Carey, Sean 294
Cargen, B 56
Cargill, G 71
Carlaw, Arthur 19, 38, 66–8
    as player 15, 25, 29–30, 33, 37, 38, 66
Carlaw, James 19, 62, *62,* 66–9, *67,* 76, 120, 361
Carlaw, William Owen (Owie) 66–8, *110*
Carlaw Park xiii, *xiv,* 26, 62–6, *63,* 69, 72, 79, 181, 214, 291, 304
    ground conditions 63, 132, 151, 157, 183, *183,* 195, 207, 212, *212,* 228–9, 230, 242
    floodlights installed 212, 230
    ownership 221
    test hosting ends 287, 323
    closure and redevelopment 333, *333,* 335–7, 361, 362
Ode to Carlaw Park 65
Carmont, George 328, 337
Carroll, Alphonsus 87
Carson, Arthur 187–8, 192, *192*
Carson, Eric 194, *194,* 196, 206, 208, 213
Carter, Herb 98, *106*
Carter, Mark 359
Carthy, Patrick *xiv,* 318, 326, *326,* 361
Casey (1923 City) 72
Castle, Bruce *182,* 183–5, 188, 201, *201*
Cawdron, Kurt 343
Central Districts (Auckland) 175
Central Districts (of New Zealand) 246, 253
Challenge Cup (New Zealand, 1997) 317
Chanfreau, Marcel 310
Chapman, Arthur 152
Chase, Rangi 116–17, 119
Chase, Tom 116–17
Chatfield, S *44*
Chatham, Eric *130,* 139
Cherrie, Les 168, 170, *171*
Childs, Harry 33, *34,* 37, 38, *41, 51*
Cholly, J 33
Chorley, Alf 13, 25, 29, 37, *40,* 392
Christenson, R 34

INDEX

Christian, Roy 191–2, *191*, 194, 199, 201, 206, 208, 213, 216–17, 222, *222*
Church, Stephen 312
City Rovers 7, 19, 25–6, 33–5, *34*, 43, *51*, 53, 62–3, 72, 83, 85, 125, 154, 173
   1924 transfer wrangle 77–8
City-Newton club 174–5
City-Point Chevalier 312
Clapp, Don 158, *158*
Clark, A *91*
Clark, Brian 208
Clark, C 56
Clark, Dean 280, 288, 291, 297, 300, 303, 314, 323, 328
Clark, Dominic 296, 308, 312, 316, 317, 320, 323, 330
Clark, Graham *178*
Clark, J 120
Clark, Jim *44*, 47, 49, *49*, 57–8, 88, *152*
Clark, John 328
Clark, Roy 129, *130*, 133–5, *135*, 137
Clark, Stan 99, 103
Clarke, Alan 81, 89, 92, 93, 98, *100*, 101, 103–5, *105*
Clarke, Jeff 271, *271*
Clarke, R 63
Clarke, Warwick / W S 129, *129*, 132–5, *135*, 137, 139, 141, 145–6
Clarkin, Neil 142, 147, 152–3, *152*
Cleary, Ivan 358
Cleary, Mick 199
Cloke, Bill 61
club competitions (Auckland) *see* Fox Memorial Shield; Roope Rooster; Stormont Shield
   inter-club trophy winners 368–71
club competitions (national) 354, 373–4
   see also Bartercard Cup; Lion Red League; Rothmans national club tournament; Tusk Cup; Wrangler Cup
clubs, past and present 18–20, 24–5, 97, 125, 173–5, 326, 367
Coghlan, M *130*
Cole, S 33–4, 37, 38
Collicoat, Warren *219*, 220, 224–6, 229–30, 232–6, 246
Collins, Ben 349
Collins, Frank 133
colours and uniforms 9, 16, 22, 31–2
Colts teams 101, 146–7
Conlon, Nadene 313
Conroy, Tom *219*, 224, 228–30, *228*, 232–3, 251, 255
Cook, Andy 332
Cook, Jamie 323
Cook Islands 330
Cooke, Bert / A E *102*, 103–5, *103*, 108–9, *110*, 112, *118*, 120
Cooke, Mel 160, 176, 186, *186*, 355
Cooke, Morrie 147
Cooke, Reg *182*, 185–6, *186*, 189–90, 192–3, *193*, 199, 213
Cooksley, Graeme 207–8
Cooney, Dr Leo 205
Cooper, Bob 229, 252
Cooper, Shane 257–8, *259*, 262, 266, 272, *273*, 274–8, 280
Copestake, Lamond *331*, 332
Cordtz, Peter 357
Cotter, H 76
Counties-Manukau Heroes 305–6, 311–12, 314–15, *314*, 317
Counties-Manukau Jetz 341, 344
Coutts, Graeme 272, 273
Cowan, Joe 224
Cowan, Ricky 259, 262, 265, *290*
Cowan, "Shorty" 116
Coyle, Craig 266–7
Craike, Royce 163–4
Cranch, Ray 136, 139–40, *141*, 147, 153–4, 156, 209, *219*
Crequer, Marty 266, 271, 272–3, *273*, 276, 278, 283
Crewther (1923 City) 72
Croawell, Bob 259
Crockett, Michael 353
Cronin, Mick 220, *233*, 234
Cronulla 223–4, 227, 246
Cross, A *44*
Cross, Tom 49, *49*
Cross, W *44*
Cubitt, Les 58
Culpan, Ivan 57, 62, 67, *67*, 69–70, *69*, *71*, *91*, 99, *110*, 120, 361
Cunningham, Rex 133–5, *135*, 137, 140, *141*
Cunningham, Wendy 313
Curran, Billy 41, *42*

D

Dacre, Ces 53
Dagg, John 213, 220
Dalton, Ted *294*
Dance (1921 Maritime) 63
Dane, Quinten 306, 310–11
Danielson, Oscar 199, 201, 204, 208, 213
Dannevirke 38
Davidson, Ben *71*–2, 75, 78, 79, 80, 82, 84, 103
Davidson, Bill / W 57–8, 60–1, 63, 72, *72*, 82–4, *82*
Davidson, Charles (Bunny) 83, *84*
Davidson, George 56, 58, 63, 72, 76, 82, 84, 137, 141–2, 146, *146*, 151, 154–6, 158–9, *158*

Davidson, Reg 84
Davidson brothers 82–4
Davies, Michael 294, 295
Davis, Dylan 350
Davis, W 116
Delgrosso, Frank 44, 56, 58, 75, 76, 79–82, 79, 93, 120
Dempsey, Claude 111–12, 115, 118
Denize, R 33, 34, 37, 38, 51
Dennison (1910 City) 33
Denton, Neville 162, 162, 165, 169–72, 171, 176, 181–4, 186–8, 188
  as coach and selector 199, 219, 228
Devine (1939 Richmond) 107
Devine, Bill 87
Devonport Domain 27, 27
Devonport United 19, 20, 81, 85, 100–1, 100
  see also North Shore Albions
Dick, Gary 208
Dillamore, C 8–9, 9
Dimitro, Mike 158–9
Dines, Kerry 196
district scheme (Auckland) 173–5
Dixon, H 89–90
Doble, Bob 138–9
Dodds, Des 152, 152
Dodds, Frank 167
Dodds, Norman 147
Dodds, Steve 273, 276
Doherty, Carl 328
Domain Cricket Ground xiii, 42, 47, 60, 62, 73, 76, 107
Donnelly, Brian 229
Donovan, H 93
Donovan, Jack 100
Doran (1910 City) 33
Dormer, Peter 147, 152, 152
Doug Price Memorial Medal 332
Douglas (1924 Devonport) 85
Douglas, H 76
Douglas, Peter xiv
Douglas, Roger 167
Dowsett, Shane 216–17, 222–4, 222, 234
Draper, Bobby 166, 166
Driscoll, Michelle 313
Dryland, Phillip 236
Duane (1929 Marist) 93
Duff, Jason 343
Duffy, Ron 185
Dufty, Craddock 56, 76, 78–81, 79, 86–7, 89–90, 91, 99
Dufty, John 8, 47
Dunn, Billy 152, 152
Dunning, Charles 4, 5, 7–9, 9, 16, 16, 19, 25, 29–30, 33, 37–8, 38, 41
Dyer, Barrie 229–31, 230, 234

E

Eade, Murray 215–16, 219, 224–6, 225, 229, 232–3
Eagleton, R 18
Eastern City Districts 174–5
Eastern Suburbs (Auckland) 174–5
Eastern Suburbs (Sydney) 100–1, 100, 107, 168, 226, 235, 238, 283
Eastern Tornadoes 319, 327–8, 331, 341, 344
Eastern United 175, 189, 189, 192–3, 193, 257
Eastlake, Cyril 156, 158–60, 162–5, 164, 167, 168–70, 173, 176, 181–3, 194, 194, 393
Eastwood, Greg 360
Eden club 173
Eden Park 42, 56, 56
Edmondson, Karl 341
Edwards, Jimmy 143, 151–3, 152, 155, 156–7, 159, 162
Edwards, Logan 289, 290
Edwards, Sam 172, 183, 187, 194, 199
Edwards, Shane 312, 320, 323, 328, 330
Edwards, W 43, 44
Ekepati, Steve 312, 314, 316
Elia, Mark 264–7, 269, 294, 295, 295, 300–1, 303
Ellerslie 173, 175, 177, 199, 313, 341
Ellis, Fred / F W 67, 69, 99
Ellis, Mark 359
Ellwood, Doug 183–4, 188, 192–3, 196, 199, 201, 213
Emery, Maunga 183–5, 187
Endacott, Frank 308, 313, 317
Endean, John / J jun 18, 18, 20
England, games against
  1910: x, xiii, 32, 35–7, 36
  1914: 47–9, 47–8
  1920: 60–1, 60–1
  1924: 78–80, 79, 88
  1928: 63, 78–81, 80
  1932: 101–3, 102, 105
  1936: 113–15, 113–15
  1946: 124, 132–4, 132
  list of results 378
  see also Great Britain
Enoka, Ruben 335
Epiha, Eva 313
Ericsson Stadium 308, 309
Eriksen, Len 162, 170, 172
Eru, Syd 298
Eustace, A 71
Evans, W M 18
Ewe, Jack and Sally 142
Eyre, Ernest 24, 27

INDEX

F

Fa'afili, Henry 322–3, 338
Fa'alogo, David 333, 337, 350, 360
Fa'alogo, Sala 333, 350–1
Fagan, Jack 170, 173, 181, 185, 193, 197, *198*, 199, 202, 252
Fahey, Ben 312
Fai, Sonny 350, 358
Faitala, Sinave 322–3, 330, 341, 350
Fakavamoenga, Cheaf Lee 316
Farrant, Len 25, 33–4, 37
Fatialofa, David 304
Fatu, Vince 347
Faumuina, Mark 312
Faumuina, Sione 338
Fenton, Ray *191*, 192
Fepuleai, Toa 236, 248
Ferguson, A *130*
Ferguson, Archie 31–3, *32*, 62, 120, *120*
Ferris, Kane 343
Field, T *130*
Field, Victor 347
Fien, Nathan 349, 358, 360
Filipaina, Olsen 227, 236, 240–1, *243*, 244–6, *247*, 248
Filipo, Lafaele 306, 310–11
Filipo, Phill *294*
Filitonga, Mikio 332
Finnerty, Lee 333, 337
First World War 50–1
Firth, Steven 305
Fisher, Jack 143, 147, 153
Fisi'iahi, David 328, 343, 349–51, *351*
Fisi'iahi, Paul 328–9, 341, 343–4, 351, 353
Fiu, Junior 312, *319*, 320, 323, 330
Flanagan, J 112
Flavell, Joe 330
Fletcher, Eric 105, 108, 111–12
Flett (1929 Marist) 93
Flinkenberg, Roy *141*
Floyd, Daniel 330–2, 337
Flynn, N 63, *71*
Fogarty, Dick 128
Fogarty, Jim 128, *128*, 135, *135*
Ford, Jim 185
Ford, Lionel 166, *166*
Foss (1924 Marist) 85
Fox, Deryck 275, 300–1
Fox, Edward 49, *49*, 89, 97
Fox Memorial Shield *vi*, 368–71
    1930s: 100, 107, 115, 118–19
    1940s: 125, 127, 142
    1950s: 151, 170, *172*, 175
    1960s: 189, *193*, 199
    1970s: 222–3, 237
    1980s: 257, *258*, 267, 268, 269, 271, *271*
    1990s: 293–5, *294–5*, 312, *312*, 315, *315*, 316, 318–20, *318–19*
    2000s: 328, 329, 331–2, *331–2*, 333–5, *334–5*, 339–40, *339*, 342, *342*, 347, *348*, 350–1, *351*
    grand final winners 372–3
France, games against xii
    1951: 150–1, 154–6, *155*
    1955: 163–4, *164*
    1960: 180–2, *180*
    1964: 193–4, *194*
    1975: 230–1, *230*
    1977: 242–4, *242*
    1981: 254–5, *255*
    1995 v North Harbour 310–11
    list of results 379
France, Marvin 355
Francis (1930 player) 98
Francis, Arthur (Bolla) 4, 39, 68
Francis, Harry 62–3
Fraser, Daniel 7, 23
Freeman, A *71*
Freeman, Gary 266, 269, 271–2, 273, 274–6, *275*, 299, *299*, 304, 313, 356, 392
Freeman, Warwick 237, 246, *246*
Fricker, H 37, 38, *41*, 49
Friend, Cathy *xiv*
Friend, Clayton 262–4, *263*, 272–4, *273*, 275, 276, 300–1, 314
Fue, John 271
Fue, Peter 271
Fuimaono, Frank 310–11
Fuimaono, John 317
Furnell (1939 Richmond) 107

G

Gailey, Doug 203, 205–6, 208, 216, 219, *219*, 230, 248, 251
Galavao, Joe 330
Galbraith, Stuart 283, 288, *294*, 295, 297
Gallagher, Bert 72
Ganley, Khamal 332
Gardiner, George 75, 79, 80, 82, 85, 87
Garrett (1924 Devonport) 85
Gascoigne, Bing 196
Gaudin, F E N 18
Gault, Angus 114–17
Gemmell, Brent 351
Gentles, Remus 328
Ghent, Billy 58
Gibbons, Joe 170
Gibson, Doug *140–1*, 141
Gibson, Jack 238
Gilchrist, Dan 5
Gillam, Ken *166*
Gillespie, Mark 255
Gillett, George 4, 39, 42, 49

Gilmour, Robbie 335
Giltinan, James J 3
Giltrap, Barry 170
Gladding, F G 8–9, 9, 12, 25
Gleeson, Jim 23
Glenora 175, 189, 192, *192*, 220, 237, 269, 272, 318–20, *318–19*, 327–8, 344
Glover, A E 18
Goddick (1924 Devonport) 85
Godinet, Pita (Peter) 353, 358
Gold Coast 303
Goodall, Vern 90
Gordon, John 251
Gordon, Tony (Tank) 238
Gore, Allen 167, 170
Gore, David 190
Goulding, James 265–6, 272, *273*, 275
Goulin, Bill 153, 159
Goulter (1910 North Shore) 33
Goulter, E 45
Gow, Sid *130*, 141, 147
Grafton Athletic xii, 49–50, 53, 88, 173
Graham (1929 Marist) 93
Graham, Abbie 109, 135, *135*, 137, 143, 146
Graham, B *130*
Graham, Bruce *132*, 133–4
Graham, J 34, 45
Graham, Keith 159, 166, *166*
Graham, Mark 222–3, 225–6, 231–2, *233*, 234, 236, 240–1, *243*, 244–6, 251, 255, 272, 303, 355–6, *356*
  as coach *320*, 321
Grainger, Jeff 227
Great Britain, games against xii
  1950: 150–1, *150*
  1954: 161–2, *161*
  1958: 168–70, *168*
  1962: 187–8, *188*
  1966: *200–1*, 201
  1970: 212–13, *212*
  1974: 228–30, *228–9*
  1977: 240–1, *241*
  1979: 247–8, *247*
  1984: 262
  1988: 276–8, *277*
  1990: 287–8, *287*
  1992: 300–1
  list of results 378–9
  see also England
Greenall, Dougie 161
Greengrass, John *217*, 232, 253
Greer, Richard 294
Gregory, Andy 277
Gregory, Charles 79, 80, 82, 85, 89–90, 92, *92–3*, 99, 120
Grey, Andrew 316

Grey, C D 18
Grey, Eric 61, 62–3, *162*
Grey, Ian 160–5, *162*, 169–70, 199
Griffen, Jim 29–30, 36–7, *41*
Griffin (1910 North Shore) 33
Griffiths, Fred 191
Grundy (1909 player) 30
Gurnick, Peter *219*, 222, 228, 229–30, 233–4
Guttenbeil, Awen 314, 338, 359
Guttenbeil, Karl 340
Gwynne, Joe *193*, 222, *222*, 291

H

Haddon, A 56
Haddon, Tom 56
Hadfield, Tom 167, 168, *171*, 176, 182–5, 355
Hafoki, Savinata 349
Haggie, Dick 163–5, 170, *171*
Haira, Ariki *see* Stanaway, Alex
Haira, Hone *see* Stanaway, Jack
Hale, Dennis 252, 265, 301–2, *301*
Halifax 104
Hall, Bob 321
Hall, C 112, *118*, *128*
Hall, Juanita 313
Hall, Len *219*, 229–30
Hall, Robert 294
Hall, Trevor 80–1, *80*, 89, *91*, 103–4
Hall, Wilson 74
Halliday, A *44*
Halsey, R *128*
Hambly, Brian 198
Hammill, W J (Bill) 69, 70, 99
Hammond, Don 160, 173, 176, *178*, 182, *182*, 185–7, *186*, 194, 197, 209, 236
Hancox, Claud *128*, 137
Hanlon, W 76, 80
Hanna, Pat 196
Hansen, Alby 230–4, *233*, 236, 238–9
Hansen, Shane 271, 277–8, *281*, 282–3
Hape, Shontayne 359
Hapi, Shontayne 331
Harbour League 344, 353–4
Hardgrave, Arthur 29–30, 41, 49, *49*, 104
Hardgrave, Roy 80–1, 86, *91*, 94, 104
Harding, David 295
Hardwick, Travers 129, *132*, 133–5, *135*, 137, 141, 156, 158–9, *219*
Hardy, Don *128*, 135, *135*
Harford, Billy 196, 198–9
Harley, J C 33
Harley, R 63
Harper (1924 Devonport) 85
Harris, Cliff 156
Harris, Darren 278

INDEX

Harrison (1910 North Shore) 33
Harrison, Bronson 360
Harrison, George 33, 37, 38, 50–1
Harrison, M 51
Harrison, Rata 182, 185, 188
Hassan, Wilf 92, 93, 102, 103–5, 105
Haswell (1910 Newton) 33–4
Hattaway, Bill 170, 176
Hawkes, Harry 62–3, 71, 76
Hawke's Bay 38–9, 40, 56, 70, 82
Hawthorne, A 34
Hawthorne, Phil 207–8
Hayward, Bob 152, 152
Hayward, Harold 41, 49, 49
Hayward, Morgan 41
Healy, D 41
Heatley, Eddie 214, 218, 220, 222
Helander, Keith 56
Hellesoe, Patrick 294, 296
Hemi, Jack 116–17, 119, 126, 127
Henare, Bryan 304, 311
Henare, Darryl 278
Henderson (1910 Newton) 33
Henry, Frank 87
Henry, Ricky 338, 340–1, 343
Henry, W 91
Herangi, Aoterangi 341, 343
Heremaia, Aaron 353
Herewini, M 91
Hermansson, Terry 358
Herring, Des 111–12
Herring, Ernest (Ernie) 58, 61, 79, 80, 82, 122
Herring, John 147, 153
Heta, Paul 312
Heta, William 347, 348, 350, 357
Hibiscus Coast 258, 319, 327–8, 331–2, 331, 333–5, 334–5, 339–40, 344
Hickey, Don 294
Hiley, Greg 277–8, 283
Hill (1910 North Shore) 33
Hill, Gavin 304, 309, 309
Hill, Owen 166, 166
Hill, Tom 223–4
Himiona, Darren 349
Hindman, Geoff 271
Hohaia, Lance 338, 359–60
Hohaia, Tama 317
Hollis, A 116
Holman, Keith 143
honours board 120, 366
Hooker, Gary 236
Hooker, Lindsay 262, 272, 273, 275
Hooper, Matt / M J 8–9, 9, 13, 32, 45, 120
Hoppe, Sean 283, 293, 295, 300, 304, 308–9, 358
Horo, Mark 267, 269, 272–3, 273, 275–6, 280, 358
Horo, Shane 266–7, 269, 271–2, 273, 274–9
Hotchin, Mark 321
Hough, Bevan 151, 153–6, 153, 166, 166
Houghton, Joseph 14
Houghton, Thomas 14–16, 25, 29, 33
Houston, Phil 302, 306
Howard, Cyril 305
Howells, Steve 262
Howick Hornets 347
Hughes, Del 314, 319, 330
Hughes, Jonathan 304
Hughes, Kevin 227
Hull 39, 255–6, 260, 260, 274, 276
Hull Kingston Rovers 256
Humphries, Bert 178
Humphries, Graham 178
Hunt, G 34, 51
Hunt, H 130
Hunt, Karmichael 360
Hunter, Stu 186
Hurndell, Clarence (Sandy) 109, 136–7, 136, 140, 141, 146, 151–6, 152
Hutt, Lou / L S G 81, 89, 103–4, 111–12, 118, 171

I

Ieremia, Simon 349
Ifwersen, Karl xii, 47, 49, 49, 51, 53, 55, 57–8, 61, 120
Ikeroma, Morris 349
Ikihele, Archie 333, 337
Iles, George 56, 58
Immortals of Auckland league 356
Innes, Craig 296, 314
inter-districts national championship 246, 253–4, 264, 269–70, 377
international matches, results of 378–80
international records 392–4
international tours 286
    by Auckland 272–6, 273–5
    see also touring teams, games against
inter-provincial games xii–xiii
    1908–09: 7–14, 8–10, 13, 23, 28–31, 29–30
    1910s: 37–8, 38
    1920s: 70, 71, 86, 86, 94, 94
    1930s–40s: 96, 129, 134–5, 135, 139–42, 140–1, 148
    1950s: 152–3, 152, 157, 160, 162–3, 166
    1960s: 186, 186, 190, 190, 193, 202–3, 203
    1970s: 218, 218–19
    1990s: 296–7, 296, 320, 322
    2000s: 349, 357–8

Auckland's increasing dominance in 1960s
204
see also inter-districts championship;
national first division championship;
National Provincial Cup; Northern
Union Cup; Rothmans inter-provincial
tournament; Rugby League Cup
Inu, Krisnan 360
Ioane, Raymond 358
Ioani, Casper 294
Iobu, Kimi 328
Iro, Kevin xi, 256, 272, 273, 274, 276–80, 279, 307, 358

J

Jackson (1910 North Shore) 33
Jackson, A 82
Jackson, Alf 29, 37, 38, 40–1, 56
Jackson, Fred 37
Jackson, J G 45
James (1912 City) 51
James, C 71
James, Fred 135, 135
Jamieson, Cory 295, 311
Jarvis, Bob 219, 222, 225, 229–30, 232–5, 234–5
Jellick, Brian 261, 319, 323
Jenkinson, Des 219
Jenkinson, R 80
jerseys *see* colours and uniforms
Joe, Leroy 312
Johnson (1924 Marist) 85
Johnson, Albert 61
Johnson, Cliff 151, 153–6, 155, 160, 161, 162, 165, 167, 168, 170, 176, 182, 183, 355
Johnson, Ivan 128, 128
Johnson, Joffre 128, 128, 132, 133, 135, 135, 137, 141
Johnson, Karl 343
Johnson, Mick 128, 128
Johnson, Nelson 166, 166, 180, 181
Johnson, Norm 128, 128
Johnson, S 128
Johnson, Ted 170, 171, 172, 183–4
Johnson brothers 128
Johnston (1929 Marist) 93
Johnston, B 79–80, 82
Jolley, Brian 234–5
Jones, H G 18
Jones, Jim 75
Jones, Lewis 161
Jones, Spencer 53
Jones, Stacey 308, 310, 313–14, 315, 317, 323, 323, 338, 355–6, 359, 359
Jordan, Chris 202, 230–1, 236, 239–41, 243, 244, 251
Jordan, Len 134–5, 137, 139, 140, 140–1, 146
Joyce, Neil 319
Jujnovich, Joe 170
Junior Kiwis 304
junior representative teams 168, 168, 224

K

Kailea, Paea 328
Kaiser, Steve 273, 273, 275–6
Kapi, Harry 322, 330
Karam, Joe 226, 236–9, 237
Kaulima, Jason 294, 306, 310
Kawe, Len 116
Kay, Arthur / A G 110–11, 111–15, 118, 126
Kay, Eddie 139, 147
Kay, J 39
KB Cup 227, 378
Kean, Sid 37–8, 38
Keane (1935 player) 122
Kearney, Stephen 308–9, 313, 317, 358, 360
Keat, R 128
Keene, S 33
Kelly, Bill 101–2
Kelly, George 145, 157, 162
Kelly, Peter 266
Kem, Billy 177, 178
Kemble, Gary 236, 238, 240–1, 243, 244, 248, 251, 255, 256, 256, 260, 260
as coach 295, 317, 337, 353
Kemp, Tony 221
Kenealy, D 41
Kennedy, Charlie 315, 317
Kerr, David 236
Kerr, W 91
Kesha, Neville 234, 244
Key, Dennis 202–3
Keys, Graham 170
Kingham, Brett 308
Kingsland club 89, 173
Kini, Mike 301
Kiri, Solomon 305, 307–8
Kiro, Anthony 328, 330
Kirwan, Jack 82, 93
Kirwan, John 310, 359
Kirwan, Pat 142
Kite, Ronald 315, 316
Kiwis and predecessors
Auckland captains 120, 394–5
Auckland coaches 395–6
Auckland criticism of selections 240, 245, 250–1
clubs with most Kiwis 396–401
games against Auckland 42, 42, 82, 139, 140, 207–8, 208, 379
players selected from Auckland, by clubs 380–90

INDEX

players selected from Warriors 390–1
related Kiwis from Auckland 401
Knowling, Ted 135, 195, *195*
Koloi, Paul 323
Koopu, Wairangi 338, 353, 359
Kriletich, Tony 196, 198–9, *199*, 205, 206, 208, 212–13, *214–15*, 216–17, 224, 228–30

L

Laing, Bert 56, 72–3, *73*, 76, 85, 120
Laing, J 85
Laird, Allan 109, 140, 146
Laird, Jim 104, 112
Laiseni, Sunita 357–8
Lambert, G *41*
Lang (1924 Marist) 85
Lang, J (Tiffy) 9, 31, *31*
Lang, John 80
Langlands, Graeme 199, 252
Lasher, John 167, 188, 193, 194
Latu, Tevita 330, 337–8
Lauaki, Epalahame 338, 341
Lauitiiti, Ali 318, 338, 359
Laumatia, Bryan 308
Lavea, Saulimai 316
Lavea, Tasesa 393
Law, D 56
Lawless, Ray *102*, 103, 105, 108, 112
laws of rugby league *see* rules
Le Scelle, J *130*
Leavai, Eddie 349
Lee, Brian 183, 185, *212*, 213
Lee, John A 99, 120–1
Lee, Shannon 320
Leeds 258, 273, *274*, 276
Leger, Francis 355
Lemafa, Herman 322, 330
Leota, Francis 278, 282, 288, 300–1
Lepper, Dave 226, 238, 240, *243*, 251
Lepper, Jack 139, *141*, 147
Lester, Aaron 307
Leuluai, Eddie 350
Leuluai, James 248, 251, 253, 255–6, *255–6*, 260, 274, 276, 279, 328
Leuluai, Phillip 323, 328, 330, 337–8
Leuluai, Thomas 338, 359–60
Lewis, Peter 322, 328
Liavaa, Josh 229–30, 238
Lile, Adam (Addie) 11, *11*, 13
Lile Shield 11
Liles, Bland 208, 213–14, *214*
Lima, Danny 304
Lima, Peter 304
Linkhorn, C 16, 25, 29, 33
Lio, Alan 319, 322–3, 330, 355

Lion Red Cup 286, 295, 297, 302, 305–7, *310*, 314–15, *314*
  grand finals 373
Lion Red League (national club competition) 267–9, 271, 283, 291, 292, 293, 295, 374
Lion Red Showdown (1991) 297, *298*
Lions *see* England; Great Britain
Lipscombe, Ken 152
List, Claude 75, 80–1, 89–90, *94*, 98, 103–5
Little, M 89–90, *91*
Littlewood, Ivan 62–3, 75, 76, *81*, 82
Littlewood, R *71*
Liversidge, M 120
Lockwood, Brian 247
Lomax, David 350, 354
Lomax, John 298, 354
Lonergan, Dean 265–6, 273, *273*, 276, 321
Longbottom, B 120
Loveridge, Norm 61
Lovett, Cedric 259, 262, *262*, 268
Lowe (1910 City) 33
Lowe, Graham 222, 224, 246, 256, 303, 320–1, *320*
Lowe, Mark 240–1, *243*, 244
Lower Waikato 39, 60
Lowrie, Jason 283, *294*, 301, 303–4
Lowrie, Sam *43–4*, 56–8, 80
Lowther, Bernie 129, 214, 216, 220
Loza, Te Manawa 312, *314*, 315–16
Luck, Micheal 358
Lunn, Herb 62–3
Lupton (1910 Newton) 33
Ly, Chan 350
Lye, Trevor *172*
Lynch, F 33
Lythe, Ben 315–17, 319–20, *319*, 328–9, 333, 337

M

McCarthy, Alan 236, 239–41, *243*, 244, 248, 251
McCarthy, D *44*
McClennan, Brian 257–8, 266, 267, 278, 283, *284*, 288, 289, 308
  as coach 316–17, 331–2, 342, 344, *346*
McClennan, Mike 199, 202, *203*, 206, 208, 213, *214*, 216, 257–8, *257*, 283, 321
McClymont, Thomas (Scotty) 43, *44*, 47, 49, *49*, 51, 57–8, 60–1, 80
  as coach and selector 55, 109, *109*, 120, 136, 175
McCook, Bill 139, 141, *141*, 152, *152*
McCracken, Ken 185–6, 190, 192–4, 199, *200*, 202
McCulloch, Steve 328
McDade, Wayne 333, 341, 350, 353, 358
McDevitt, Conrad 52–3

McDonald (1929 Marist) 93
McDonald (unspecified) 33, 72
McDonald, Hec 80
McDonald, R 33
McDonald, R W 33
MacDonald, Ronald / R A 8–9, 9, 14–15, 29, 37–8, 38
McEwen, Ashley 219
McGahan, Hugh 257, 261–2, 261, 283, 321, 392
MacGowan, Bill 317
McGregor, Cameron vii, xiv, 66, 361
McGregor, Dougie 56, 58, 143
McGregor, F 44
McGregor, Jack 63, 66, 71
McGregor, Ron 66, 109, 133–5, 135, 137, 143–5, 143–4, 167, 221, 361
McGregor, Steve 245
McGregor, Tracey 265–6
McGuinn, Bob 216, 222
Machee, Loi 294
McInnarney, Arthur 121, 137, 140, 141
McInteer, Arch 163, 166, 166
McIntosh, Ken 294, 295, 301, 306, 354
McIntyre, A 91
McIntyre, Greg 351
McIntyre, H 89
McIntyre, Jonaree 294, 295
McIver, Ken 152
McKay, Ron 156, 162–3, 165, 168–70, 172, 181
Mackenzie, H 76
McKewen, Trevor 321
Mackie, E 63, 72
Mackie, Jason 306, 309
McKinnon, Wade 358
Mackintosh, Dave 294, 295, 297, 301
Mackintosh, H 130
Mackrell, Bill / W H C 4, 7, 8–10, 9, 29–30, 33–4
Mackwood, Dean 314
McLaughlin (1923 City) 72
McLean, Ben 311, 311
McLean, Duncan / D W 7, 18–24, 20, 23, 45, 51, 56, 120
McLean, Willie 312
McLeod, A 91
McLeod, Don 141, 151–2, 152
McLeod, Jack 108
McLeod, Peter 272, 273, 276, 291, 291, 302
McLeod, Trevor 312
McNamara, S 44
McNeight, Bill 120
McNeil, Clarrie 108
McNeill, M 71
McNicol, Colin 147
McPherson, Guy 349

McRae, Duncan 167, 178
McRae, Ron 178
MacReynolds, Tom 23
Maddison, L 43
Maea, Aleki 310
Maea, Des 307
Maera, Jason 328
Magatogia, Carl 269, 282
Mahima, Peter 116–17
Mahuta, Tonga 74
Maiava, Hutch 333, 334, 337
Maki, F 33
Malam, Brady 301
Malam, Gus 221
Malametinos, Kosta 319, 323
Malesala, Malesala 312
Malietoa-Brown, Gus 304, 315, 342
Mangere East 271, 283, 293, 318–19, 339–40, 339, 342, 350
Mangos, Therese 313
Maniapoto, Rewi 16
Manlane-Roskill 175
Manly 173, 225, 270, 270, 297, 303
Mann, Don 194, 199, 214, 216, 219, 223–4, 229–30
Mann, Duane 277–8, 280, 296, 304, 306–9, 306, 311, 314–15, 317, 319, 328
Mann, Esau 305, 314–15, 314, 327, 328
Mann, George 266, 271–2, 273, 278, 280, 282, 288, 300
Mann, H 130
Mann, Warren 272, 273, 288–9
Mannering, Simon 359–60
Mansson, Paul 303, 308
Manu, Misili 342
Manukau 97, 115–17, 126–7, 259, 263
Manukau-Greenlane 175
Manurewa 316, 327–8, 341, 347, 348, 354
Māori involvement 25–6, 115–17, 142, 203
Marist club 53, 81, 85, 85, 100–1, 100, 118, 136, 142–3, 172, 175, 327
    1929 vs South Sydney 91–2
    1933 defeat of St George 106, 106
    great 1965–66 seasons 199
    influx of Pacific Islanders 160
    players selected for Kiwis 104–5, 105, 399–401
Marist-Richmond Brothers 328, 340, 341–2, 344
Maritime club 62–3, 237, 238
Marjoribanks, Tyson 330
Marsh, Wayne 238
Marsh, Wilson 306, 308
Marshall (1908–09 player) 14, 16
Martin (1912 City) 51
Martin, R 128
Martin, Stan 224, 306, 311, 314, 323, 330

INDEX

Martin, Tania 313
Mason, Len 82
Matai, Steve 340, 360
Matautia, Vila 288, 291, 296
Matete, Paul 213, 222, 234, 236
Matthews, Howie 351
Mattson, Graham 188, 191–2, *192*, 194, *194*, 199, 288–9
Matua, Rusty 283, 291, *292*, 347
Matulino, Ben 359
Maxwell, Henry 158–9, 165, 167, 168, *171*, 176, *178*, 181, 183, 213
Maxwell, Trevor 220
Meates, Bill 157
Meates, Jack 157–9
Meates Cup 157, 182
Meehan, Pat 101, 103, 105
Meli, Francis 338, 359
Menzies, George 142, 162, 176, 184, 186, 239, 355
Menzies, Joe 79–80, 82
Messenger, Dally 5
Meyer, Ted 98
Middleton (1939 Ponsonby) 121
Midland Districts (Auckland) 175
Midlands-Bay of Plenty 235
Mildenhall, Daniel 322
Miles (1910 City) 33
Miller, O 33, 56
Mills, Brian 361
Mills, Jim 232
Mills, Laurie 107–8, 121
Mills, Lester 196, 201
Millward, Roger 212–13, *212*
Milne, W *44*
Mincham, Bob 197, 204, *204*, 207–8
Mincham, Ted / E T 105, 108, *108*, 111–12, *118*
Mincham, W 120
Minogue, W 62–3
Mitchell, Alf 105, 108, 112, 160
Mitchell, George 107–8, 160
Mitchell, J 63, 72
Mitchell, Robert (Bob) *34*, 37, 38, 41, *41*, 49, *49*, *51*, 58
Moana, Martin 309
Moimoi, Fuifui 332, 337
Moimoi, Robert 271, 283
Moisley, Dick 80, 92, *93*, *94*
Moki, W *34*, *51*
Moncur, Gordon 167
Monie, John 304, 308, 313, 317
Monteith Shield 368
Moon, Dennis 166, *166*
Mooney, Owen 167
Moore (1929 Ponsonby) 93

Moore, Eddie 197–9, 201, 205–6, 213, 222
Moore, Ewan 192
Moore, Harold 147, 166, *166*
Moore, Roy 154, 156, 158, 165
Moorwood, Michael 259
Morgan, E *118*
Morgan, Len 196, 199, 204, 208, 213
Morman, G *91*
Morrison, Daryl 253, 259–60
Morse, Frank *34*, *40*
Morton, Geoff *294*
Moselen, Doug *178*
Mouat, Neil 87
Mount Albert
    1930s–40s: *116*, 119, 136, 142–3, *148*
    1950s–60s: 154, 174–5, 177, 190, *193*, 199, 203
    1970s–90s: 226, 257, 258, 259, 268, 295
    2000s: 327–8, 333–4, 340, 341–2, *341–2*, 344, *345–6*, 350–1, *351*, 353–4
Mount Roskill 175
Mount Smart 291, 304–5, 308, 357
    see also Ericsson Stadium
Mount Wellington 231, 319
Mountford, Cecil 126–7, 129, 131, 245
Murphy, Justin 331
Murray (1943 Manukau) 127
Murray, David 305, 308
Murray, Joe 167
Murray, Mark 328
Myers, Sir Arthur 35, *35*, 62, *62*
Myers Cup *34*, 35, 368
Myler, Frank 212
Myles, David 331, 338

N

Napa, Stan 222–3, 241, *243*, 244, 246
Nathan, Vern 351
national first division championship 279–80, 289, 296–7, 349, 377
National Panasonic Cup 227, 378
National Provincial Cup 320, 322–3
Neal (1924 Marist) 85
Neal, George 56
Neal, H *44*
Neary, Clive 192
Neighbour (1909 North Shore) 25
Nelson (1924 Marist) 85
Nelson, Boycie 315, 317, 320, 323, 328–9, 333
Nelson team 37–9
Nepia, George 26, 117
Nesbitt, Bill 243, 273, 276
Netzler, Murray 227, 235, 248
New South Wales Country 197, 220, 323, 343

New South Wales, games against 41–2, *41–2*, 73, 76, 77, *77*
list of results 380
New South Wales Premier League 352
New Zealand Māori 260
New Zealand Rugby League 206–7, 234, 286–7, 289
    formation 19, 28
New Zealand Rugby Union
    discontent with 2, 10–11
    reaction to league 4, 7, 11, 14–15, 23
New Zealand team *see* Kiwis
New Zealand Warriors *see* Warriors
Newcastle country district 225
Newdick, L 56
Newton Rangers 19, 21, 25, 33–4, 77–8, *91*, 112, 119, 173
Ngamu, Gene 295, 304, 308–9
Ngawati, Kevin *171*
Nikau, Tawera 282–3, 287, 288–9, 291, 296
Nixon, Terry 152, *152*
Noble, Jack 349
Nolan, L 37–8, *38*
Noonan, Bill 270
Noovao, Meti 304, 311
Nordgren, Brian 129, 131, *131*
Nordmeyer, Rene 270, 273, *273*, 278
Norgrove, D *44*
North Auckland 96
North Harbour Sea Eagles 305–7, *306*, 310–12, *310–11*, 315
North Harbour Tigers 340, 344
North Island division two 330
North Shore club 18–21, 24–5, 27, 33–4, 43, 56, *130*, 174–5
    see also Devonport United
North Sydney 272, 297, 298
Northcote 21, 174–5, 258, 271, *271*, 283, 284, 291, 293–5, *294–5*, 327–8, 331–2, *331–2*, 340
Northern Districts (Auckland) 174–5
Northern Districts (of New Zealand) 246
Northern Division (Australia) 227, 239
Northern Storm 344
Northern Union Cup 39, *39–40*, 56, 74–5, 86, 89–90, 96, 98–9, *98*, 119, 134, 139–40, 182, 186, *186*, 190, 193, 202–3, 266
    list of holders 375–6
    see also Rugby League Cup
Northern Union (in England) 3, 7, 28
    influence in New Zealand 6, 10, 14
Northland 75, 98–9, 218, 344
Norton, Graeme 293, *294*, 295, 306, 310–11, *310*, 352–3
Norton, Stewart 230–1, 236
NSW Cup 352–3

Nurse, Roy 129, *132*, 133–6, *135*, 141, *148*
Nuuausala, Frank-Paul 343

O

Oakley, Harry / H B 19, *19*, 33, 37, 38
O'Brien, Jim (Devonport) 81–2, *81*, 85, 89
O'Brien, Jim (Marist) 81–2, *81*, 85, 92
O'Brien, Jim (unspecified) 80–1, *80*, 98
O'Connell, Richard 312
O'Donnell, Claude 58
Ofanoa, Robert 304
Ofsoski, Bob 223
O'Hara, Dane 224, 236, 241, *243*, 244, 251, 255, 256, *256*, 260
Okesene, Hitro 307–9
Olliff, Laurie *178*, *182*, 183, 185
O'Neill, Julian 350
Orchard, Phillip 165, 205, 208, 355, 394
Orchard, Robert 196, 214, 216–17
O'Regan, Ron 250, 251, 253, 255–6, 260, 262, 264–7, 268, 269–70, 272–3, *273*
O'Shea, Terry 267, 269, 283
O'Sullivan, John 216, *219*, 223–4, *223*, 225, 226, 229–30, 232, 234–5
Otago 22, 38, 89–90, 94, *94*, 166
Otahuhu
    1910s–40s 50, 88, 125, 128, *128*, 136
    1950s–70s: 170, 173, 175, 189–90, *193*, 199, 222–3, *222*, *231*, 246
    1980s–90s: 257–9, 291, 292, 295, 312, *312*, 313, 315–16, 318–19, 323
    2000s: 327–8, *329*, 333–5, 347
    players selected for Kiwis 398–9
Otahuhu-Ellerslie Leopards 341, 344
Otara 315–16, *315–16*, 319
Owen, Bruce *171*

P

Pacific Cup 160
Pacific Islands' influence 160
Pai, Jeremiah 338, 358
Paki, Brownie 74, 79–80, 98
Paki, George 61, 72
Pakuranga 319
Paleaaesina, Iafeta 331, 338
Palmada, Jason 306, 308, 311, *311*
Panapa, Sam 256, 264–6, 269, 272–3, *273*–4, 275–6, 282, 287–9
    as coach 349–50, 355, 358
Papakura 175, 334–5, 347, 354
Papakura, Riki (Dick) 26, 31
Papalii, Junior 312
Papalii, Lafu 308
Parkes, Jim 87
Parkin, Jonathan (Jonty) *61*, 78, 79
Parnell Girls' Club 70
Parramatta 192–3, *192–3*, 214

INDEX

Parry, J *128*
Pascoe (1930 player) 98
Pascoe, Craig 351
Paterson, Murray 176, 182
Patterson, J 18
Patterson, Jim *168*, 170, *171*, 181–5
Patterson, Murray 167, 181
Pattillo, E *128*
Patton, Michael (Mike) 272, *273*, 275–6, 278, 280, 282–3, 288, 301, 303
Pau, Tyrone 330, 337, 341
Paul, Clarrie 246
Paul, Henry 256, 304, 307–8, *308*, 323, 359
Paul, Robbie 359
Paul, S 56
payments 38, 245, 259
Payne, Bert *188*
Payne, J 80–1, 89, *91*
Pearson, F 56
Pearson, Lou 168
Peckham, Bill 80, 82
Peckham, T 63, *71*
Pele, Eric 323, 330
Penney, Ted 177, *178*
Penrith 227
Pera, Robert 271
Percival (1909–10 player) 25, 33
Percival, John 252–3, *252*, 302, 356
Percy, Rex 165, 167–8, 170, *171*, 173, 176, 213, 393
Perenara, Bernard (Bernie) 340, 343–4, *345*, 353
Perenara, Henry 323
Perenara, Marcus 331
Perrett, Sam 360
Perry (1930 player) 98
Pert, Bruce 167
Petersen, Clarrie *130*, *135*, 135
Petersen, Lou 87
Phelan, E J *34*, 69
Phillips (1912 City) 51
Phillips, Gary *168*, 168, 176, *176*, 182–4, 188, *188*, 201
Pickering, James 301
Pickrang, Frank *114*, 115–17
Pilcher, Earle 205–7, *205–6*
Pine, Chappie 259, 266, 271
Platt, Andy 275, 308, 314
Player of the Year award 374–5
Poasa, Pat 251, 255
Poching, Willie 295, 308
Point Chevalier 175, 177
Pollock, R *91*
Polson, Clarrie 61, *61*, 74–5, 76, 79, 80, 88
Polynesian Rugby League Festival (1993) 305
Pongia, Quentin 297, 358
Ponsonby club

1908–19: 19, 21, 25, 33–4, 43, *43–4*, 52–3, 56, 57
1920s–40s: 85, *91*, 92, 93, 126, 131, 143, *148*
1950s–60s: 157, 170, *170*, 172–3, *172*, 175, 199, *200*, 203, *203*
1970s–2000s: 222–4, 223, 332
most Kiwis selected 396–7
Pooley, A *44*
Potter, Kevin 238
Pouesi, Marcus 255
Pouha, Sione 351
Pouwhiuwhiu, Te Keepa *see* Asher, Ernie
Powell, Roy / R H S 105, 108, *110*, 112, *114*, 115, *118*
Powley, Alf / A J 23, *45*
Prentice, Stan 81, 105, 108, 112, *141*
Prescott, Phil 343
Presland, Nicole 313, *313*
Price, Doug 139, 141, *141*, 151, 153
Price, Graham 230–1
Price, Hayden 351
Price, Steve 358, 360
Proctor, Lyndsay *219*, 225, *225*, 232, 240–1, 243, 244, 255
professionalism 289, 307
  player drain in 1980s 255–7
Proffit, Danny *178*
Prohm, Gary 222–3, 246, 248, 251, *251*, 255–6, 306
provincial competition *see* inter-provincial games
Pulieata, Kevin 280, 282
Pye, Les *130*, *132*, 133, 135, *135*, 137

Q

Queensland, games against 81–2, 220, 278, 380
Queensland Country 227
Quirke, A *118*
Quirke, W 112

R

Rae, A *44*
Rae, Laurie 142, 153
Rae, Peter 177, *178*, 182
Rae, Tommy 139, *141*
Railway club 52–3
Rainey, George 63, *64*, 220–1, *220*, 234, 238, 243–4, 254, 289, 361
  criticism of Kiwis selection 240, 245, 250–1
Raisbeck, Don 177, *178*
Rakena, Hona *171*
Rakena, Tai *178*
Ramsay, Neville *280*, 282–3, 297, 301, 315
Rankin, Eileen 313

Raper, Johnny 207–8
Rapira, Sam 359, 360
Ratima, Joe 156, 161–2, 164, 170, *170*, 172, 176
Rattenburg, Graham 342
Raudonikis, Tommy 234, 238
Rauhihi, Paul 295
Raumati, Tangi 236
Rawiri, Richard 259
Rawiri, Terry 259
Raynes, C 120
Raynor, George 82
Read, Arthur *130*, 133, 135, *135*
Redcliff (Brisbane) 226
Redmond, Dave 109, 140–1, 143, 146
Redmond, Wayne 213, 234
Redwood, Jack 103, 136, 137–9, *137*, 144
Redwood, P 8–9, *9*
referees 28, 31–3, *31–2*, 252–3, 301–2, 374
    assaults and incidents 182, 205–7, *205*
    test referees 402
    three players sent off in three minutes 172
Reid, G 63, *72*
Reid, Tom 183–5
Reidy, Brian 168, *168*, 172, 176, 184–8, *188*, 190, *190*, 197, 199, 201
Reke, Rukingi 41
Retzlaff, Herman 353
Rewha, Peter 259
Rhodes, George / G E 67, 70, *91*, 93, 97, 99
Rich, Morris 140–1, *141*
Richards-Jolley, Doug 148, 153–9, 161–2, *161*
Richmond
    1930s–40s: 97, 103–4, 106, 107–9, *107–9*, 115, 136–7, 142–3
    1950s–60s: 151, *153*, 167, 175, 199
    1970s–90s: 223, 291, 295
    2000s: 326–8, 331–2, 339–40, 347
    players selected for Kiwis 104–5, *169*, 397–8, 401
Riddell, Jim 159, 163–5, 167, 181, 213
Ridge, Matthew 314, 359, 392–3
Riechelmann, Alan 156, 166, *166*, *171*, 172
Riley, Brian 82, *111*, 112, *118*
Riley, C *128*
Riley, Mark 291
Riley, Syd 8–9, *9*, 33–4, 37, 38
Ripley (1925 referee) 81
Ririnui, Pita 126–7, 129
Risman, Gus 132–3
Ritchie, R *128*
Riverina 227
Robarts, Fred 303, 320
Robarts, Phil 301
Roberts, Ron 145
Roberts, Roy 192, 197, 201

Robertson, Bob 152, *152*
Robertson, Bruce 155, 156, 165, 201
Robertson, Maurie 109, *109*, 133–5, *135*, 137, 141–3, 145–6, 151, 156
    as selector and coach 168, 173, 191, *198*
Robertson, Wayne *219*, 223, 229, 233–6, *235*, 248
Robinson, G *34*
Robinson, Mark 359
Robson, Ian 304, 317
Rodger, W *128*
Roff, Roy 140, *141*, 152–3, *152*, 156, 158–9, 162
Rogers, E 56
Rogers, Percy 152
Rogers, Ra 146
Rogers, Steve *141*, 147
Roope, Dick 52, *52*
Roope Rooster 52, 92, *93*, 107, 115, *193*, 295, 350, 368–71, *vi*
Ropati, Feu 293
Ropati, Iva 202, 270, 278, 288–9, 293, *293*, 296, *296*, 298, 300–1, 304
Ropati, Jerome 338, 340, 359–60
Ropati, Joe 262, 264, 270, 293, *293*
Ropati, John 270–2, *273*, 275, 293, *293*
Ropati, Peter 266, 270, 272–3, *273*, 275, 282, 287, 288–9, 293, *293*, 297, 298
Ropati, Romi 293
Ropati, Tea 202, 258, 266, 270, 272, *273*–4, 275, 280, 282, 293, *293*, 296, 308–9
Ropati brothers 293, *293*
Rota, Don 223–4
Rota, Glen 340
Rota, Roger 223, 227
Rothmans inter-provincial tournament 195–6, 204, 213, 218–19, 235–6, 376
Rothmans national club tournament 189–90, *189*, 373
Rotorua 19, 31
Rowe, Harold / H F 4, 7–9, *9*, 13–15
Rowe, Phillip 192–4, 196
Ruby (1930 player) 98
Rugby League Cup 39, 203, 264, 266, 279, 289, 296, 308, 312, 316–17, 357
    list of holders 375–6
    see also Northern Union Cup
Rukutai, Jim 26, *34*, 37, *41*, 67
Rukutai Shield *vi*, 26, 368–71
rules 2, 7, 12, 21, 31, 78, 129
Runanga (West Coast) 125, 142
Russell-Green, Jack *130*, 139–40, *141*, 146, 156
Rutherford, John *130*, *132*, 133, 135
Ryan, Des *132*, 133, 135, *135*
Ryan, Gerald 167
Ryan, Kevin 167

INDEX

S

Samoa, Tui 349
Samuela, Noora 295
Sanderson, Alan 170
Sanderson, Doug *171*
Sanderson, N *128*
Sargeant, Dave 224, 253
Satherley, Cliff 105, 108, *108*, 111–12
Satherley, Jack 107–8, 115
Satherley, Jeff 192
Satherley, Warren 190, 192, 224
Savory, Charles 39, 44–7, 49, *49*
Schaumkel, Guenther 349–51
Schaumkel, Kevin 255
schools
    1990s championships 315
    opposition to league 89
    schoolboys competition 88
    secondary schools tournament in 1970s 202
    St Paul's College in Australian competition 339
Schultz, Bill 176, 194, 196, 199, *200*, 201
Schultz, Len *106*
Schultz, Paul *182*, 192, 196–7, 199, 201–2, 204, 206, 208
Schuster, Fred *212*, 213, 216
Scott (1924 Devonport) 85
Scott, Bob 126
Scott, Len 79–81, *80*, 94, *94*, 101, 103
Scott, Verdun 117, *117*, *130*
Seagar, Allan 75, 85, 86, *86*, 98, 99, 101, 103
Seagar, George 25, 29–31, 33, 36–8, 38, 41, *41*, *45*, *50*
Second World War 109, 120–1, 124–5
Seeling, Charles (Bronco) 4
Setefano, Mike 311, *311*
Seuseu, Anthony 328, 330, *331*
Seuseu, Jerry 312, 314–15, *314*, 317, 338, 359
Seymour, R *128*
Shaw, F 33
Shelford, Kelly 259, 265, 277–8, *277*, 280, 282, 298
Shortland (1930 player) 98
Shortland, Ryan 353
Shrimpton, Bill *273*, 282, 328
Shrimpton, Ray 262
Siddle, Colin 185
Silcock, Nat 161–2, *161*
Simons, K *128*
Simons, Peter 251, 259
Simpson (1910 Newton) 33
Simpson, E *118*
Simpson, Johnny 126
Simpson, Vic 93, *122*
Sinclair, Jim 178

Sinel, Ray 192, *196*, 197, 202, 206
Singe, Arthur 82, 87
Singe, Barry 158, 173
Skelton (1929 Ponsonby) 93
Smith, A 33
Smith, Adrian 322
Smith, C E *130*
Smith, Chris 191–2, 194
Smith, D *128*
Smith, G *81*
Smith, George (1) 3–6, *3*, 23
Smith, George (2) 25, 37, *41*
Smith, Graham 229–30
Smith, Jeremy 330, 332–3
Smith, John 224, 234, 236, 239–41, *241*, *243*, 244, 251
Smith, Jonathan 328
Smith, R *130*
Smith, Tom 13
Smyth, Ron 170
Snedden, Cyril / C A 20, 137
Snowden, Bill *171*, 176, 181, 183–5, 188, 197, 199, *199*, 202
Solomon, Brendan 330
Solomon, Dave 108, 119, *121*
Solomona, David 315, 318
Solomona, Se'e 278, 280, 288, 296, *296*, 308–9
Somers, W 18
Somers, Wally 60–1, 76, 79, 80–1, 89, *91*
Somerville, Jim 153
Sorensen, Bill 153, 156–60, 162–5, 167–8, 170, 172, *172*, 181–4, *182*, 187–8, *188*, 213, 393
    as coach and selector 225, 230, 233–4, 236–7, 240, 242, *243*–4, 245
Sorensen, Bill junior 160, 227, 234, 236, 238–9
Sorensen, Dane 160, 214, 225, 227, *231*, 232–3, 239
Sorensen, Dave 160, 216, *219*, 220, 222, 230–2, 239–41, *243*, 244
Sorensen, Kurt 160, 214, 225, 227, *231*, 232–4, 236, 238–41, *243*, 244–6, 261, 392
Souter, Fabian 344, 350
South Africa, games against 380
    1963: 191–2, *191*
South Auckland 74–5, 79, 82, 90, 96, 98–9, *98*, 129, 140–1, 152–3
South Island inter-districts team 246, 253–4, *254*, 264
South Sydney 91–2, *92*–3, 203, *203*, 227
Southern Districts (Auckland) 175, 189–90, 192
Southland 7, 38
Sparnon, Jack 178
Sparnon, John 202, 205–6

Speedy, Jack 128, *128*
Speedy, Royce 128, *128*
Spence, Bill 143, 146, 151–2, *152*
Spencer, George 9, 12–13
Spooner, Kevin 192
Sprague, Reg 39
St George, Neville 80, 82, 85, 103
St George (Sydney) 106, *106*, 177, 246, *246*
St Helens 104, 238, 258, 263, *263*, 274–6
St Paul's College 315
Stack, R *91*
Stanaway, Alex (Ariki Haira) 16, 26, *30*, 32–3, *34*, 37, *41*, *51*
Stanaway, Jack (Hone Haira) 19, 26, 32–3, *32*, 35
Start, Miguel 344, 350
Steel, Kevin 252
Stephenson, Bob 75
Stevenson, A 56
Stewart (1924 Marist) 85
Stewart, Dennis 265–6, *265*
Stewart, Don *294*, 306, 310–11, *311*, 320
Stewart, Doug 52
Stewart, Ivan 58, 60–1, 72
Stewart, Ossie 151–3, *152*
Stewart, Richard *294*, 311, 316–17
Stewart, Troy *294*
Stirling, I *130*
Stirling, Ken 215, 216–17, 220, 224–6, *225*, 229–30, 232–3, 236, 245
Stockley, W 114–15
Stonex, Ivan *135*, 195, *195*, 221
Storey, Ray 152, *152*
Stormont, Bill / W 60–1, *71*, 79, 80, 85, *85*
Stormont, J 85
Stormont Shield *vi*, 85, 107, 115, 118, 172, 222, 350, *350*, 368–71
Stuart, Brent 298
Sturm, Matthew 312, 314, *314*, 351
Sullivan, Jim 80, 101, *102*
Super 10 and 12 319–20
Super League 286, 310, 313, 317, 320
Superleague (New Zealand) 302
Sutton, A 33
Sutton, Tom 278
Swann, Anthony 311, 351
Swann, Logan 311, 338, 359
Swann, Willie 304, 311
Sweeney (1924 Marist) 85
Swift, Bill 167
Sydney Metropolitan 235, 238–9, 330

T

Taewa, Whetu 298, 307–9
Tagaloa, Lawrence 312
Tagaloa, Taime 282, 288–9
Tainui Māori Trust 320–1
Tait, Roger 191–3, 197, *200*, 201
Talaepa, Fale 349
Talamaivao, Abel 351
Talamavao, Louis 343
Tamaki Leopards 344
Tamaki Makaurau 142
Tamati, Howie 246, 279
Tamati, Kevin 246, 262, 356, *356*
Tamatoa, Bleu *319*
Tamatoa, Lee 319–20, 343
Tancred, Henry (Harry) 72, 120
Tapuai, Auvae 311
Taranaki 11–14, *13*, 28–30, *29*, 39, *40*, 203, 218, 253, 322, 330, 357
Tatana, Henry 204, 208, 214–17, *217*, 220, 270
Tatapu, Tony 300–1, 303, 306–9
Tate, Brent 360
Tau, Joe 343
Taufa, Una *305*
Taulapapa, Misi 343
Taumata (1943 Manukau) 127
Taunga, George 349
Taurua, Doug 230–4
Tawhai, Latham 306, 310–11
Taylor (1924 Devonport) 85
Taylor, A *130*
Taylor, Alan 201, 212
Taylor, F 33
Taylor, Glenn 222–4, *231*, 240–1, *243*, 244, 246
Te Atatu 257, 267–9, *268*, 320, 326
Te Kawa, Jack 170
Te Kawa, John 170
Te Mata, Karl 330, 338
Te Rangi, Hare 322–3, 328–30
Te Tai (1943 Manukau) 126
Te Whata, Bill 80, 82, 86
Teague, Kevin 266
team of the century 355
Telford, Bill (Snow) 105, *108*, 109, 111–12, *141*, 167, 182, 185, *223*
Temu, Jason 307, 330
Teniseli, Paolo 328, 330
Tetley, Harold / H G 105, 108, *108*, *110–11*, 111–12, 114–15, *118*, 120, 165
Tewheoro, Taffy *xiv*
Thacker, Dr Henry 43, *61*
Thacker Shield 43–4, *43*, 154
Thomas, H *130*
Thomas, V 56, 63, *71*, 72
Thompson, Aubrey 126
Thompson, F 120
Thompson, Manoa 309
Thompson, T A 19
Thompson, W T 18
Thomson, Mike 280, 282, 298

INDEX

Thornett, Dick 207–9, *208*
Tierney, Lynley 313
Tikinau, Monikura 358
Timms, Tom 75
Timoko, Nahu 277–8, 283
Tinitelia, Frank 259, *259*, 265
Tittleton, George 98, 111–12, 118
Tittleton, Wally 108, 111–13, 115, 118, *118*
Toagaga, Kennedy 259
Tobin (1910 City) 33
Toby, Ed 322
Tocker, Bill 147, 153, 154
Todd, Brent 264, 266, 270
Todd, Lance xi, 4, 6, 23, 28, 30, 256
Tofu, Meke 349
Toloa, Luther *243*, 244
Tomlinson, Arthur 170
Tonga 323
Tonga-Tama, William 223
Tongia, Sione 357–8
Tony, Motu 328–9, 331, 338
Tookey, Mark 331
Toopi, Clinton 323, 331, 338, 359
Tooth Cup 227
touring teams, games against 63–4, 96, 180
  see also Australia; England; France; Great Britain; New South Wales; New South Wales Country; Queensland; *and individual visiting clubs*
Townsend, Alf 63, *71*, 82
Townsend, Dave 271, 296, 303
Townsend, Ray 192
Tracey, Brian 199, *219*, 223–4
transfer issues 23, 131, 167, 213, 221, 234–5
Trevarthan, Tom 116–17
Trevarthen, Bill / W M 4, 5, 7–9, *9*, 15
Trott, Jarod 323, 343
Trumper, Victor 3
Tuakura, George 328, 337, 341, 350
Tucker, Aaron 319–20, 323
Tucker, R *91*
Tufeao, Siali'i 343
Tuia, Pena 349
Tuia, Tony 349, 355
Tuigamala, Va'aiga 256
Tuimavave, Evarn 338, 340, 359–60
Tuimavave, Paddy 264–6, 272, *273*, 275–8, 280, 283, *284*, 288, 297
Tuimavave, Paki 310–11, 317
Tuimavave, Tony 278, 283, 288, *294*, 297–8, *298*, 300, 303, 309
Tuisamoa, Matthew 301
Tuohey, T *91*
Tupou, Alex 316
Tupou, Tame 341
Turner, George 166, *166*, 168, *171*, 176, 181–4

Turua, Henry 340, 343, 350
Tusk Cup 258–9, *259*, 374
Tyler, Billy / W T 4, 5, 7–9, *9*, 13–14, 16, 19, 25, 30, 33
Tyne, Edward 11–13, *11*

U

uniforms *see* colours and uniforms
United States All Stars 158–9, *159*, 380
University club 167, 202
Ussher, Percy / P S 19, 45–6
Ussher, S *91*

V

Va'asa, Hale 341
Vagana, Joe 304, 306, *306*, 310, 314, 315, 323, 359
Vagana, Nigel 311, 313, 315, 392
Vaigafa, John 328
Vainikolo, Lesley 317, 359
Valeni, Ben *319*, 320, 343
Varley, Shane 236, 240, 248, 251, 255, 256
Vasau, Daniel 343
Vatuvei, Manu 261, 338, 359–60
Veart (1924 Devonport) 85
Veikoso, Mike 305
Veivers, Greg 224
Victoria Park *x*, 8, *8*, *10*, 29–30, *41*
Villasanti, Richard 331
Vuna, Cooper 350

W

Wade, G 89
Waikato 182, 203, 213, 218, 235, 317, 320, 349, 357
  see also South Auckland
Waikato Cougars 311, 315
Wainuiomata 207, 283, 291, 295, 327–8, 354
Waitakere City Raiders 305–6, 312, 314–15, 317
Waitakere Rangers 344
Wales 231–2, 380
Walker, Dave 153
Walker, W J 37, 38
Wallace, Grant 303
Wallace, W 76
Walsh, W (Bill) 43, *44*, 57
Walters, Stan *xiii*, 49, *49*, 58, 60–1, 120
Wanganui 38
Warner (1912 City) 51
Warrington 273, 276
Warriors 317–18
  creation and preparation 302, 304–5, 308
  games and performance 309–10, *309*, 313–14, 317, 320–1, 338, 358
  impact on the sport 286–7, 359
  ownership 318, 320–1, 326

reserve grade teams 308, 313, 317, 320, 352
Warriors Colts 311–12, 314, 317–18
Wātene, Frank 311, 314
Wātene, Steve 97, 98, 99, 113–17, *115*, 120, 126–7
Watkins (1938 Richmond) 107
Watson, Dave 266, 272, 278, 280, 282
Watson, Eric 321, 326
Watson, J W 70
Watts, Teddy / E W 18, 21, 23–4, *23*, *34*, 37, 38
Webb (1921 Maritime) 63
Webb (1924 Devonport) 85
Webb, Brent 119, 358
Webb, Charles 42, 49, *49*, 72
Webb, Stan 81–2, 89–90
Webber, Ray 168–70, *178*
Weir, Vinnie 305, 308
Weiss, Col 205, 207, 220
Wellington xii, 6–7, 21–2, 43, 57, 96, 139, 203, 213, 227, 253, 291
    games against
        1908–09: 8–13, *8–10*, 23, 28, 30–1, *30*
        1910s–20s: 39, *40*, 70, 89–90
        1930s–50s: *118*, *122*, 129, 140, 152
        1960s–70s: 195–6, *196*, 218, 235–6
        1980s–90s: 279–80, *280*, 289, 296–7, *296*
        2000s 330, 349, 357
Wellm, C *128*
Wells (1909 player) 25, 29
Wells, B 33
Wells, C 33
Welsh, Gavin 312, *312*
West Coast 99, 125, 136
    games against
        1920s–30s: 70, 86, 89–90, 96, 104, 109, 119
        1940s–50s: 129, 134–5, 139–42, 151–3, 157, 160, 162–3, 166, *171*, *176*
        1960s–70s: 182, *182*, 186, 193, 202–3, 218, 235–6
        1980s–2000s: 312, 355
Western Districts / Western United 174–5, 177, *178*
Western Springs 291
Western Suburbs (Sydney) 107, *108*, 142–3, 168, 227
Weston, S 56
Wetherill, Maurice 63, 71–2, 75, 76, 79, 80–2, 86, 87, 89, 98–9, *98*, 111, 120
Whaiapu, Greg 142
Wharepapa, Arapeta *see* Asher, Albert
White, Des 139, 147, *147*, *150*, 151–62, *152*, 158, 167, 261, 355–6, *356*, 392–3
    as selector and coach 168, *171*, *182*

White, Neville 166, *166*, 223, *231*, 236
White, Rachel 313
White, Richard 322, *331*, 332
White, Sara 313
Whiting, Graham 237, 238
Whittaker, F 76
Whittle, Terry 223, 227, 246
Wigan xi, 4, 6, 39, 68, 77–8, 84, 86, 101, 127, 131, 256, 274, 275, 276, 299, 308
Wigg, Regan 332, 337, 342, 344, 351
Wiggs, Albie 197, 199, 203
Wiggs, Ernie 190, 192–4, *194*, 196–9, 201–2, 204, 206–8, *206*, 212–13
Wiki, Ruben 303, *303*, 352, 353, 355–6, *356*, 359, 392
Wiles, Allan 140, *148*, 154–6, *155*
Wilkie, Dave / D A 70, *135*, *141*
Wilkinson, Jack 161–2
Williams, Bill 58
Williams, Darrell 262, 265–6, 270, *270*
Williams, Dennis 214, 216–17, *219*, 225–6, *225*, 230, 232, 234, 236, 239–42, *239*, *243*, 244–6, 251, 392
Williams, Ray 203, 213–14, 216, 220
Williams, Sonny Bill 392
Wilson, F 72
Wilson, Jack *xiii*, 60–1, 89–90
Wilson, John 240, *242*, 244
Wilson, Sean 311, *311*
Wilson, Tammi 313
Winfield Cup 286, 289, 302
Winter, Warren 226, 230–1, 236, 240, *243*
Winters (1910 Newton) 33–4
Witehira, Leah 313
Wittenberg, John 205–6
Wolfgramm, Willie 305
women in league 70, 305, 313
Wood, Edith 120
Wood, J 71
Wood, Nathan 331
Wood, R H 120
Woodward, Frank 16, 24–5, 29–31
Woollard, Gary 202, *205*, 206, 208, 216
Woolley, Charles 49, *49*, 61
Woolsey, Bill 166, *166*
Woolsey, Gene 192, 214, 216
World Club Challenge 317
World Cups xiii, 162, 202, 239–42, 245, 327, 338, 358, 360, *360*
Wrangler Cup 258, 374
Wright, Hercules (Bumper) 30–1
Wright, Jack 87, 147, 151–3, *152*, 158, 202
Wright, Joe 170
Wright, John 222–4, 246
Wright, Keith *193*
Wright, Kelvin 333, 344, 350–1, *351*
Wright, Murray 222, 231, 233–6

INDEX

Wright, Nick 222–3, 227, 236, 246, 253, *254*, 255, 260, 264–5, *265*
Wright, Owen (1) 170
Wright, Owen (2) 223–4, 246, 248, 253, 257, 259, *260*, 262, 264, 266, 296–7, 300, 303
Wrigley, Edgar 5
Wynyard, Billy / W T 4, 7–9, *9*, 12–13, 16, 22–4, 26, 56
    as administrator 18, 23–4, *23*, 31, *61*
Wynyard, Dick / J R 4, 5, 7–9, *9*, 13–14, 22, *23*, 24, 26–7, 29–31
Wynyard, G A 18
Wynyard, George 22
Wynyard, Henry 22
Wynyard, William (Tabby) 22

Y

Yandall, Jacob 349
Yardley, G 63, *71*
Yates, John 161–2, 165, 167, 170
Yates, Simon 166, *166*, 170, 222
Yates, Victor 196, 199, *200*, 201–2, 206
Yaxley, Peter 252–3
Young, John 205–6, *205*

Z

Zwart, John 259, 262

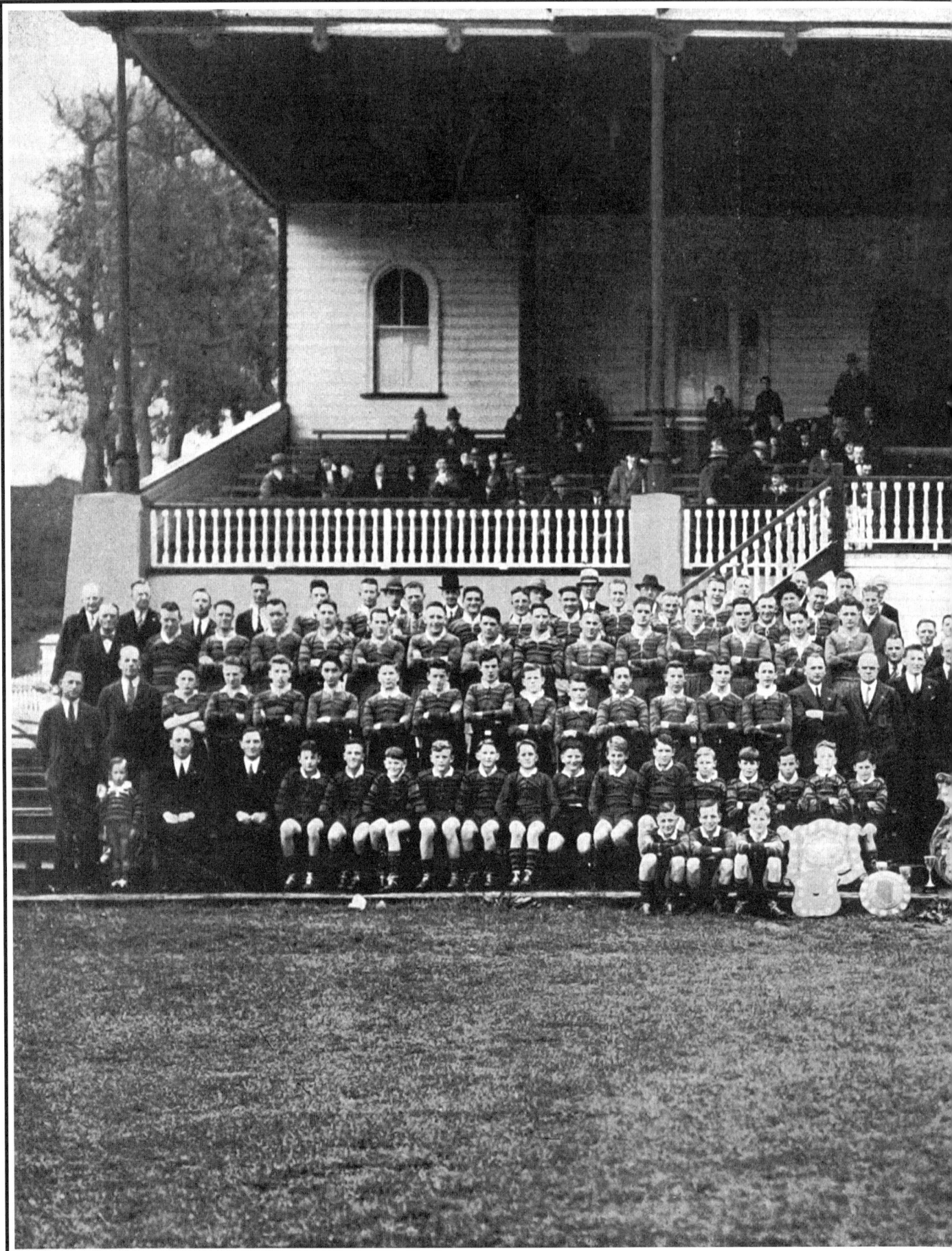